GW00670542

To my true friend
"Pre-war" Pete
Peter McGuinness
Very Truly
Gusty Spence

GUSTY SPENCE

Gusty Spence on his release
from the Maze prison, 1984

GUSTY SPENCE

ROY GARLAND

THE
BLACKSTAFF
PRESS

BELFAST

First published in 2001 by
The Blackstaff Press Limited
Wildflower Way, Apollo Road
Belfast BT12 6TA, Northern Ireland

Typeset by Techniset Typesetters, Newton-le-Willows, Merseyside

Printed in Ireland by Betaprint

A CIP catalogue for this book is available from the British Library

ISBN 0-85640-698-8

www.blackstaffpress.com

to

Louie Spence

They suffer in our coming and in our going.
It is they who have the most courage.

from Gusty Spence's letter
to Joe McCann's widow, 15 April 1972,
and based on the words
of Patrick Pearse (1879–1916)

Contents

Acknowledgements

My main conversations with Gusty Spence took place from the beginning of 1999 until near the end of 2000, although some took place as far back as the late 1980s. The earliest research was related to my thesis for a master's degree in Social Science in Irish Studies entitled 'The Ulster Volunteer Force Negotiating History' (1991). This was completed through the Department of Social Anthropology at the Queen's University of Belfast (QUB) under the supervision of Dr Graham McFarland.

I have used the word 'conversations' deliberately, because 'interview' seems much too formal a description of our many discussions. These were never an onerous task for either Gusty or myself. When I first mooted the idea of writing Gusty's story he was very hesitant. I stressed the importance of making the experiences and thinking of grassroots loyalists available to a wider audience. Trevor West of Trinity College Dublin, an old friend of Gusty, encouraged me to persist, maintaining that the story had to be told. Eventually, Gusty agreed and I wish to thank him for the many enjoyable hours we have shared on this project. All unattributed quotations in this book are taken from these conversations with Gusty.

During this time Gusty and his wife Louie regularly welcomed me into their home until one dreadful day in August 2000 when people claiming to be loyalists attacked their home.[1] Despite such difficult circumstances, Louie has always had a cheerful smile and I appreciated her warm hospitality. I would like to thank Louie and her daughter Elizabeth for contributing to this work through interviews with Maura Lee of the Irish broadcasting organisation RTÉ in 1996.

Among those who had a major input into this study were Billy Mitchell, Billy Hutchinson, David Ervine and Jim McDonald of the Progressive Unionist Party (PUP). Each gave me invaluable insights into the life and character of Gusty Spence and the roots of change in loyalism. My many convesations with Billy Mitchell were extremely helpful. I would like to thank each of them for their contribution in the midst of busy work schedules and, in the case of Billy Hutchinson, dangerous developments in the context of the loyalist feud in the late summer and autumn of 2000.

Among those who contributed but do not wish to be named were 'John', 'Mark', 'Victor', 'Jack' and 'Robert'. I could never fully express how much I owe to their contributions, trust and friendship. 'John' and I go back many decades and had it not been for him I might never have dreamed of doing this work. It was 'John' who first gave me an insight into the world of the Ulster Volunteers and the humanity that could overcome the inhumanity threatening to engulf it. I spent many enjoyable hours talking and listening to 'John', as well as appreciating brief conversations with his wife at her home, where there was always an open door.

On numerous occasions I have spoken with Philip Dean, Gary McMichael and David Adams of the Ulster Democratic Party (UDP), and I would like to thank them for their friendship and insight down the years. They have played an enormously positive role in relation to the events that are described in this book and I wish to acknowledge this. My thanks are also due to Andy Park, an Ulster Unionist and former leader of the Ulster Clubs who works with Community Dialogue.

I would also like to thank members of the Workers' Party, some of whom have had long-established contacts with Gusty. Tomás Mac Giolla gave me a copy of his crucial 1971 speech at Carrickmore in County Tyrone and Dessie O'Hagan, who first met Gusty shortly after his release in December 1984, was extremely helpful. Art McMillen, brother of the late Billy McMillen, welcomed me into his home and gave me valuable insights into the character of his brother who was one of the first republicans to engage with Gusty in Crumlin Road prison. I wish to thank both Dessie and Art for providing and/or confirming various details relating to republicans in the past. Their help is greatly appreciated.

Martin Meehan, a member of Sinn Féin, who, like Gusty, spent many years in Crumlin Road and Long Kesh, spoke freely of his experiences. As an Irish Republican Army (IRA) officer in both prisons he met Gusty and contributed further to my understanding of Gusty's role. Jim Gibney of Sinn Féin not only facilitated the meeting with Martin Meehan but he and Tom Hartley enabled me to understand something of the humanity within republicanism. Thanks are also due to Jake MacSiacices of the *Andersontown News* for the cheerful way he provided me with relevant historical details.

I owe particular thanks for encouragement to Dr Maurice Hayes, Lord Blease, Professor Brian Walker of the Institute of Irish Studies, QUB, Alister McReynolds, Director of Lisburn Institute of Further and Higher Education, and to Dr John Fairleigh of the Institute of Irish Studies, QUB, who in the 1970s introduced academic lectures to Long Kesh prisoners. John A. Moses, Adjunct Professor in History at the University of New England in Australia, also encouraged me in this work in 1997 by pointing out that the story could have a long-term impact. The late Paddy Devlin, Minister for Health in the short-lived Stormont power-sharing executive of 1974, who shared a similar background to Gusty, opened his home to Gusty and me and contributed to my research. We are grateful to Paddy's widow Teresa for the warm welcome we received.

Chris Hudson, the Dublin trade unionist who played a significant role in liaising with the leadership of the Ulster Volunteer Force (UVF) and became a conduit between the Irish Government and the UVF during critical developments in thc preace process, was most helpful. I would also like to thank Terry Harkin of the Irish Republican Socialist Party (IRSP) for confirming details about former Irish National Liberation Army (INLA) prisoners in Long Kesh.

Trevor West of Trinity College Dublin has been an unfailing source of encouragement and inspiration since he read my thesis on the UVF in 1991. His contribution to the successful completion of this work has been immense. Eddie Spence gave me ready access to his collection of loyalist magazines which I found most helpful.

This book would not have been possible without substantial financial assistance from the Ireland Funds toegether with the Joseph Rowntree Charitable Trust. A research fellowship which I held at the Institute of Irish Studies, QUB, from 1999 to 2000 was also invaluable in allowing me to complete work on the book and I would like to acknowledge the help and encouragement I received from everyone there. I also owe particular thanks to RTÉ and Maura Lee for access to recordings for a radio programme entitled 'A Tap on the Shoulder', broadcast on 25 April 1996.

The Governors of Lisburn Institute were generous in granting me an extended period of leave and I would like to thank members of staff and students for bearing with me during this period. Thanks are also due to Deborah McArthur and Ita Connolly and to the staff of the Linen Hall Library Belfast who unearthed factual information for me, while the library itself generously made its resources available. Thanks also to Elizabeth Mullan of Dairy Farm Library in west Belfast and to the staff of Lisburn Library.

I am also indebted to Marian Gallagher of the Public Record Office of Northern Ireland and to Nelson McCausland for their help with research for this book. The *Irish News* provided ready access to their files, and in particular I would like to acknowledge the help of the editor Noel Doran. Presbyterian Church House in Belfast also helped with information and I wish to thank Hazel Legge of Ulster Unionist Party headquarters for her help in seeking out historical details on former officers in the party. I am grateful to the Royal Ulster Constabulary at Knock for trying, albeit without success, to locate sources of information relating to the UVF which I believed were in their possession.

I would also like to thank Keith Baker for his editorial work on the book and to thank the various members of staff at Blackstaff Press for their support, particularly Patsy Horton and Wendy Dunbar.

Last, but by no means least, I am grateful for the forbearance of my own family during many long days and nights.

ROY GARLAND

MAY 2001

Abbreviations

B Specials	Ulster Special Constabulary
CLMC	Combined Loyalist Military Command
CLPA	Combined Loyalist Political Alliance
CO	Commanding Officer
DUP	Democratic Unionist Party
INLA	Irish National Liberation Army
IRA	Irish Republican Army
IRSP	Irish Republican Socialist Party
LOL	Loyal Orange Lodge
NICRA	Northern Ireland Civil Rights Association
NILP	Northern Ireland Labour Party
NIO	Northern Ireland Office
OC	Officer Commanding
PIRA	Provisional Irish Republican Army
PUP	Progressive Unionist Party
RHC	Red Hand Commando
RTÉ	Radio Telefís Éireann
RUC	Royal Ulster Constabulary
RUR	Royal Ulster Rifles
SDLP	Social Democratic and Labour Party
UDA	Ulster Defence Association
UDP	Ulster Democratic Party
UDR	Ulster Defence Regiment
UFF	Ulster Freedom Fighters
UPA	Ulster Protestant Action
UPV	Ulster Protestant Volunteers
USC	Ulster Special Constabulary
UUP	Ulster Unionist Party
UVF	Ulster Volunteer Force
UWC	Ulster Workers' Council
YCV	Young Citizens Volunteer Force

Chronology

28 June 1933	Born at 66 Joseph Street in the lower Shankill area of Belfast
1938–43	Attends Riddel Memorial Public Elementary School
1943–47	Attends Hemsworth Square Primary School
1947	Starts work at a Belfast mill
20 June 1953	Marries Louie Donaldson
May 1957	Joins Royal Ulster Rifles and serves in Cyprus
April/May 1961	Leaves army after developing asthma
October/November 1965	Joins UVF as Commanding Officer of the Shankill unit
26 June 1966	Peter Ward killed early Sunday morning outside the Malvern Arms in Belfast
27 June 1966	Questioned at Brown Square police barracks from approximately 7.30 a.m. to midnight
28 June 1966	Charged with murder and conspiracy at 1.00 a.m. on thirty-third birthday
18–26 August 1966	Preliminary hearing at lower court (taking depositions)
26 August 1966	Informations are refused and Gusty Spence is freed then rearrested
6 October 1966	Trial proper begins
14 October 1966	Found guilty of murder but not conspiracy. Sentenced to life imprisonment on 15 October
4 January 1967	Appeal dismissed
11 January 1967	Leave to appeal to House of Lords refused
1 July 1972	Granted parole from Crumlin Road jail to attend daughter Elizabeth's wedding
2 July 1972	Abducted by UVF

11 October 1972	Arrested with UVF leaders but unrecognised and walks free from Castlereagh Holding Centre
4 November 1972	Captured on the Glencairn Road by the Parachute Regiment and taken to the Maze prison
13 April 1974	Mother Isabella dies
October 1974	Becomes committed to peaceful means after UVF ceasefire collapses
Early 1978	Resigns from UVF
Christmas 1982	First parole
June 1983	Second parole
13 December 1984	Released on licence
17 April 1991	First Combined Loyalist Military Command (CLMC) ceasefire
November 1993	Gusty meets Irish politicians
13 October 1994	Reads CLMC document at press conference in Fernhill House, Belfast
15 October 1994	Meets taoiseach Albert Reynolds in Dublin
23 October 1994	Arrives in New York
10 April 1998	Good Friday Agreement reached
19 August 2000	The Spence home attacked during loyalist feud

1

Introduction
Gusty Spence Declares Peace

Gusty Spence has been associated with the Ulster Volunteer Force (UVF) since 1965. He was the first leader of the Shankill UVF, an extremely secretive organisation about which relatively little is known. Following his arrest and trial for the Malvern Street murder in 1966, he was given a life sentence, which was intended to mean at least twenty years' incarceration. He was released in December 1984, having served almost nineteen years, during most of which he was commanding officer (CO) of the UVF prisoners.

In October 1994, ten years after his release, he was once again rocketed to prominence when he publicly announced the ceasefire of the Combined Loyalist Military Command (CLMC),[1] heralding years of protracted talks and negotiations about peace.

The ceasefire was designed to initiate a new beginning in which sectarianism would end and a more radical form of unionist politics could flourish. It seemed appropriate that Gusty, the father of modern Ulster loyalism, was chosen to read the statement. He was one of a small number of 'thinking' UVF men, some of whom had family links with the old Northern Ireland Labour Party or were in other ways influenced by left-of-centre concepts, who were to steer the UVF towards democratic socialist and unionist politics.[2]

As Gusty read the ceasefire statement, he was flanked on either side by leading members of the Progressive Unionist Party (PUP) and the Ulster Democratic Party (UDP). These political parties were confidants, respectively, of the Ulster Volunteer Force/Red Hand Commando and the Ulster Defence Association/Ulster Freedom Fighters,[3] meeting under the auspices of the CLMC.

Gusty had resigned[4] from the UVF leadership in the Maze[5] prison as long ago as 1978 but it is a reflection of the respect in which he is held among his loyalist peers that he was chosen to read, and indeed write, the CLMC declaration.[6]

Although not everyone was reassured by the words, most people greeted the statement with relief. The text of the document reads:

> After a widespread consultative process initiated by representation from the Ulster Democratic and Progressive Unionist Parties, and after having received guarantees in relation to Northern Ireland's constitutional position within the United Kingdom, as well as other assurances, and in the belief that the democratically expressed wishes of the greater number of people in Northern Ireland will be respected and upheld, the CLMC will universally cease all operational hostilities as from 12 midnight on Thursday the 13th October 1994.
>
> The permanence of our ceasefire will be completely dependent upon the continued cessation of all Nationalist/Republican violence; the sole responsibility for a return to war lies with them.
>
> In the genuine hope that this peace will be permanent, we take the opportunity to pay homage to all our Fighters, Commandos and Volunteers who have paid the supreme sacrifice. They did not die in vain. The union is safe.
>
> To our physically and mentally wounded who have served Ulster so unselfishly, we wish a speedy recovery, and to the relatives of those men and women we pledge our continued moral and practical support.
>
> To our prisoners who have undergone so much deprivation and degradation with great courage and forbearance, we solemnly promise to leave no stone unturned to secure their freedom.

To our serving Officers, NCOs [non-commissioned officers] and men, we extend our eternal gratitude for their obedience to orders, for their ingenuity, resilience and good humour in the most trying of circumstances, and we commend them for their courageous fortitude and unshakeable faith over the long years of armed confrontation.

In all sincerity, we offer to the loved ones of all innocent victims over the past twenty-five years abject and true remorse. No amount of our words will compensate for the intolerable suffering they have undergone during the conflict.

Let us firmly resolve to respect our differing views of freedom, culture and aspiration and never again permit our political circumstances to degenerate into bloody warfare.

We are on the threshold of a new and exciting beginning with our battles in future being political battles, fought on the side of honesty, decency and democracy against the negativity of mistrust, misrepresentation and malevolence, so that, together, we can bring forth a wholesome society in which our children, and their children, will know the meaning of true peace.

The statement came approximately six weeks after the Irish Republican Army (IRA) announcement of its own cessation of military operations. But, unlike the loyalist statement, the IRA cessation contained no expressions of regret for the carnage that characterised much of the IRA campaign.[7] This may reflect a genuine fear among republicans of being held solely accountable for the whole conflict, but it has fed suspicion within the unionist community.

In this book my intention is to tell the story of Gusty Spence and how he played a pivotal role in the attempts to initiate the transition from an abnormally divided society into a society at peace.

He first came to my attention in 1966 after the murder in Malvern Street. Since then I have followed his contribution to the developing peace moves and I was encouraged by snippets of information filtering out of jail. The most significant of these were the condolences he expressed to the wife of Joe McCann, an Official IRA man killed by security forces in 1972, and his friendship with Cardinal Tomás Ó Fiaich.

My own background in loyalism began with membership of the Orange Order from 1964 to 1972. I was a member of Belfast County Grand Orange Lodge and Worshipful Master of St Mary's Churchmen's Loyal Orange Lodge (LOL) which became Ireland's Heritage LOL 1303 in 1970. I was also press officer of the Ulster Young Unionist Council and a member of the

Ulster Unionist Council and Standing Committee. I was a regular visitor to the Reverend Ian Paisley's Free Presbyterian Church and was involved with Paisley in a number of protests and demonstrations.

From the autumn of 1969 to the summer of 1971 I was a senior officer in Tara, a loyalist paramilitary organisation led by evangelical Christians associated mainly with Ulster Young Unionists and with the Free Presbyterian Church. The UVF in substance became part of Tara in 1969 but continued to operate as a separate unit. After leaving Tara in 1971, I remained in contact with 'John', who eventually introduced me to Gusty early in 1985.

It was never Gusty Spence's intention to commit his experiences to paper but since the late 1980s, and frequently on a weekly basis, he and I have discussed our hopes for a resolution to the political crisis in Northern Ireland. He always believed that sooner or later a new day of peace would dawn. At times the breadth of his experience, his perception of the nature of Northern Ireland politics, and his unfaltering hopes for political progress have astonished me.

2

The Cradle of the Ulster Volunteers

Gusty was born at 66 Joseph Street in the Shankill Road area on 28 June 1933, and it was in that house that he was raised. He was the sixth of seven children, five boys and two girls. The oldest was Billy, then came Cassie, Jim, Bobby, Ned, Gusty and Lily.

Joseph Street was almost totally enclosed by the small terraced houses of Malvern Street, Hopeton Street, Clements Street and Malvern Place, and it had little to boast of apart from a Plymouth Brethren mission hall.

Malvern Street, which paralleled Joseph Street, was renowned for elaborate colourful decorations on festive occasions like the Twelfth of July[1] but apart from that there was not much to brighten the lives or lighten the burdens of the people. While there were elements of deprivation throughout the Shankill, squalor and poverty were more common here in the lower Shankill, particularly around the adjacent Old Lodge Road, which could be seen from the top of Malvern Street. It was mainly from this area, known locally as the Hammer, that many early recruits joined the ranks of the UVF in the 1960s. Many families had strong military traditions, and most early UVF men had served in Britain's armed forces.

Gusty's father had been in the army. William Edward 'Ned' Spence took great pride in saying he was from Mackey Street in the Tiger's Bay area of north Belfast. However Gusty discovered that his father was actually born in Whitehaven in Cumbria and that his grandfather appears to have been a transient worker.

Ned became a member of Edward Carson's Ulster Volunteer Force and fought during the First World War. On his return in 1919 he married Isabella (Bella) Hayes. According to Gusty:

> He fought right through the First World War, was present at the big battles like the Somme and Ypres. He returned after being promised 'a land fit for heroes' but found nothing but grinding poverty and unemployment. As a result, he joined the Royal Artillery before the end of 1919.[2]

Gusty's father died in November 1965. On 21 November 1971, to mark the sixth anniversary of his death, Gusty wrote to his brother Billy, indicating through his words the powerful nature of his commitment to unionism and his father's influence. He wanted, he said:

> ... to acknowledge and confirm all those loyalties so carefully nurtured and handed on to us. When fate picked me to 'soldier' in this prison it could have indeed pointed the arrow at any one of us, any one of Ned Spence's five sons. I am glad and proud to be the one son chosen to be here for Ulster and I am in a privileged position and I am humble.

When Ned returned home again in the early 1920s he once more faced unemployment. He had been illiterate when he went into the army but not when he came out, and so he took great pride in a precious third-class certificate in education which was placed on the wall with solemnity. However, it proved to be of little value during the depression of the 1930s when he worked on the outdoor relief schemes. Ned's deep sense of bitterness was frequently talked about in the home:

> After a grinding week's work on the outdoor relief scheme he was handed a piece of paper that he had to take to a shop that had purposely inflated prices. At the bottom of that piece of paper it stated, 'no tobacco or snuff to be issued'. This was the only relief from the tedium of life in those days and was looked upon as a privilege. My father felt extremely bitter that a country for which he had fought and for which thousands had died should treat them so shabbily.

These memories remained deeply implanted in Gusty's mind. He remembers seeing the marks of the pits dug at both ends of Joseph Street to keep the police from attempting to enforce the relief schemes when local people refused to work them:

> The pits at the top and the bottom of the street had been filled in and weren't properly cobbled. They were designed to stop the Lancia cars patrolling the streets. A pit was dug at the top and bottom of virtually every street in the Hammer. They were like tank traps and the Lancia cars couldn't traverse them.

Shankill Protestants in those days suffered as much as their Catholic neighbours, but loyalists felt they could not complain. Those who did so were regarded as disloyal:

> That was the first slippery slope. The border would fall, the Jesuits would move in and all hell would break loose. Even now when, as a member of the PUP, I would put forward a political point of view, people tell me that I am being disloyal. But it won't work. We will not go back to the touching of the forelock. We will not go back to subservience.

However the atmosphere generated by this kind of thinking was repressive. Gusty passed a remark to his brother Billy in the early 1960s:

> 'I don't think everything is all right on the Prod side and everything all wrong on the Taig [Catholic] side.' Billy said, 'Watch that, that's dangerous talk.' Then I thought to myself, 'Are we living in a quasi Nazi state?' He was the secretary of the West Belfast Imperial Unionist Association. I said, 'Well that's what I believe.' He respected that.

Many years later Gusty realised that this restrictive environment with its 'thought police' had inhibited his personal development:

> I had all these embryonic feelings, all this personal development, which should have had its beginnings when I was a child. And here I was, a grown man who had fought in the British army but it was only then that these openings within me began to grow.

Yet there was dissent in the Shankill. Gusty's father disliked the Ulster Unionist Party (UUP) and had never been a member of the Orange Order, saying 'I can't think of why I should join that organisation, people who shake each other's hands on the Twelfth of July morning and stab each other in the back for the rest of the year.'

Ned Spence saw the unionist people as gullible and the unionist politicians as gulling the people. When he voted, he did so to please Bella. He would vote for Tommy Henderson, who had a social conscience and fought to have basic amenities like running water introduced into small terraced houses in the area. Alternatively he might vote for the notoriously sectarian former Royal Ulster Constabulary (RUC) District Inspector J.W. Nixon (Nixon had also been in the RUC's pre-partition predecessor, the Royal Irish Constabulary). The choice illustrates the confused nature of the politics of the Protestant working class at that time.

Both Nixon and Henderson were Orangemen and independent unionists. There was, however, a great gulf between them. Gusty talks of Henderson as 'a working man, mildly socialistically inclined', while Nixon hated Catholics and was reputed to have been involved in the infamous massacre of the McMahon family in 1922. Henderson's popularity reflected his work for the unemployed and needy, whereas Nixon's was related to a militant sectarian unionism for which he was eventually dismissed from the RUC. The difference between Henderson and Nixon was reflected at a meeting of Northern Ireland Parliament in Belfast City Hall in 1932. Jack Beattie who was a Labour politician, seized the mace shouting that his motion on unemployment was being ignored. In the uproar that followed Tommy Henderson joined in condemning the Government's treatment of the unemployed as a 'disgrace to civilisation'. Beattie shouted, 'The House indulges in hypocrisy while there are starving thousands outside.' With that he grasped the mace and threw it on the floor. Henderson roared, 'What about the 78,000 unemployed who are starving?' Government benches retorted, 'God save the King' to which Henderson replied, 'God save the people' and left. Only J.W. Nixon was left on the opposition benches.[3]

There were, of course, many people in the Hammer who identified with the Ulster Unionist Party. In fact, success for the UUP in the area depended on the willing cooperation of working-class supporters.

'John' described Gusty's brother Billy as 'a red hot socialist'. However Gusty said:

> 'Socialist' gives the wrong impression. Billy had not read any socialist politics but he was always up in arms because the Unionists chose candidates from factory owners or managers from outside the area. He was fiercely working class and fiercely proud of his roots.

John's own socialism was related to social deprivation in the Hammer. As he recalled:

> Water was running down the walls and the houses had been condemned before the war. Yet at that time Harcourt [a Stormont Unionist MP], and other Unionist figures were in my mother's home because they depended on people like my mother and father to get them elected and do their dirty work. They couldn't wait to get down to the Reform Club, to get the whiskeys and clear their nostrils.

There was severe economic depression in Belfast during the 1930s:

> The great shipyards, then among the finest in the world, and the ancillary engineering firms in the Lagan Valley were all in chronic depression. World trade was in steep decline. No shipping orders were on the horizon. Belfast's other great industry, linen, was equally badly affected, with the mills either closing down or on halftime. One in four was out of work, and thousands of skilled and unskilled workers dug trenches in the streets for grocery chits of token value. There were no wages being earned and little actual cash around, so rent went unpaid. For a time the bailiffs were rampant, until the unemployed workers organised resistance to them.[4]

Resistance took the form of street demonstrations. On Tuesday, 11 October 1932 there was an attempt to form up in procession in east Belfast:

> At Templemore Avenue an attack was made by a crowd armed with stones on an isolated party of police. They drew their batons, but things were looking very ugly when police reinforcements in a caged car appeared on the scene.[5]

As these Protestant protesters were being taken away, in the midst of baton charges, Catholics from Seaford Street attempted to rescue them by joining in the rioting against the police. However, the worst violence took place in the lower Falls where the police used live rounds. Samuel Baxter, a Protestant, and John Geegan, a Catholic from Smithfield, were both mortally wounded.

Reporter James Kelly was sent to the Shankill area by the *Irish Press* to cover a march from Tennent Street:

> I remember a woman with a shawl come running to the people I was talking to. She shouted: 'They're kicking the shite out of the peelers up the Falls. Are you going to let them down?' And that seemed to be the

> flashpoint for the riot . . . I took refuge in a shirt factory in Agnes Street and we saw some of the Protestant workers actually shooting at the police.[6]

A big march was held followed by a meeting of people from the Falls and the Shankill at St Mary's Hall in Bank Street. Gusty's mother was present and she told him that an 'Oul doll from the Falls' had said, 'It's all for Ireland', but my mother said, 'Fuck Ireland, it's all for bread'.

In the end, increases in relief were granted and the workers saw this as a great victory. Although these particular events were over before Gusty was born, vivid stories were passed on to him. The extent of Catholic–Protestant cooperation may have been exaggerated but that it took place at all was a remarkable part of Shankill history.

The diversity within the Shankill community was illustrated in 1934 when a contingent of Shankill Road Protestants attended the annual commemoration at Bodenstown of the United Irishmen leader Wolfe Tone. They carried a banner reading, 'Wolfe Tone Commemoration 1934 – Shankill Rd Belfast Branch – BREAK THE CONNECTION WITH CAPITALISM'.[7] Members of the Tipperary IRA attacked them and tried to grab their banner. The Shankill men resisted. Part of the irony of that incident was that Wolfe Tone himself was a Protestant.

In Belfast, sectarian divisions remained beneath the surface but in 1935 they reasserted themselves with a vengeance during the return journey of a Twelfth of July Orange parade. A relatively trivial incident in York Street ignited intercommunal violence which continued for days. The UVF was surreptitiously re-formed,[8] but as Gusty said:

> People do not wish to know that their government hired gunmen at ten bob a day to shoot Catholics and to ignite sectarianism in order to break the fleeting unity between Prods and Taigs. The Orange Order played a part in this because they insisted on marching along York Street, where an Ulster government reinforced by the Royal Ulster Constabulary barred them.

Fierce riots followed and:

> For over two hours battle raged between the opposing forces and scenes that almost beggar description were enacted. Armoured cars, firing machine guns, while police, armed with rifles or revolvers, fired upon gunmen and stone-throwers at all points, but from the corner of Donegall Street to the middle of York Street the fighting raged uninterruptedly for two hours.[9]

It was nearly the end of August before the violence ceased. These were not the last riots Belfast would witness; nor had they been the first. A.T.Q. Stewart refers to riots of various intensities throughout the nineteenth and twentieth centuries.[10]

The Shankill consisted of a number of close-knit communities in which relatives lived near each other. Gusty recalls that they would have said, 'Oh God, they live away up in Belgrave Street,' though that was a matter of only a few hundred yards.

The centre of the Hammer was a playground on the other side of Hemsworth Square senior primary school in Malvern Street, which was known locally as the Henhouse. Joseph Street itself was known as the Banjo. One theory relates the name to an old Belfast expression meaning getting a beating: being 'banjoed'. Indeed, many a fight took place there. Contestants would strip to the waist and fight with bare knuckles. Gusty has a different explanation for the name. 'It was derived from what they used to do to the peelers. The cops were detested; we only saw them when they came to lift someone or to back up the bailiffs.'[11]

His schooling began in Malvern Street:

> I remember the Riddel School with fondness. Miss Irvine, who had taught my mother, taught me. She was a wonderful woman who would bring sandwiches for her own lunch and a few extra ones for the really poor kids. We called the head Daddy Barnes and he gave us some hammerings.[12]

After Riddel, Gusty went to Hemsworth. The headmaster was Daddy Glass:

> He was an Orangeman and he used to take us for algebra – everyone hated it, so lads like Hango Devlin and Jimmy Cosgrove would invent some argument about the Battle of the Boyne at the start of the algebra lesson and ask him to sort out the row. That was the end of the algebra lesson for the next thirty minutes. Anything about King Billy crossing the Boyne stopped Daddy Glass in his tracks.[13]

Gusty was bright at school and gained a leaving certificate, entitling him to a grammar school education. However, costs would have been approximately 52 shillings (£2.60) and as far as the Spence family was concerned the money just wasn't there. The family could not afford basic things like a school cap, blazer, grey shorts and a few books. Some families did manage this, and Gusty explained the difference thus: 'I suppose the secret was having only one child in the family with the mother and father both working. Economic circumstances were different.'

Those who went to grammar school from the Shankill were few in number. Like Gusty, most Shankill children left school at the earliest opportunity, often before they reached the age of fourteen. Many of the previous generation had left school at twelve or thirteen, and some had had no education whatever.

> The 'boxers' had middle shades and short haircuts, the 'intellectuals' wore Brylcreem and had clean knees and no scars. You kept clear of them.
>
> Status was based on how far you could throw a stone or climb a lamppost, how good you were at marlies [marbles] or how fast you could climb the Hammer railings.[14]

Gusty's mother, like most mothers on the Shankill, tried to keep her children out of trouble by sending them to various youth organisations. Gusty attended the Lower Shankill Boys' Club on Monday nights and the Church Lads Brigade on Tuesday evenings. The brigade was the Church of Ireland equivalent of the mainly Methodist and Presbyterian Boys' Brigade. It was a military-style organisation that had contributed to the original UVF. Gusty remembers parading with dummy rifles:

> Always in the back of my mind were the First World War, the Somme and the men of the UVF. We were brought up with the sound of the drum and the flute. Old soldiers sat on a bench outside Stewart's barbers, covered in a sea of blue smoke from pipe tobacco. They talked about the trauma of the Somme and of the men who died. My own Da fought from 1915 to 1918 and had only 27 days' leave but at least he did come back.[15]

Being in the Junior Orange Order was a popular activity in the area:

> Every youngster at seven or eight years of age was in the Orange Order. In Joseph Street they joined the Alexander Blair Memorial Lodge. But that's not where I learned my politics. My Ma told me about the Prods and Taigs ambushing the cops in Northumberland Street during the 1932 hunger riots.[16]

Gusty joined the Junior Orange Lodge. He says:

> We looked upon it as a social activity. We didn't sit round tables cursing the Pope or anything like that. We went through the ritual, which was intriguing, even for a boy, and sometimes laughable. We went to Clifton

Street Orange Hall and smelt this slightly fusty smell and went round these big rooms with big ornate chairs. We wondered at the importance of those 'betters' who sat in these chairs. It's different when you're young and life's a whole new experience. Now and again we had parades which were colourful and noisy and for a day we were important.

It always rained during the Easter Tuesday parade but we got a wee roughness [money] somewhere along the line. I maybe had sixpence in my hand or thrupence [three pence]. Perhaps someone gave you a penny and you finished up with a shilling going down to Bangor. You had four lads going round Bangor gathering willicks [whelks], and then we marched home exhausted, proud that we had defended Ulster once again. I suppose it was a little bit of supremacy. You always felt a wee bit better than the Taigs.

Gusty however was not entirely at home within Orangeism and 'didn't really take the full package'. Gusty's brother Ned joined the Junior Orange Lodge at the age of twelve and like his other brothers, he joined Prince Albert Temperance LOL 1882 in his late teens. However, unlike Gusty, Ned broke from Orangeism and became a socialist. For a time he was even a member of the Communist Party. He shared the same poverty and slums as the other members of his family, but it had a different impact on him.

According to Gusty, Sunday School was a must. At first he attended the mission in Joseph Street:

There were obligations on me to go to church. If I didn't go I couldn't play for the football team so I joined the Church Lads Brigade in St Michael's Church of Ireland. I went to the first service at half past nine and then to the half past eleven service. If I attended both, I ran home after the first service, got a piece of bread and jam and ran to the second service. My mother went to wee cottage meetings organised by some people in the street who were 'good-living'. Sometimes she took me to the Deacon Memorial Hall in St Michael's. I didn't want to go but it was the only time my Ma could go and so I was trailed along. I was showing those who picked the football team how good I was – churched three times in the one day.

While playing football Gusty was in contact with 'John', who lived a few streets away. 'John' said:

We all played for the schools and the local teams. When I came out of my time [apprenticeship], I moved to England to work round the sites. Gusty

> hit the army trail so our paths divided and didn't cross again for some years. When I came back I got married and saw him regularly. His brother Ned – Nicko was his nickname – was a great Blues [Linfield Football Club] supporter so I always saw him at the football matches.

Gusty recalls that his mother, like many mothers on the Shankill, started to work in the mill at the age of twelve:

> It was unforgivable for those so-called captains of industry with their expansive waists and gold watches to employ underprivileged and undernourished children from six in the morning to six at night and half past twelve on a Saturday for the princely sum of two shillings and nine pence. Nineteen new pence for sixty-six and a half hours of slavery.

Bella stopped working in the mills while her children were young. However when they reached the age of ten or twelve, she went back.

If a woman got work in a factory, rather than a mill, this represented a step up, even if wages remained the same. When Gusty's future wife Louie Donaldson first expressed an interest in working in the mill, her father said, 'No one belonging to me will ever work in a mill,' so she worked in the Blackstaff factory. This carried more prestige and was a bit cleaner than the mills. Gusty also worked in the mills – in his bare feet – and he remembers a Catholic woman from the Pound Loney getting special permission to go to the gatehouse twice a day to breast-feed her baby:

> I worked in Craig's Mill, also known as the New Northern, at the corner of Northumberland Street on the Falls Road. I worked in Greeves's Mill or Conway Mill where the republicans are at the moment. Greeves's Mill was split in two, Cupar Street and Conway Street, and I worked in both. I also worked in Brookfield Mill, Edenderry Mill, York Street Spinning Mill and Rosebank Factory. In those days you could move from one mill to another but it was menial work with scab wages.

A few hundred yards from Joseph Street was the Old Lodge Road and Lonsdale Street, infamous for its poor housing, which was to be devastated by German bombers during the blitz of 1941. The destruction highlighted the extent of poverty in Belfast. One clergyman, on observing the scene, said:

> I hope and trust that they will never be rebuilt again ... A minister said to me, whose congregation had been bombed ... if he could get the people

entirely out of the way, he would be happy if the Germans would come and bomb the place flat.[17]

In Lonsdale Street in 1941, 190 people were living in twelve houses. A health report for that year described working-class housing in Belfast thus:

> Damp, mouldering walls, many of them bulging, rickety stairs, broken floors, crumbling ceilings were common defects. Some of the 'houses' were mere hovels, with people living in indescribable filth and squalor ... rents were 1/9d a week for a small attic which it was an adventure to approach.[18]

A number of other Protestant areas in the Shankill were bombed, as were some Catholic areas, but it appeared that it was mainly the Protestant streets that experienced the devastation. The rumour was that Catholics had kept their lights on during the blackout to guide the German bombers into Protestant areas. Gusty heard these stories:

> The famous rumour at the time was that the Catholics were burning newspapers and ringing the place round with flames to guide the bombers. A lot of nonsense of course, but you'd be surprised how many people actually believed that, including myself.

Fighting often took place between various streets within the Shankill:

> The Hammer and Beresford Street were sworn enemies as were the people of the Nick on the other side of the Shankill.
>
> I idolised the man who would give you justice. If someone hit a wee fellow the hard man would mark his card. It was a kind of one-man paramilitarism.

Some houses in Lonsdale Street and adjacent streets became brothels and during the 1960s pimps and prostitutes became more common. Respectable people preferred not to know about this side of life on the edges of the Shankill:

> People worked all kinds of moves and schemes but were accepted. They had to get a living but they didn't get a living off each other like the moneylenders.

Rosie Connor, a popular lady who spoke in local mission halls, lived in a tiny house in Campbell Street:

Rosie was a fighting woman; she could have fought like a man and did fight men. She was a hard woman and had led a chequered life when she was young. Rosie had been on the game and drank the wine, she lived a full life and had worked in the mills, but Rosie changed. She had a big rough countenance but she was a good woman. Rosie, Maggie White and my Ma had been friends for over sixty years.

Whenever women were in my mother's house there was always a squad of kids. The women would say, 'Wee pigs have big ears' so the kids were bucked out, but sometimes we heard things. My mother and these women had the highest praise for Rosie because she had pulled herself from the gutter.

Many people were preoccupied with staying alive and when Gusty's father met old soldiers they would say:

'Well Billy, what do you have?' 'I'm having the bins, its not very good but it's constant. Your money's not worth a damn but it's coming in every week.' The problem for the whole street was getting a reserve, having a job and retaining it.

I delivered the mail in Carrick Hill, a nearby Catholic area and it was awful as were the wee Prod streets in Brown Square. You walked from the street into the living room where you could have two chairs but no room for a settee, one bedroom upstairs and you walked out to the yard, there was no scullery [working kitchen].

A horse falling in the street brightened your day. It was a change from the drabness. Men in our street had to get a coat over the horse's head to make it rise to its feet. That was something out of the norm, out of this grey squalor.

Politics in those days was colourful however and there were fistfights and running battles between unionists and independent unionists on the Shankill Road.

The terraced house where Gusty, his four brothers and two sisters lived with their father and mother was as inadequate as the rest:

You couldn't have swung a cat in the scullery where all cooking and washing was done. We had a bath of course – it hung on a spouting hook out in the yard, a big tin bath. It was brought in on a Saturday night and everything was washed, the kids and clothes and everything else. We had an outside toilet and on Sundays my father sat down and studiously cut up newspapers and strung them along a piece of cord for the toilet. On winter nights we went out with a candle and as a child you were naturally scared and sometimes your ma or your da stood at the door until you went to the toilet.

In our house we had a thing called the English cup, a big tin bucket brought up the stairs every night. The oul fellow used to say, 'Right childer, gather up your parrots and monkeys [an old Army expression] and don't forget the English cup.' The English cup was placed strategically on the landing. We called it poulaying, but at different intervals in the night you heard the rattle, like a kettledrum, of the English cup. Some of my mates said, 'English cup, have youse got an English cup?' I would explain what it was. My mates had different names for the receptacle – Aunt Jenny or Bridget. My father and mother always discreetly used the downstairs toilet.

We were like sardines in the front bedroom with two double beds. Two of us brothers lay up and two lay down and I always got some fellow's toe up my nose in the middle of the night or somebody had eaten a heel of bread and the bed was full of crumbs. The bed consisted of a palliasse [mattress cover] stuffed with straw, which was religiously changed twice a year with straw from Sarah Cathcart's shop in Downing Street. My mother and two sisters slept in one bed and my father and my eldest brother slept in the back room. How there were seven of us is beyond me. I don't know when opportunities presented themselves during my sojourn on this earth, because my mother and father never slept together.

For a blanket Gusty and his brothers had their father's First World War greatcoat; sheets and pillowcases were made from bleached flour sacks stitched together. For heat in the beds the family used a hot stone wrapped in cloth or even a lemonade bottle filled with warm water. The legs of the bed were placed in shoe polish tin lids filled with paraffin oil to prevent bugs and cockroaches from crawling up. Walls were sometimes treated with red lead from the shipyard in an attempt to kill the bugs; while this was happening the children would be farmed out for a few days.

The houses were firetraps. Sometimes at night Gusty was awakened by the sound of pigeons in the roof space. There were no divisions between the houses and once birds gained entrance they could fly internally from one end of the street to the other.

Many children were riddled with diseases such as rickets, malnutrition, measles, diphtheria and scarlet fever, all of which could be life-threatening. Yet the hovels in which the people lived were rented at about four shillings and three pence a week, a substantial sum in those days.

The Spence family was able to survive on a basic diet of stew and broth, with occasional treats of 'pigs' cheeks, ham shanks, pigs' feet, pigs' tails, oxtails, tripe, bacon ends and parings'.

> At night the nine of us used to eat on the stairs. The youngest boy, me, sat on the bottom stair, with my saucer on the next step. Ned was up above me and then Bobby and so on right up the stairs.[19]

Other items on the menu included offal, while sausages were a staple diet. People also fed on elder – cow's udder – and at times armies of people gathered whelks from the seafront at Holywood, a few miles down the coast on Belfast Lough. Only a few men in Joseph Street could afford the half-crown rent for plots of land on which to grow vegetables. Others went up the road to gather watercress on a Sunday evening.

Gusty never stayed at a hotel or even a boarding house, and it was virtually unknown to go out for a meal:

> The nearest thing we ever got to that was the stew shop at two pence a bowl and we thought it was great. Ma and Da and the family went there once or twice a year. There was my Da, hoking in his waistcoat pocket to fetch a half crown or florin for the bowls of stew, and I thought we were 'no goat's toe'. We got down to an ice cream shop at Christmas, and that was a great treat.

The ice cream was served in a very 'basic restaurant':

> There were big trestle tables and hard wooden chairs where you'd get a skelf in your bum if you weren't careful. Salt and pepper was in jam jars but this was the nearest thing to heaven that I knew. There was my Da sitting with his cap off and we felt like lords.

Gusty's friend Billy McIlvenna worked in a small shop at Downing Street called Trimble's and it was here at the end of the war that Gusty, aged twelve, had his first bottle of Coke. Coca-Cola had a factory in Rumford Street but the drinks were intended solely for the American troops. Billy McIlvenna and Gusty each had two jobs and when school finished at 3.30 p.m. they ran down to W. & G. Baird's *Belfast Telegraph* premises in Royal Avenue from where they delivered newspapers in big horse-drawn carts until seven or seven-thirty.

On their return, Gusty helped Billy washing and shaving pigs' feet. They used large scrubbers and cut-throat razors and washed the pigs' feet with a water hose. The trotters were then taken into the yard and boiled in a large vat before being drained and cooled and sold in the shop. One Catholic fellow from Albert Street sold pigs' feet in threes. He went round the pubs with a bag shouting, 'Pigs' feet half a crown a yard.'

As a perk the shopkeeper would give Gusty a few pigs' feet and on a Saturday night he was seated at the top of the table while the whole family ate heavily salted pigs' feet. The feet were even incorporated into a local version of the national anthem:

> God save our gracious King,
> Long live our noble King,
> God save the King.
> Send her victorious,
> A pig's fut between four of us,
> Thank God there are no more of us,
> God save the King.

Some people kept pigs and hens in their back yard where a large pot was also kept for potato peelings and other leftovers to feed the pigs. Chicks were sold freely from pet shops in Gresham Street, and Shankill people were often awakened in the early mornings to the sound of a cock crowing in a neighbour's back yard.

And there were the street games. In the summer there were peeries – spinning tops – kept in motion by being whipped. Sometimes the tops of the peeries were coloured with chalks, and the colours produced intriguing patterns as they spun. Boys played with hoops and cleeks (shaped wire hooks) and sometimes old tins with lengths of cord attached could be used to make stilts.

Catching spricks – sticklebacks – from the rivers was popular. The Forth River at Glencairn was a favoured spot. There was a dam near the Springfield Road and one further up the Ballygomartin Road, as well as the Waterworks on the Antrim Road. Girls played with tennis balls against a wall and would try to keep as many moving as possible. Then there were skipping games, accompanied by street songs such as 'I'll tell me ma when I get home'.

Divis Mountain, the Antrim hills and open countryside overlook the Shankill, and much adventure was to be had up there. Children could look down and see Belfast shrouded in a pall of smoke from many factory chimneys. This was the great escape. Gusty often ventured there, and during his years of imprisonment he could dream:

> When we got beyond the Shankill and into the old Glencairn Road at Forth River we were in open countryside. There were trees to climb, long grass to hide in and clear, cool water to drink. You gathered a big bunch of bluebells for your ma on the way home.

From up there you could see all of Belfast. You could see the Shankill – and the Falls:

> Both sides could have spoken with authority on poverty but unfortunately that never happened. Poverty on the Shankill was every bit as grinding and sometimes more so than on the Falls but if people are in a wretched state they like to look upon others as being in a worse state. People said, 'Did you see the Taigs? I saw a couple of motor cars sitting outside their houses.' or 'Some of the houses were lovely, they had a three-piece suite and their house was decorated and painted on the outside.' People were amazed at that and said, 'And then they say they're downtrodden and everything else!'

Whenever working-class people from the Shankill managed to rise above their manifold disadvantages, they faced the snobbery of a middle-class society reluctant to accept that anything good could come from the 'back streets'. (When PUP activists eventually moved into the political arena, there were those who said, 'Who does he think he is? Sure he was brought up in such and such a street.') Talent was assumed to reside in other places, and Shankill loyalism was despised as unadulterated bigotry – at least when it was not needed.

3

Dark Recesses of Sectarianism

The Falls and the Shankill were separate worlds. Most Protestants and Catholics proceeded along each other's roads with caution, conscious at every turn of being in enemy territory. When boys from the Shankill went to the Falls baths they remained vigilant. Young Protestants could be assaulted. The medallions that Catholic youths wore, even in the water, identified them, and their absence might prove significant.

Gusty recalls tales of Protestant boys being asked to recite the Hail Mary, a Catholic prayer. If they couldn't repeat it, 'they got their pans knocked in'.

The streets between the Shankill and the Falls were then unimpeded by high walls (the Peaceline) and steel gates, and were to remain so until 1969. The young Gusty Spence was in one of these connecting streets when he saw the future Roman Catholic Cardinal, then Father William Conway:

I was a boy. We were all smokers who had gone to this little Catholic shop at the bottom of Dover Street. They sold Free State cigarettes and cigarettes were scarce during the war, especially Woodbines. We were getting them a halfpenny cheaper. Sometimes seven or eight of us went down. We'd pool our pennies to buy four fags between us. Then we would stand around in little huddled groups smoking and someone would say, 'There's that big man, that priest,' and Father Conway would glance in our direction. I don't think he glowered or was reproaching us but he certainly paid particular attention to the pall of smoke emanating from the huddle of young fellows.

Many years later, Gusty and Conway were to meet. It was 1974. One of them was by then a cardinal, the other a prisoner in Long Kesh.

As a boy of twelve Gusty also met Paddy Devlin, who had been interned during the war but in 1974 became Minister of Health in the Stormont power-sharing executive. In 1945, Billy Spence asked him to play for Old Lodge and he told Gusty: 'Aye, you must be going bad, coming down for a Taig from the Falls to play for a Shankill Road team.'[1]

When Gusty went with his mates to the Falls baths he faced a problem. He had a union jack tattooed on his right arm. In order to hide this telltale sign, he covered it with a large sticking plaster so that it seemed 'I'd half lost my arm.' His Catholic friend Jimmy McKenna tried to protect him. If anyone made sectarian comments, Jimmy would say, 'Come on now, I don't want any of that old nonsense.' Jimmy also had a tattoo on his arm, but his depicted an Irish tricolour. When they went to Peter's Hill baths in the lower Shankill, he had to cover that up with a plaster.[2]

Jimmy came up the Shankill on the Eleventh Night for the bonfires. Gusty says, 'You got a bit of bullying but there was quite a number of Catholics and there were Protestants who went down to the Falls on the fifteenth of August for Our Lady's Night'[3] and the Catholic bonfires:

I couldn't really dance as such but I remember going down to Townsend Place, to the bonfire down there, when the Taigs were out with accordions. We got a drink of sarsparilla [soft drink] and I might have got a wee sip of wine and was dancing round the bonfires and the Taigs were singing oul rebel songs but it didn't affect me. I suppose there was a tolerance there but sectarianism was there below the surface. If anything happened, both sides automatically took up positions within their own communities.

Catholic girls from the mills came up the Shankill at the Twelfth:

They came round the bonfires and Malvern Street Arch, dancing, and no one was offended. The Pope was kicked but the Catholics were not kicked. Nobody attacked a Catholic because they were a Catholic when he or she came round the Orange arches.

However despite these frequent close contacts there was no meeting of minds:

Once I was going to beat a fellow because he told me Jack Beattie was a Prod. I nearly had yer man by the throat, 'He couldn't be a Prod, he's an all-Irelander.' In my simplistic mind I couldn't comprehend that a Protestant could be in favour of an all-Ireland.[4]

Division lay all around, even when it came to going to the cinema. The 'picture houses' included the 'Shank', 'Wee Joe's', the Stadium on the Shankill, the Gaiety in North Street and the Savoy and Crumlin on the Crumlin Road. Both Protestants and Catholics frequented the Gaiety Picture Theatre in North Street, but on different evenings, as Gusty recalls:

On Monday night Protestants went, on Tuesday night Catholics. Wednesday and Thursday nights were neutral, on Friday night Catholics went and Saturday night Protestants. The Gaiety never played the national anthem. They played 'Goodnight Sweetheart' which seemed very strange

When the deluge of people came out they automatically crossed the road to the Millfield side, which was inclined to be Prod. But if there were enough of us, I was as hardy as anyone else and we ran the gauntlet past Carrick Hill to show our hardihood and manhood. But if enough Taigs were throwing stones we took the far side until we were out of range and ran up the Shankill.

Occasionally Gusty went to cinemas in the Falls area including the Arcadian in Albert Street, the Clonard and the Diamond. He recalls the patrons standing and clapping whenever something was shown on the screen favourable to Catholicism, while they booed at the royal family or anything else British.

The streets were Gusty's world and as he wandered them he made comparisons. For example, there were only muted displays of Protestant patriotism, in the shape of flags and bunting, in the predominantly Protestant Old Lodge Road. This was very different from nearby Malvern Street and Brown's Square which had lavish Orange arches and decorations.

The Old Lodge Road was a strange place. It was a kind of second string to the Shankill. There were virtually no decorations at the Twelfth, perhaps because there was a fair smattering of Catholics, especially on the right-hand side going up from North Street. They weren't seen as Catholic streets; they were loyalist districts with a smattering of Catholics. Then again, you had a good-sized Jewish element too and some of the streets had professional and semi-professional people like doctors, lawyers, dentists and the usual moneylenders.

In those days the peace walls were invisible. But in the streets stretching from the Shankill to the Falls even children could tell where the Protestant homes stopped and the Catholic ones began.

Once you passed a particular point in Northumberland Street you were into hostile territory and vice versa. You were always conscious of being in hostile territory even though there were no guns thundering in those days.

One of Gusty's nightmares was to find himself lost on the Falls with no way out. In these dreams he was always in abject fear that Catholics or the IRA would apprehend him.[5] Such fears had been strengthened by stories from previous Troubles:

Taigs were bad, never mind the IRA. That was the section from which the IRA came. I was confused and didn't want to contemplate the idea that Catholics were my equals. Not that I saw myself on a lofty pedestal, I was just the normal five eight on the street, but there were things that were wrong. You said to yourself, 'Flip me, that's wrong but they're Taigs and it'll fucking do them rightly.' We had to maintain this barricade at all costs and we cowardly acquiesced. If there had been normal politics we would have had voices, but there was no real alternative.

4

Marriage and Military Service

Gusty began his school career at the age of five in 1938 and finished at the age of fourteen in 1947. On the Sunday morning that war broke out Gusty was being bathed with his brothers and sisters in front of the fire:

> Men went to Clifton Street to enlist and the police had to make a baton charge to keep them back. Many were already in the reserve forces where they got a pair of good boots and items of clothing to be pawned when not needed. But war was declared on a Sunday morning so Mary Leathem had to be contacted so the men could get their army boots from her pawnshop.
>
> Every house did their duty by sending volunteers into the forces. My brother Willie joined the Navy, Jim joined the Gordon Highlanders and our Bobby joined the Navy. The women were at their doors, 'juking' out to see them go.

After they left their mothers feared the approach of the telegram boy:

> He was hated when he arrived with his red bike and wee peaked hat to

deliver the telegram. Sometimes he brought good news that a son was coming home on leave, but my ma dreaded the telegram boy. If someone said, 'Ma the telegram boy's in the street,' she froze and turned weak at the knees. She told her boys, 'If you're coming home on leave, don't send any telegrams, just come.'

People refused to go into a shelter after the Percy Street shelter collapsed killing seventy-four people:

After the blitz I went down to the Shankill where people were bringing bodies from Percy Street. A pub had gone up in flames and I could smell the drink. Miller's confectioner shop next door had sold toys. I found toy soldiers in the street and began lifting them up.

Suddenly I felt a tap on my back and turned round to see a peeler, who seemed sixteen foot high. 'What are you doing there?' I showed him the toy soldiers and a look of compassion came over him. 'Who do you belong to?' Says I, 'I live in Joseph Street.' 'Get to hell home where you belong.' The boys were soon all around me looking at the soldiers.

Later they put up signs, 'Looters Will be Shot' but even though the people on the road were hungry they renamed Berlin Street Spitfire Street, in a burst of patriotic fervour.

The children of Joseph Street were evacuated to Glenavy, about fifteen miles from Belfast, in County Antrim:

We got into a three-ton army truck and went up the Falls Road with this big Union Jack singing, 'Hitler thought he had us with his ja, ja, ja. Hitler thought he had us but you see he never got us, with his ja ja, ja ja ja.' Nobody paid a blind bit of notice. When we got to Glenavy we had a wee bit of adventure, things to investigate, an oul prison and a river.

Next day, Ma says, 'Right up you get and come on with me.' 'Where are we going?' 'Belfast.' A wee countryman said, 'Oh you couldn't go.' My Ma says, 'Are you going to stop me?' We hit the road along with the three Smith children whose dad had been taken prisoner. They clung to my Ma and someone said, 'We'll have to hand them over to the orphanage.' Says my Ma, 'I'm their aunt, I'm looking after these children, come on.'

Jean, Bo McClelland's wife, was there.[1] Eddie McKenzie waved this big open-back lorry down. What did they put us on top of? Dead cows! They must have been transporting them to feed the people of Lisburn. We were shit scared but I paughled through and there was me sitting on top of a dead cow.

The first stop was Lisburn about eight miles from Belfast:

> We stayed there overnight and next morning we were bucked on to a truck and taken to Belfast. A bomb in Hopeton Street had wrecked all the houses in Joseph Street. There were no windows left in my Ma's house and my eldest sister who hadn't been evacuated had made a fire. My Ma says, 'You're making a fire in the middle of the floor?' Cassie says, 'Ma, our house is wrecked.' She was making chips on the fire.

It was accepted that as soon as children left school they would contribute to the family income. Gusty was destined for the mills:

> Everyone worked and subscribed. We were unskilled labour. Ach, I was still a school kid when I went into the dark Satanic mills strategically placed in the catchment area for the Falls and the Shankill. The bosses didn't ask if you were a Prod or a Taig. You kept your head down working in your bare feet in the spinning rooms and earned your sixteen shillings and eight pence a week. I detested those mills. They were dangerous places. People lost fingers, but of course the bosses got over that. They didn't offer compensation but gave them a job for life and because of economic depression people often accepted this. I couldn't get out of the mills quickly enough, but the economic needs of the family demanded I stayed there.

Eventually he did manage to get out and find employment elsewhere:

> A friend introduced me to house repairing and I worked in various building jobs until I was eighteen or nineteen and went into the Belfast shipyard. The money and the rapport were better. I was working solely with men and it was a man's atmosphere, which helped to formulate attitudes. Some of the formulation wasn't all that good. We had to stand up for ourselves. I had entered a man's world. Most of the workforce was Protestant. This was probably a carry-over from the 1920s and the 1930s when there was internecine warfare, sectarian riots, and the shipyard was looked upon as a loyalist domain.

This was the first of several spells of employment Gusty had in the shipyard, some of them lasting only a few months. He worked as a stager:

> A stager was the equivalent of a scaffolder in the shipyard. He put wooden planking up in stages for riveters and welders and others. Only wood was used at that time. They were called stagers because they lifted the fitting up for the different trades in stages, every six foot.

When Gusty and 'John' were about sixteen they courted two girls who were mutual friends from Disraeli Street. The girls were forgotten however when 'John' began to serve an apprenticeship and Gusty found other work.

Gusty Spence was married to Louie Donaldson from Hertford Street on the Grosvenor Road in 1953, Queen Elizabeth's coronation year.

> I met Louie on the Shankill Road. She probably knew where to come if she wanted to get a proper man! I was nineteen and she was eighteen. We courted and we hadn't a halfpenny between us. We saved ten pounds and borrowed another ten and that's what we were married on. I was grateful that Louie accepted me, without being too maudlin about it. Best move ever I made.

In those days droves of young people walked up the Shankill Road where Gusty and his friends gathered on Sunday evenings:

> Life was passing us by and we were saying hello to Tom, Dick and Harry or Rosie and Sarah. We were full of life but Belfast must have been one of the most miserable towns ever. No cinemas or pubs were open on Sundays and the done thing was to walk up the Shankill Road, up the Ballygomartin Road and round the side of the hill, about four miles. There was a big green square there and literally hundreds of young fellows and girls were pairing off and sitting having a yarn or smoking wee butts.
>
> Louie Donaldson was friendly with a girl called Jeanie. They worked together and often walked up the Shankill on Sunday evenings. We did a bit of whistling and walked up the road with them before sitting down and having a yarn or smoking a butt or two. I courted her since January 1952 and we were married on 20 June 1953.

Pastor Sammy Cromie officiated at the wedding in Wellwood Street Mission in Sandy Row:

> Billy McCoubrey took four photographs of the wedding with a Brownie camera because we couldn't afford anything else. After the wedding we caught the Bangor train in Station Street, spent a day in Bangor and caught the last train back to Belfast that night. We walked to Hertford Street in the Grosvenor Road area where Louie took off her high heels as we slipped quietly into the street lest the neighbours heard.

The Grosvenor Road, where Gusty and Louie began their married life, was very different from the Shankill because Catholics were living close by:

> I found it an alien atmosphere. After living in the Shankill Road all those

years I was suddenly transported to the Grosvenor Road and I didn't like it at first but it grew on me. It finished up that I loved the Grosvenor Road because I was exposed to a different culture, whereas the Shankill Road was only the domain of loyalists. There was more coming-together than I had known outside of the mills. There was a level of tolerance. Facing Leeson Street, which was Catholic, was Little Grosvenor Street where you had an Orange arch every year. Catholic people would come from Leeson Street and dance at the bonfires and the pubs stayed open a bit late and people had a reasonable time.

When the shipyard became slack, Gusty began working in Mackie's engineering works on the nearby Springfield Road. In 1954, on 14 October, Gusty and Louie became parents when their first daughter, Elizabeth, was born. Sandra was to be born two years later in 1956, Catherine in 1960. Gusty and Louie seemed happy.

Well, happy is not the word; I was content. Happy in those days depended on economic circumstances. People were always amazed because Louie and I were always laughing and joking, and even Louie's cousin said, 'I don't know what you're laughing about. You haven't a penny between you.' And Louie says, 'Ach, there's more to life than money.'

Living on the Grosvenor Road widened Gusty's world. It meant meeting all sorts of people:

One day I was with Harry Millar and we did a wee bet in Walker's bookies. We then went up to see how it had done and found that two of the horses had actually won. While we were waiting on the third horse we called into McCavanagh's Bar at the corner of Distillery Street. Billy McMillen was there with two other fellows and he said, 'Are you down on business or pleasure, Gusty?' Says I, 'A wee bit of pleasure, Billy.' So Billy set us up a drink and of course we set one back again. I didn't know the big fellow there but I knew some of the others including Billy McMillen who was in charge of an IRA battalion, although the IRA was virtually defunct at that time.

Before Easter of 1966, there was a bomb explosion in a telephone kiosk at Smithfield. B Specials captured the man who did it. He was sitting there in the bar with Billy McMillen. It quite amazed me, having lived in the racially, religiously and in every other way sanitised society of the Shankill. It opened new vistas for me, showing that people could live cheek by jowl. I recall in amazement saying to Louie, 'I've come down Elizabeth Street and I saw a union jack, tricolour, union jack, tricolour on alternate houses.'

Lord Blease, formerly Billy Blease, a prominent trade-unionist, says the Spence family were 'good trade unionists'. Gusty says:

> We were a unionist family but also a trade union family. We believed in collective bargaining and work being safeguarded. My Da belonged to the Municipal Union. I belonged to the Transport and General Workers' and the Municipal Union. Those were the days of collective bargaining and you had to have a strong trade union. You couldn't have got a job in the shipyard without being a trade unionist. Our Willie was also a member of the Transport and General Workers' and the Municipal. Bobby joined the navy when he was young but later worked in the power stations and became a member of a trade union there. Jim was a member of a union, and Ned was also a Communist.

Gusty rejects any suggestion that those were 'good old days':

> Children were birthed in different hospitals and went to separate schools. The only time they came together was under the 'great' captains of industry in the mills. When people died they were buried in different graveyards. We read different newspapers, reflecting different political points of view. Even the great trade union movement was divided. Those people who taught our children could not agree on one union. We had the Irish National Teachers' Organisation and we had the Ulster Teachers' Union. Even now we have separate teacher training colleges. If the teachers are separated, what can we expect from the children?
>
> There were subtleties that never permitted us to be a wholesome society. There were political machinations and the border was hammered deep into the Protestant psyche. When the political bosses wanted a manifestation of support they ensured that there was a threat to the border. That energised the electorate to put their Xs where they were supposed to put them.

Gusty was out of work again in 1957:

> The shipyard had hit a hell of a slump and I then worked at everything and anything that turned a shilling. I smile to myself when people talk about forced migration. We took economic migration as the norm. I worked in England, Scotland, Wales and further afield. When work was slack I went away for a period of months and sent money home. I saved up a couple of shillings, came back and took up where I had left off. I thought nothing of it. We just took it with a pinch of salt but when I joined the army in 1957, there was a big big depression and there was no alternative. I had to have a reasonably constant wage because I had two children then.

But it was not entirely for economic reasons that Gusty and his brothers joined the armed forces. Writing in July 1981, Gusty reflected on his motivation in a letter to Bob Hynds, a fellow inmate from Compound 21 of the Maze prison.

> I got involved because it was the done thing at that time. We had been reared on a diet of duty and country. That is why Willie, Jim, Bobby and myself had joined the forces. Deep down you looked upon anyone who did not join as being a traitor. It's laughable nowadays, but so are many things.

Gusty joined the Royal Ulster Rifles (RUR). Army experience broadened his mind as well as assisting in his general education, and the Irish elements in army ritual and tradition left a lasting impression upon him. Occasionally he heard the officers giving the Sláinte (toast) in Irish. Gusty enjoyed this expression of Irishness, which was as pronounced in the RUR as it was in the Royal Inniskilling Fusiliers and the Royal Irish Fusiliers. Some soldiers in these regiments would later join the IRA while others, like Gusty, joined the UVF.

Perhaps it was this 'natural' Irishness that eventually enabled Gusty to communicate to loyalist prisoners and others a sense of pride in things Irish that sat easily with their unionism. David Ervine, who was with him in Long Kesh during the 1970s, believes that the unionism he espoused was 'a unionism that was not anti-Irish, not anti-Catholic and a unionism that says, "I'm an Irish citizen of the United Kingdom."'

There was, of course, some expression of Irishness in the old UVF. One of Gusty's souvenirs from that time exhibits a slogan in Irish: 'lámh dhearg na hUladh' (red hand of Ulster). This document is dated 2 May 1914 and it records the presentation of the colours to the west Belfast Regiment of the UVF at Glencairn, where Gusty was to read the CLMC ceasefire declaration many years later. It is part of Gusty's extensive collection of memorabilia, mostly British military badges, the bulk of which he inherited from his father.

> St Patrick's Day was a big day in the Ulster Rifles. We marched to two tunes: an Orange song, 'The Sash my Father Wore', and a republican song, 'Kelly the Boy from Killan', representing both traditions in a cultural sense. Then on Rifles Day we commemorated the Somme. The Sláinte was given, and the pipe major drank the last drains of Irish whiskey. The dress of the Royal Ulster Rifles included the standard saffron kilt. We had Tara brooches, the shamrock and the Maid of Erin harp. All those things awakened

in me the feeling that we're Irish. We're British, of course, but we're also Irish.

The RUR also stimulated an interest in history:

I was always very interested in the regimental history of the Rifles and all the Irish regiments. It's a wonderful colourful history. All these wars were fought, with all the suffering, killing and dying, and there was a great *esprit de corps* and comradeship. There was a big division between 'other ranks' and officers. I suppose I felt insulted having to go to the back door of the officers' mess. It was like a tradesmen's entrance. There were always social divisions, but less so in the Rifles than in the more elite regiments like the Guards.

I belonged to a hard regiment that drew its recruits from the working-class areas of Belfast as well as Dublin and Liverpool. They were tough men. The professionalism of the training and the physical aspect, as well as the handling of firearms, was thorough and the regiment gained a very good reputation as far as fighting men were concerned. We didn't care much for the Paras or any others.

Gusty and his regiment were sent to Cyprus, and there he experienced a deeply divided society in the throes of upheaval. It was in Cyprus that he became friendly with a southern Irishman whose father had been in the IRA:

I've always considered it ironic that on many occasions my life depended on someone who was born and reared in the Free State and who had republican inclinations. Tony O'Rourke and I were full corporals and he carried his father's two IRA medals with him. He never wore them of course, he couldn't, but even whilst he was in the British army, an anachronism in itself, he was fiercely republican.

Political discussion was frowned upon, but Gusty could retain his pride in Orangeism:

I carried my Orange collarette with me in the small pack. No matter where I went the sash went with me, and on the Twelfth morning I put it on and one of the boys would pipe me round the hut. Some of the locals thought I was mad, but I was only trying to keep up a tradition, the tradition of those who went over the top on 1 July 1916 wearing their collarettes.

The collarettes could not be displayed otherwise. Politics were taboo but there was a high level of tolerance and in the corporals' mess someone would sing, 'We're off to Dublin in the Green' and then someone else sang

'Derry's Walls'. I don't remember any fights over religion or politics. Sometimes we joined in singing the opposition's songs.

For Gusty, 'peacetime soldiering just represents a drab life broken up occasionally by moments of absolute terror when you're in action and under fire'.

He recalls coming into contact in Cyprus with The National Association of Cypriot Fighters (EOKA) terrorists who had escaped detention, including one leader named Joseph Ashiotis.

A fellow from the Falls Road named Burns was on guard duty one night when a young fellow came up to him saying, 'My name is Joseph Ashiotis. I want to give myself up.' Ashiotis was on a wanted list but Burns said to this big tall thin fellow, 'Better get out of the road there or I'll hit you a good kick up the fucking arse.' But your man repeated, 'I am Joseph Ashiotis. I want to see the intelligence officer,' and he mentioned the officer by name. Burns immediately put him under arrest. He had turned informer and the company went up next day to the terrorist hide which was littered with booby traps. They drove a flock of sheep up and set all the booby traps off.

There was quite a bit of that because of internment. We carried the names and photographs of wanted men and were always on the lookout. One night there was a line-up and an informer was handcuffed to myself and another fellow. As we went down the line he nodded and picked out three men who were taken for interrogation. Then there was a cordon and search sweep but when we got back into our billet and took the handcuffs off we discovered he was a British army major and an intelligence officer. There was all types of divide-and-conquer pranks played, and there were dirty tricks.

Gusty was a member of the regimental police.

There is the military police service, which is the Royal Military Police Corps, but I was a military policeman within my own regiment. We were known as regimental police and didn't wear the red hat. I wore the ordinary dress of a Royal Ulster Rifleman with insignia indicating that I was a policeman. I was still a corporal, under the head of policing. He had senior men under him, one of whom was yours truly, and my friend Tony O'Rourke was a policeman too.

In Cyprus certain areas were out-of-bounds for soldiers:

The only place we could frequent socially was the old city Famagusta. It was Turkish and they weren't shooting us in the back. The Varosha area was inhabited by Greek Cypriots and was like the Falls Road in Belfast is to

British soldiers.

Yet I found the army a liberating experience in many ways and after facing active service, things you once thought dangerous did not seem dangerous any more, and you took chances.

One experience in Cyprus, which Gusty described as a 'telling moment', stayed with him down the years.

Cyprus represented an internal security situation and wasn't seen as a war – it was always 'an emergency'. People have great euphemisms for these things. Someone fired two shots at us and we put the patrol into the side, radioed for instructions, and did the normal thing, a cordon and search.

While waiting for orders, Gusty's attention was drawn to the faces of people passing by:

As I looked into their eyes I could see fear and hatred and began to wonder – what am I doing here, thousands of miles from the Shankill? These people were walking past me, ordinary people, and I could see hatred in their eyes for me. I couldn't understand this. Here was I, three thousand miles from Belfast, and I asked myself the question, 'What the hell am I doing here?' And it may have been a spark that led me to question.

Gusty also spent some time stationed in Germany.

I admired the German people and obviously Britain and America had learned from the First World War not to rub peoples' noses in it when they were defeated. There was big economic investment by Britain and America to ensure that there would never be such an obnoxious thing as the rise of Nazism again. I never met a Nazi while I was there; at least they didn't admit to it. But sometimes when they got a liquor or two in them, we could have heard the old marching songs.

While talking to Gusty about his army experience, I encouraged him to reflect on how it had influenced his life. Had it resulted in the development of a professional code which may have enabled soldiers to respect their enemies?

The Ulster Rifles was one of the toughest regiments in the British army and discipline had to be extremely strict to keep such men in line. But whenever it came to fighting prowess, all you had to do, as General Ken Breedin said, was point them in the right direction while reasonably sober and away they went to give a good account of themselves.

> There are, however, lines that are never crossed, because it was not decent. That was further instilled into me in the army. Even though we saw people abusing their position, we knew it wasn't right. We weren't always in a position to protest if they were superior officers. But in my section I ensured that no one abused their position. With us being a rifle regiment we became extremely proficient in firearms and, to a lesser degree, explosives. I imagine that was one of the reasons why I was approached in 1965, as well as me being a 'stalwart loyalist', whatever that means.

After developing asthma, Gusty left the army in 1961. The following year his son Andrew was born. That year, 1962, was the fiftieth anniversary of the signing of the Ulster Covenant by many thousands of Ulstermen opposed to home rule, so Gusty and Louie gave their son the middle name Carson after the Unionist leader of the time Edward Carson.

But Gusty's return to civilian life was not easy:

> I had no house, no job and no vote but yet there were people who looked upon me and people like me, as being part of the Protestant ascendancy. You can't get any luckier than that. In those days we had universal franchise for Stormont and Westminster elections. But many couldn't vote in local elections. I knew a man who had twenty-seven wallpaper shops so he had twenty-seven votes in local elections. I had none. If a man and wife lived in the same house, whoever's name appeared on the rent book, the man or the wife, they had a vote but the other spouse had none. That was the case in England at one time but they did away with it years earlier.

This system was not confined to Protestants. Catholic businessmen also had multiple votes. The slogan 'one man, one vote' was used as a political rallying cry. It was misleading, and there was generally a failure to acknowledge that in most elections 'One Man, One Vote' was already in operation. Those who lost out included both Protestants and Catholics. When universal franchise was eventually introduced in local government elections it made little, if any, noticeable difference.

As an ex-serviceman, Gusty soon found himself in a relatively privileged position of having a choice between applying for work in the Post Office, the RUC or the Prison Service. In the end he chose the Post Office because it paid three half-crowns (37½ pence) more each week. As in many places of work at that time, there were opportunities to exploit the system. In the Harland and Wolff shipyard, people had friends clock them in so that they could claim a day's pay but actually stay at home.[3] In some cases they carried on a private business. According to Gusty:

> I worked in the Post Office until 1965 and I claimed overtime that I hadn't worked, which was the norm. If I had been prepared to give other names to the authorities I may only have got a slap on the wrist but I wouldn't do that, so they gave me six months' imprisonment and I got the sack from the Post Office.

This kind of practice was common in those days. In one large organisation in which I was employed for a short period, workers were constantly clocking each other in and out and the bosses turned a blind eye. It became easier during holiday periods when the workers were paid double, or even treble, time. I can still recall one worker singing his heart out with the words, 'On the good old double time'.

> . . . The boss would have said, 'Look, stay on for two hours and I'll pay you for four.' So whenever the bosses were pulled in, they ratted and said, 'Ach no, we didn't say that at all,' so you were left holding the baby. There were others involved but I was the only one to get time because I wouldn't make any statement or admit anything. The bosses in the Post Office knew but the managers didn't know, or pretended they didn't know, because they themselves were bosses at one time, and they had come through the ranks.

Gusty was going to jail for the first time. But he took his sentence philosophically:

> I prided myself that I had not been responsible for anyone else going to jail, including some of the bosses. I was getting jailed for something I did, all right, but it was custom and practice.
>
> When I came out, some of those who could have been caught said, 'Well done, Gusty lad,' but they didn't bring a loaf or anything else to my wife.

5

Politics and Personation

Gusty served four months of his sentence. He found prison harsh, but he did not look on himself as a criminal. Instead, he felt he was someone who had been caught out in a misdemeanour. After he came out, he found employment where he could, including the shipyard again. But gradually he was becoming more directly involved in politics of a kind.

For him, the central issues facing Northern Ireland were the border with the south and the Union with Britain. To safeguard them he would do whatever was required.

> So come election time, we were always impersonating votes. I was an impersonator, I'm not proud of it but I'm not particularly ashamed of it either. It was the norm in those days. The Prods did it, the Taigs did it, everybody did it. Perhaps some of the steam and fun has gone out of voting. It has become the norm to vote legitimately, although there are those who would contest this.

We examined the electoral rolls and if we found any Catholic names we went to the polling booth first and voted in their name. These were names like Sean O'Toole. We stole Sean's vote while Sean was stealing Billy's vote. Everybody was stealing each other's votes and the slogan was 'vote early and vote often'. The dead were resurrected and the sick were miraculously made whole. Personation was organised, but these majestic parties nowadays would tell you that impersonation was reprehensible. Yet they were the paymasters and if you were arrested, they paid the fine. We did it out of patriotism, misguided or otherwise. I saw it as a continuing service to the Union – the end-all and be-all of everything.

Unionist personation can only be understood in the context of the Ulster Protestant mindset. Gusty saw 'the wolf at the door' in the shape of nationalism, republicanism or the Roman Catholic Church. The threat could also take the form of socialism. Even the mildest of socialists could be classed with republicans as dangerous because they were less sound on the border:

We were born into corruption. We didn't know any better. It's like being born in a pit and you claw your way out of it. Politics in Northern Ireland was the politics of fear, in which one side frightened their band of people into voting for them while the other side did exactly the same thing. What we did, and it was reprehensible, was that when we got the first grasp that things were wrong we stayed mute, lest the spotlight of attention was brought to bear on us.

The spotlight could shine on anyone who questioned that which was expected to be taken for granted. Some had always questioned, but the main alternative was seen as some form of socialism and that could lead to what Gusty called the 'white buffalo' or Lundy syndrome.[1] Anyone who questioned was seen as a potential threat to the whole Protestant community. Gusty was well aware of the process:

The great term in my day was red-flagger. The 'powers that be' scared the shit out of people by resurrecting various ghosts. One ghost was the Catholic Church, others were fascism and Communism. The latter was promoting world revolution and all governments saw themselves as under siege from that source. So they had to scare the people with this Communist threat.

Gusty, 'John' and 'Robert' were later branded Communists by right-wing unionists, as 'John' discovered:

> I got stopped by an ex-internee and he said, 'We've been told that you and Gusty and "Robert", are three commies.' The man is a friend yet even he believed it.

Politics in Northern Ireland has been described as a zero-sum game. If one side gained, the other side had to be losing something. Gusty saw personation as 'striking a blow for the cause by making sure that the unionist candidate was returned'.

At the 1964 general election the candidates in West Belfast, a marginal Westminster constituency, were Harry Diamond for Republican Labour, Liam (Billy) McMillen, Republican, Billy Boyd of the Northern Ireland Labour Party, and Jim Kilfedder of the Ulster Unionists. Unionists feared that the British Labour Party would win the general election: the party leader, Harold Wilson, had promised to act against discrimination in Northern Ireland if he were elected.

Kilfedder's election agent and secretary of the West Belfast Unionist Association was Gusty's brother Billy. Gusty decided to help out and was a 'station captain' at St Catherine's School on the Falls Road. His role was to prevent personation but he had another role too. He says of his brother, 'He did the legitimate stuff and I did the illegitimate stuff.'

In the end, Kilfedder was to be successful. It was at this time that I heard about Gusty's exploits at the Ancient Order of Hibernians hall on the Falls Road. He had gone there to check reports that nationalist personators were being organised from there. According to him, unionists had already found 'racks of coats and wigs and shoes because my wife and others had been in the hall and seen them'.

Gusty travelled there with his brother Billy while another Unionist drove the car. He approached a greengrocer's shop beside the hall to discover that the owner had gone to town. Gusty asked the owner's wife for the key and she obliged and he went about his investigations. 'Kilfedder knew exactly what I was at.' His brother Billy said:

> 'He knows but he doesn't want to know, he's a barrister and he doesn't want to have any knowledge of this.' But [said Gusty] he knew the next day when he was in the car with me and we went to the Falls Road. They never got out of the car, but I was carrying a firearm. You don't take all that many chances.

Gusty was armed:

Posing as a Post Office investigator, I went along to the addresses on the polling cards. 'Is there anybody in the house entitled to vote who is not going to vote for whatever reason?' 'Yes, there is,' this wee woman said. 'Our Sean's in the army and people came round and collected his card.' She had handed over Sean's polling card which finished up in our hands so there was going to be a police investigation over it.

A big meeting took place and we presented overwhelming evidence of election fraud, which we were also involved in. O'Neill was there, Faulkner, and [Brian] McConnell and others. The meeting was held in Glengall Street to consider whether or not to take the West Belfast election to an electoral court but they decided against it.

That may have been for obvious reasons. Nationalists would have said, 'Well, we've won an election hands down and these people are going to do everything they can to remove it from us.' The word came down the stairs that no one would be taken to the electoral court because they had no balls. We were incensed at that time and the police investigation ran into the sand.

I went down to Chichester Street to the offices of John G. Edwards who was a Catholic, incidentally, and solicitor to the Ulster Unionist Council. I was interviewed there by Robert Porter, a County Court judge who later became Minister of Home Affairs, to elicit the facts. We had to admit that we had personated and could be jailed. We certainly went to the Falls to undercover this nefarious activity, but it was a fact that we were personating people and indeed we personated the votes on the stolen poll cards.

I remember newspaper headlines in those days: 'The Well Oiled Unionist Election Machine Swings Into Action'. I'll tell you what the well-oiled unionist machine was. It was Gusty going to a wee woman and saying, 'Come on and stick a couple of votes in here.' 'Ach,' she says, 'Gusty, I have his supper on.' Says I, 'Well, put it on a low gas. Sure it won't take you two minutes.' I brought her round to Malvern Street where she was sticking in a vote or two. That was the 'well-oiled unionist election machine'.

People will say, 'That's terrible,' and there would be the tut-tutting from predictable sources. But they were halcyon days in many ways, times of excitement and passion. Both sides were at it a mile a minute.

Gusty had his own team of personators consisting of fifty to sixty people. There were other teams throughout Belfast, but Gusty's people boasted that they were the most efficient. One of them claimed to hold a record at seventy-four votes in one day.[2] Gusty recalled, 'Even my mother was at it, a wee innocent woman, an old staunch unionist who saw it as part of her duty. You could always expect two or three votes from my ma.'

Gangs of personators could become vicious rivals but there was also honour between the gangs. Sometimes there was an acknowledgement that 'You fought your corner and I fought mine.'

> It was unusual, unless someone had a previous conviction for the same offence, for him or her to be sent to prison, and if they were sent to prison it might be for a month. The last five arrested were from my team and they were fined £150 a piece.

In those days, £150 was a lot of money so Gusty tried to get help from the Unionist Party secretary in Glengall Street:

> I went down to Jim Bailie and put it to him – 'Jim, these people have been fined £150 a piece and they don't have two pence. What are you going to do about it?' 'Well now, I don't know,' he said. But it finished up that I got the money from the Unionist Party to pay the fines. There must have been slush funds. I liked Jim Bailie and Billy Douglas, his predecessor. They reckoned that Billy Douglas was the equivalent of Daly in Chicago. He was the boss. He hired and fired and ruled with a ruthless hand.
>
> A lot of the sport and a lot of the craic has gone out of elections. There were humorous aspects. When people got a name and address to personate, they used to rhyme it over and over. It was like monks intoning a prayer as they kept rehearsing. They would mutter within themselves, 'Sam Cairns 48 Denmark Street'. Once when I was station captain, this person who was on our side got right up to the table and then forgot the name and address. He says, 'Fuck it' and walked out muttering, 'I'm not voting the day.'

Once a vote had been tendered there was nothing further that could be done:

> This fellow had the vote in his hand and the personation officer was following him right into the booth, saying, 'You're not so and so.' And he was saying, 'How do you know?' He forcefully put his X on the paper. Once he got it in the ballot box and knew he was safe, he turned round and chinned your man before the police could do anything about it and ran out of the polling station.

But the practice of personation was not always so humorous:

> There was a very hairy time in 1966. Feelings were high in Belfast and we

> always prided ourselves that no matter how tight the polling stations were in nationalist districts, we always fully manned them. But people became trapped in polling stations in republican areas and the police had to force their way in to get our people out. The same thing happened on the Shankill and I remember having to get republicans out of Malvern Street. They had been personation officers there.
>
> There was always an element of risk and a threat of violence. Nationalists had a good slick team and I remember reports coming in on how well they were organised. That moved me into action, saying to our teams that the nationalists were so well organised we would have to be better organised and put more votes in.

In Gusty's view, most politicians would have used whatever methods worked and whichever words could get them elected. It is his opinion that unionists never attempted to educate their people and unionist politicians had no real understanding of what passed for normal politics elsewhere. 'It's only now that they're on the threshold of practising what passes for politics.' I suggested to Gusty that unionists had taken much of the progressive legislation that Britain passed, adopted it, and sold unionism as being the source of these benefits. He responded thus:

> Well, that's right, but they didn't have much choice. When they're tied to the country it would be illogical not to pursue the same policies as the mother of parliaments. But there were still gross anomalies and the household vote persisted in Northern Ireland. It persisted for one reason only – for patronage. And many unionist politicians opposed the enlightened legislation brought in by a Labour government after the war, including family allowances and the National Health Service.

Unionist politics revolved around the constitutional issue and the border. This was not amenable to negotiation and compromise. Politics had all the markings of a religious conflict in that it seemed to be centred on supposedly ultimate and sacred things. In the mind of many protagonists such issues could only be solved through violence and bloodshed.

6

The Formation of the Modern UVF

The original Ulster Volunteer Force did not end in 1914 when it was incorporated into the 36th (Ulster) Division, but was resurrected from time to time, albeit never on the same scale. During the 1920s Sir Basil Brooke was horrified at the anarchy he had observed in Dublin and was determined that such lawlessness would not spread to the new Northern Ireland, so in June 1920 he proceeded to organise his 'illegal vigilante force'.

> He began with the formation of a nucleus of fourteen on the demesne at Colebrooke. They were armed, using the UVF guns 'run in' by Crawford at Larne. They had never been surrendered but carefully concealed, he claimed later, for just such an eventuality ...[1]

Brooke's action in forming a local protection force was certainly not unique. It was paralleled by similar groups formed by northern unionists elsewhere, as the need was widely and independently felt.[2]

Ulster unionists officially reactivated the UVF for the protection of life and property.

> On 25 June 1920 therefore, the UUC [the Ulster Unionist Council, the central authority of the Unionist Associations] Standing Committee decided to revive the UVF and Wilfred Spender was asked to command the force. He himself regarded it as 'the best and safest way' to avoid 'serious trouble'. From police reports, it can be seen to have been active in all six north-eastern counties except Down by August.[3]

Lieutenant-Colonel Wilfred Spender, an officer in the UVF during 1913–14,[4] said the raising of the UVF in 1920 was at the suggestion of Edward Carson. However Fred Crawford reportedly advised Carson that it was necessary to re-form the UVF and get recognition for it, otherwise Protestants would be 'killing a lot of Sinn Féiners'.[5]

> ... the Army and the RIC [Royal Irish Constabulary] were to cooperate not only with the Black & Tans but equally with the UVF in Ulster. After this there was an improvement in the situation, and I was able to allow the UVF to resume their patrols with the Military forces ... All these duties, mainly at night, were unpaid, and were putting a severe strain on our men, and I then put forward the proposal that the UVF should be changed into three types of Special Constabulary.[6]

Reorganisation took place before the end of 1920[7] and the UVF was transformed into A, B and C special constabularies.[8] The C Specials and the A Specials were disbanded as soon as a degree of security was achieved. The B Specials remained until 1971 when they were disbanded.

The UVF was apparently reactivated in the 1930s. According to Gusty:

> The UVF were called upon about 1934 when it seemed likely that Northern Ireland was on a point of rebellion. Protestants and Catholics were coming together and men were hired to shoot Catholics to promote sectarianism and drive a wedge between them. They were paid a half a quid a day. At least three of the old gunmen told me from their own mouths at separate times that was their role.

Among those who spoke with Gusty were Buck Alec and Bobby Moore. They said:

> There was an element of the UVF reconstituted in 1935 and some were covertly enlisted by the Ulster government at a fee of ten shillings a day to promote a sectarian war, which they did do.

Buck Alec in time became critical of the Unionist government and was tempted to lift the lid on the past:

> A couple of times he pronounced that he would denounce them and tell some of the things that he had been involved in. However the government would have had him in the courts and he could have served a lengthy sentence. It's one of those things that the unionist/Protestant/loyalist people will not admit to. The Ulster government did employ people to start a sectarian war and it was successful because the rapprochement between them was quickly blown up and the IRA became involved in order to protect the Catholic community.

Buck Alec was a legendary figure in Belfast, famous for keeping lions in his back yard in York Street. Gusty recalled:

> His son Danny and I were trained in St Patrick's Barracks at Ballymena and were in the same regiment. We came up to Belfast for weekends and Danny would call round and I saw his father and we had a yarn. After I came out of the army we remade contact, getting arms and ammunition and stuff like that, because Buck Alec had very wide contacts. As far as I know he was a professional gunman and during the twenties when things got a bit tight Buck Alec went to America. He ran with the mobs there. Danny, who was my mate in the army, was named Danny Devargo Robinson after a gangster in Chicago.
>
> Buck Alec was in the UVF when it was reconstituted in the 1930s. He was a very secretive person and the mere fact that I elicited that much information was a revelation in itself. He virtually never spoke about that and lived for forty years under threat from the IRA. He never sat with his back to the door but always sat where he could have the full panoramic view. Bobby Moore was the same, and although Bobby became a Christian in his later life, they were both old gunmen.

A number of authors have suggested that the re-formation of the UVF in 1965 was linked with Ulster Protestant Action (UPA), but Gusty rejects this. 'No indeed, it wasn't. The UPA was a ginger [pressure] group. They had no firearms or anything remotely like that.'

However when the UPA had been formed in 1956, there was growing concern about Northern Ireland's position within the UK. The IRA began a violent border campaign that year and it continued until 1962. The end of the campaign did not reduce tensions, and some loyalists were aware that there was a turning 'towards left-wing politics and social agitation' among republicans, which increased fears of subversion.[9]

A number of other events helped to stimulate fears. In 1958 the Queen Mother and Princess Margaret visited Pope John and were attacked by Ian Paisley for 'committing spiritual fornication and adultery with the Anti-Christ'.[10] This visit was followed in the early 1960s by high-profile visits to the Pope by the Queen and the Archbishop of Canterbury, among others. For some Ulster Protestants, the Queen's visit represented the ultimate betrayal because it conflicted with the Williamite settlement and the Bill of Rights of 1689.

Ancient fears were being rekindled and they were compounded by a virulent new fundamentalism associated with Ian Paisley. In 1962 a tract was produced and distributed by a Belfast evangelical Protestant, William McGrath, which spelt out the message:

> ... we will be labelled as bigots and our actions described as undemocratic. When our fathers ran the guns into Bangor and Larne, their action was undemocratic, illegal and unconstitutional but God blessed their efforts and gave us the victory – the spirit of our fathers must live again in us.[11]

The year 1962 also saw a massive celebration at Balmoral in Belfast of the fiftieth anniversary of the signing of the Ulster Covenant. The gunrunning of 1914 was celebrated in 1964 and Ian Paisley held a 'Thanksgiving Service' in the Ulster Hall on 26 April of that year. His sermon was later printed in the *Protestant Telegraph* and illustrates the mindset of right-wing unionists at the time:

> When Colonel Crawford suggested to the leaders of the Orange Society of the day that they should arm the Orangemen, the leaders almost passed away with fright. Yes and many of them in our day are of the same kind. Then part of the Ulster Unionist Council resigned when the decision was made to bring in the guns. Many in church and state are acting similarly in this day of crisis. They are afraid to face the issue so they take the easy way and simply run away.[12]

That year Belfast faced the first street riots of the modern Troubles. An Irish tricolour was placed in the window of a shop in Divis Street being used as an election office by Billy McMillen, the republican candidate for the Westminster election. The tricolour was seen as an affront to unionists, a reflection of an imperialistic claim by the southern state over Northern Ireland. However, according to McMillen's brother Art, Billy McMillen was not being sectarian and in fact he had erected a large banner in his offices reading, 'Let the Orange lily be the badge of you my patriot brother, the everlasting Green for me and us for one another.'[13]

In fact a radical reappraisal within republicanism had been in process since before the end of the 1956–62 IRA campaign. Loyalists generally were unaware of these developments, and any knowledge that was gleaned was filtered through Orange-coloured spectacles that showed that the IRA had not changed at all or had gone communist.

Paisley demanded the removal of the offending tricolour and he and others threatened to bring loyalist protesters into the area. I at that time observed a big loyalist man taking to the centre of the street at Belfast City Hall and calling upon others to follow him to Divis Street singing, 'For we'll buy a penny rope and we'll hang the fucking Pope on the Twelfth of July in the morning.' The man got six months' imprisonment but was later 'saved' and began giving his testimony at gospel meetings. The RUC removed the flag to avoid serious disturbances but riots followed and water cannons were soon in action in the lower Falls.

On 14 January 1965, Terence O'Neill, the Northern Ireland prime minister, welcomed the Irish taoiseach, Seán Lemass, to Stormont. He did this without consulting most members of his cabinet – in reality there would have been little prospect of such a visit being welcomed by the majority of them – and this was regarded as an unforgivable sin.[14] Ian Paisley and some of his supporters travelled to Stormont with placards reading 'No Mass, no Lemass'; 'Down with the Lundies'; and 'IRA murderer welcomed at Stormont'. He handed in a letter of protest suggesting that O'Neill had adopted the tactics of a dictator and had forfeited his right to be prime minister.[15] Opposition to O'Neill was not, however, confined to Ian Paisley and his people. There was growing opposition to O'Neill within the Ulster Unionist Party.

William McGrath, who had been preaching in mission halls, church halls and Orange halls since the 1950s, was also fomenting an atmosphere of suspicion. His message was that the IRA had gone communist and that there were deeply laid plots to destabilise and overthrow the Northern Ireland state. For at least a decade he had been predicting that blood would be flowing in the streets of Belfast. The scene was being set for the reintroduction of armed militias, and in 1965 he told me that the UVF was being re-formed to meet the perceived threat.

In March 1966 Belfast newspapers reported that the UVF was under investigation by the Government because of rumours that it was being re-formed to oppose Republican Easter Rising parades.[16] In fact the previous year, two people had approached Gusty, one of them being a Unionist Party politician. He was told that the UVF was to be re-formed throughout Northern Ireland and he was to be responsible for the Shankill. Gusty's staunch loyalist reputation, along with his military experience, explains why he was approached.

> I can't possibly say that I knew the ins and outs of the political machinations in the background because I didn't. I was approached to join the UVF. The way the story was put to me was that there was incipient rebellion and I had taken an oath to Her Majesty the Queen to defend her – it seems grandiose – against enemies foreign and domestic. I saw my service in the UVF as a continuation of my British army service.

This sentiment was reflected in a letter Gusty sent from Long Kesh in 1981 in which he wrote of his reasons for joining the UVF after explaining why he joined the army. 'Going into the UVF appeared an extension of that duty i.e. to oppose the Queen's enemies foreign and domestic.' In this sense Gusty did not join the UVF for sectarian reasons and he was not intending to fight a sectarian war. He does not deny, however, that there was an element of sectarianism involved. That was almost unavoidable in either community but Gusty's motivation, like the motivation of most early UVF men, was to defend Ulster in the context of an assumed threat:

> I didn't join the UVF for sectarian reasons. Sectarianism might have snuck into it in some shape or form but I joined the UVF purely for patriotic reasons and during my whole time in prison I never allowed any form of sectarianism.

Gusty and three others travelled to County Tyrone to be sworn in:

> It was a stormy night in November and it was an unlikely setting. It was outside Pomeroy, County Tyrone. There were groups of people there whom I didn't know and there was a general swearing-in ceremony held in a barn.[17]

An ex-army colonel performed the ceremony after thirty or forty people had gathered:

> Who they were or where they came from, I just don't know. There was a thing that always intrigued me – the secrecy of the UVF – very secretive. It

was on a kind of a need-to-know basis. There was no dialogue, perhaps for security reasons; they didn't want the groups in contact with each other.

After this Gusty was occasionally given instructions. 'But they were subject to interpretation. Number one – we were never getting any firearms. We had to purchase our own. We were told to procure and to hold ourselves in readiness.'[18]

This account fits with a later statement made by Hugh McClean to the police in relation to the UVF Malvern Street shootings in June 1966. He said he had 'joined the Shankill Road Division' of the UVF and that 'Gusty Spence was my immediate boss in the force. He [Gusty] told me he was taking orders from another person but he did not mention any names.' (Incidentally, none of the three UVF men who travelled with Gusty to Pomeroy was ever charged with an offence.)

Little is known about the UVF beyond Belfast at this time. A senior loyalist member of Tara, from County Down, told me in 1971 that he knew 'respectable' members of a rural organisation who called themselves the UVF but they were quite different from the UVF men of the Shankill.

Gusty agrees that some of those initiating the UVF in 1965 were middle class. They were not 'physical force' men but were holding themselves in readiness for a doomsday-type situation. Once physical force was mentioned 'most of them bolted for cover'.

The oath used at Pomeroy was similar to that later used by the modern UVF and written by Gusty:

General Command
Ulster Volunteer Force

To be Administered by a Brigade Officer
or Senior Rank Delegated by said Officer

I swear by Almighty GOD to bear true allegiance to my homeland. I promise to obey all lawful commands directed to me by my superior Officers according to the principles, rules and regulations governing the Ulster Volunteer Force and administered by the GENERAL COMMAND.

I undertake never to betray a comrade or give any information to whomsoever which could prove detrimental to my Cause and if I fail in my obligations I shall truly deserve the just deserts befalling me.

> I further promise to portray courage, forbearance and tolerance during my enlistment in the Ulster Volunteer Force and never to besmirch by word or deed the Cause which I am sworn to uphold.
>
> As a volunteer of the Ulster Volunteer Force, I have no mental reservations whatsoever and to all the foregoing resolutions I do so swear.
>
> For God and Ulster
>
> God Save The Queen[19]

Formal and informal meetings of the Shankill UVF took place throughout the winter of 1965–66. They consisted of a small group of no more than twelve people who were loosely organised. Few communications were received from Pomeroy, and Gusty found this exasperating. A countryman once brought an order to shoot a nationalist election worker, and Gusty said, 'OK, we will have to steal one or two cars.' The man reacted in astonishment. 'We're going to shoot somebody,' Gusty replied. The man was aghast at the idea of stealing a car.

The Shankill UVF had to think about procuring arms:

> We bought our own firearms. We garnered funds whatever way we could and I think there was at least one bank done in those days on the far side of the town and I think it was six or eight thousand pounds.

The bank referred to appears to have been a sub-office at the old Supermac shopping centre on the Saintfield Road. According to press reports, £8,000 was taken and the UVF issued a statement signed by Captain William Johnston 'assistant adjutant of the 1st Belfast Battalion of the UVF'. The statement claimed that two junior officers of the UVF carried out the raid and the money was 'for further arms to be used against the enemies of Ulster'. Press reports suggested that the statement might be genuine but it could have been a hoax or even from the IRA.

For people like Gusty, a fine line had to be drawn between robbing banks, related 'procurement' operations, and racketeering.

> I never hesitated to slam sectarianism, gangsterism and extortion. However it seemed fair enough for the UVF to say, 'We can't collect taxes the way legitimate governments do and we have to get the money from somewhere, so we rob banks.' At that time I wasn't against robbing

banks or raiding for arms, but it had to be planned so that no one got injured or hurt.

Weapons could be obtained in other ways. They could disarm local B men:

> They knew where the B men lived and it was a matter of going in and taking their arms. Virtually every bank in Northern Ireland at one time also had a legitimate firearm. I remember as a boy going to get change of thrupence and seeing the big gun sitting on the counter in the bank in Malvern Street. These weapons were withdrawn but it was known where they were kept. The Harbour Police could also be disarmed. The UVF had to have weapons.

Some firearms had been hidden away in loyalist areas since the 1920s and 1930s. Some of these made an appearance in the early days of the Troubles:

> I was always pestering this man for firearms and I bought the first Thompson submachine gun that was ever seen on the Shankill Road. I paid thirty quid for it and twenty rounds of ammunition. A .45 Webley pistol cost a fiver, which was big enough money in those days for working men. Dues were paid and codes were used. It might seem a wee bit childish but it wasn't.
>
> There was a group in Carrick but I didn't know these fellows. North Belfast men were in the west Belfast group. I'm not conscious of anybody in south or east Belfast, although it was said there was a group in east Belfast.

The fiftieth anniversary of the 1916 rising in Dublin was on the horizon. This generated fears which brought the UVF on to the streets:

> There's no doubt whatever that the Ulster Unionist Party and the police were anticipating civil disturbance at Easter 1966. The UVF was stood to and they were armed and on duty at interface areas. I remember going to visit two men in Cupar Street. There were also two at the top of Denmark Street and there were men on duty on the Springfield Road and at both ends of Cupar Street. There were about eight or ten men in a house ready to be drafted in.[20]

The UVF leadership expected the Shankill men to create 'incidents', but in Gusty's view these were not meant to involve fatalities. UVF men were largely left to their own devices, however, and some incidents were the work of individuals. The perpetrators did not regard their activities as criminal but rather as doing one's duty for one's country:

It wasn't illegal at that time. We were following in the steps of our fathers and there was nothing more sinister. As a matter of fact it was seen an honourable, if misguided, thing to do. The first thing we set out to do was to get as many old UVF lapel badges as possible to be worn openly. It wasn't a boast – there had been no violent attacks at that particular time.

Violence was, however, part and parcel of what the UVF was about and soon there was a fatality, albeit a non-intentional one. A UVF man threw a petrol bomb through a window at the rear of a Catholic-owned pub on 27 May 1966. He had thrown the bomb into the home of Matilda Gould, a Protestant. Her home was an annexe to a pub in Charleville Street and painted in the same colours. She was burned to death.

Although those behind the formation of the UVF may not have wanted to see deaths, they needed 'violent acts to hype the situation up' if plans to destabilise O'Neill were to succeed.[21] According to Ed Moloney and Andy Pollak, RUC Special Branch had come to the conclusion that:

Billy Spence had formulated the UVF's strategy for 1966 – a clever plan that was designed to mislead the authorities into thinking that bombings and gun attacks carried out by the UVF were really the IRA's work. The idea was to halt O'Neill's 'bridge building' policies and maybe even cause a reaction against him within the Unionist Party, which would force his resignation.[22]

But Gusty insists that his brother was not the originator of the organisation and that only some UVF actions were to be presented as the work of the IRA. The UVF, in 1966, stated publicly that their intention was to kill known IRA men.[23]

Billy Spence was certainly a respected adviser to unionists and to people associated with the UVF. Both Gusty and 'John' speak in glowing terms of Billy Spence's wisdom. Billy Hutchinson, who came to know him in the early 1970s, also appreciated his advice in relation to recruitment policy for the Young Citizens Volunteer Force, a youth wing of the UVF.

On 9 June 1966, the following report appeared in the *Belfast Telegraph*:

A body calling itself the First Shankill and Sandy Row Ulster Volunteer Force said today it had sent a telegram to Capt O'Neill stating it had no longer any confidence in his leadership.[24]

This report supports Gusty's denial that the motivation behind the formation of the UVF was related solely to threats or perceived threats from the IRA. In his view the UVF was re-formed largely as a consequence of internal rivalries within unionism:

> There always was an implied threat from the IRA but I believe the UVF was reconstituted to oppose or be used as a bargaining counter against some of the things O'Neill had brought into debate. People do not realise how heavy the opposition was to O'Neill. I suppose in working-class areas some of the things might have been welcomed, although I question his motives. Probably he was only trying to keep the wolf from the door, but there was great concern within the Unionist Party that he was going too far, especially when he brought Lemass to the North. His overthrow was to take the shape of violent incidents in Belfast and Northern Ireland to hype up communal and political tensions.
>
> I joined the UVF in 1965 when I didn't have enough maturity or knowledge but others could see on the horizon the fiftieth anniversary of the [1916 Easter] rising. So here you had the UVF reconstituted in 1965 and it's getting close to the fiftieth anniversary of the rising. A lot of things were confirmed. All the Catholic streets were decorated and we saw barricades at the end of streets.

Green-white-and-gold decorations, including thousands of tricolours, decorated the streets of the Falls Road, seeming to confirm the validity of unionist concerns:

> The IRA issued a few bellicose statements and it was put out (by unionists) that the City Hall would be taken over. There may have been something in it because there was a police guard put on the City Hall. The area where I lived (Grosvenor Road) had murals of 'flames of fire' and everything else to make the Catholic people cognisant of what had happened in the blood sacrifice of 1916 and perhaps rekindle public opinion.[25]

The major concern of unionists was fear that the constitutional position of Northern Ireland was being undermined. To articulate this fear and to identify the traitors within unionism is to curry favour with the electorate. Dangers are therefore heightened or even invented. In a society riven by siege and victim mentalities, touching the heart of antagonism and suspicion by raising concerns about the border involves no great difficulty. Once fears are generated, violence can easily be spawned – and others are drawn into its orbit.

When Terence O'Neill met the Irish taoiseach this was seen as the ultimate betrayal. His other 'crime' was to visit Catholic schools and speak with nuns. Gusty regarded these things as inconsequential, even at that time, although the meeting with the taoiseach in 1965 had been groundbreaking:

> As a result there was uproar in unionism. Members of O'Neill's own party set up the UVF, a clandestine organisation that would commit violent acts to put pressure on the prime minister. O'Neill would be removed and someone more amenable to this group's thinking would be put in place.

By the beginning of June 1966, the late Brian McConnell, Minister of Home Affairs in the Stormont Government, admitted to having seen reports of the formation of what was being called the 'First East Tyrone Division of the Ulster Volunteer Force'. Surprisingly, however, he regarded the UVF as a benign organisation whose aim, as he understood it, was to defend Northern Ireland's constitution by peaceful means. This apparent view gives credibility to the suggestion emanating from the Tara leadership in 1971 that the UVF in rural areas had a more 'respectable' character.

Only after the Malvern Street shootings did the government's public assessment of the UVF change. In Belfast, O'Neill was briefed at an emergency cabinet meeting and told Stormont:

> Information which has come to hand in the last few days makes it clear that the safety of law-abiding citizens is threatened by a very dangerous conspiracy prepared at any time to use murder as a weapon ... The Minister of Home Affairs has this morning made regulations under the Civil Authorities (Special Powers) Act (NI) 1932 to declare an organisation, which has misappropriated the title 'UVF', an unlawful organisation ... This organisation now takes its proper place alongside the IRA in the schedule of illegal bodies.[26]

On 29 June, the political correspondent of the *Belfast Telegraph*, reporting on the proscription, wrote, 'I understand that from information gathered by police they are convinced that the UVF are in being and that there are branches and divisions attached to it.' And the writers Ed Moloney and Andy Pollak refer to UVF cells at this time in south Antrim, Portadown and Pomeroy.

Gusty's belief is that the growing opposition to O'Neill was based mainly on resentment that Brian Faulkner had not become premier. When Gusty was arrested in 1966 he was surprised to be questioned about 'the plot':

The Special Branch kept on referring to 'the plot', 'the plot'. I hadn't got a clue what they were speaking about and it was only later on, in putting things together and getting titbits from here and there, that I realised that a heavy element within the Unionist Party was discontented with O'Neill's 'liberalisation'.

I had my first encounter with members of the UVF in the mid-1960s. I met two men separately and discovered that they were members. Both had grown up in or near the Hammer. 'John', who became a senior member of the organisation, told me that they were 'doing something practical for Ulster'. This comment was made after I had told him of work I was doing promoting evangelical Protestantism.[27] I had a fair idea of the meaning of the word 'practical' and didn't ask for clarification. 'John' had met up with Gusty, having lost touch with him since the early 1950s. He joined the organisation in 1966. Many years later, I asked 'John' about the size and organisation of the UVF as he knew it then:

Very, very small, loose. I didn't know of any other cells, never met them at that particular time. All I know and all I can talk about is my cell. There were maybe eight to ten people. McClean obviously was one of them but it was Shankill-orientated and Hugh McClean had married into the Shankill.

I could see Ulster becoming part of an all-Ireland structure at that particular time and I hadn't the sense to think politically then. I was politically naïve and that's an understatement. It was in preparation for the event of Armageddon and trailing us by the tongues into an all-Ireland. Seems stupid to look back on that.

'John's' motivation was not as straightforward as it might seem, however:

I had an inbred hatred of these people who used my parents. I had watched them being used and I watched my uncle being delighted to get a job digging holes in roads and I could never get over that. My mother and father had captained Malvern Street station for the Unionist Party for many years. They worked for the Unionist government, but we still found ourselves in a house with a bath hanging on the entry wall and the swings at the top of the street closed on a Sunday, while these people were down in their country houses, playing polo and going out in their boats.

I would say I was always socialistic in my thinking. I think it would be very difficult to have come from my background and my home without having commonsense attitudes.

There was a tendency to label thinkers like 'John' communists. He recalls:

'If you didn't vote unionist, weren't in the Orange Order and didn't support the Blues [Linfield football club] on the Shankill Road, you were regarded with suspicion as probably a communist.'

'John' confirmed that the early UVF remained composed mainly of ex-servicemen after Gusty's imprisonment:

> The top people at that time were special ex-army people, very very special, ultra-special. They were the original ones that done it and not one of them got caught, not one, and now the main players are dead and buried.

They had expert knowledge in various military fields and some had been in elite regiments. The intention was to confine membership to ex-soldiers, but this proved impossible and others became involved at an early stage. They were working-class men who were not politicised and were prepared 'to serve Ulster'. Most, but not all, were members of the Orange Order. I asked Gusty if this implied a religious as well as political motivation. 'It was a mixture of both, the same as my father would have had in the UVF. It was for God and Ulster.'[28]

The UVF was not generally concerned with issues of left and right. It was with the defence of Ulster in mind that the UVF announced its 'declared war on the IRA' on 21 May 1966. 'Captain William Johnston', again described as assistant adjutant of the 1st Belfast Battalion the Ulster Volunteer Force, signed the statement:

> From this day on we declare war against the IRA and its splinter groups. Known IRA men will be executed mercilessly and without hesitation. Less extreme measures will be taken against anyone sheltering or helping them, but if they persist in giving them aid then more extreme methods will be adopted. Property will not be exempted in any action taken. We will not tolerate any interference from any source, and we solemnly warn the authorities to make no more speeches of appeasement. We are heavily armed Protestants dedicated to this cause.[29]

Captain Johnston was reported to have said that a UVF campaign would begin in the immediate future and that a list of known IRA men had been drawn up by the UVF.

On 27 May, less than a week later, the UVF killed John Patrick Scullion, a Catholic who lived off the Springfield Road. A republican named Leo Martin was the real target but he could not be found, and it seems that they had come across Scullion inadvertently. It was not immediately apparent that this was a sectarian shooting. It was assumed that John Scullion had been stabbed. He survived the shooting for fourteen days.

On 11 June police appealed for information about a car seen in the area.[30] On 23 June, John Scullion's body was exhumed and the evidence suggested a bullet wound. Harry Diamond, Republican Labour MP for the Falls area, raised questions at Stormont. He referred to various theories including one that it might be a loyalist killing. On the other hand, he said, there had been suggestions that the killing might have resulted from an internal republican feud. Later a number of people, including Gusty Spence, were placed on trial for the killing. (William McGrath offered a different explanation. He claimed that John Scullion was a communist and alleged that he was part of a communist conspiracy centred on the International Hotel in Belfast.)

The next murder took place immediately following the annual Whiterock Orange parade at the end of June. At this parade evangelical leaflets of McGrath's Christian Fellowship and Irish Emancipation Crusade (CFIEC) were distributed. They were entitled 'The National Crisis of Faith' and proclaimed that a major crisis requiring armed defence was facing Northern Ireland:

> This crisis ... will eventually break into armed conflict between those who fight the 'battles of the Lord against the mighty' and those who know nothing of 'the glorious liberty of the children of God'. Blood had ever been the price of liberty ... Oliver Cromwell once said 'Choose ye out Godly men to be Captains and Godly men will follow them.' We must do the same.[31]

During the early hours of the following morning, 26 June 1966, the killing of Peter Ward and the wounding of two others took place.

Four Catholic barmen, Andrew Kelly, Liam Doyle, Richard Leppington and Peter Ward, had been drinking at the Malvern Arms in Malvern Street on the Shankill. Off-duty RUC constables had also been in the bar at the time, as were a number of UVF men who believed that the four were members of the IRA.

The UVF men decided to set up an ambush at the side door. When the four barmen came out, they were fired on by a number of UVF gunmen. Liam Doyle and Andrew Kelly were wounded while Peter Ward was shot dead. Shortly afterwards, Gusty Spence and two other men were arrested.

Peter Ward and the others had been working at the International Hotel, which was a venue for socialist meetings of various descriptions.

Communists, and even socialists, were seen by most evangelical Christians as anti-God people who were engaged in subverting not only Northern Ireland but the whole of Western democracy. A number of evangelical fundamentalists joined various Orange lodges in the early 1960s to steer the Orange institution away from compromise with Catholics, communists and 'ecumenical' clergy, who were seen as agents of darkness.[32]

After Gusty was arrested, William McGrath expressed concern about his fate, and during the trial at the Crumlin Road he produced an anonymous tract. This was widely circulated throughout Northern Ireland and beyond, as far afield as the Soviet Union.[33] McGrath hoped that the letter would reach and influence the trial jury and others close to the case. Lord Chief Justice MacDermott, however, told the jurors at the trial:

> It has come to my notice that certain communications – through the post or otherwise – have been sent to various members of the community regarding this case and other cases that still have to be tried at the Commission.
>
> You should disregard all communications of that kind – they may be anonymous or not but disregard them completely. If by their nature they give you any concern, your best course would be to bring them to the attention of the police. The important thing is, any of you who serve as jurors should act on the evidence of the case and nothing else.[34]

Part of the communication read:

> The Official Unionist Party saw the UPA as a possible basis for underground movement to counter IRA activity. Eventually the UPA was infiltrated by Official Unionist Party agents who in a short time took over complete control. The Ulster Volunteer Force was then formed as an armed underground movement by those who had gained control of the UPA. During the Kilfedder Election in West Belfast arms were issued freely by the Party to members of the Ulster Volunteer Force.
>
> Ward was an enemy agent who was working in cooperation with [Paul] Rose, the Anti-Ulster MP at Westminster. The International Hotel, Donegall Square, Belfast is a favourite meeting place for Enemy Agents and in many ways is their HQ, Ward was employed here.

Gusty does not believe the UVF victims were anything other than innocent Catholics. Nor is he aware of the Unionist Party handing out weapons during the Kilfedder election, although he accepts that this is a possibility.

The document reflects the concerns of the conspirators. The truth about the plot could have become public knowledge so the victims had to be demonised. There was of course also a paranoid fear of communist infiltration among sections of the unionist community.

McGrath's tract was designed, he claimed, to save Gusty from the death penalty, which was a real possibility because he was facing a charge of 'seditious conspiracy'. However McGrath also said he wanted to protect Ian Paisley's name by suggesting that the UVF was an Ulster Unionist outfit, rather than a Paisleyite body. By claiming that the victims of the UVF were communist, McGrath was implying that they were *ipso facto* legitimate targets.

In the years after the Malvern Street shootings, other secret paramilitary groups began to emerge. Some of these were under the control of local Ulster Unionists and businessmen. Most were ostensibly formed to defend Ulster but Gusty insists that the UVF was not reconstituted because of any threat from that quarter.

When the Malvern Street killing took place in 1966, statements were issued to the press claiming responsibility on behalf of the UVF. Some of the Shankill UVF men I have spoken with resented this publicity and would have preferred an entirely secret organisation. One man, however, told me about the buzz he got from watching TV pictures of some of the things in which he later became involved in; he also enjoyed the fact that friends were unaware that he might have had a part in it. However, publicity was essential to the purpose of those who were lurking in the shadows.

If the UVF plan in 1966 was designed to destablise Prime Minister O'Neill, it proved a failure. However, the matter did not rest there and three years later in 1969 members of the UVF collaborated with Ulster Protestant Volunteers (UPV) agents in bombing water and electricity installations. The bombings were deliberately misattributed to the IRA and/or the Irish army. In his book *The UVF 1966–1973*, David Boulton pointed to the irony then current: it was said that the UVF was arming the UPV, when in reality Loughgall UPV had supplied gelignite to the Shankill UVF.[35]

7

Trial and Imprisonment

Gusty Spence believes that the police knew about his involvement in the Ulster Volunteer Force:

> They knew I was the CO [commanding officer] of the Shankill unit, which incorporated parts of Highfield and the greater Shankill, right into north Belfast. When the police came on the Monday morning, 27 June, they raided my house in Hertford Street and took me in for questioning.

It was reported that on being arrested, Gusty responded with the words, 'That's what you get for being a Protestant.'

> When they searched my home at half past five or a quarter to six that morning, there were various photographs on the wall. During the search one of the policemen passed remarks about King William on the wall and the Orange and Black certificates. 'This is a good Protestant home,' he said. I agreed. 'That's right. Is that why this house is being searched?' He says, 'Well, partly' and it was then that I made the remark, 'That's what you get for being a Protestant.'[1]

Shortly after his arrest and questioning Gusty wrote detailed notes on what seems to be prison notepaper.[2] There are two versions of these notes, one of which seems to be a copy and is endorsed by Gusty's mother: 'A statement written & sent to me by my son Augustus A. Spence'. There are no dates on the documents but Gusty confirms that they were written at a very early stage after his arrest in 1966.

In these notes Gusty records that when the police came to his home he asked them to produce a warrant. They replied that if he did not open the door it would be forced open. Gusty let them in and they said the search was taking place under the Special Powers Act, the same basis under which they then brought him to Brown Square police barracks.

Gusty claims that he faced serious threats during his questioning. He was then questioned about what went on in his Orange lodge room and why a 'sentry' was posted at the door.[3] 'Was he there to prevent anyone from interrupting the weapons training?' 'I told him to watch his filthy mouth and I got a slap on the mouth for my trouble.'

Gusty was refused requests for food even though Louie had already left sandwiches and cigarettes for him. However, they granted his request for asthma tablets because he was experiencing difficulty in breathing.

They then threatened to release him on the Falls Road where 'the IRA, who had my description, would blow holes in me'. They produced a written statement but Gusty refused to sign. He offered to write a statement himself, accounting for his movements, which they could sign as witnesses. They declined this offer and began to question Gusty about his having been 'in charge of a team of personators in the recent West Belfast election. He asked me how twenty-two stagers could all get the day off work from the shipyard. He took a note of my foreman's name.' Gusty records in his notes that a detective alleged that a named politician 'was the legal brain that prepared UVF members to withstand police interrogation and he made foul remarks regarding [this politician's] private life'.

They said that John McQuade MP was a high-ranking officer in the UVF, and that a well-known businessman was 'a supplier of arms and ammunition easily obtained because of his USC [Ulster Special Constabulary] connections'. A Shankill Road shopkeeper was named as 'a supplier of finance' and a unionist councillor was alleged to have 'sought to solicit certain information from various police officers'. It was claimed that 'all of these men held high posts in the UVF'. The detectives also alleged that:

> Tennent Street Unionist hall was a den of subversive iniquity and it was being used to drill and hold meetings in. [A named detective] asked me about the funds of Shankill Youth Centre and why a large sum of money had been withdrawn from the bank lately. He alleged this money was being used to purchase arms.

They asked how much money Gusty had received for personating for the Unionist Party. He treated this with contempt. But he admitted being in various republican tally rooms and the Hibernian hall on the Falls Road during the day of the election.

The police then returned to the UVF. Gusty records that one of them said:

> This was an organisation being used to overthrow the Ulster government. The brains behind this UVF were even at cabinet level and consequently I was afraid to speak, to get the big fish involved. He asked me did I know any old gunmen employed by the government during the Troubles. A Mr Alec Robinson was named [Buck Alec]. I told him I knew him to see but I knew his son better.

Gusty was asked about Ian Paisley and what connection he had with him. He told them he did not agree with Paisley and had no connection whatever with him.

After further questioning one of the detectives brought in some articles including a wallet belonging to the dead man, Peter Ward:

> The wallet was covered in blood. There were army badges fixed to the wallet which was a tan colour. There was an army discharge paper in it belonging to the deceased who bought himself out after approximately 75 days. There were numerous photos in it, one of which was coloured, portraying the deceased in the Army cookhouse amidst pots and pans. On the back were the words – Christmas 65.

Gusty claims that one of the detectives said he would give him his freedom if he would only indicate where the guns that did the job could be found. His note says, 'I still have the utmost regard for the uniformed police but this is my first ever contact with plain clothes men. I think they are bloody awful.' He told me:

> They asked me to account for my movements, which I did do because I had nothing to fear. I had been at Joe Watson's bar [the Malvern Arms] that night. I had a couple of drinks and in actual fact I had a couple of drinks with the men who were later charged with the offence. But I had left and gone home and when they cautioned me, they said about the murder of Peter Ward and I said 'No'. I denied all knowledge of it and continued to deny all knowledge of it.

John McKeague, writing some months later in the *Loyalist News,* referred to the complaints made by Gusty about his treatment by the police:

> He asked for a solicitor and was laughed at, he asked for food and was sneered at, he asked to see the officer in charge of the station and was told he had 'no chance'. He was told the phones were out of order when he requested the use of one. Twenty-four detectives working in relays of four grilled and questioned him, threatening him, so as to make a statement, for over 18 hours. He refused to make any statement, he was struck on repeated occasions and we have the names of the police officers who used the brutality.[4]

Gusty claims:

> I don't know how many there were – quite a number. Special Branch and other detectives questioned me from about half past seven that morning ... There was no rest in the barracks. It was continuous questioning. One person passed a remark to which I took exception. I passed a pretty vicious remark in turn and he hit me a slap in the face. I was no mug in those days with boxing and I'd fought in the streets and I said, 'If you hadn't your big brothers with you, I'd fix you in about two minutes.'

In total the questioning went on for most of eighteen hours. Gusty had indeed asked that a solicitor be present but this was refused. The police later implausibly denied that such a request had ever been made. No solicitor was present throughout this period, nor was a solicitor present during the questioning of the other accused. Even in those days this would have been considered unthinkable.

Gusty eventually decided he had had enough:

> In the afternoon I said, 'Right, am I under arrest?' I hadn't been cautioned and I wasn't under arrest. Says I, 'Well I'm prepared to leave this station now.' I got up to leave, and there was panic stations. They physically restrained me. There was no kicking or fighting, but four or five of them

physically restrained me and put me back in the seat. I said, 'I demand to know under what circumstances or under whose jurisdiction I am being held here.' They told me it was under the civil authorities' Special Powers Act and under the direct orders of the City Commissioner of Police.

I said, 'He hasn't got the authority to order you to hold me, to interrogate me. You told me I was here to assist in your inquiries. I have assisted you as far as in me lies because I will not make a written statement, putting on paper what you want me to say. This is why you're preventing me from leaving this barracks.' I never saw a solicitor and was without rest or food all day.

Something similar may have been happening to Hugh McClean over a longer period:

I surmise that because McClean was arrested the previous day, on the 26 June. He made a number of statements over a two-day period. What I can gather was he had been up all night. He arrived home in Carrickfergus in the early hours of the morning and the police raided his home quite early. They brought him to the barracks and he was subject to interrogation.

McClean's statements, which I have examined, appear to confirm this.

Gusty was becoming increasingly sceptical about the RUC and the legal system:

The RUC in those days were not prepared only to apprehend and place before the courts. They were intent on conviction before they reached the courts. Statements were seldom, if ever, ruled inadmissible. Between 1922 and 1972, virtually 50 years, there wasn't one *cause célèbre* over a miscarriage of justice in Northern Ireland. That doesn't happen in any normal democratic society. The police did concoct evidence and verbal statements. I made no verbal or written statements.

I asked Gusty about allegations of ill-treatment during questioning:

I was roughly handled and received one slap in the face. There was no other form of physical attack. There was intimidatory abuse. Derogatory remarks were passed about my personal circumstances and my family. There were no inducements although inducements were held out to others. There were twenty-two judges' rules which stated that certain things should not happen. All those things were dispensed with and RUC Special Branch was a law unto itself. Some people would still say that, in relation to drugs today, the Special Branch remains a law unto itself.

Gusty made it clear to the detectives that he was prepared to defend himself:

> 'If anybody lifts their hands to me, I'm going to get tore into them and I'm going to suffer injury and you're going to have to explain how I received those injuries.' It would have been said that the prisoner struggled or he assaulted a policeman and had to be restrained. But I was going to buck a chair through the window on to Peter's Hill on the Shankill Road.

The good cop, bad cop routine followed:

> They backed off after that and sent in this sergeant who told me he was good-living.[5] He had accepted the Lord and asked me why wouldn't I cleanse myself by telling him everything? We were being questioned in different rooms in Brown Square barracks. There were questioning detectives and listening detectives. The detectives who listened would have gone into the other rooms and put things to the different prisoners. Interrogation is a big game.
>
> The door burst open and a detective walked in saying, 'It's all over. Spence has confessed.' He'd walked into the wrong room. He was supposed to walk into somebody else's room. There were looks of horror on the faces of the detectives and what did I do, it wasn't a laughing matter, but I burst out laughing and he was quickly hustled out by the other detectives.

Gusty always denied killing Peter Ward but never denied involvement in UVF activities. 'Some people called it poetic justice that I had done things for which I had not been apprehended. Maybe that was keeping me sane.'

Later, as he sat in court contemplating the workings of the justice system he thought:

> Here's a country that I was prepared to give my life for and they're doing this on me. My mother and father taught us about embitterment, you didn't hate because it's soul-destroying, but I felt a burning sense of injustice. My counsel called for police notebooks in which they were supposed to have written everything down.

Gusty says he was amazed that these notebooks were so full. He had urged his defence counsel, John Creaney, to insist on an identification parade in which the wounded young men could identify their assailants. Bob Williamson, Hugh McClean and Gusty Spence were placed in line and the two wounded young barmen, Richard Leppington and Liam

Doyle, together with Andrew Kelly, their manager at the hotel, picked out McClean and Williamson as two of the assailants. Another man, coincidentally known to me, was picked out but was absolutely unconnected with the UVF or the killing. He had been brought in from the street at random.

Gusty stood in four identification parades but was never picked out. The police remained convinced they had 'the boys that done the job', especially 'this fellow Spence'. McClean's statements implicated him:

> Whether [McClean's] statement was true or not – and I'm telling you the statement was not true – it should not have been admitted as evidence against me. But because it was a conspiracy trial the judge ruled on it and there was never any danger of the judge ruling any other way. Including the statements was the only way they could find me guilty.
>
> Hugh was under heavy pressure, facing constant interrogation by Special Branch for two or three days, he would have written and signed anything. 1966 was quite different from today in relation to police procedures, or should I say lack of them.

The 'constant interrogation' of McClean was the basis of a claim by his counsel that the circumstances in which they were made violated Judges' Rules, that 'Anything said [by McClean] was the result of threats of physical violence and that he was in such an exhausted state that he did not know what he was doing.'[6] However Lord Justice MacDermott chose to admit McClean's statements.

According to one RUC statement, the use of which was objected to by McClean's counsel, McClean had been asked how he came to join the UVF and had allegedly replied, 'I was asked did I agree with Paisley and was I prepared to follow him. I said that I was.'

McClean also reportedly told a detective, 'I'm terribly sorry about this. I am ashamed of myself. I am sorry I ever heard of that man Paisley or decided to follow him. I am definitely ashamed of myself to be in such a position.'

Gusty says he later asked McClean why he said this but McClean denied it. 'I never said that, Gusty; why should I say it?' Gusty suggests that:

> The police and certainly the government were trying to find a link between the UVF and Paisley and I'm saying, in fairness now, nearly forty years after the event, that to my knowledge Paisley had no connection with the UVF.

> He may have had other connections, but to my knowledge Paisley had no connection with us.

McClean had faced days of intensive questioning and he told Gusty,'I literally would have said anything and signed anything.' As far as the remarks about Paisley are concerned, McClean also said, confusingly, 'I never said it, but if they said I said it, I probably did say it.' Gusty claims that:

> Police always made at least three deliberate mistakes in a statement, always misspelt a word or scribbled something down to get your initials on it. So whenever you claimed that, 'Oh no, I was forced to sign it' or 'They'd kept it covered', you could never account for the three sets of initials.

In McClean's first statement he said he had been in the Malvern Arms with a man called Spence, whose first name he didn't know. They were talking outside and there were four men in the street talking about four 'IRA men' still drinking in the pub. The four men left the street and Spence also left. Later, as the four suspected IRA men were leaving the pub, he said an unknown person placed a gun in his hands. He fired some shots but 'I know I did not hit anyone. I panicked and ran away.' This statement was apparently taken about 4.30 to 5.00 p.m. on Sunday, 26 June 1966. In it McClean said he had not slept since the killing in the early hours of that morning and had been 'worried stiff'.

Despite his exhausted state, another statement was extracted from him about shooting through a window of a house in Carrickfergus. This statement was apparently taken between 5.10 and 5.40 p.m. on the same day. McClean made a further statement during the following morning and early afternoon. In this he said he had not slept and had 'been thinking about this thing all night', and would now 'make a clean breast of everything' and 'tell the whole story'.

On the morning of the killing, according to this statement, he was given a revolver and told there would be a meeting that night. He went to the Shankill, had a drink, and watched an Orange parade. Gusty Spence chaired the meeting during which two men were sent to Claudy to collect two volunteers and bring them along. These two men 'belonged to a country division of the Volunteers'. Later an attempt was made to locate and shoot an IRA man in Baden-Powell Street in the Oldpark Road area but he was not at home. Another man reportedly said, 'I have torched the place.'

Later there was talk about the need to get arms. They then went to Watson's Bar and during that evening saw four men drinking at the bar. A discussion followed about whether they were Catholics. He said that Spence listened to their conversation, decided they were IRA men and that 'they will have to go'. The shooting occurred as they left by the side door.

It was common practice for the police to write statements and ask the accused to sign them. Sometimes this took place after extensive interrogation and even physical intimidation. The suspect, perhaps while extremely confused, would be asked to sign. In that context the person facing the interrogation might be so disoriented that he or she would be prepared to sign anything.

Even after implicating Gusty, the police were not yet finished with McClean and he made a number of other statements about his activities. One of these related to the collection of gelignite in Portadown to be used, he said, to destroy a monument to Saint Patrick in Downpatrick. McClean told Gusty in prison that he had never said these things but Gusty pointed out, 'Hugh, whether you did or whether you didn't is beside the point. Your name's at the bottom.'

Seven years later, while in Long Kesh, McClean wrote a retraction of his 1966 statement in the form of a poem acknowledging that Gusty Spence was not involved in the killing:

One night some 'Volunteers' did meet
In a house on the Shankill Road.
Their aim, the IRA to defeat
Was their vow in that humble abode.

One man stood out above the rest.
As a leader he's a must.
We picked you Sir 'cause we need the best.
In you we placed our trust.

We made our plans and all went well
Until, a mild June morn
Tis a sad sad story that I tell
And I alone must mourn.

They said we shot an enemy down
And two more on the street.

Why charge our leader? He was homeward bound
When the enemy we did meet.

Our trial was a political hoax
A rigged up court and that's true
They must be guilty, twelve fools said,
Ah but for the grace of God there goes you and you.

A cruel judge he bade us rise.
Do twenty years he said.
But take heed old one with your rheumy eyes
We'll be free while you are dead.

Tis sad to see as years go by
An innocent man still jailed
But no complaint have I heard from him
And it's nigh on seven years.

As in this wretched place we dwell
He keeps our hopes alive
By helping us to beat this hell
To help each man survive.

So Long Kesh, Long Kesh, here's my prayer
May your shambles decay and rot.
'Cause Gusty Spence will see the day
When Long Kesh is all forgot.

DANDY McCLEAN
29 MAY 1973[7]

'Dandy' was Hugh McClean's nickname. Here he states that at the time of the Malvern Street murder, Gusty was on his way home to Hertford Street. This belated admission was of little comfort.

Gusty Spence, Bob Williamson and Hugh McClean were charged on 28 June 1966 with murder and with murder in furtherance of a seditious conspiracy (a charge that carried the death penalty), in that they

> On divers dates between March 1 and June 27 1966 conspired together, and with other persons unknown, to incite ill will among the different classes and creeds of the Queen's subjects, to create a public disturbance and

> disorder and to injure and murder persons who might be opposed to their opinions.[8]

While on remand in Crumlin Road Gusty decided to go on hunger strike. This was for two reasons: 'To try and get an early trial and to protest against the behaviour of the police. I fasted for a period of ten days.'

It had still to be decided whether there was a case against the UVF men. The authorities 'knew' they were the culprits although in theory a presumption of innocence is supposed to prevail.

> Before a lower court, they went through the taking of depositions, which were recorded in longhand by a clerk. Police presented their evidence and the defence presented theirs. At the end of the submissions, the resident magistrate Gerard Lynn, who was a Catholic, makes a decision that there is either a case to answer or not a case to answer. This is called 'informations'. A *prima facie* case was found against Bob Williamson and Hugh Arnold McClean but in my instance informations were refused. There was no *prima facie* case to answer and consequently I walked out a free man.

Gusty's relief at finding his freedom was short-lived:

> District Inspector Sam Bradley arrested me on the steps and charged me with being in possession of a firearm. That was enough to hold me. I remember saying to my counsel, John Creaney, 'Surely to God they can't do this?' He says, 'Well, they can, in actual fact.'

The intention was to place Gusty on remand so that he could be tried again. Gusty found this incredible and said to his counsel:

> 'There's no evidence against me. I'm going to be freed again.' He said, 'Well, I wouldn't be too sure about that.' Says I, 'What do you mean?' He says, 'You can rest assured the Attorney General is down at the books now to see what he can dig up against you.' And he did. I was indicted under the grand jury system of the 1850s, which had been instituted when they couldn't get local juries to convict.

The grand jury consisted of members of the landed gentry and those sympathetic to them. It had been reactivated in relation to a traffic accident case immediately before being used in Gusty's trial. This seemed like a deliberate attempt to hide the reality that it was being used to ensnare Gusty Spence.[9] The accident involved an articulated lorry which had jackknifed on the Lisburn Road, resulting in fatalities:

The police had charged the driver with careless driving but the evidence demonstrated that the man was not responsible so informations were refused. The Grand Juries were prepared to indict me but they indicted this driver first, so they were in a position to say, 'Oh well, we're not using it solely against Gusty Spence in particular; we indicted this lorry driver.' The accused doesn't appear in front of the grand jury. The case goes in front of it and the only ones to present evidence are the police. In the driver's case they returned a 'no bill', and he was a free man. In my case they returned a 'true bill'.

The offence was committed on 27 June 1966 and they brought in legislation during August and September making it retrospective to January 1966. Anyone found guilty in relation to a seditious conspiracy would be hanged. I remember the words of the Lord Chief Justice, MacDermott, an ex-Attorney-General, a Unionist Party hack and a former B Special commandant. He says, 'The grand jury have returned a true bill against Spence. Whether it's a good bill or not, has yet to be determined.'

MacDermott took this particular case himself and Gusty believes he did this for political reasons. They were determined to have a successful prosecution:

They were trying to get away with murder with supreme arrogance and not one person questioned it anywhere. What price investigative journalism? Attorney General E.W. Jones, MP for Derry City, the most gerrymandered city in Western Europe, was railroading me in the name of justice.

I suggested that in those days Protestants assumed that the legal system and its protectors were legitimate:

Yes, there was no rights watch, no human rights concerns, nothing, and when they charged us 'in cause or furtherance of a seditious conspiracy', this meant whoever *they* deemed or said were involved in the conspiracy. You want to see the people they dug up, people I had never heard of in my life.

Gusty also found himself aligned with a number of UVF men like Leslie Porter from Carrick. Henry Hayes turned Queen's Evidence and was not charged:

There were all types of things introduced and Barry Shaw, who became the Director of Public Prosecutions, was my QC. We opted for a separate trial, which the Lord Chief Justice said there was merit in but would not grant.

> We asked for a trial without benefit of a jury because it was a legal case and again this was denied. I made no statements of any description except those of complete denial and innocence.

Gusty never spoke to his QCs until about two days before the trial and feels that some significant details were missed.

The men were found guilty. Had they been tried separately there was no evidence to convict Gusty Spence:

> In a case of a conspiracy you could be sitting in a room with a person without having a clue as to who he is. You don't know what he's doing there but if he nods and winks at you, he doesn't even have to speak, he's part of the conspiracy, and I found myself in the dock with these unknown people.

Leslie Porter, who was convicted of firearms offences, said, 'Spence is the Colonel of the Shankill Division so far as I know and his official name is Colonel William Johnston.' 'Captain William Johnston' was the name used on all statements made by the UVF.

The charge in relation to the death of Scullion was withdrawn because there was no evidence, but despite this, Gusty felt, 'The writing was on the wall. They weren't going to let me go anywhere and I was found guilty. I appealed the case but there were no separate appeals. The three judges said in all probability Spence was there.'

The jury had had little choice:

> There are three decisions that a jury may make here. Obviously the shooting wasn't manslaughter because it was premeditated. The jury was left with two choices: either guilty in cause of furtherance of a seditious conspiracy – punishment hanging – or guilty of simple murder. What choice would they make between hanging and someone going to prison for life? They were left with Hobson's choice. They did their damnedest to prove there was a seditious conspiracy and at the same time the Crown approached my counsel, saying that if I would plead guilty to simple murder that would be it finished.

Gusty said the case 'was scaring the shit of those people who were conspiring against O'Neill'. People had to be made accountable and the UVF had to be stopped in its tracks. Ian Paisley's profile was rising and his stunts were damaging unionism, so by linking Paisley with the UVF, perhaps he could also be damaged. And the circumstances of the trial and the determination to secure a conviction, whatever the cost, were exposing the fragile nature of the justice system. The *Loyalist News* of 7 August 1971 stated with some justification that 'Gusty Spence is a scapegoat, Gusty Spence is a political sacrifice.'

But Gusty remained defiant:

> What inspired me was – here were principled men, bastions of virtue, belted earls with robes and ermine and power, and they could stoop to such levels. I felt myself a king compared to that scum. I did, honestly, without being embittered. I told my ma, 'Ma, you never brought me into the world for an oul bastard like that to say to me that after ten years you'll be morally and physically and intellectually degraded. So there. Fuck them.'

Gusty was recalling the words of the Lord Chief Justice who, in passing sentence, said:

> It may well be that circumstances will alter but I fix it now, although it well may be that before this period is up, you will be worn physically, mentally and morally – the general experience being that after a period of imprisonment something like ten years a man goes down in all those directions.[10]

These remarks put steel into Gusty's determination:

> Says I, 'I'll fucking prove that rheumy-eyed oul bastard wrong.' Hopefully I did but my mother never lived to see it. I suppose he didn't have much choice either. Did he not have to go with the flow?

Long after the sentencing and the appeal, one or two jurors questioned the decision they had made. One was the foreman of the jury, who contacted the Northern Ireland Office (NIO) in May 1972 about his troubled conscience. The reply from the NIO, dated 19 May 1972, said:

> Further to our telephone conversation last week about the case some years ago in which you were foreman of the jury, I have as I promised looked into the aspect of this matter which has been troubling you.
>
> The position is that the document signed by a foreman of a jury simply records the jury's findings on questions of fact. The sentence is the responsibility of the Judge, and it is the Order of the Court, as recorded by the Court Clerk, which is the authority for the detention of the accused in prison.
>
> I hope that this information, together with the fact that your present

> attitude has now been clearly recorded here as a result of our conversation, will ease your conscience in the matter.

During his trial Gusty was approached on three separate occasions to plead guilty to simple murder. The ironic situation was that if Williamson and McClean had pleaded guilty to simple murder, Gusty would have stood trial alone and would have been a free man, yet no such approach was made to them:

> It was absolutely sown up. If they had had a chance initially to plead guilty to simple murder they probably would have done so and it would have got me off the hook of the conspiracy charge.

Gusty told me:

> It was farcical but people don't recognise injustice unless it happens to them and of all the campaigns that have been waged on behalf of justice most were of a Catholic or nationalist persuasion. I suppose there are historical reasons for that, but even when there was gross injustice in Northern Ireland, if it happened to Prods there was never the same will to see things through to their logical conclusion. While these things were happening, my elder brother said, 'I can't believe this is happening in our country.' Says I, 'Go to the Falls Road and they'll believe it.' They even brought a man whose pub had been robbed to see if he could pick me out and I was as much mortified at that as at anything else.

Gusty's sense of injustice was relieved to some extent by the fact that he had been involved in other UVF activities:

> I was up to my eyes and ears in it, yes. If I had been just plucked off the street without any paramilitary involvement and stuck in jail for something I didn't do, I would have been the most embittered person in the world. Now, even though there was an injustice, but poetic justice, done to me, it never really embittered me. If anything, it made me cynical of the RUC. Not because of their detective prowess or because of their upstanding humane behaviour. I saw them for what they really were. I'm not embittered against them, it's just a matter of fact, as far as RUC detectives and Special Branch are concerned, they've had a good innings. They're about to get their comeuppance.

Gusty was haunted by these things for a very long time:

> When I went into jail I was obsessed with my case, absolutely obsessed. I

ate it, drank it, slept it and smoked it and even in my dreaming hours I dreamt about it. Absolutely obsessed with the question, 'How can they do this?'

Not a single voice was raised in protest. Unionists were too closely identified with the state (or perhaps with the conspiracy) and were unlikely to issue a challenge that might have brought into question the validity of 'their' legal system. Many nationalists would have assumed guilt and were reticent to defend a member of what republicans have since referred to as 'loyalist death squads'.

The O'Neill administration felt a need to deal with 'the plot'.

Terence O'Neill and his government had to show the conspirators that they were the bosses. And whatever minions, and I was a minion, came into their path they would be steamrolled, just as simple as that. I was a football between the conspirators and the government. I'm not crying in my beer here. No moaning, no girning from me. In many ways I got my just desserts.

Senior Unionists had always resented O'Neill who became friendless and aloof. As prime minister he made gestures towards reconciliation but this did not enhance his popularity. Gusty Spence is convinced that some Unionists, 'many of whom are still living', engineered the 'plot' including the formation of the UVF. O'Neill records that while in Norfolk in 1966, news reached him of the backbench conspiracy and of secret meetings in the homes of politicians. Signatures had been collected demanding his resignation.

On our return from England I was given a list of those who were supposed to have signed this mysterious piece of paper. The trouble was that officially no one knew anything about it. The next morning when a Cabinet meeting was over, I threw down the gauntlet and told my colleagues I was going to fight this conspiracy ... One Belfast MP, who had undoubtedly signed the 'piece of paper', issued a statement saying he had withdrawn from his previous position. One sentence in that statement was most revealing. 'He regretted that because of the indirect pressures of extremism, democratic decision within the Party was made more difficult.'[11]

The conspirators ran for cover after the Malvern Street episode.

Meanwhile the belief that Gusty Spence killed Peter Ward has dogged him for much of his life, despite his repeated denials.

In a letter dated 11 November 1977, from 'St Quentin Compound 21, Long Kesh Camp', Gusty refers to himself as 'apparently making good copy in which I play no part and to which I do not contribute':

> Unfortunately, the mother of young Peter Ward has been trailed into the morass of words and someone ought to be ashamed of themselves for doing so. I can only apologise to this lady for the heartache she has been caused. To keep the record straight I wish to state that I wrote two letters to Mrs Ward in 1966 and at that time the then Deputy Governor of the prison informed me that the then Ministry of Home Affairs would not permit such letters to leave the prison. The contents of the letters are both personal and confidential and were for the eyes of Mrs Ward alone. I also wrote to the families of Andrew Kelly, Liam Doyle and Richard Leppington (three other lads involved in the Malvern Street case), but these too were refused by the authorities.
>
> With the help of God I will leave prison in June 1986, never having asked favours from any source, and I will continue to do what I can for all prisoners, whatever their affiliation or calling, since Northern Ireland has been twenty years behind in reform and might I add that whoever does not like it will have to start getting used to it. I will never try to be all things to all men. In conclusion I would like to state for the very last time that I did *not* murder Peter Ward.
>
> People in Ulster have a peculiar habit of believing what they want to believe but they must now and again search their conscience and face the truth as it is and not as they would wish it to be. The knowledge of my innocence has been the main factor in me serving almost twelve years in the most manly way I know possible. I am an Ulster Loyalist who desires continued union with Britain and I am proud of having worn the Queen's Coat, but I will not wear blinkers for anyone and pretend that our society is not sick and in need of cure.'

Gusty continues to deny the killing of Peter Ward. The latest occasion was in 1999 when journalist Peter Taylor alleged that Gusty had apologised to Mrs Ward for her son's murder. Taylor drew Gusty's attention to the 'abject and true remorse' for victims expressed in the 1994 CLMC ceasefire statement. He asked if this remorse included the suffering of Mary Ward. Taylor records Gusty's response:

> 'The most important thing to do was apologise to Peter Ward's mother', he said, 'and to apologise to all the mothers.' Mary Ward told [Peter Taylor] that Spence had telephoned her. 'He said he wanted me to forgive him. I said,

> ''Yes, I'll forgive you on one condition – that you bring peace to this country, because I don't want any other mother to go through what I have gone through. My Peter is in my mind every day and every night.'' I said, ''I know it's not going to bring Peter back, but please try and bring peace here.''' I asked Mary if she now forgave Gusty Spence. She said she did.[12]

In fact Gusty had not made an apology for the murder of Peter Ward. Unknown to him, contact was made with Mrs Ward by a man from Belfast now living in Dublin. This man was an emissary between Dublin and Belfast during the lead-up to the CLMC ceasefire. After Gusty announced the ceasefire, Tommy [the Dublin emissary] came back to Gusty's home. While there, he was given permission to use Gusty's phone. Without warning, and while still holding the receiver, he turned to Gusty and said:

> 'I want you to speak to someone.' I says, 'Who is it?' He says, 'Mrs Ward.' I says, 'Tommy, I didn't want to be any source of embarrassment to anyone.' Says I, 'Hello, Mary,' and I remember her words. She said, 'God must be in me this morning because I forgive you.' And I says 'Mary,' without acknowledging what I had done or didn't do, I said, 'We're all in need of forgiveness and for your forgiveness.' 'You know,' says I, 'I too offer my forgiveness to all people that have done me harm.' It was a short, short conversation.

Gusty felt uncomfortable about this sudden encounter but he respected Tommy and his main concern was for Mrs Ward. Later he said to Tommy:

> 'You might have given me warning about what you were doing, hi boy.' 'Ach,' he says, 'I never thought.' An *Irish News* reporter learned about the conversation and wanted me to meet Mrs Ward. I says, 'I would meet Mrs Ward any day but certainly not in the glare of publicity.'

While on the phone, Gusty had heard voices, possibly of members of Mrs Ward's family:

> They weren't too pleased with what she had said and done, and I didn't want to compound her problems. Even Louie said, 'Did you ask her for forgiveness?' I says, 'No Louie, I didn't,' because I really had much to be forgiven for but certainly not for the killing of Peter Ward.

Shortly after Gusty's conviction, the Orange Order chose to expel him. It has often been claimed that there was no choice involved, because the rules are said to require the expulsion of members found guilty of criminal offences. But this is far from clear. Attempts were made to prevent Gusty's expulsion and his brothers came to him saying:

> 'Right, you're being expelled from the Orange Order. What do you want us to do?' I said, 'I don't want you to do anything. You continue.' There was no point in the world collapsing round them because the world had collapsed round me. They were dedicated Orangemen. They weren't Orangemen in an old bigoted style. They really believed in it.

Gusty's expulsion was opposed in numbers 2 and 3 district lodges in Belfast. The opposition was to no avail, and so the Orange Order disowned him.

He was sentenced to life in prison on 15 October 1966, with a stipulated minimum term of twenty years. He and his family faced a very problematic future. Louie and their four children had no visible means of support and now had the added stigma of a husband and father in prison for murder.

In 1996, Louie Spence and her daughter Elizabeth spoke with Maura Lee of RTÉ about their experiences. Elizabeth was eleven years old when her dad was arrested. She recalled that day vividly:

> I remember everything, the house being searched, my daddy being arrested. I remember what we were told to tell the wee ones. They always thought he was in a military hospital. I remember everything because my Mummy took sick after it with her nerves and my daddy was actually sentenced on my birthday, my twelfth birthday. I remember the police coming in that morning and getting us out of our beds to search underneath the mattress and my daddy being taken away.

Maura Lee then asked if she had expected her father to come home again:

> Oh yes, I did then, but I started reading the papers when I wasn't supposed to. The first few days we took it in our stride until I actually knew what my father had been charged with. Now it was hard at first when he was sentenced and at school people taunted us. My mother had to go up to the school a few times. People taunted you about your daddy being a jailbird. That part of it was hard, but we had to be strong because we had my mummy there. So you had to just keep it up, get up and go on. You had no other choice because then we knew that he had been sentenced to twenty years.

Louie said:

We just had to manage. There was nothing else to do. You kept thinking of your children. Well, to be honest, I took a nervous breakdown and it was my sister pulled me out of it, for she told me that if I kept on the way I was going I would end up in hospital. She couldn't look after the children and they would be put in a home. That was the first thing brought me to my senses.

They grew up very quickly, especially the two oldest ones. Elizabeth worked in the mornings. She went out at six o'clock and worked in a shop round the corner, until she had to leave for school about half past eight. When she came out of school at three o'clock or half past three she went back round to that shop, and worked until it closed at seven o'clock. After Sandra came out of school she worked in a fish-and-chip shop from four o'clock, and through the week she worked until twelve o'clock at night. At weekends it was one o'clock and two o'clock the following morning before I was going up to pick her up.

Elizabeth recalled:

The visiting was difficult, especially for us as children. It was a very small room and there was a table in the middle and my daddy sat at one end, the prison officer sat at the other and we sat at the side. We could only speak about things that the prison officer approved of. There was no such thing as bending over to give him a kiss. We weren't allowed to do that. The prison officer sat and listened to the whole conversation and if there was something that he didn't agree with us talking about, he stopped us from speaking about it.

We had at least four years of that. This was before political status came in and we got open visits then, but visiting was hard for us, being young.

Other children said their daddy took them places, or they got presents that my Mummy couldn't afford. Sometimes we were a wee bit jealous but we realised we just couldn't have it. It brought our family closer together, we respected our mother and father a lot more than many children do now and we're still a very close family.

Had Louie been lonely?

When I was rearing four children, I was never lonely and my house was never empty. But I had lonely moments when they were all out and I was sitting alone. I had my sister just across the street and that helped.

I'm not politically minded, we were reared in a mixed district and I always had Catholic friends. My children played with Catholics and we thought nothing of it until the Troubles. We couldn't understand this fighting with each other.

Five years after her father went to jail, Elizabeth Spence was married. Soon she was facing added difficulties because her husband, Winston 'Winky' Rea, was jailed. 'I was pregnant when my husband was in Crumlin Road jail and my daddy was in Long Kesh.'

In 1976, Louie committed some of her reflections to paper. She writes of deep feelings of hurt and confusion:

> My first reaction was one of great sadness – a sadness that I have never experienced before – and this sadness was accompanied by extreme sleeplessness. My husband had always had the job of shouldering the main responsibilities whilst I was concerned solely with caring for the children and making day-to-day purchases. The trial lasted for ten or eleven days but for the life of me I could not understand it and was dependent on the lawyers to keep me informed. My husband kept telling me that things would be OK. He believed in British justice.
>
> After he was sentenced I thought that I would die and was inconsolable. I felt a great anger initially with those who had taken my man away but I did not allow that anger to embitter me and I resolved that despite my plight I would attempt to carry on life as normal as possible.
>
> All the while, on visiting days, my husband kept on encouraging me and I suppose it's true that we helped each other over our respective 'black' periods. Troubles are easier handled when you understand them. At this time I was forced to move house because I lived in a contentious area. After a visit by certain 'gentlemen' who tendered me advice to leave, I did so. The house had been attacked on several occasions.[13]

Louie's sister, who was living nearby, suffered worse. Her home was maliciously burned down.

Gusty recalled how Louie

> . . . was intimidated out of her house in the Grosvenor Road and had to take flight and was moved in a lemonade van. Johnny Havern and Charlie Harrison and two other men came with an empty lemonade van and moved the furniture up to Highpark Crescent at Highfield where she got a place that was infested with rats. She never went back to the Grosvenor Road but she visited her sister who still lived close by in Naples Street. Hertford Street was eliminated to make way for the new motorway. Where the Grosvenor Road and the new motorway meet, there's a set of traffic

> lights. That would virtually have been the site of our house in Hertford Street.

Gusty never returned to the Grosvenor Road. But in 1972, while on parole, he visited his mother in Joseph Street and they danced in the street for joy. For Louie, the bad old days are a distant memory:

> I've just blocked everything out. With him being out now, even though I know he's been away for nearly nineteen years, to me he's never been away. I'm just that sort of a person. I tried to block everything out during the bad years.

8

Prison Life
Resistance and New Beginnings

Gusty Spence had been living in Hertford Street. A few hundred yards further up the Grosvenor Road, in Distillery Street, a 21-year-old man was startled to learn of the Malvern Street killing. Martin Meehan was to become a leading militant Irish republican and, like Gusty, to spend most of twenty years, intermittently, in Crumlin Road jail and Long Kesh prison. He told me that the Malvern Street killing and the UVF had a profound effect on him:

> I remember seeing this thing on the wall – UVF. I kept walking down the street but I couldn't understand. What does it mean, this UVF? It was on a gable wall facing my house. The next thing this incident with Peter Ward happened and it had a massive impact on me. 'Why would somebody do that?' I said to my mate, 'I'd love to go to that trial to hear why these people did that.' I had never been in a court or a police station and was lily-white at that stage.

As we walked into the big courtroom and towards the public gallery, the three heads looked in our direction. We sat there for up to two hours, listening. After that I started delving into the history of the place, started reading books about the twenties and further afield. I got a perspective on why it happened. The trial had a profound effect on the whole nationalist community. It was like a bolt of lightning out of the sky.

The same events had a profound effect upon members of the Protestant community and left a number of burning questions.

Gusty had appealed but the Court of Criminal Appeal dismissed this on 4 January 1967, together with the appeals of Hugh McClean and Robert Williamson. Gusty then sought leave to appeal to the House of Lords but on 11 January 1967, Lord Justice Curran, Lord Justice McVeigh and Mr Justice Lowry rejected this also.

He was left with many questions to reflect upon during the long years of incarceration that were beginning:

I had to do something. We tried through politicians but they really weren't interested. Those of the unionist tradition who might have been sympathetic kept their head well down after the failed *coup d'êtat*. If they had taken the case up, they would have been seen as some kind of traitors.

Fortunately Gusty was able to discuss the situation with his brother Billy:

My brother was a great mentor of mine, a very wise and intelligent man and we weighed up all the pros and cons. Billy said, 'They probably would let you down. If they were willing to acquiesce in your hanging, they would let you down now. Whatever political clout you had has all flown for cover.'

Billy Spence began writing letters to various people in an attempt to get the case reopened.[1]

While Gusty was on remand from June to October 1966, he was not required to work. However once he was sentenced, he had to appear before Major Mullin, the governor at Crumlin Road, who assigned work to him. Gusty immediately refused:

I saw the absolute shock on the man's face when I said 'no'. He said, 'What did you say there?' 'I said no.' He said, 'No one has ever said that before.' Says I, 'Well I'm saying it. I'm not working for the prison. If you give me trade union wages I'll work, but I won't work for half an ounce of tobacco a week, not under any circumstances.'

Gusty was accused of being arrogant and confined in isolation to a small cell. While there his health deteriorated. The cell was approximately eight feet by twelve feet and he was locked up for twenty-three hours each day, leaving one hour for exercise. The only items in the cell were a bed, a chamber pot, a chest of drawers, a bible, which Gusty read, and a 'water gel', a big tin containing a gallon of water for drinking and washing.

> The first seven months were done behind the door in solitary confinement because I wouldn't work for them. Seven months was unprecedented in those days. I was a prisoner and I wouldn't work for my captors. People were trying to make me into something I wasn't. I resented and defied that.[2]

I asked Gusty how he coped:

> I had all this feeling bubbling up inside me and it's very hard to explain. It was a deeply, deeply emotional time. Traumatised would be too strong a word. I had been in various sticky situations before and had my feet well on the ground but in those days you would have seen a different person in front of you. I was completely and absolutely defiant, I wasn't going to take any shit and I didn't give a fuck. You do your worst and I'll do my best. My main concern was not for me, my concern was for my wife and my family, for my mother and my brothers and sisters.
>
> My burning sense of injustice was kept in perspective because I was conscious about embitterment and all those things that are self-destructive. Once you master those you're on the road to recovery. I still got my visits once a month but when I left my cell it was searched and so I used to leave little notes – 'ha, ha, you're at it again, some Prod you and some loyalist', that type of thing.
>
> Some of the prison officers were sympathetic. 'That's desperate. If you'd even take a wee job, we'd get you a wee cushy number somewhere.' Says I, 'A cushy number is not the point. It's working for the prison. I'm not prepared to work for the prison.'

Gusty's mother and father had the same defiant spirit:

> My mother especially was a defiant wee woman who would have fought like a tiger for her young. If you hurt or molested or maligned any of her young she fought like a tiger. I was determined to maintain my dignity. Seven months was a short period compared to Terry Waite and others who spent five or six years in solitary with no medical care.
>
> It helped me to see myself for what I was. It led me on the road to find

me. I remember some of those Hollywood films whenever someone says, 'At long last I've found myself.' The seven months put me on that quest. It was my first tottering baby steps towards me finding Gusty Spence, to get all my priorities right and come to terms with myself. There are a lot of people at war with themselves but I found peace with myself. Whereas before there was always turmoil and I was saying or doing things I knew weren't right. I was saying them to please or I wanted to be part of the herd. After this I said and thought as I felt.

His confinement raised acute and embarrassing questions for the authorities. Politicians and others were asking why. It was difficult to justify such a long period in solitary confinement:

The governor said to me, 'Spence, you're arrogant.' I says, 'No, Governor, don't mistake pride for arrogance. Don't mistake defiance for arrogance.' I was defiant when anyone did or said anything to demean me. I would never allow myself to be treated other than as a man.

In the end, the governor was forced to negotiate:

The governor and I made a deal whereby when I went to the shop, I didn't do any work. I just sat there in the tailor's shop and when he came around I threw a pair of trousers on my knee and went through the pretence of working. But I didn't work. It showed that bargains could be made and kept.[3]

This bargain reflected the efforts of the Chief Officer of the prison, Eddie Jones. Jones had served in the Second World War with the Irish Guards and was something of a diplomat:

He was used to handling men and as time went by he would approach me in my cell, asking what circumstances might permit me in conscience to leave my cell and work. There were all types of formulae to inveigle me but I always rejected them and would put counterproposals, which they in turn rejected. After some time we reached an agreement that I would go to the prison workshop.

I suggested to Gusty that he had gained a kind of political status before it was officially granted:

I never looked upon myself as being anything other than a political prisoner. I'm suggesting to you in humility, and the prison officers of the time will confirm it, I behaved as a political prisoner. It was a question of struggle; struggle to achieve the most stupid things, to have sliced bread, for instance. There were two-pound loaves of bread cut in four and we each got half a pound of bread a day. We had this big heel of bread and could do whatever we wanted with it.

We found we could manipulate the system by showing the governor how to save money. An awful lot of bread was being wasted and we demonstrated that if bread was sliced the men would only take what they required. Whereas half a pound of bread had been thrust upon them, they could now take four or six ounces. The governor came before the whole of A wing in a breathless state announcing in a loud voice, 'As from tomorrow lunchtime, sliced bread will be served.' They cheered him and it was terrific. Very soon after that we devised means to get brown bread introduced.

We began to introduce variety into that terribly depressing menu. This was a small thing but there were other struggles that went on and on.

Thus a form of politics began within Crumlin Road jail. But Gusty continued on the journey of self-discovery that would shake his preconceptions to their foundations:

I had known nothing of the historical circumstances that led me to be there. I knew that William had crossed the Boyne in 1690 and I knew there was a rebellion or a rising in Dublin in 1916. I knew about the Somme but I knew nothing about Irish politics and it became a personal quest to determine the political circumstances that led me to be serving life imprisonment.

Such a journey required a detailed examination of past and present and books, especially Irish history books, were essential aids:

The first time I went to the governor he said, 'Oh well now, it was politics and historical circumstances which have you here and I don't want to exacerbate the situation by allowing you to read Irish history books.' I persisted and we brought a little bit of political pressure from the outside from genuine people, including men within the judiciary who didn't see any harm in education. Others saw education as a very dangerous thing.

Gusty's quest led him into an inner debate with himself. Opportunities for discussion were limited but he met with a 'non-political' Catholic prisoner named George:

In his youth he was in a street fight at the Plaza Ballroom in Belfast. Someone was stabbed and George got life imprisonment. He was extremely well-read and intelligent, and he was taciturn. I was pretty taciturn myself in those days because I was in prison and there was only about ten politically oriented prisoners. You kept your own counsel because the place was a chatterhouse of talk and small things were blown up out of all proportion.

I was feeling my way forward and George and I would launch into Irish history as we walked round the exercise yard. We could only stop to go to the toilet for a few minutes' respite and roll a cigarette to have a smoke. We would just hit on a subject by accident and the subject that day was imprisonment. We were debating how good or how bad it was and George asked, 'How do you look upon imprisonment?' Says I, 'The way I look upon it is that I'm on a troopship and every day of imprisonment is like a day on a troopship that is bringing me nearer home.'

Gusty's experiences could have demoralised him. Alternatively he could have become a model prisoner and accepted himself as a criminal. This could have ruined his capacity for anything else. He chose to resist all attempts to control him and to follow his quest into every area of life. He asked himself questions that most people have neither the time nor the inclination or perhaps the courage to face:

I had to find out what put me in jail in the first place. I went into it at half-cock at first. You can't just take a thing in the middle – you have to begin at the beginning. It was always a set of historical circumstances. I went right back to Strongbow, although I quickly dispensed with that. It really started with the plantation times. That's when the troubles in Ireland had their origin. With the Reformation having left Ireland virtually untouched, it was almost completely Catholic. Here you had an alien people, an alien race with an alien culture, alien everything, rejected ...

I wanted more knowledge, more, more and more. The more that I investigated, the more I found that, OK, there's a justice on the Catholic side, but one side was as bad as the other. There were atrocities on both sides and there was intransigence on both sides. Each was responding to a violent movement coming from the other side.[4]

Prison experience has the potential to diminish the prisoner's humanity and replace it with a type of collaboration that is damaging to self-respect, so it must be resisted if the prisoner is not to be damaged psychologically. Gusty was defiant and it was this that probably saved him from the kind of destruction that prisons impose. This need to resist is recognised by sociologist Erving Goffman:

> The recruit comes into the establishment with a conception of himself made possible by certain stable social arrangements in his home world. Upon entrance, he is immediately stripped of the support provided by these arrangements. In the accurate language of some of our oldest total institutions, he begins a series of abasements, degradations, humiliations, and profanations of self. His self is systematically, if often unintentionally, mortified.[5]

The abasements referred to include: being stripped naked, washed, disinfected, given a number, a cell, a minimum of food and a prison uniform. This happened in Crumlin Road. Gusty adds, 'All your possessions, rings, lighters, cigarettes, everything, is taken from you.'

Then there was an attempt to intimidate. When Gusty was brought to his cell for the first time:

> There were twelve or fourteen officers, a show of force lined up and stern-faced ready to receive us and show us who the bosses were. It was a constant fight to retain one's dignity. Some prisoners fell to the wayside because, while they wanted people to acknowledge their dignity, they did not bestow dignity on their fellow prisoners. Prison is a different world. Modes of behaviour and morals are different, principles are different, the whole approach to living is different. Prison has destroyed men and when some of them came out they wanted to get their own back and they did.

The uniform would become a matter of grave concern to loyalist and republican prisoners in years to come. It consisted of a striped shirt and a pair of denim trousers but for Gusty the precise nature of the garb was inconsequential:

> It wouldn't matter what it was. If it was a silk shirt it wouldn't make any difference. When Margaret Thatcher announced that all prisoners would be allowed to wear civilian clothes one naturally assumed that their families would send their clothes in but that wasn't the case. The prison issued the clothes and they were still prison clothes.

On one occasion a prison officer tried, without success, to get Gusty Spence to make a pair of trousers for Ian Paisley:

> When Paisley got jailed in 1969 a fellow brought a pair of trousers and gave them to me to be made for him. I put my arm out through the window and threw them as far as I could, saying, 'What are you going to do about it?'

He put me on a charge and there was a lot of diplomacy before everything was assuaged.

Gusty said he did this 'just for badness'. He would not make any prison uniform or do any work. It wasn't because they were Ian Paisley's trousers:

No, no, they just happened to be for Paisley. Your man picked them out specifically to bring to me in order to try to humiliate me, to make me do some work. 'Ah, you'll do prison work and, even more, you're going to make Ian Paisley's trousers.' So I bucked them out as far as I could and he said to the other officer, 'Did you see that?' He said, 'Well what do you expect the man to do?' We played these little games but they were serious games.

Gusty was provided with a small aluminium bowl for his food:

The diet tin was about four and a half inches in diameter and approximately two inches deep. We got a small round of meat in that and a scoop full of turnip or cabbage or some other vegetable. There were also haricot beans that looked like Heinz beans but were like bullets. We got two potatoes and a mug of soup. That was our dinner and it was terrible. We then got watery custard with what we called a wad. The wad was baked on flat trays and it was a type of sponge cake. It was called a wad because it tasted like cotton wool.

We had a mug of tea at night and in the morning. For breakfast we got a bowl of porridge and, before we got the bread sliced, an eight-ouncer, a quarter of a two-pound loaf. We could cut the eight-ouncer into three slices but we had insufficient margarine to cover the three slices – so we made do. Half a pound of bread a day was our ration, with as much water as we could drink. Breakfast never varied, no such thing as fries. Nothing ever changed except for Christmas morning when we got cornflakes and milk. We had roughly a quarter-pint of milk a day.

Everything was measured to provide sufficient sustenance but the prisoners were hungry. When men are locked up there's no need to be overfed but there's no need for them to be hungry. When we went to bed hungry at night, we always saved a little bit of something through the day, maybe half the meat from the dinner. If I got tea at night I might save a piece of cheese. Later on, things improved but in those days that was our diet. When we complained, the stock reply was, 'There's a dietician in the Royal Victoria Hospital who worked that out. The person is a professional.'

The Crumlin Road jail was on the edge of the Hammer district where Gusty had been born and raised. As he recalls, 'I could look down from D wing and see Joseph street and could see my kids playing in the street when they were up seeing my mother.' Gusty's children missed their father and sent occasional notes to keep in touch with him. Three of these remain in Gusty's old scrapbook. The first is dated 31 May 1968 and was written from Hertford Street by Sandra who was then eleven years old.

> Dear Daddy xo
>
> I hope you are keeping well as it leaves us the same, please forgive me for not writing but this last while back, I have not been in the mood for writing. I have been up to see my granny quite often this week, daddy xo. I would like to know if you could make me a skirt? If you have not got my measurements I will send them up on my letter next week. Please hurry and write me a letter.
>
> Your faithful daughter
>
> Sandra XOXO
>
> PS Hope I see you soon.

The second note is from Catherine. It is undated but was presumably written when she was seven or eight years old, in 1968:

> Dear Daddy
>
> I hope you are getting well. We are coming up next week to see you. I am going to the Sunday School trip on Saturday. We get 5 times tables and we have to learn them. The skirt was lovely and I fell tonight and Margaret Smith put a plaster on my knee.
>
> All my love
>
> Catherine XOXO

Andrew was only six in 1968. His father was in hospital when he wrote an undated letter:

> Dear Daddy
>
> I like going to the Hospital. I like the sweets you give me dear daddy. I will bring you some chocolates. You are getting out of hospital. Are you

keeping well? When I bring the chocolates, I will bring you some sweets.

Love

Andrew XOXO

The family of Gusty and Louie were warm and loving. Women, in Gusty's view, played a crucial role amidst the insanity of Northern Ireland:

> They kept the home going. They picked up the pieces. If a man goes into jail, the family becomes a one-parent family and she has to deal with the economic situation and with the children's schooling. I cannot praise those women highly enough. I'm talking about both loyalist and republican women in the prisoner context. The only sanity in Northern Ireland for a number of years was the sanity women injected into the situation.
>
> The burden was on the family as was the stigmatisation, because a Provisional man's wife is looked upon as the extension of the Provisional and the loyalist man's wife is seen as the extension of loyalist paramilitary. But in many cases they didn't even know what their husbands were involved in.

The Twelfth of July was always a particularly emotional time for Gusty, who had been steeped in Orangeism. In 1966, while he was on remand in Crumlin Road, members of his family initiated a tradition by gathering outside the prison. Prince Albert Orange Lodge also stopped outside, as a mark of respect:

> I remember June of 1966 just coming up to my first Twelfth in Crumlin Road jail. I was on hunger strike, incidentally, and it tore the guts out of me. With my face jammed against the bars, the big tears running down, a certain amount of self-pity knowing that all my brothers in my lodge and all of Ulster was on parade. Here was I, only thirty yards away from the event, and couldn't participate or even see it. The Prince Albert Lodge stopped outside the jail that first year. Belfast County said that if they did such a thing in future their warrant would be taken from them. They refused to expel me at first and the Grand Lodge said, 'If you don't do it we'll take the Lodge Warrant from you.'

The protests of Grand Lodge did not stop Prince Albert Temperance from paying their respects again in 1967 en route to the Twelfth demonstration. They stopped outside the jail to convey 'fraternal greetings' to Gusty Spence and to James 'Rocky' Burns and Henry Miller. John Bryans, the

Belfast county grand master, was reportedly shocked.

Other Orange lodges joined Prince Albert Lodge, including Old Boyne Island Heroes, who also had men in jail. Prince Albert was not the first Orange lodge to express respect to people in Crumlin Road jail. However, whereas Prince Albert and Old Boyne were decidedly working-class Orange lodges, earlier lodges saluting at the 'Crum' were further up the social ladder, or would have seen themselves in that light. The prison warders had their own lodges, such as Whitewell Temperance and Cloverhill. As these lodges passed by Crumlin Road on the Twelfth morning, the governor took the salute. Gusty recalls, 'The eyes-left was given. It's absolutely true. Of course it ceased in 1966 whenever Prince Albert Lodge stopped for me.'

Orangeism continued to pull at Gusty's heartstrings:

> ... but through the years it faded after we saw some of the machinations. They weren't the defenders of the faith. They made no response even to the looting that was going on in some loyalist districts and they stayed outside the Troubles. They continued making bellicose, belligerent speeches, that's all they did. A section of the Protestant population began to have a closer look at the Orange institution and to ask what they were doing.[6]

In July 1967 Gusty's mother came to the corner of Agnes Street, about a hundred yards beyond the prison itself, with his brothers and brother-in-law:

> With the grace of the governor I was allowed to exchange cells for one night only, the Eleventh night. I gave some tobacco to a wee man called 'Apple' Sammy who was a willing partner in changing cells. On the Eleventh night I could barely see my mother and my brothers and brother-in-law at Madden's pub. My brother-in-law stood flicking his lighter to let me know that the family was there.

As Gusty stood peering in the hope of glimpsing flashes from the cigarette lighter, his eyes fell upon a small piece of graffiti scratched in the corner of the small window:

> Some IRA man with a nail or a pin had etched the words 'God save Ireland' in the corner of the glass. Well, if it was good enough for an IRA man to save Ireland, it was good enough for Gusty to try to save Ulster. It was an inspiration and a challenge in many ways.
>
> There were many people from whom I drew inspiration. I remember one

> prisoner who had polio, a very dignified person and a disabled thief. He bore his illness with great dignity and he eventually died. I saw him walking in extreme pain but he had an old saying, 'Don't let the bastards grind you down. Don't let them see you suffering in any way.' That helped me to keep my head up. Those little things added to the makeup of what was me.

The following day, twenty-six members of Gusty's family gathered outside the jail. They issued a statement on Prince Albert Lodge headed notepaper. It was addressed to 'Dear Gusty':

> Fraternal and Loving Greetings from your family assembled outside the walls of Crumlin Road Prison. We will leave presently to celebrate our Forefathers Glorious Victory at the Boyne. We know you will be with us every step of the way. Long live the spirit of Carson, Long Live our War Cry. *No Surrender.*

On the following Twelfth, members of his family were joined by members of the wider kith and kin outside the jail and presented another statement of support. The document depicts a union flag at the top and begins:

12th July 1968
278th Anniversary of the Victory of King William III
(of Glorious Memory) over the forces of Popery and tyranny

To Augustus Andrew Spence Fraternal and Loyal Greetings

From the members of your family assembled outside the walls of Her Majesty's Prison, Belfast. Our physical contact with you may be stopped, but our love, regard and respect for you will never cease and will remain unconquered.

This was followed by a version of the Ulster Covenant and a pledge to resist any imposition of an Irish republic and, if so imposed, to refuse to grant it recognition. The statement ended with the words 'NO SURRENDER' and a poem:

Brave boys he said be not dismayed
At the losing of one Commander
For God will be our guide this day
And I the General under

WILLIAM III, 1ST JULY 1690

A list of signatures of those present follows, headed by the signature of Gusty's wife Louie, followed by his mother Bella. The children are among the sixty-three family members who signed. Such gatherings continued outside the prison into the 1970s.

Louie at first was permitted one visit and one letter each month. Later this was increased to two visits and two letters, Gusty thought these restrictions were ridiculous:

> A person could only see his family once a month for a half-hour, six hours per year. How could that contribute towards keeping the family unit intact? If we infringed any rules or regulations we could get a visit withdrawn as a punishment but they didn't withdraw any of my visits, even when I was refusing to comply. It was because our Willie could have mustered a certain amount of covert political support. People would have asked, 'What's happening in the Crumlin Road jail?' Or someone 'of standing' would write a letter. The prison authorities always lived in mortal dread of people 'of standing' finding out what was happening, and it curbed them to some extent.
>
> If Boxing Day fell on a Sunday the TV was removed because the Deputy governor was 'good-living' and also forbade the playing of cards and darts on Sundays. I could never equate this with any form of Christianity, yet all types of ministers and pastors – and chancers – came and went, more or less with free access.
>
> We had the *Belfast Telegraph*, but on a Sunday we weren't allowed the *News of the World*. At one time if there was a picture of a semi-naked woman in a newspaper someone was delegated to cut another piece of paper and paste that over the top of it.
>
> There were other comical aspects, you saw a wee man running about with a little stick, it was marked with nine inches. When we wanted a bath, we got nine inches of hot water, not a centimetre more or a centimetre less. 'Will I put another wee drop in?' He made sure it just came up to the nine-inch mark.
>
> When you got a scoop of tea it wasn't unusual to find some lentil and barley in it. Somebody had emptied the tea into the remainder of the soup. It was abominable; Crumlin Road was not a nice place.

Billy Blease, the trade unionist who became Lord Blease, visited the prison during these early years and some thirty years later he could still recall his first meeting with Gusty Spence:

> We were taken round the various parts of the prison, the workrooms, the

> prison cells, the different types of cells, the little hospital and meeting rooms and the open spaces, the playground and the football playing area ... Gusty was there alone. I met him many times after that, of course.

Blease described his impression of the conditions thus:

> Not too good, in my opinion – sitting in rows, sewing and making material. The cells were sometimes tightly packed with two and three men. My impression of the cells was that they would provide difficult living conditions for any man. Even for people who'd been used to living in the small homes of the Shankill Road, they were pretty hard and grim and it wasn't a pleasant place to be. Our general consensus was of cramped conditions. The warders and the system were trying to do their best in the overcrowded situation. We saw three in some cells. There was a prison chapel, of course. I certainly didn't see any concert hall but I understand there was a cinema show or a general meeting room for special occasions. Maybe that's where the church services were held, it appeared to be just a drab sort of meeting hall and there weren't any pretensions about it.

Lord Blease gave an assessment of Gusty Spence's contribution to Crumlin Road:

> I know from the governor and others that he was highly respected. He saved many situations. He represented the prisoners in an honest and open way and he became a leader in that sad situation, which is to his credit ... I visited him during an upsurge from the political prisoners. I recall him explaining that this was not the way to resolve their problems.
>
> He was highly regarded as a man of his word, a man who could stand out and in that way he got the respect of the governor, the prison warders and those that managed the prisons and, of course, many of the prisoners. He became a very ill man in prison. He had a heart complaint and I think a chest complaint and that led to representation for remedial reasons.

Gusty's health began deteriorating immediately after his incarceration. This was a consequence partly of his work in the mills and partly of the shock of separation from Louie and the children and from his friends on the Shankill. His diet was hardly adequate, and medical support was limited. At a very early stage he launched himself into hunger strikes that would take a heavy toll on his health.

His first heart attack happened in Crumlin Road in 1971. He had felt ill and was examined by a Doctor Girvan:

He was a caring doctor if you were ill but there were many prisoners swinging the lead. He would give them two number nines, which was a laxative, and send them to their work. But when you were really ill the man looked after you, and he and I formed a good relationship. He examined me and said, 'How do you feel?' Says I, 'I feel all right. A bit woozy and a wee bit short of breath.' He said, 'Sit down there for a minute or two.' So I sat down. I must have been sitting there ten minutes when two young fellows came in wearing white coats. I said 'God bless us' because all types of things were racing through my mind. Says I, 'Who are you?' They said, 'We're from the cardiac unit in the Royal Victoria Hospital.' 'What are you doing here?' They said, 'We'll have to have you over to the prison hospital.'

I says, 'That's OK. Do you want me to go now?' 'Oh no, you can't, you have to go in a wheelchair.' Says I, 'You're not pushing me out of here in a wheelchair. I don't want the prisoners to see me,' but they said, 'I'm afraid we insist. You're going in a wheelchair.' So they brought me over to the hospital and they put me on the ECG and so on.

Being in hospital gave Gusty more time to think. Years later, in July 1981, he explained his thinking in a letter to Bob Hynds:

Finding myself in jail I had to face a long time and many questions. I did it constructively, I think, and set out to educate myself with whatever was required in my quest. I am not interested in qualifications except that of experience, and the more experienced I became the more questions I asked and the less answers I got. I wanted to get particular answers but it does not always work out that way and I got 'hooked' on finding out the truth whatever that might be. I questioned everything, from Louie to politics and, however unpleasant, I faced the facts.

Deeply held and lifelong opinions on most matters changed dramatically, if slowly at first, and I learned not to be afraid of the truth, however embarrassing and whatever the cost, although I must admit I was quite cowardly sometimes. It was not sufficient for me to know the truth. I felt I had to convince others, especially the young fellas who came into this place. This was resented in some quarters at first because I did not fulfil the image of the 'Gusty Spence' of the newspapers and what passes for so-called folklore. They had to be won away from the gun, which my image had helped to romanticise. Coward that I am, at the time I did nothing to 'right' the image since my ego had taken off and I was a hero. Poor fool that I was.

9

Hunger Strike

After the failed appeal in early 1967, Gusty discussed his situation with Louie and then made a decision. Not only would he continue refusing to cooperate, he would refuse to eat:

> I began a hunger strike while pretending to work in the prison workshop and was soon visibly weakening and could see it in the mirror. I was becoming somewhat disorientated. My dinner was always brought into my cell and I was being watched closely by the prison authorities to make sure I wasn't drinking tea or eating behind backs. I was drinking water but I was true to my hunger strike. I think it was about August 1967 and it was very hot. I became so weak they moved me to the prison hospital.
>
> I was on hunger strike for a multiplicity of reasons – to get the case reopened, to get better conditions introduced because conditions were bloody awful. There were a myriad of things wrong with Crumlin Road jail. I had to put pressure on the governor and this is why the prison conditions were brought in. It wasn't only for me, it was for the whole

prisoner population. My appeal had been turned down about January 1967 and this was the basis of my burning sense of grievance. I had to take into account my family's feelings and the logic of having a case reopened.

Gusty received some indirect encouragement from an unexpected source while listening to two leading republicans speaking on Radio Ulster:

They interviewed Jimmy Steele and Hugh McAteer about me being on hunger strike and they said, 'We understand why the man's on hunger strike. The conditions in Crumlin Road jail are absolutely Dickensian.' One was a lieutenant-general and the other was adjutant-general in the IRA. Both were ex-Chiefs of Staff and I took great heart from what they said. Here was the so-called enemy recognising me as a soldier and as someone who was striving to bring about a more humane regime in Crumlin Road jail.

Gusty was to go on hunger strike on three occasions. At the beginning he was on hunger strike for one week, then for ten days, and finally for thirty-five days in 1967.

Many people in the unionist community neither understood nor sympathised with Gusty's plight. They saw him as an embarrassment, and his agitation for changes in the prison system was beyond their comprehension. Yet Gusty retained his sense of loyalty, even when the state he loved was inflicting punishment on him.

They threatened to bring doctors in from the Royal Victoria Hospital to force-feed me. But I said that if anyone contravened my person they would be charged with grievous bodily harm. I told them straight, 'Go ahead, you attempt to enter my veins and I'll resist.' That put them off the force-feeding bit and we came to a quid pro quo. The governor would have no compunction whatsoever about bringing in moderate reforms within his scope, and he was a pretty powerful person in those times. He could have granted parole and didn't have to go through the Minister of Home Affairs. But the governor told me, 'Gusty, I have no control whatsoever over the jurisprudence or whether your case is reheard.'

Gusty had made a decision. 'I mean this and it's not a boast, I was prepared to die. I was prepared to sell my life dearly.' But Louie was far from impressed:

I could not understand why my husband had to be a leader – I know that he did not want to be – and why he had to hunger-strike first and be on strike longer than anyone else. I resented this, I did not want to share him with anyone and I felt that other people had first call on my husband. I remember one hunger strike he commenced. I threatened that if he did not come off it I would refuse to see him again. He told me that he had to do his duty, and I suppose I was stubborn. I did not go to the prison to see him for six months, although I got daily reports on his condition. I thought he was putting Ulster before me and I thought, 'To hell with Ulster, what about me and the kids?'[1]

On this occasion and after approximately ten days, Gusty came off hunger strike because, as his brother suggested, the prospect of generating real political clout was remote. He could generate support on the streets but this could lead to riots and disturbances. Gusty was not prepared to go down that road. Deaths could have ensued and it would have drawn attention to Northern Ireland in a retrograde way. 'I saw things so clearly, as if I were on drugs or was removed and looking at myself and at the situation,' he later recalled.

My mind was as clear as a bell and I reached heights I never thought possible. Not that I'd any form of clairvoyance, but seeing things in their proper perspective was a wonderful experience. I could see that as being a turning point in my life. Not the fear of death but the lucidity that came from the hunger strike.

Gusty's experience of hunger-striking gave him an understanding of republican hunger strikers:

People later kept on asking me about the hunger strikers of 1981. Says I, 'I respect those men because they were doing something I had done myself.' How could I disrespect them? I agreed with their goals and that they were noncriminal prisoners. They wanted to make a life for themselves within prison. Whatever they did they did in pursuit of a cause.

I was still a patriot but at the same time I was getting my patriotism into proper perspective, that was the important thing. Better men than I had died in pursuit of what they believed. My patriotism became narrower, sharper and more concise. The process began with the hunger strike and it's still continuing and will continue till the day I die.

Being on hunger strike was not a pleasant experience:

After a while you lose hunger. You're in a constant everlasting battle, not so much with yourself or about dying, although dying was important and I won't understate that. It was the effect it was having on my family. I had a wife and four wee children, I had my mother and my brothers and my sisters. It was also what effect would my death have in political terms. I couldn't really see to the end of that.

Maybe I didn't want to overestimate my own importance. This was something I never did. When people speak about Gusty Spence I don't equate with that person at all. You equate with Gusty Spence, not the myth or the legend. I was very conscious of that, and the pressure was enormous.

On one occasion Gusty also experienced a kind of hallucination:

Before getting into bed I had a habit of throwing my trousers and my shirt over a chair. I was sitting reading a paper and had wee roll-ups. Thankfully we still got our wee butt. I was reading the paper and I glanced over it and there was a fellow sitting there. I could see him as clear as I can see you but I couldn't even describe what he was like. For all intents and purposes, it was a person. I got the paper up again; it frightened the living daylights out of me but when I put the paper down again there was nothing but a pair of trousers and a shirt.

Various attempts were made to get Gusty to stop his hunger strike. A psychiatrist was sent, as were a number of clergymen. One of these was the Reverend William Hoey, a Church of Ireland clergyman:

This big fellow came in like a bull in a china shop. He didn't know where he was and asked, 'Gusty Spence?' Says I, 'That's right, who are you?' He says 'I'm the Reverend Hoey and I'm standing in as a substitute.' Says I, 'Are you a bought man?' 'No,' he says, 'the only person has bought me is the Lord Jesus Christ.' Says I, 'Well that's good enough, sit down.'

So we talked for hours. We got on so well the authorities would not let him come back to see me. He didn't fill the criteria which was, 'Get Gusty off the hunger strike.' We never even spoke about that. He just asked, 'Are you resolved in what you're doing?' Says I, 'Yes, I'm absolutely resolved.' We talked about life, we talked about religion, we talked about virtually everything, but they wouldn't let him back even though I made different requests.

I asked Gusty why he brought his hunger strike to an end:

Firstly they agreed that conditions would change in the prison. But as far as my case was concerned various lawyers said, 'Gusty, what you are doing, you're putting a gun to the head of a state and the state can't tolerate that. Even if they wanted to look at your case, they would be doing so under pressure and they couldn't do that. You'll die, make no mistake about it.'

The dying did concern me but it would have been the futility of the dying, the futility of what I was putting my family through. At the heels of the hunt, there was going to be no return. That's what I determined in my state of lucidity. It made common sense and it was practical. I had been so filled with defiance that nothing else mattered. What if I died? I would have been a martyr but how would that have affected my wife and children and my mother, who was aged? All those things had to be taken into consideration.

Gusty wrote a letter to his brother Billy on 11 September 1967, although Billy has written at the top that he only received it on 1 May 1971. This was on official prison note paper, at the top of which Gusty's number is given as 1124. Gusty began by thanking his brother for a recent letter and went on to express his annoyance with the fact that cards sent to him had been lost. He had accidentally discovered two postcards hidden by an officer in the jail.

In the letter Gusty asks Billy to thank his brother Jim for two books, one of which was *Old Soldier Sahib* which he said:

Brings back old memories of my father and his favourite army sayings. Both he and Mother had a hard old life but their fierce independence won through and with the help of God I will attempt to follow in their footsteps. Those people will never understand us. It's not egotism, it's pride and sheer Ulster guts and stubbornness. We can never be beaten because we will not admit defeat and we have not been taught how to surrender ...

Old Jim Burns was asking to be reminded to you all, he still retains the old spirit that keeps this Bog British. He, like myself, makes no apology for being what he is. To slip apologetically through life is no existence at all. If such a philosophy, mean as it is, went abroad we would soon find the land a place of shivering creatures without the capacity to live or the courage to die – a calamity surely. Amid apathy and treachery, cold friends and active enemies, worn-down frame and sometimes baffled mind, we are still to plead the same old sacred cause, voices crying in the wilderness.

But the blood will warm again and people will recover their imaginations when they think of how another voice 2,000 years ago cried out in the wilderness and how the message is still potent and inspiring today when 'practical' man sends no whisper across the years. We are loyal yet, even in prison, even after humiliation, lies, perjury and scorn.

During 1967, Gusty's mother began organising a petition for his release.

The petition stated:

> This man was sentenced to twenty years' imprisonment for murder and the evidence against him was entirely negligible. He has always denied all knowledge of this crime. He was denied the right of a separate trial and also denied an appeal to the House of Lords. Being convinced that this man is completely innocent
>
> WE DEMAND HIS IMMEDIATE RELEASE

The first page of the petition contains names of people mainly from the Grosvenor Road, Donegall Road, Sandy Row and Ormeau Road areas, streets like Roden Street, Hertford Street, Grosvenor Road, Coolderry Street, Matilda Street, Windsor Drive and so on. Some people, including nationalist MP Thomas Gormley, complained that the petition was organised by the banned UVF and that people were forced to sign it. In response Bella wrote to the newspapers denying the allegations:

> I am a woman of 71 years of age so would hardly be eligible to join the UVF, although my deceased husband was a member in 1912 and served gallantly at the Somme as a member of that historic division. Maybe Mr Gormley forgets that many UVF members gave their lives at the Somme, thereby making this country the democracy it is today and giving him the opportunity to say the things he does. I am the person who is organising the petition for my son and I will continue to fight for his freedom while I have breath left.

Bella went on to say that she would remove the names of anyone who so requested but she didn't expect many requests.

Despite the failure of the petition and Gusty's hunger strike, the latter was to have an unforeseen effect on a member of the prison staff. He was a nationalist Catholic prison officer who began to take a close interest in Gusty's demeanour at the time when the prison authorities were trying to influence Gusty's wife to persuade him to call his protest off. Gusty remembers:

> I would never ask a favour from a prison officer in my nineteen years in jail and I think this is how I gained respect. I never even asked for a light. If a prison officer wanted to do me a turn, and there were those who did, it was they who approached me.

The prison officer was observing him carefully. 'I saw the respect, I saw the sympathy in the man's eyes as I was going through the excruciating experience of a hunger strike.'

At some level Gusty's resolute determination had brought distant memories of other resisters and hunger-strikers into the mind of that Catholic prison officer. The Minister, as he was later code-named, was well read in Irish history. It was a time when Gusty was beginning to ask questions and delve into Irish history, and eventually the Minister struck up a conversation.

> One day the Minister said, 'Can I do anything for you?' I says, 'Well no, not really.' He said, 'Now, if there's anything I could do for you, let me know.' 'Yes, I'll do that.' He came back to me the second time, and he said, 'Can I do anything for you?'
>
> Louie and I had – unusually – fallen out and there was a period when Louie didn't come to see me, not because she didn't love me, because she did love me. She was trying to bring influence on me to end my hunger strike and it was only later that we got this into perspective.
>
> There was a deputy governor who was supposedly 'good living' – 'I'm a Christian and I've been saved so many years.' He would say to Louie, 'Wait till I tell you Mrs Spence, we're doing our best for this man but he won't let us help him. Now if things were kept quiet, who knows what'll happen in five years time. Will you have a talk with him?'
>
> Little ploys were brought to bear on people when they bucked authority. One day I collapsed in the prison hospital. I wakened up and this loyalist prison warder was saying, 'Here quick, drink this, this'll help you.' It was milk, and I spat it out and said, 'No.' If I had have taken a drop of milk that was the hunger strike broken.

Gusty however decided to trust the prison officer who had offered help:

> Whenever he said, 'Can I do anything for you,' I said, 'Yes, you can, you could see my wife.' He didn't live in Belfast and to see Louie was far out of his way. So I gave him instructions to assure my wife that I loved her. It's a very personal thing but it was also to make her aware of the pitfalls and the lengths the prison authorities would go to undermine what I was trying to do.
>
> Whether what I was doing was right or wrong was beside the point. To use one's nearest and dearest to influence me wasn't for the greater good. He went to Louie and I learnt how she felt. Part of the pressure brought on me during the hunger strike was because Louie wouldn't come and see me

because she didn't want to see me suffering. It's absolutely a human circumstance.

By this stage Gusty had lost weight and he was wasting away in bed. This created added pressure because although he wanted to see Louie and the children, he didn't really want them to see him like that. The Minister talked with Louie and came back with a message, 'Yes, I will see you.'

The Reverend Charles Sansom was the prison padre so I saw him and the governor agreed to a fifteen-minute special visit when Louie and I talked over our problems, which were really my problems, as opposed to hers.

That was the only time that Louie did not come to see me. She herself was suffering horribly because of me being removed and rearing the four children ...

The pressure was not just because of the demands of being the sole parent to our four children but because of the sideways looks of people on the street and the occasional snide comments. The children also suffered some abuse in school.

My wife, my mother and the family had nothing but love and consideration for me but of course they were putting pressure on me. My brothers understood and they knew it was a principled stand I was taking. Being men, they didn't have the same feelings as women. They respected me and supported me 100 per cent. But women are different. When they saw a loved one going through what I, and other people later on were going through, they wanted them off it as quickly as possible, and as far as they were concerned, to hell with principle.

The Minister who liaised with Louie was more than helpful:

He would buy her extra sandwiches but I said, 'I don't want to be taking your bread.' He said, 'Don't worry about it. Is there anything else I can do for you?' Says I, 'Well my mother lives in 66 Joseph Street, my brother-in-law lives in 32 Belgrave Street and our Billy lives in 50 Joseph Street.' I gave him all the names and said, 'Feel free to call and tell them who you are. We'll give you a code name. Your code name is "Minister".'

The code name stuck. More recently Gusty's son asked him:

'Da, you keep on talking about codename Minister.' Says I, 'My source had to be guaranteed with my life because his life was at stake.' Slowly the Minister got to know all my family. He was a terrific man even after the Troubles really exploded. He was an ordinary man with all the fears and aspirations anyone would have yet he went through those barricades into the middle of the Shankill Road when things were extremely tight and him being a Roman Catholic.

I thirsted for news from home and only got one heavily censored letter a month. We couldn't mention anything of worth. We are a non-demonstrative people, don't like to mention certain things in front of strangers. We didn't want a family problem to reach the eyes of strangers so we devised a method. He would carry half a packet of sweets and I would write my letters invariably on toilet paper in very small writing. They were squeezed up tight and moulded into the shape of a caramel so that if the security staff stopped him he could say, 'It's only a packet of sweets.' Caramels were carried out and in for years. You would be surprised how much information or queries could be condensed in a caramel.

Gusty had also found in the Minister someone with whom to share his interest in Irish history. 'The conversations I had with him were long conversations, almost invariably about Irish history, and we became firm friends.' This friendship crossed the barriers between Catholic and Protestant, nationalist and unionist, prison officer and prisoner, city dweller and rural dweller. Gusty recalls:

The Minister's name was guarded and he was treated absolutely anonymously. It was like spies during the Second World War who were never referred to by their proper names. Even close members of my family never knew his name, although they would have rendezvoused with him. Even now we don't refer to him by his name, so deep was the secret. Not because he was a Catholic. As a matter of fact I was very proud that one of my closest friends could be a Catholic and was prepared to assist me in a nonphysical way. I would never have compromised the man by asking him to bring in armaments or anything like that.

It was a personal service he gave to our family. He kept us in contact with each other. We also did role-play from time to time. We would be in the place of so-called employment, and the prison officers there were invariably loyalist. A certain amount of hostility emanated from that source and the Minster would sound out each man for me, saying, 'Look at that Spence fellow. Who does he think he is, strutting about the place?'

These prison officers were 'respectable' loyalists while Gusty was seen by some as disrespectable. He was seen to have brought causes into disrepute by those who would say, 'Wait until *we* start.'

The Minister also sounded out other prison officers, Gusty told me.

> Some of the reaction was, 'Ach well now, the man's doing no harm' and 'I mean to say, if you were serving a lifetime maybe you'd be the same.' But some were hostile and we sussed out their hostility. There were super-Prod officers and I would have said to them, 'Look at that Fenian so and so. Who does he think he is and he's getting a living from the government. I'll guarantee he's not loyal.' Sometimes there was no response and sometimes they would say, 'Oh no, I don't even want to talk about that. That man's doing his duty.'
>
> Never in a million years would they suspect that a Roman Catholic prison officer and I were close friends. To me, friendship means a person who's there whenever you need them – and he was there when I needed him and I was there when he needed me. There was an incident in Ballynahinch when one of his daughters had married or was living with a bloke in Ballynahinch and some super-Prods were giving problems. The girl was a Catholic and men were dispatched to disabuse them saying, 'These people are all right. Leave them alone.'

The friendship continued long after the Minister left the prison service. After Gusty's release:

> Louie and I went down to his home town. We picked him up and went out for a very pleasant day. Louie was driving and we shared a couple of beers and reminisced about things that happened in the prison, some very sad things, and from time to time not only was there mirth but there were tears in our eyes. There were people in prison who had left and been killed or there were tragic events on either side. I'm speaking even about prison officers, for many of whom I had the greatest respect.
>
> Eddie Jones and Bert Miles and people of that calibre and decent Roman Catholic officers like Gerry Melville. Gerry lived for a pint. He was a single man who played a saxophone in an orchestra and he was shot dead. There was a Liverpool officer, Paddy Mackin, a Catholic who married a Congregationalist lady and lived on the Oldpark Road. They had a son in the RUC and the son was visiting and had been ringing the doorbell but there was no answer. He went into the house on a Sunday morning [3 February 1979] and found his mother and father both shot to death.[2]
>
> Paddy was a decent inoffensive man who would have gone out of his way to help anyone. He wasn't a hard, vicious man, he wasn't someone who demeaned people. I can't understand the taking of their lives. Maybe it was to dissuade other people from becoming members of the prison service. It had an effect because there weren't all that many Catholics in the

prison service and quite a few left. Catholic officers were prime targets for the IRA, but other officers were shot as well.

We spoke about these things and we kept in contact. I was extremely conscious of his position being a Catholic.

He was a nationalist who abhorred any sort of violence. He was a devout Catholic, a communicant, and he used to tell me, 'God forgive me I missed mass.' 'Ach,' he says, 'The Lord knew I was having a couple of pints and enjoying myself.' He was a happy-go-lucky person and I suppose it started with him. I began to have respect for people who were not the same as myself, who were not unionist. It was through listening to him and watching his demeanour. We had nothing else to do except watch people and guess their motives. I found the man's motives pure and I said to myself, 'Well, all Catholics are not the same, all Catholics are not raving IRA men.' This was in the throes of change in the early days but the rapport didn't develop overnight.

I had just begun to have a taste for Irish history and we spoke about historical facts. He said, 'If the unification of my country costs one drop of innocent blood, I don't want it.' I paid particular attention to it, and we used to quote poetry to one another. We didn't do it openly but there were wee surreptitious moments, when I would repeat, 'Who dares to speak of '98?' He would repeat the next line. We were two flies on the wall, looking in on prison life ...

I was very sad when he passed away. I wanted to go to his funeral but there were physical force nationalists there and I didn't want any pressure to come on the family. So I viewed it at a distance.

The Minister gave Gusty a small booklet entitled *The Ghosts of Kilmainham* published by the Kilmainham Jail Restoration Society in 1963. It contained republican poems and brief details on various heroes ranging from Henry Joy McCracken right through the pantheon of nationalist heroes to Eamon De Valera who was still living when the book was printed. The first poem is *The Felons of Our Land*, by Arthur M. Forester and the last is *1916*, by Monsignor Pádraig de Brún.

It contained factual material and romantic idealism. Both aspects helped Gusty gain an insight into the things that inspired republicans. He loaned the book to me in February 1996 and I found it dog-eared with use. Irish history had opened a new door as Gusty indicated in his letter to Bob Hynds in 1981:

Irish history enthralled me because it was 'new', because I had never read it

> before even though it was old. It's a bloody shame you know that it was never – and still isn't – taught at school.

The Minister helped prepare the ground for much that was to follow. Gusty developed new contacts with republican prisoners. His capacity to empathise with opponents was evident in his letter to Joe McCann's wife after the Official IRA man was shot dead by the security forces in Belfast in 1972. As the journalist Peter Taylor said, Gusty 'saw himself as a soldier and soldiers did not massacre innocent civilians. Spence, whatever his enemies thought of him, lived by a code and respected IRA men who lived by it too.'[3]

But how did others react? 'Victor', who had not then reached senior rank in the UVF, said:

> That whole thing didn't cause me a problem. It was just a soldier relating to a soldier, which I could do quite easily. I had read stories about the First World War and the Germans coming out of the trenches and playing football on Christmas Day with British soldiers. Whether they're actually true or not, I'm not sure.
>
> Things could be appreciated inside prison but not if they had happened outside. The prison was sacrosanct and anything done in prison was put into a different category. Nothing unites people like common suffering. Therefore the nonaggression pact of 1971 made sense. You didn't have to lose face or credibility. Cooperating in the prisons didn't diminish your own ideals. It was uniting in a common suffering. If you claim to be a prisoner of war then you are a prisoner of war and you can't carry on a war within a prison.

The sacrosanctness of prison gave Gusty Spence space for personal development and change. His friendship with the Minister, his freedom from the constrictions of intercommunal rivalries, were of crucial significance in his quest.

From almost the first day of his imprisonment Gusty questioned many things that are usually taken for granted. He began to talk with Catholic and eventually republican prisoners. For many years he remained wedded to violence as the means of protecting Northern Ireland's integrity and stymieing British attempts to extricate themselves from the Ulster problem. He remained in contact with the UVF through people like 'John', and Bo McClelland who became UVF Commander in his absence. However he was inevitably somewhat isolated from the conflict on the streets although he heard the shooting at the height of the confrontations of 1969:

> When I heard this prolific shooting my face was jammed against the bars. I hadn't heard so much gunfire since I was in the army and it went on right through to the early hours of the morning.

This was during October 1969 when two civilians and one RUC man, Constable Arbuckle, were killed during a UVF battle with the army. Some sixty-six other people were injured, thirty-seven from gunshot wounds; of these, fourteen were soldiers, three policemen and twenty civilians.

Most of the UVF men firing towards the army lines were themselves ex-army. Gusty heard of these activities from a radio inside the prison. He heard army reports of UVF resistance while they were being pressed back into the Hammer. The soldiers cordoned off the area and found petrol bombs, guns, other offensive weapons and ammunition, and the illegal Shankill pirate radio. But they got little of substance.

Generally he obtained only titbits of information, carried to him by members of his family – titbits such as, 'The boys are still intact and they were asking about you.' Gusty remained resolute in his defiance and his loyalism, and in a letter dated 9 November 1969 he wrote, 'I'm an awful man for tradition.' In the letter he paid 'tribute to those gallant men who didn't stop to count the cost – the forgotten men'. He was writing of soldiers who died in the wars but saw himself in the same tradition of self-sacrifice. After quoting poetry about the fallen, he wrote:

> I write of course of those men who, a few short months before their inception into the British army, belonged to an organisation formed to combat the forces of rebellion and sedition besides the actions of misinformed and selfish Englishmen. I mean, naturally, the glorious and immortal Ulster Volunteer Force. Memories last so long as the mind lasts. This is our heritage and I dare anyone – no matter who they be – to take it from us. FOR GOD AND ULSTER.

In another fragment of a letter from the same time Gusty writes about 'the rebels':

> They think they are on the point of overthrowing Ulster, think they have foreseen everything and have provided against everything but they have forgotten the most important items of all – the indomitable tenacity of the Ulsterman and his refusal to accept defeat. So until all rebels realise and give cognisance to these traits – Ulster shall never be at peace ...

> I am as God made me and I thank him for it. An uncompromising man is so rare a phenomenon in Ulster today that the appearance of one takes his generation by surprise and he dies broken-hearted, is shot or is jailed before his people have made up their minds whether to crown him, condemn him or simply to ignore him.

While Gusty had begun to question many things, he remained a resolute and determined Ulster loyalist.

10

Political Status

In Crumlin Road jail, prisoners were able to visit the 'cinema' once a month:

> The old fellow who ran it was Chuff McCullough, a good man who went out of his way to get films acceptable to the prisoners. They called him 'Chuff' because if you said, 'That was a good film, Officer McCullough,' he was 'all chuffed'. If you said, 'That was a lot of crap, Billy' – 'Oh now,' he would say, 'they can't all be good.' The projector was a cinematograph donated to the prison by the old Classic Cinema in Castle Lane and the films were shown in the gym.
>
> We weren't allowed to smoke outside our cells and that's why I started chewing a wee bit of tobacco, which gave me the same satisfaction as a smoke. The prison worked in a spider system. All the wings branch out like a cobweb and everybody's marched in from the separate units, A wing, B wing, C wing and so on.
>
> A wing and D wing would go together because they were old hands.

> Prisoners in B wing and C wing who were star men [first-time prisoners] would go in together. Talking was extremely limited. When the lights went out and we were sitting conveniently, we could smuggle stuff back and forward. It was a pretty tough regime, but the prison officers on the whole were a decent bunch of men, most of them ex-service. The officers that I found oppressive and who didn't give much countenance to human feelings had been screws during the war. They were invariably B Specials and very ignorant, sectarian men.

On one occasion a prison officer in an interview began asking Gusty:

> 'If a child is born on the Falls and a child is born in the Shankill ...' He was beating about the bush and I was a wee bit puzzled, then it hit me and I said, 'Are you attempting to lecture me on sectarianism?' He said, 'No, I don't want to hurt your feelings.' Says I, 'Hurt my feelings? You've something like one hundred and twenty prison officers here and four of them and two principal officers are Catholic, and you wouldn't have them about the place only you need them to administer the chapel.' He says to the chief, 'There's no talking to this man. March him out.'
>
> The principal officers were John McCoy and Paddy Mackin, and four other Catholic officers were McComskey, Rogan, Gerry Melville and Joe Lavery. They were decent men but they wouldn't have had them about the place only they were needed to administer the chapel. Prod officers wouldn't officiate in the chapel.

Prisoners could borrow one book for as long as a month, but couldn't get another until it was returned. Around Christmas, books could be exchanged once a fortnight. They were wellworn and any books considered harmful, politically or otherwise, were excluded. The librarian brought a selection of books round the wings to the long-term prisoners on a small trolley or prisoners could ask for a particular book. Tales about Africa were very popular. After Gusty's hunger strikes in 1967, he began to have access to a wider range of books, but they remained restricted even in Long Kesh in the late 1970s. Gusty, however, had some success:

> I put about nine points to the governor and the Chief Officer. One was for the admission of political books because that was also part of my quest. I could get *Treasure Island* and Shakespeare but they weren't the type of book I needed. I wanted something to point me in the direction of why I was sitting in a prison cell at thirty-three years of age serving life imprisonment. I had escaped hanging and I wanted to know why this had happened. The

first book I got was *My Fight for Irish Freedom* by Dan Breen, which was naïve in the extreme. Books on Northern Ireland politics were extremely rare.

Gusty's reading and reflection enabled him to teach other prisoners. The governor at first wasn't sure when Gusty proposed to teach Irish history lessons:

> He misunderstood at first and said, 'Are these for paramilitary lessons?' I said, 'Have a prison officer present if you want. He will probably learn something, coming from a working-class unionist background.' So at first they brought a prison officer for the Irish history lessons, which were open to everyone.'

Gusty quickly came to see that history is less a matter of facts than a matter of interpretation:

> I was extremely careful. Only by comparing the lies could you approximate to the truth and you never hit the truth spot on. When one is teaching one has got to be absolutely factual as you could be called to account. After about six weeks the prison officer was quietly withdrawn and I was left to get on with it. Other aspects of education kept impinging. People wanted basic English language or literature or advance in both subjects. Political science was unobtainable and there was no danger of it being put on the 'curriculum'.[1]

There was no formal education, but for a loyalist to be teaching Irish history in any situation was a novel experience. Working-class loyalists, and indeed many nationalists in those days, had no access to their own history in a formal sense:

> There had been no education of the Protestant mass and the Protestant working-class man or woman was often in complete ignorance of Irish politics and indeed of any politics. Hence there was contempt from republican prisoners, not for loyalist prisoners but for their lack of knowledge.[2]

Gusty began to reduce this deficit by reading as widely as conditions permitted:

> Various authors gave me inspiration: St John Ervine whenever he was doing a biography of James Craig, later Lord Craigavon. Terence McSwiney who died on a seventy-four-day hunger strike belonged to Oglaigh na

h-Éireann, the Irish Volunteers, and was the first Lord Mayor of Cork. *Gaol Journal* by John Mitchel, who was a Protestant and a Young Irelander, and many others.[3]

On one occasion in 1972, Gusty received an unexpected present from a Dublin man, Joe Colgan:

> I received a book out of the blue, *A Seat Behind the Coachman*. It related tales of old Ireland the way it was, humorous tales and tales of a social and cultural nature. It was endorsed 'Joe Colgan', but I hadn't a clue who Joe Colgan was. I couldn't even send a letter of thanks because I didn't know who the man was and letters were very precious in those days.

Many years later Gusty and Joe Colgan were to meet, and through Joe a meeting was arranged in Dublin that was to lead to a significant link between the UVF and the Irish government during a vital stage in the peace process. Back in 1972, when Gusty received Joe Colgan's book, he had no idea that it had been sent by a Dublin republican.

I have known Joe Colgan over many years and I spoke with him on Saturday, 2 September 2000. I asked why he had sent the book to Gusty, whom he did not meet until the 1990s. He told me it was 'because he was the most hated figure in the Republic at that time'. Gusty remembered Joe's act of generosity and when he eventually met him, he immediately recalled the book and the card he had sent. This left a lasting impression upon Joe, who later facilitated dialogue between loyalists and republicans.

People who begin to radically re-examine their assumptions can find this a lonely experience. It is particularly so in claustrophobic political or religious contexts where to question is painful not only to oneself but to one's friends. The UVF had little inkling of what was happening in Gusty's mind, although there were those who privately shared much of his thinking. Beyond the UVF, the Protestant commitment to civil and religious liberty and freedom of conscience was not very deep, and people of conscience could be dismissed as traitors and expelled from the community. Others, in both traditions, were rethinking their positions, but people in the throes of change do not readily share their questioning. Gusty found this a lonely experience:

> I'm not sure that others were going through the same rethinking. Some were only doing five or seven years and hadn't thought about the situation as I had, but I would think many went through a similar experience. Most

screws came from the country districts and brought their sectarian attitudes with them. That could mean not giving a prisoner a glass of water or not letting him out to the toilet. They were fighting an obscure fight and were not always the professional people that the NIO and the Prison Officers' Association said they were.

Gusty frequently thought about his mother with great fondness:

> She was always a defender. God knows, in the back streets of the Shankill Road in the 1930s you had to have someone to defend you. I don't mean physically, I mean from people being disparaging because we had nothing, barely shoes on our feet and sometimes no shoes on our feet. She was the bulwark. She did the hammering, for instance, while my father never touched such things. All he did was look over the glasses. My mother was the manager, the comforter, the lover and in many instances the provider. She did all those things with one thing in mind, love. Nothing else. It was the care and attention of the family ...
>
> There was pride there too and we were warned, 'Never tell lies, never steal.' If my mother caught us stealing, we would have got killed. She didn't have to get the bible out but might have said, 'If you tell a lie it will come back to haunt you. It won't haunt me and I'll never trust you again.' We did tell wee white lies and when my mother suspected it was a lie, she accepted that it was for the greater good. When I was lifted that time, ach, it nearly killed her.

If the love and support of his mother sustained Gusty in his early years, Louie's constancy through almost nineteen years of imprisonment was the crucial factor in his survival. She found it difficult, but she gave Gusty the space to find a way forward.

Members of the wider family circle also played a part, and the support of key people within the leadership of the UVF who understood the need for change was vital. Despite hardship and difficulties, relations within the family remained strong and they sustained each other. Louie's refusal to visit and watch her husband destroying himself through starvation may have saved his life.

Gusty reflected on his family:

> Even when I was in Long Kesh, decisions were still made as a family. I was not a patriarchal figure but they came up if they had problems. Sandra or Catherine would come up, explain the problem and ask, 'What'll we do?' We all sat down and worked it out. Louie once said to me, 'Did Andrew

make you a promise?' I says, 'What do you mean?' 'Did he promise you he wouldn't get married until you got out of prison so that I wouldn't be left alone? Andrew told me he's going to get married to a nice wee girl down the street.' I said, 'Well there's no problem with that.'

In fact there was a problem in that they had no money to finance the wedding. However, a solution was found in the form of a krugerrand Louie had purchased on Gusty's behalf.

Someone said, 'That South African krugerrand is worth a few quid.' I was in Long Kesh and as far as I was concerned it was my wife's coin. Andrew was being married and had nothing so we said, 'What about the krugerrand?' It was sold and the proceeds went a long way towards financing the wedding. He was married in the City Hall and they had a wee bit of a reception afterwards.

Money was always a problem, but the family held together:

I always told the children, 'I love you. Make sure that you tell each other that you love each other.' I'm very proud of them. Andrew was only four when I went away and when I came back he was a grown man. My family had all grown up. Louie kept that family together. It wasn't easy for me in Long Kesh but it was a hell of a lot harder for her.

Elizabeth and Sandra and Catherine helped out. Andrew had his paper round and worked in the loyalist club collecting bottles. Louie worked in the loyalist club peeling potatoes. She also scrubbed floors and her hands were red. The work ethic was always there and sometimes they were taken advantage of. But no more so than ordinary working-class people are.

Although in jail the pull of Orangeism remained, Gusty decided it was not for him. But he accepted that there were well-intentioned people who wanted to see him back within the fold:

'You should be back in the Orange Institution and we'll get you back.' I wouldn't offend those people but I would ask, 'What for? Are you taking leave of your senses? What would I want to join the Orange Order for? There's nothing in it that I want. There are many things in the Orange Order that I do not want.'[4]

Gusty did not deny that positive elements existed within Orangeism but he questioned its value. Most Orange lodges did little more than discuss mundane aspects of the Twelfth demonstration and other social activities.

In prison Gusty was able to meet all kinds of people. He met with a

Jewish man who had been in the Nazi concentration camps as a boy:

> He was a Jewish ex-paratrooper who received a prison sentence for trying to smuggle cannabis into Northern Ireland. That was virtually unheard of in those days. He broadened my horizons and encouraged an awareness of world affairs. He gave me a better perspective because I was tunnel-visoned. I asked him about the Holocaust and I think he was in Ravensbruck. He remembered running through the snow at night between his mother and his grandmother, who were holding him like grim death. There were dogs barking and Nazi SS shouting and yelling. That image stayed with him. I knew about the Holocaust because I had followed the Second World War closely.

Despite the deprivation and pain of separation from loved ones, Gusty found prison an invigorating experience:

> It might seem strange to hear me say that, but we had to divert our minds in so many ways that we didn't have time to think about our own particular circumstances. I found both political and nonpolitical prisoners intriguing. I'm not too sure what a criminal prisoner is. Most people in prison were not completely bad, they weren't all evil. Some had been subject to sociological pressures and there were men who started by mitching [playing truant] off school before progressing to the training school and borstal and then to prison. Some came to look upon crime as a profession and some treated prison as punishment for following their profession.
>
> I felt great pity for some prisoners, especially when there were deaths in the family or difficult family circumstances. I felt compassion. My door was open and if people knocked they were never turned away and they were listened to. I would like to think that was one of the good things I did in my life.
>
> Humanity was encompassed in it all, there's always a spark of humanity. If they asked me for a cigarette paper or a piece of bread, I'd give it to them. Any time a prison officer said, 'Gusty, so and so has asked my permission for you to write him a letter,' I said, 'Well, he's already asked me would I write the letter, and that was OK.' They knew I would write the letter because the man was illiterate.
>
> There was no education whatever in Crumlin Road prison or in the early days at Long Kesh, none whatever. What I wished to do in Crumlin Road jail was to teach men, to relate Irish history so that they would have a better grasp of the political circumstances that led them to jail and why they were fighting.

Most of the people Gusty found in jail were working-class with little or no education:

> There were no middle-class people in the UVF. One or two people had gone to university but they too came from a working-class background and were susceptible to the pronouncements of politicians. If politicians said something was true, it was true, and the newspapers in Northern Ireland didn't go out of their way to deny it. I suppose it goes back to Tennyson, 'Theirs not to reason why, theirs but to do and die.' Even now at this moment sitting in the heartland of the Shankill Road, scholastic academic achievement is rare.

Gusty met Frank Gogarty, a former chairman of the Northern Ireland Civil Rights Association, who was jailed for six months in September 1970 for using abusive language with intent to cause a breach of the peace.[5] He also met Frank McManus, who had been elected Westminster MP for Fermanagh and South Tyrone in June 1970 and was imprisoned in January 1971 under the Special Powers Act. McManus was also involved in the civil rights movement. Gusty got to know both men:

> When Frank Gogarty came, we struck up a relationship through smuggled notes. I would send a couple of cigars across to Frank who smoked French cigarettes. He returned some of his cigarettes. I had a surreptitious conversation with him as he was being brought through A wing and we touched on points of identification and agreement. We were both agreed that Northern Ireland society would have to become more equitable, with more input from the minority. Frank Gogarty and Frank McManus weren't in any paramilitary organisations. Jail is a great leveller and when people came into prison I saw them as persons, not as the notorious myths that surrounded them.

Until 1970 there were no republican prisoners in the jail. Most loyalists had come in as a result of activities in 1969, including reactions against the Hunt Report on the RUC and street battles against the British army. This situation gave Gusty a certain amount of strength in the long-term A wing and throughout the prison:

> Prison couldn't function without prisoners, and people who weren't in the UVF but had loyalist inclinations and who were in jail for throwing petrol bombs or fighting the army, the police or even republicans, were scattered throughout the prison in A wing, D wing, and C wing. They had posts in

> the cookhouse or with the maintenance staff and we could have started and stopped the jail. In fact we did start and stop the jail.

The first republican prisoners were members of the Provisional IRA (PIRA), which was formed in January 1970. Gusty got to know individual Provos but

> Some were obviously bigots and didn't want to know me or people like me. They made it very obvious, whereas the Official IRA would go out of their way to have dialogue with us and we did exactly the same with them.

During a curfew in the lower Falls on 3–5 July 1970, soldiers were fired upon and they used large quantities of CS gas in return. A house-to-house search ensued and weapons, explosives, ammunition and two-way radios were discovered.[6] The Sinn Féin leader Maire Drumm led a march down with bread and milk for the kids because people were confined to their houses.[7]

> You're talking about a block, bordered by the Grosvenor Road, Cullingtree Road, Albert Street and the Falls Road, which would have been 'Sticky' or Official IRA land.

As a result, about three hundred people were lodged in Crumlin Road jail before being charged with offences. Gusty recalls the prison being near to bursting point with people sleeping all over the place. The new remand prisoners were held for at most a few weeks. They were mainly lodged in B and C wings, away from the sentenced loyalist and republican prisoners in A wing.

Some members of the Official IRA had been arrested, and although they were separated from loyalists, some contact was possible. The new prisoners had to have access to the exercise yards and were designated the use of C and D wing yards, as well as A wing yard when it was not in use. In order to get to A wing yard they had to pass through A wing, where Gusty was incarcerated. Billy McMillen, leader of the Official IRA in Belfast, was among those on remand, and Gusty managed to have quiet chats with him:

> I was ill about this time and they had begun leaving my cell door open for prolonged periods of time because I wasn't going anywhere and was incapable of working. They were afraid of another heart attack and me dying. As the remand prisoners were being brought through each day, my cell door was ajar and Billy would nip in. I had the coffee going and the

cigarettes and the pipe and we kicked ideas about and had a good friendly relationship.

This friendship formed the basis of a new relationship between UVF and Official IRA prisoners. As a result, Gusty says:

> The Official IRA men coming in during 1971 and '72 deliberately sought us out, and it became a very inspirational time for me. Here you had the commander of the Official IRA being more than reasonable and absolutely nonsectarian. He wanted a united Ireland, no doubt about that, but Billy McMillen was very positive in his attitude to unionism and Protestants.

Like the Minister, McMillen told Gusty that in relation to a united Ireland, 'if it cost one Irish life, it wasn't worth it'.

On 9 August 1971 the Crumlin Road prison population was significantly strengthened by an influx of republican prisoners following the introduction of internment. Gusty said this was not his first experience of internment:

> I remember the first detention of twenty-two men in 1969. They were only held for five days and released. One of them finished up as a friend, Malachy McGurran, from the older republican movement. Malachy was one of the main political thinkers of the Official IRA and the Workers' Party. I met him on several occasions but we didn't have as much time together as we would have liked.

Two leading Provisionals were sentenced under the Explosive Substances Act on 15 April 1971. These were Francis Card, otherwise Proinsias Mac Airt, and Billy McKee, a veteran Belfast IRA leader. Gusty is convinced these men had been set up: 'Francis Card and Billy McKee had been targeted by the security forces who brought in Scotland Yard detectives. In their view this was ordinary crime and they were going to solve it.' Gusty found that the Provos had little to offer loyalists:

> The Provos didn't have a political agenda. If they had any agenda, it wasn't even 'Brits out'. I remember asking Billy McKee, 'What is it you want, Billy, a place in the sun? The all-Ireland bit is just not on, but it's not only that, what have you got to offer Prods?' He agreed there was a vacuum but said it was about to be filled. They came out with the ÉIRE NUA document.[8]

Loyalists could gather intelligence from the new prisoners in various ways:

> After internment in August 1971 the new prisoners were billeted in Girdwood Barracks adjoining Crumlin Road jail. The authorities decided to break down the wall between the jail and the barracks. Men were beaten, there's no question about it, and they were lodged in C wing which became the internment wing. I had a mole in there – Plum Smith – who was an orderly. He was a member of the Red Hand Commando serving six months.

While Gusty regarded republicans as the enemy, all prisoners had a common adversary in the prison authorities and they had no intention of making war on one another in prison. Billy McKee was trying to move beyond the old agenda:

> He was emphasising the nonsectarian aspect of the Provos. I believe he was genuine enough but it wasn't borne out by the Four Step Inn, the Balmoral and the Bayardo Shankill bombings. One Provo said to me, 'We'll fight alongside loyalists against communism.' They were extremely wary of the so-called communistic aspect of the Official IRA and there was great anger with the Official IRA for not having protected Catholic areas in 1969 …
>
> I'm not politically naïve as far as Northern Ireland is concerned, but I didn't have any interest in Marxism. I wasn't really aware of it. There were only embryonic socialist stirrings within myself at that time.

Gusty saw a possible basis for a new understanding between members of the Official IRA and the UVF who shared the same working-class underprivileged background and a growing commitment to nonsectarianism. Thus whenever Gusty met members of the Official IRA, he found there was 'an immediate empathy'.

> The first day that P.J. Monaghan, the OC of the Official IRA, came into prison he came down to my cell, knocked the door and introduced himself. I invited him in and we had a cup of coffee. We had a good yarn and it became a friendship. The purists would say, 'How could you be friends with an IRA man?' Of course you can, providing it's understood, and the Official IRA were always very strong on this, 'We don't want to engage ourselves in a campaign against loyalists, it's against the army who we see as being oppressors.' But it is virtually impossible to fight a war without incurring civilian casualties, which they learned to their cost in Aldershot and other places. They called a ceasefire in 1972 [on 29 May], after Ranger Best was killed.

The people of the Shankill and the Falls shared the same lifestyle and similar levels of poverty.[9] Gusty discovered that:

> They didn't look any different from me, they didn't talk any different from me, and their background was very similar to mine, working in menial jobs. It was then that something else began to arise in me. I was always afraid of this word 'socialist'. A socialist in Shankill Road terms was always a 'red flagger', someone who was going to bring in Moscow at the drop of a hat.

In 1981 Gusty reflected in the letter to Bob Hynds on his talks with IRA men:

> I started to have dialogue with the IRA men in jail and was surprised how much we had in common tho' they were the enemy. Some people did not like my talks but I spoke as an individual and was entitled to my opinion. We began to cooperate on prison matters and consequently began a campaign of prison reform. I do not regret it and take much satisfaction knowing that such dialogue and cooperation could be carried even further, and perhaps a basis for bigger things could be achieved namely the ultimate – Peace!

Despite such developments, life in the jail could be very difficult when violence flared outside. On Saturday, 4 December 1971, the UVF gave their response to the IRA bombing of the Four Step Inn on the Shankill Road where two Protestants had been killed in September. McGurk's Bar in North Queen Street was demolished by a UVF bomb. The death toll reached fifteen, with eight injured. Riots followed and a number of people, including members of the security forces, were injured. McGurk's public house was close to the jail and the explosion was clearly heard. Gusty remembered that night:

> When explosions were heard the Provos in the prison always cheered. Men showed a fair face in the morning but they let themselves go at night. There was a bit of shouting out of windows then at the end of the night: when the 'Soldier's Song' was played on Irish radio, somebody countered it with 'God Save the Queen.'
>
> That night there was an extremely loud explosion and they cheered it to the echo. We all tuned in to the police radio until news started coming in that it was an explosion in McGurk's Bar. The silence was deafening. The next morning at half past seven the atmosphere was electric. You could have felt the electricity on your tongue. I saw McKee and I saw P.J. Monaghan and we were agreed there had to be strict discipline.

This became known as the 'no-conflict' policy. Fighting had broken out in the dining hall and although it was quickly broken up and only a few injuries were sustained, the danger was obvious. A verbal agreement was made that there would be no fighting in the prison. This agreement was almost always adhered to.

Martin Meehan, OC of the IRA remand prisoners, was regularly in consultation with Billy McKee, OC of A wing, and says that McKee sought to reassure loyalists as well as accepting the need for mutual safeguards. Meehan, however, says that while

> there was no major trouble among the sentenced prisoners, there was some fighting among remand prisoners because there was no discipline among them. There were fist fights on the visits and fist fights coming from the visits. I was involved in a few incidents myself. I was picked on because there were maybe two or three of them and when I was on my own they would make a go for me.

As Gusty recalled, the general absence of violence in Crumlin Road jail contrasted with life outside:

> There was a war going on. Prods were being shot dead, Taigs were being shot dead. There were awful explosions – fifteen people killed in one explosion, people killed in the Four Step Inn, people killed in the Balmoral Showroom. Imagine the discipline needed to keep the lid on that situation. It's only one hundred yards long and forty yards broad and you have men packed in that place like sardines.[10]

Monaghan, the Official IRA OC, came regularly to Gusty's cell:

> We had a strong relationship with P.J. Monaghan because before our men had started to talk together, he and I talked together quite a bit. We took so-called physical exercise together and would go to my cell to theorise over a cup of tea or coffee. He would have been the first Official IRA man I got to know in depth.

While the discussions with Billy McMillen were of major significance, Gusty's relationship with Monaghan was of longer duration and facilitated the beginnings of dialogue among ordinary loyalist and republican prisoners:

> What Monaghan had to do was to encourage his men to speak to my men, to initiate debate. They began to explore each other's perceptions in depth.

> This exploration was very important for people from different violent sides who had suddenly been thrown together. People imagine UVF men as being six foot four with four foot six broad shoulders but were amazed to find they were little slight men from all walks of life.
>
> Prisoners were completely integrated in those days, with my men subject to my discipline, the Provos were subject to theirs, and the Officials to theirs. But we had ordinary Catholics and Protestants who were bigots. News time at six o'clock was always hyper-sensitive because of the explosions and shootings and petrol bombings. Some of these Taigs or Prods would pass snide remarks and cause hyper-sensitivity.
>
> One night after a particular incident, a lot of the Provo prisoners rushed down. I heard there was trouble in the canteen and of course my men had rushed down too, including myself, to see what this trouble was, and to quell it. A non-paramilitary prisoner had passed a remark at which people took offence. There was an altercation that could have become a general melee in which men would have been killed. But McKee was down and Francis Card and Peter Monaghan and myself had quelled the disturbance. We resolved that in future anybody wishing to listen to the news would do so in their own or someone else's cell. TVs would be turned off at six o'clock.

New prisoners needed help to come to terms with their situation. This was provided to some extent by the discipline and structure that Gusty, in cooperation with republican leaders, instituted. Prisoners on remand had particular problems:

> Remand prisoners came in full of defiance – 'I'll beat this and I've got witnesses lined up and the police really don't have anything.' That is until the dawn of realisation comes in, what I called the mincing machine, a court of law. Slowly, through logic and the presentation of facts, the aspirations of the prisoner were cut down to size. He was left in stark terms with guilt or innocence, the preponderance being heavily in favour of guilt. He could admit guilt and face plea-bargaining, or he could continue knowing that the judge would find him guilty and he would be penalised for wasting the court's time.

The discussions with the Official IRA were of major significance. The Official IRA were on a serious mission to engage with loyalists in genuinely nonsectarian politics. They became committed to a socialist ideology that was foreign to the UVF. However there had always been UVF men with socialist inclinations or even a background in the Northern Ireland Labour

Party. This provided a potential basis for understanding and a context within which Gusty could express sympathy to IRA Volunteer Joe McCann's widow on the death of her husband at the hands of security forces on 15 April 1972:

> My dear Mrs McCann
>
> I would like to tender to you my deepest and profoundest sympathy on the tragic death of your beloved husband, Joe.
>
> There are those who would find it strange to hear from someone such as myself but I can assure you that whilst your husband and I may have been opposed to each other in politics, we shared that common bond that is known only to those who fight their own respective corners to the best of their ability. He was a soldier of the Republic and I a Volunteer of Ulster and we made no apology for being what we are or were.
>
> Joe once did a good turn indirectly and I never forgot him for his humanity, and even though I never got the chance to thank him personally, I am almost sure that he knew how I felt and that I was grateful to him.
>
> In such circumstances, my inept words are little comfort to you but if you believe that these words are from the bottom of my heart it may go some little way to enabling you to understand them.
>
> I, too, am a family man with a wife and four lovely children and this aspect is the most heart-rending of all because the women suffer in our coming and in our going and it is they who have the most courage.
>
> May God bless your 'wee' ones and yourself in your hour of extreme grief and may He give you the strength required to face the future as Joe would have wished it.
>
> I salute your husband as an honourable and brave soldier.
>
> Very sincerely and truly,
>
> Gusty Spence

Gusty's reference to the women suffering 'in our coming and in our going' comes from Patrick Pearse and demonstrates his growing appreciation of Irish history.

He had known Joe McCann, who once lived in the loyalist Highfield estate in the upper Shankill. Gusty still recalls the good turn referred to in the letter:

> There were Official IRA armaments held in a house in north Belfast. The UVF knew about this and the guns were taken and passed over to the organisation. The Official IRA then swept into Sandy Row and lifted three fellows. They then released one man, saying, 'Tell the UVF that if we don't get these

guns back we're going to shoot these two fellows.' Through my contacts I was told that the two fellows were not UVF men although the man they released was. I sent word to Joe McCann, 'Joe, you'd be shooting them for the wrong reasons. Don't do it. Do me a turn and I won't forget about it.' One Official IRA man wanted to shoot them dead but Joe released them, a magnanimous gesture.

Gusty's letter to Mrs McCann sent a positive and potentially helpful message to the unionist community, suggesting that while IRA men were the enemy, they were not alien creatures. Rather, they were soldiers, even 'honourable'.

It was particularly helpful for loyalists that in 1972 Official Republicans accepted the principle that a thirty-two-county Irish republic could only be achieved with the consent of Protestants. Tomás Mac Giolla, at Carrickmore in 1972, rejected the attempted coercion of Protestants into an Irish republic in the following words:

> The Irish revolution, which must continue and to which we pledge ourselves, demands the support of the Protestant working-class. People have talked about the Provisionals trying to bomb one million Protestants into a Republic; but they would not – could not – and no one can – and no one as far as we are concerned would try – to bomb them into a socialist republic. That would be the ultimate contradiction and stupidity. We need those million Protestant working people on the workers' side in the Irish revolution ... The Protestant workers ... do not wish at the present time to have a united country. Let us understand them.[11]

Gusty has frequently quoted Mac Giolla's words. They helped create space for the UVF and other loyalists to work together in prison for common objectives.

Gusty told me that in prison, 'the real opportunity to talk, and talk long into the night, only came after the achievement of political status on 20 June '72'. There was a paradoxical element in this because at around that time, sectarian assassinations began to intensify and there was intense concern among loyalists about the intentions of the British government. The fear was that the PIRA had achieved something in their talks with British ministers. At about this time, according to Gusty, the paramilitary groupings divided the wings of the jail by mutual agreement:

> In Crumlin Road jail there were four wings, A, B, C and D, with three floors to each wing. The long-term prisoners had had A wing consisting of A1, A2

> and A3. An arrangement was agreed between Billy McKee for the Provos, P.J. Monaghan for the Officials and myself as OC of the UVF. A1 and half of A2 would go to the Provos – that's the landings. The other half of A2 would be distributed to the Official IRA. The whole of A3 would be taken up with loyalists.

Gusty was aware of certain advantages in having control of the top floor of A wing:

> It was an excellent defensive position and that was one of the reasons why I chose it. The two stairwells could easily be blocked and we were on the pig's back unless everybody vacated A wing and set it on fire, but even then there was still an escape route.

He estimated that there were about 20–25 Official IRA, 100–150 Provisional IRA and 50–60 loyalists on A wing. The Provos decided they needed two floors: A1 and A2. It seemed that the Provos were not prepared to share cells as the loyalists did. Gusty would have been happy to have A3 exclusively for loyalists but he didn't want to get involved in the intra-republican conflict:

> The Provos in my opinion welshed on the agreement. They said, 'No, no, we've too many men – we need A1 and A2.' It was a fallacious argument because they really wanted rid of the Officials. There was great enmity there and the mere fact that warfare hadn't broken out, not only between the loyalists and republicans but between republicans and republicans, was due, in my opinion to the 'no-conflict policy'. I said we would give a third of our landing to the Officials, which we did.
>
> I doubled my men up, two men to a cell – in some cases trebled them up, but it was mostly doubled up. It was then that the real dialogue began with the Officials because political sessions and cultural arguments and debates could take place more easily. The initial debate therefore began in Crumlin Road prison.

This sharing with the Officials had very positive consequences:

> Not only was our defensive position strengthened, my men had exposure to a more enlightened political group. It was all right Gusty talking about politics but now it was coming from a different source which was confirming and giving credibility to some of the things I was saying. The Officials were nonsectarian even though they slagged about Prods and Taigs.

> There are not too many instances of the Official IRA taking Prods out and shooting them because they were Prods. I would sit with P.J. Monaghan and a couple of the senior UVF and Official IRA officers and they would engage in discussions which amounted to kicking political ideas about. The younger element in the Official IRA came into contact with a similar element of the UVF. Ten or twelve might sit down in a cell where there was good political exposure one to the other. Most of my men were politically naïve.

There was only a limited time each day when prisoners were free to associate with other prisoners on their wing:

> Lock-up was at seven o'clock at night, but as we gained strength in the jail, we put certain propositions to Major Mullin, the governor, who was an enlightened man who did some progressive things. But the jail was in turmoil and there was more than double the numbers there should have been. There was a control problem because the three organisations were controlling their own men. Loyalists in other parts of the jail were looking to A wing while the Provisionals and Officials were looking to their [leaders in] A wing for leadership. It suited us to put the jail into a period of disequilibrium from time to time. The electric would go out and meals were not cooked.
>
> Prisoners wouldn't work and men with posters paraded round the laundry demanding trade union wages. The whole place was in chaos and they brought the paratroopers in. They and the governor were concerned about containing it through perimeter security. Internal security depended a big lot upon the discipline of the UVF or IRA troops. They were pretty well disciplined because McKee and Monaghan and myself were all people who adhered to discipline. There were no fist fights or wanton damage or vandalism and the place was spotlessly clean.

A delegation of Social Democratic Labour Party (SDLP) people came to the Crumlin Road jail and met Gusty Spence early in 1972. Those involved included Austin Currie, John Hume, Ivan Cooper, Gerry Fitt and the late Paddy Devlin. The meeting was productive:

> Later Paddy made a public statement that Gusty Spence was making sure that all the Protestants in the jail had good jobs. I got on very well with two brothers in the jail, Mal McDonagh, a well-known Northern Ireland footballer, and his brother George, who was ex-air force. I said to George, 'When you next meet the SDLP tell Paddy Devlin that what he said in the *Irish News* is completely erroneous. Never once in that prison did I make any form of sectarian utterance.' The next time he came up he told me that

> Paddy was only going on the information supplied and if he was wrong he apologised.

The SDLP visit was not related to the political status issue, but Gusty said:

> Anyone who had knowledge of Irish history knew that once loyalists or republicans gathered enough strength they would opt for political status. They are, after all, political prisoners. Paddy Devlin was an ex-prisoner himself and the SDLP played a pivotal role.

I spoke with the late Paddy Devlin about Gusty:

> Prisoners had complained about food and living conditions and we were invited by the governor to see what the jail was like. When we got there he gave us a room and said, 'I'll send the prisoners in and you can interview them.' They were all green [nationalist] prisoners but quite suddenly there was a sharp knock at the door and a man appeared. 'I'm Gusty Spence. Are you going to do anything for us?' I said, 'I'm Paddy Devlin.' He said, 'I know who you are – I remember you playing football.' So I says, 'That's right, I played with your brother Billy for Old Lodge. We'll do the same for you as we're doing for everybody else.'
>
> Gusty said, 'OK, I'll arrange interviews in here. Are you going to the Maze?' I said, 'We hope to go there too.' 'We have prisoners up there and I want you to gave them a fair deal as well.' I says, 'They'll be interviewed and we'll do the same for them as we're doing for everybody.' He says, 'That's fair enough,' and we shook hands. When we went to the Maze he had all the leaders lined up to do the interviews on the conditions they were living in.
>
> That was probably the most important contact I had with Gusty Spence at the time and we knew each other for some time prior to that. Afterwards when I went to the boxing and other places and his relations or friends were about, they would come over, tap me on the shoulder and say, 'Gusty sends his regards.' That went on for some time, and finally a man said he had been told by Gusty to come to see me. They wanted to get someone to go to Mountjoy prison in Dublin where there was a neglected loyalist prisoner. I went down on two occasions and got him extra writing gear and a few other small things.

In 1972 the *Orange Cross* organised collections and set up a stall selling loyalist literature and other items. With the proceeds they were able to lodge small amounts of money for each loyalist prisoner. They also supplemented parcels destined for the prisoners with basic necessities like soap, a comb, hair cream, face flannel, shaving soap. These items were greatly appreciated, and in a leaflet the *Orange Cross* said:

> We have heard that more than one silent tear was shed because 'Our Boys' have discovered that they are no longer forgotten. We in the *Orange Cross* fully intend to see that indeed they will not in future feel forgotten ... Our 'Christmas cards for the Boys Appeal' produced many hundreds of cards. For this response we are also grateful. The retort of James 'Rocky' Burns to all the Christmas Cards was, 'I feel like a film star.'[12]

But 1972 was a difficult year for loyalists. Stormont was suspended on 28 March but it was the prison officers rather than the prisoners who were most concerned about this. One of them sought advice from Gusty Spence. Gusty recalls: 'This prison officer came to me virtually in tears and said, "Gusty, you know we're sold out. What are we going to do now?" This man was locking me up every day of the week.' It was Gusty's view that the ending of Stormont had the potential to set loyalists free from their reluctance to criticise 'their' government. It represented a form of liberation, though it was not generally recognised as such.

Political status became a more pressing issue in the spring of 1972, as Gusty explained:

> The normal routine was that once a prisoner completed half his sentence he was qualified for, but not entitled to, parole twice a year, a week in summer and a week in winter. Some of my men, who had been out for a week in July 1971, expected Christmas parole, but an order came through that those who were in prison in connection with the present Troubles were not to be given parole.
>
> This meant we were not being treated as normal prisoners. I decided they had to be treated as special prisoners. I was down to the governor like a shot. 'Governor, can you explain that?' He says, 'yes' and read it out to me. I said, 'I don't know what this means. If my men are not to be treated as normal prisoners they must be a special type of prisoner. I'm telling you now that in the very near future, I'll be opting for political status.' He says, 'Well that's the way you look at the situation.' Says I, 'There's no other way to look at it.'
>
> I sent for Billy McKee and Peter Monaghan, 'What are we going to do about this? We'll have to carry out some form of campaign to get special recognition.' We thought McKee would contact the PIRA Army Council in Dublin but he came back and said, 'We don't think we could pursue a

> policy of political status at this time.' I was bitterly disappointed. However there are always little things that set off big explosions.

The prisoners knew they had strength in Crumlin Road because it had become almost uncontrollable. Billy McKee, however, regarded opting for political status as a grave step. He would have to be sure of his ground as well as of Gusty Spence and Peter Monaghan. A degree of trust was required between all three and McKee needed the approval of the IRA Army Council. Martin Meehan agrees that there was some reluctance, particularly about the possibility of hunger strikes. He told me it had been no light action to contemplate, but a groundswell of opinion gathered among the new prisoners, favouring a campaign for political status. Gusty said the catalyst appeared to be a row over cigarettes:

> A prisoner who was in for causing an explosion, in which he blew himself up, attacked a prison officer and gave him a beating. He received an unprecedented sentence, nine months' loss of remission and a number of days in solitary confinement.

It was a serious beating, in which the prison officer concerned received a ruptured spleen and other wounds:

> In a fit of pique Billy McKee opted on his own [that is, without consulting Gusty Spence and Peter Monaghan] for political status. Peter Monaghan told me this and I told McKee, 'I'm a bit angry here, Billy, because we're always shouting about consultation.' Despite this we sat down to map out a strategy and it was agreed that they could do whatever they liked on the Falls Road but the Catholics were to be kept away from outside the prison. That would be a Protestant domain.
>
> It was not in the UVF's interest to be on the streets but they could manifest themselves through the UDA [Ulster Defence Association]. Jim Anderson, a leading figure in the UDA, promised me help and soon there were thousands marching up and down outside. There was some political agitation as well and the SDLP did a good job. Paddy Devlin did an exceptionally good job but unionists played no part whatever.[13]

Some of the republicans went on hunger strike, but loyalists were determined to keep their campaign separate and did not engage in hunger strikes:

> It would have been absolutely disastrous to be seen to be on hunger strike

with them. So the strategy we used was to demand segregation. This gave the UDA and the UVF strength on the outside. We knew we'd get no support from the Unionist Party. We got nothing from those people not a thing, except to accuse us, 'They're supporting the IRA.'

The UVF began to organise inside and outside the jail. A UVF covenant was published by the *Orange Cross* in May 1972 in which thirty-five UVF prisoners, including Gusty Spence, Hugh McClean and Robert Williamson, committed themselves as follows:

> Being convinced in our consciences that our Cause is just, and our endeavours in furtherance of that Cause fully commensurate with the finer attributes of the British Ulsterman, we, the Loyalist Political Prisoners, entombed behind these walls now, in the fullness of time, assert our full prerogatives under British Liberty to opt for full status as Political Prisoners, and we shall, as far as in us lies, use every and all legitimate means in pursuance of these honourable aspirations.

The statement went on to refer to the suffering of loyalists in their campaign to remain British. They would not be found wanting or be deflected from the course they had embarked upon. They spoke of pride in their womenfolk who 'have proven their unswerving fidelity and devotion in our fight for freedom':

> We now openly and with proud aforethought pronounce our allegiance to the Ulster Volunteer Force which in Law is banned but in practice is living and real and to us is an attestation to the unquenchable and unconquerable spirit of the Ulster Loyalist.
>
> Notwithstanding sneers and insults, despite the slanders and inexactitudes YOU the Ulster Loyalist have a rare opportunity to identify yourselves with us and perhaps WE, together, can wash away the stink of servility that has marked our so-called politicians of recent years and by our understanding can perhaps erase the injustices of the past.
>
> We desire peace with JUSTICE, but not at the cost of SLAVERY. A start has to be made now and we are prepared to be willing sacrifices in order to achieve that peace but to enable us we must solicit and receive your support. Feel your own strength, justify your Cause and stand up to be counted.
>
> May God give us all the strength and guidance that is required.
>
> *The combat deepens on ye brave,*
> *That rush to victory or the grave*

Wave, Ulster all your banners wave
And charge with all your chivalry.

FOR GOD AND ULSTER[14]

The protestors achieved considerable disruption inside and outside the prison. Gusty recalls:

> We brought the jail to a standstill and turned it upside down. The first morning of the protests all loyalists appeared in civilian clothes – it was a miracle. Oh, God bless us, we took over parts of the jail; we started and stopped the jail; the lights went out and the water wouldn't work, all those things happened in order to build pressure. Not only that, there were thousands of people demonstrating outside the jail, masked men in ranks were marching up and down in columns of three, and so on. Prison officers had to sneak in through side doors to get into the prison.

The whole point of the agitation was to get the people and the paramilitaries energised:

> We wanted to have loyalists parading up and down outside the prison, to agitate and to try and force or at least influence unionist politicians by showing that these men are political prisoners – some of them are in here at the insistence of politicians who had told us, 'Ulster will fight and Ulster will be right', 'Liquidate the enemy', 'Shoot to kill'. They can't now leave them in the lurch. But it was absolutely futile because they showed no interest whatsoever. Sinn Féin was only in its embryonic stages but big pressure from the nationalist population was being brought to bear on the SDLP.

Loyalists knew that unionist politicians did not want to know about the prisoners, and it was with this in mind that they tried in various ways to highlight the prisoners' plight and draw attention to them. For example reports surfaced in May 1972 that an Orange lodge – 'Unofficial No. 1' – had been formed by loyalist prisoners in A wing. Among the alleged officers was Gusty Spence as Second Lecturer. The Worshipful Master was Thomas Rowntree, who proposed that 'fraternal greetings and brotherly affection' be forwarded to their fellow Orangemen.[15] This proposal was reportedly received with acclamation and the lodge meeting ended with the singing of the National Anthem. However such reports had to be treated with great caution: as Gusty suggests, the prisoners' lodge was a ruse to embarrass the Orange Order.

> We used all methods to promote the loyalist prisoners in Crumlin Road jail. Not only was there lack of interest within Orangeism, there was a viciousness emanating from the Orange Order: 'These are only scum anyhow. True loyalists wouldn't finish up in jail. They broke the law.' All this hypocritical observance of the law while the same people were breaking the law themselves, always behind closed doors of course. We had to do things to keep the prisoners in the public eye and were not going to let society forget about us.

At this time, however, Gusty also had other matters on his mind. His daughter Elizabeth was to be married on 1 July 1972. Winston Rea, the prospective groom, had already visited Gusty in prison, and the date was set. (Later, Rea was to become a prisoner himself.) Gusty applied for parole but by May it was still not clear whether parole would be granted. On 30 May, Gusty wrote a personal letter to Louie expressing his undying love. In the course of the letter he provided some details about the developing situation in the prison. The prisoners had not yet been granted political status but:

> We have made our moves and we are now dressed in civilian clothing, and this being the case, they shall not allow me to go on the visits with you. This breaks my heart love as each of our visits are very precious to me. We had to make this move for full segregation before trouble breaks out. The Rebels want us to move and we want to move so why the HELL won't Whitelaw give us the move that we want? The governor is powerless ... and has refused to speak with me because I am now in civilian clothes. My, oh my, isn't that a terrible crime – me wearing civilian clothes.

Gusty did not want complete separation but believed that limited segregation would be helpful. They already had separate floors in A wing and Gusty put it this way: 'It was nice to have friends visiting but it was also nice to see your friends going home. It was not that there was fear of one's neighbours but people felt safe in their own homes.'

In the same letter, he went on to write about his intentions and doubts regarding his hoped-for parole:

> I am still putting in for the parole for Elizabeth's wedding and shall kick up a hell of a row if I am refused. I don't expect anything from these people as I wouldn't trust them an inch.

He then wrote about the actions that prisoners had taken in pursuit of political status and segregation:

> We occupied the dining hall last night from 8.30 p.m. until 7.30 a.m. ... and I informed the governor that if the army attacked us we would retaliate very severely. That's a laugh, as I haven't hands to bless myself. Give the kids all my love and explain to them the whole situation ... We have taken too much from these people and we must show them that we are not dirt. We don't want violence and I am almost sure that none shall occur.

This was a typewritten letter. Gusty added in handwriting, 'everything was OK' beside his reference to 'retaliation'. At the side he added, 'Come as usual for your visits and let them turn you away – and then kick up like hell!'

The *Orange Cross* in June carried a leading article entitled, 'The UVF Reborn' in which it drew parallels with what was happening in 1972 and what had happened in 1912:

> Men marched, drilled and took orders in a disciplined and military fashion. Unarmed combat was practised. Platoons and Companies responded with responsible reaction to the shouted orders of their officers. The old Ulster Volunteer Force relives. The spirit of our Fathers and Grandfathers of 1912 is rekindled. We have taken enough. We will take no more ...
>
> On then, Ulster Volunteers. Train, march, discipline yourselves and prepare – prepare – prepare. Do it with dignity – do it with discipline – do it with honour.[16]

The groundwork had been done. The UVF had been organised and strengthened during the winter of 1971–2 when two senior officers, 'Robert' and 'John', travelled the length and breadth of Northern Ireland recruiting and building up the UVF in preparation for an expected escalation in conflict. This strengthened the political status campaign, which in the end was successful:

> Political status was achieved on the 20 June 1972 (though the government insisted it was only Special Category Status). The Provos called a ceasefire on 26 June. I was out on 1 July and I think that was part of the concession to try and cement some kind of reconciliation. The Provo ceasefire only lasted a fortnight and broke down in Horn Drive at Lenadoon. Political status continued right through to 1976 when Merlyn Rees did away with special category status, as the euphemists called it, for new prisoners.

William Whitelaw granted more visits and civilian clothes for the prisoners. He did not regard political status as a major concession, but in the longer term it became a major issue stirring deep passions.

Gusty had been involved in much of the negotiations. He explained how these took place in the governor's office in the middle of the night:

> The governor was asking me questions. He had the phone in his hand and the person on the other end of the phone, who I'm convinced was Willie Whitelaw, was listening and then the governor was clarifying any points.

However Gusty was not the only one involved in the negotiations:

> We actually conferred amongst ourselves as to what we wanted and what we didn't want. There were three-way negotiations. The Official IRA negotiated with the authorities, the Provisionals negotiated with the authorities, and I negotiated with the authorities. At the same time, the SDLP through the medium of Paddy Devlin were negotiating with the authorities.

The Chief Prison Officer at this time was called Billy Wright,[17] and he approached Gusty asking him to clarify the conditions that had been agreed. As a result Gusty typed out the details of the agreed conditions on food parcels, visits, cigarettes and so on. This was done on his own typewriter. He then supplied copies to the governor as well as to the Official and Provisional IRA prison leaderships.

In a letter to the *Orange Cross*, dated 14 July 1972, A wing prisoners explained that they had not yet achieved segregation:

> True, we are in our own civilian clothing, it's true we have been allowed other little items like extra tobacco and food parcel (at our own expense), but on the ONE thing we waged our campaign, with all your very welcome help, Segregation, we have been not only sold out on, but in fact we are now in a far worse position than before.

Agitation for segregation continued after Gusty left on parole to attend his daughter's wedding. While he was absent another CO took over his role, but he did not have the same level of understanding with McKee and Peter Monaghan and the situation deteriorated somewhat. Gusty was told that the loyalist prisoners felt themselves at risk.

> One day after all the loyalist prisoners went out to play football, they squatted on the football field and said they wouldn't go back to A wing.

> They were kept out on the football field all night until they were eventually moved to what they called the annexe, in D wing.

Loyalists had not been restricted in their contact with republicans and so

> There were those who imagined themselves vulnerable to attacks by the IRA, notwithstanding the pact that had been agreed. There was integration with a minimum of segregation and the minimum was confined to the floors. Having said that, the Official IRA were also apprehensive and when they came to Long Kesh they opted for segregation.

On 12 July 1972 a special edition of the *Orange Cross* carried a message from UVF prisoners who had won the battle to be classed as Special Category Prisoners or, in their view more appropriately, 'political prisoners'. Gusty Spence as commanding officer and twenty-seven other prisoners had signed a statement on 20 June 1972 saying:

> There is no talk of victory – No march of Triumph. Just a sigh of relief that our protracted campaign to be recognised for what we are has been fulfilled and in the cold light of Whitehall we are seen as Loyalist Political Prisoners. Granted there is still a reticence to give us full recognition, but who cares – the principle is there and that's what life is all about – Principle.[18]

The same newspaper carried another message:

> To the Loyal Ulstermen and Boys who are drilling openly on our streets we tender our Comradely compliments and regards and as brother Ulster Volunteers we have nothing but admiration for the stand you have taken in defence of freedom.

The nightmare of the 'Crum' remains with Gusty to this day. He feels contempt and hatred for the notorious prison and he has said, 'I'll dance on its grave. I always promised myself I would do that one day – and I will ... Shutting it is not enough. I want it completely razed to the ground.' Gusty described the prison to me:

> Crumlin Road jail was a dank, Victorian, austere, depressing and oppressing place. The prisoners were as thin as greyhounds. It was one of the worst prisons in Western Europe. The food was minimal and even exercise was at the minimum. While on remand we were locked up for twenty-three hours a day, but after sentencing we had relative freedom to half past six at night.

Gusty says the situation was so awful that it was necessary to hide the reality from friends and family when on visits, but it was impossible to eliminate the pervading smell of urine and excrement. Yet from that unpromising environment new light began to dawn in the minds of loyalists who were helping to shape the destiny of Northern Ireland.

For the moment, however, Gusty was outside, released on parole to attend his daughter's wedding. Events there would soon take place which meant he would never go back inside the Crumlin Road jail again.

11

Abduction

When Gusty left the prison on 1 July 1972 his intention was to return as promised:

> There was no evil intent in my mind whatever in applying for parole, nothing. It wasn't a question of absconding or anything like that. We came out that morning and we went to the wedding, which was heavily laced with UVF personnel. But right from scratch they were at me saying, 'Don't go back.'

As Gusty's son-in-law Winston Rea was to say in 1975 from within Long Kesh:

> Certain unknown members of the Ulster Volunteer Force decided that he could be a greater asset to the people of Ulster than he was behind the iron bars and stone walls of Belfast Prison. It was necessary to have a man of his calibre to help lead the fight against the IRA. So the members of the Ulster Volunteer Force kidnapped Gusty and held him and refused to let him go

back to the hellhole, Crumlin Road jail.[1]

'John' told me that in 1972 the UVF needed a morale boost and the kind of publicity and strength that Gusty's abduction would provide. Northern Ireland was believed to be facing an IRA-led insurrection and would have to be vigorously defended.[2] The need was pressing because the British government was thought to be making a deal with the IRA.

However Martin Meehan told me that many nationalists were questioning Gusty's influence at that time:

> Nationalists saw Gusty getting released followed by an upsurge in sectarian assassinations, so right away people were saying, 'There's Gusty Spence, he's been in for sectarian assassinations, he's out on the streets again and there's an escalation.' The common denominator was Gusty Spence so he would then have been classed by nationalists as a sort of a prima donna, a hate figure, there's no doubt about that.

This may have reflected the mindset of many nationalists in 1972 but, although Gusty undoubtedly remained influential, he was not the leader of the UVF. Certainly the UVF did at times regard Catholics as legitimate targets but, even so, UVF killings in 1972 remained at a relatively low level. During a year when the UVF and Red Hand Commando together are estimated to have killed 35 people in total, the UDA/UFF are reckoned to have killed 71, the Official IRA 20, the Provisional IRA 234, other republicans 26, the army 79, the RUC 6, the Ulster Defence Regiment (UDR) 1, other loyalists 15, and others 9.[3]

The following year saw a slight decline in UVF/RHC killings and a bigger decline in UDA/UFF killings.[4] UVF killings escalated during the mid-1970s but only during two years, 1975 and 1994, did UVF/RHC victims slightly outnumber PIRA victims, and they never even approached the level of IRA killings in 1972.[5]

Many murders ascribed to the UVF were the work of notorious gangs, like the Shankill Butchers, who were out of control. The UVF leadership at that time did not have the courage to stamp these out. To have done so would probably have entailed extensive bloodshed. The primary rationale behind loyalist killings was to send a signal to the British government that if the IRA could win concessions through violence, then loyalists were prepared to initiate even greater violence. The loyalist intention to pressurise the nationalist community into rejecting republican violence was of lesser significance but there had been a real possibility of more horrific and devastating violence against nationalists. This was seriously considered, but thankfully such a course of action was rejected. The progressive leadership of the UVF, and Gusty Spence in particular, was opposed to sectarian killings, as will be illustrated later in this book.

Coincidentally, at the time of Gusty Spence's abduction William Craig MP was speaking in Scotland. He was quoted as saying that Ulster Vanguard was involved in preparing a loyalist army should the need arise.[6] Civil war seemed near, and in Ainsworth Avenue, in the upper Shankill Road area of Belfast, on 3 July

> 6,000 to 8,000 masked UDA men faced units of the British Army in the rain. The UDA had iron bars and clubs but did not attack the troops who prevented them setting up another barricaded area, which the secretary of state had expressly forbidden. Major General Robert Ford, Commander Land Forces in Northern Ireland, negotiated with UDA leaders ... A compromise was reached by which both the security forces and unarmed UDA men would patrol the area.[7]

The UDA had earlier threatened to bring a further 20,000 of their men on to the streets. A few days later Bill Craig reportedly said, 'that four or five armed commando-type Protestant organisations were standing by to carry out special duties in the event of civil war in Northern Ireland'.[8]

It was in this context that it was felt that Gusty Spence was needed to boost the UVF. He was the only one capable of giving the necessary injection of energy. He had given his word that he would return to prison and the UVF leaders decided to ease his conscience: he could not be held responsible for failing to return if he were abducted by force.

> I was released on Saturday, 1 July 1972 for thirty-six hours for the wedding. I was to report back by 6 p.m. on Sunday night. Elizabeth and Winky were going to Scotland and we saw them off. I didn't drink then but a bit of a celebration was held in one of the clubs in my honour and they were into my ear right away – they had formulated a plan. I said, 'Look, I gave my word that I'll be back in prison at six o'clock on Sunday night ... But if anything unforeseen happens over which I have no control, then I have no control over it.'
>
> I set off from Springmartin, where Louie was living, with one of my nephews driving. A car pulled in in front and one behind at the Springmartin Road. Masked men got out and Jim Curry, my nephew, began

struggling with them, and I told him, 'Don't stop them.' He struggled and got a broken nose while I was bundled into the motor. I finished up in a place in County Down. They told me they had lifted me because of my intimate knowledge of the old UVF in 1912 and because of my grasp of military structure and so on.

There were fears that Gusty had been killed. The RUC said the IRA might have captured him and when a body was found near the Hammer in Twickenham Street, the police thought it was likely to be his. It turned out to be the body of John O'Hanlon, a Catholic victim of a sectarian killing.[9]

On 29 July, the *Orange Cross* carried a leading article entitled, 'We Hold Gusty – UVF.' In a short article the magazine demanded justice for him through a review of his case. At this time, Gusty told me, he, 'was ensconced in a place in County Down where I spent two to three days with UVF personnel'. The UVF then issued a statement signed 'Captain William Johnston, Adjutant of the UVF.' This stated that he was being held by the UVF against his will and that neither he nor members of his family had been aware of UVF plans. 'When we are certain his case will be reviewed – and if possible another trial agreed upon – then, and only then, will we release him.'[10]

To the majority of the Catholic population we would say, Unite and join us in defeating the IRA as a means of keeping sectarian warfare from becoming a reality. Sectarianism plays no part in our policy and we contend that the working-class people of whatever creed are the real inheritors of peace and prosperity.[11]

'John' suspects that the authorities were quite happy to see Gusty at large. His influence could bring some kind of order to a fragmenting and angry loyalist population. He recounts how Gusty 'went about very openly and attended meetings after he got abducted'. Gusty confirmed this in a statement issued through the *Orange Cross*:

In Freedom

Sisters and Brothers, I am in your midst moving amongst you quite freely and your interests are most dear to my heart. Like myself, you seek only JUSTICE and my solemn promise is that Justice will be done and be seen to be done. Abuse and vilification have been hurled at your fair name and for far too long your fears have been played upon by evil men. This shall cease and no longer shall you be exploited and used as a political pawn. You too seek peace with Justice (you never wanted anything else) and only for your

Gusty Spence, aged ten, as mascot for Joseph Street Mission Football Club

Gusty marries Louie Donaldson on 20 June 1953.

Gusty (far right) as a soldier in the Royal Ulster Rifles, 1957

BELOW
Bella with her four sons, Gusty (bottom left), Billy (top left), Bobby (top right), and James (bottom right)

Gusty on active service with the
Royal Ulster Rifles in Cyprus, 1958

Gusty, 1962, on the fiftieth anniversary of the Covenant, making a speech to Prince Albert LOL 1892 on the Shankill Road

RIGHT: Gusty 'on the run' after his abduction by the UVF in 1972

Gusty, 1975, as Commanding Officer UVF, Long Kesh

RIGHT:

Gusty with a young David Ervine (back left) and some of his men in Long Kesh, *c.* 1976

BELOW:

Gusty, 1985, on the Shankill Road. Frizzells fish shop in the background was blown up by the IRA in 1993.

PACEMAKER PRESS INTERNATIONAL

Gusty at the PUP offices on the Shankill Road in 1985

PACEMAKER PRESS INTERNATIONAL

Gusty in America after the ceasefire in 1994 with (from left) David Adams, Gary McMichael and Joe English of the UDP, and David Ervine and Billy Hutchinson of the PUP

Gusty in the poppy fields at the Somme, 1991

Roy Garland, Maura Lee and Gusty on the Shankill Road, 1996

restraint and that of the disciplined Loyalist Organisations this land of ours would have been plunged into a foul civil war long since. Without our principles impeached it is our intention to work to secure a lasting and just solution to the morass in which we are now in. We shall negotiate from a position of strength and Mr Heath and Mr Whitelaw shall use good sense and see our Loyalist Ulsterfolk in a new perspective. This is my promise to you.

No Surrender – Gusty Spence[12]

Hardline unionists would have regarded some of this as questionable. They saw no need to 'work to secure a lasting and just solution'. All that was needed, in their view, was the defeat of the IRA.

At this time Billy Hutchinson was about sixteen. Destined to become a leading member of the Young Citizens Volunteer Force (YCV), he met Gusty at Studio Ten in Aberdeen Street on the Shankill Road. Hutchinson had heard stories and songs about Gusty who had become part of Shankill folklore. Hutchinson had never expected to have an opportunity to meet him, and the meeting made a deep impression:

When I did meet him he had a presence about him. The presence was in the room whenever he was there and yet I knew he was a very friendly man and could tell that he was a family man as well, that he was interested in his family. That really impressed me about him.

I suggested to him that he could not have got to know Gusty well because he was only free for about four months. He did not agree:

I spent quite a lot of time with him and there was much talk. I heard many things that he said and did get to know him, even though it involved a short space of time. We were probably in each other's pockets for sixteen hours a day.

There was no confusion about where we were going and what the end product would be. In many ways it was a socialist view that Gusty argued. It was about looking after the community. That could mean doing something for the most vulnerable or the elderly. In those days most people had coal fires and if the elderly needed coal we procured the coal and gave it to them rather that let them freeze. It was a whole new way of looking at society and it put things into perspective for me.

However some of Gusty's ideas were perhaps premature:

Gusty was ten or fifteen years ahead of his time. If he had have been doing

> this in the 1980s it probably would have had more success but because it was during the early seventies against a backdrop of growing sectarian killings it was harder to do. People were not as focused as they became after the power-sharing government and the Workers' Strike in 1974 and the strike in 1977 which Paisley tried to kick into but didn't work. All of those things – together with the hunger strikes of the 1980s.

Gusty was being sought by journalists, who had an advantage over the security forces in uncovering his whereabouts at a time when loyalist no-go areas were impeding traffic. Several organisations, including the Red Hand Commando, were involved in enabling David Boulton, who was with Granada Television's *World in Action*, to make contact.

The crew were blindfolded and driven to a loyalist club on the Shankill Road. This was only days after Gusty's abduction. Five armed and hooded UVF men stood guard throughout the interview.[13] During the interview Gusty's UVF captors said they wanted a retrial on the grounds that the first trial was politically motivated, with the result that Gusty had been sentenced for something he had not done.

Gusty denied being Commander, Chief of Staff or leader of the UVF, and the interviewer assumed this was because he was caught in a catch-22 situation. To acknowledge UVF leadership would seem to conflict with the claim that Gusty was a captive. In fact, whilst Gusty remained a UVF figurehead, he was no longer leader of the UVF outside the jail, and any links with the wider organisation into which he had been initiated in 1965 had vanished in 1966.

The interviewer put it to Gusty that a British court of law had convicted him. Gusty pointed out that he had walked out of a lower court a free man and repeated, 'I did not shoot Peter Ward.'

Part of Hugh McClean's statement was then read out suggesting that Gusty had listened to the conversation of the young men in the Malvern Arms and told the others that they were IRA men and would have to go. In response, Gusty said any suggestion that IRA men would talk so openly on the Shankill Road was preposterous and he argued that the statement should have been seen as inadmissible. He added that Special Branch had interrogated McClean for two full days, and referred to the fact that similar statements had recently been thrown out of court.

He denied knowledge of the formation of the UVF in the 1960s and refused to say what rank, if any, he held or had held. He admitted that the UVF had guns, had used them, and was prepared to use them again against anyone prepared to usurp the constitutional position of Ulster. The prisoners in jail remained in contact with the UVF outside but Gusty refused to say how. He was asked about talks with republican prisoners and he said he could not make friends with people who were trying to overthrow the constitution.

An extract from his letter to Joe McCann's widow was read out and it was suggested that this might seem strange to his supporters. Gusty disagreed, saying that even Montgomery had paid tribute to Rommel. Gusty said that the good turn referred to in the letter was when Joe McCann spared the lives of two men at Gusty's request. Gusty insisted that there was a common bond between all honourable soldiers. He accepted that it was possible to be an honourable man and to be in the IRA.

He was then asked to comment on the leadership of unionism and he accepted that Stormont represented fifty years of misrule. Referring to the unionist leadership he said they had got us into 'one hell of a mess'. They needed to put their differences to one side and think of the people, the small people, the have-nots:

> One has only to look at the Shankill Road, the heart of the empire, that lies torn and bleeding. We have known squalor. I was born and reared in it. No one knows better than we do the meaning of slums, the meaning of deprivation, the meaning of suffering for what one believes in, whatever the ideology. In so far as people speak about fifty years of misrule, I wouldn't disagree with that. What I would say is this – that we have suffered every bit as much as the people of the Falls Road or any other underprivileged quarter, in many cases more so.[14]

This statement was to cause some heart-searching in circles beyond the confines of the UVF, especially his acceptance that Stormont represented fifty years of misrule.

Gusty said he would be active in the life of Ulster. He would like his part to be a peaceful one but he was prepared for whatever role the people asked of him. He deplored random killings and called upon people to desist from sectarian actions. He was then asked about his 'hero' status and the fact that he seemed to be saying that he had not done the things attributed to him. He replied:

> What I'm saying is this. I didn't take the actions with which I was charged. I'm not saying I didn't take any actions. Gusty Spence the hero is a myth. The person who sits before you now is truly a humble and sincere man,

some people would say misdirected. That is a matter for conjecture. I am sincere in anything I have ever done and I shall be sincere in anything I ever do. But as far as the hero bit's concerned, it's nonsense.[15]

With determination, Gusty now set about the reinvigoration of the UVF. It might be difficult to appreciate how growth in UVF membership could coincide with the emergence of democratic socialist thinking, but there was little contradiction in the minds of most of the UVF leadership. During his time of freedom Gusty was reported to be pressing young UVF recruits to help repair people's homes as well as train for militant action.[16] He recalls being asked about politics at a swearing-in ceremony in 1972:

One fellow asked me, did we have any political policies. I said, 'At this point in time we do not have any political policies because we're not a political organisation but we have a political conscience.' I didn't want to go too far because in the army politics was not spoken about. Politics is for the politicians. I went on, 'Our social conscience has to take as primacy the needs of the working-class people.' I omitted to say *loyalist* working-class people. I wanted them to read that into what I was saying.

There was a rudimentary knowledge of politics within the UVF leadership inside and outside prison and especially among people like 'John' and 'Robert'. A political study group had to be set up on the outside, which seemed unlikely at that particular time, or it had to be as a result of political science approaches within the prison.

At another swearing-in ceremony in south Belfast

There was a sizeable body of thirty or forty men and one old soldier said, 'Sir, can I draw your attention to something?' I replied, 'By all means,' and he went on, 'One of our prospective volunteers is only sixteen years of age.' I said, 'Sir, I cannot in conscience tell that lad he is ineligible for the UVF, taking into consideration how many sixteen- and fifteen-year-olds not only served in the UVF but were killed with the Ulster Division in France.'

I always smiled into myself when I heard people saying, 'The only way out of these organisations is in a coffin.' It's a lot of nonsense. As long as a man maintained his silence in relation to his service in the UVF he was free to resign at any time. It was a popular myth put about by people who were ill-disposed towards the UVF.

At another swearing-in ceremony in an Orange hall, with a more sizeable body of men, I said, 'I want you to think hard about your enlistment because you will be called upon if there is a military stand-to.' Men weren't under military orders at all times but if there was a military stand-to,

> requiring them for a physical-force operation, they had to think hard about that. One man had the courage to speak. 'I don't think I could carry it out.' Says I, 'Well, that's all right. You'll be escorted from the premises. You're free to go as long as you retain your silence.'

Support for the UVF was coming from surprising sources. Apart from politicians, some other 'pillars of civic society' provided assistance in a variety of ways. But the context then was different:

> Violent things were being done but there had been no nefarious activities such as you see today in punishment shootings and stuff like that or people engaging themselves in semi-criminal things. So there was support from middle-class people who were reasonably prominent in society. I had meetings with many prominent people who shall remain nameless.

This kind of support reflected the alarm felt within the unionist population. Many felt they were at the mercy of a pan-nationalist front, stretching from the IRA to the Irish government, and that they were facing a weak administration at Westminster:

> IRA men were being released from prison and flown across to meet William Whitelaw. The IRA didn't call a ceasefire for nothing, and we were concerned about what the IRA had been promised to bring about that ceasefire. The answer has never been given. There had to be reasons, and people put forward reasons to us and some were pretty horrendous. The British government were thought to be going to capitulate. Certainly Seán MacStiofáin, William Whitelaw and Gerry Adams were privy to the reasons. Promises were made, transport and money was made available.

During his spell of freedom Gusty reactivated the YCV and was committed to the value of military training in terms of instilling discipline and idealism.[17] He gathered other ideas from the 1912 period:

> What I wanted to do, just as Carson and Craig had done, was to set up an indemnifying fund, some form of financial and practical support for women and children who could lose husbands and fathers. We engaged in bank robberies but there is a fine line between robbing a bank while not molesting anyone, and extorting money. I remember saying to the paymaster, 'How much money does the UVF have in hand?' He quoted a ridiculous sum so he was sacked and a new one was appointed. We wanted to build up the funds for two reasons: to indemnify against injury

> and for firearms. Firearms were most important. If they didn't have sufficient firearms they had to be procured. This meant raiding for arms and taking on the army to some degree.

On one occasion while Gusty was at large, an informer passed information to the RUC which led to the capture of most of the UVF brigade staff in a club in Brennan Street:

> About sixty-two men were arrested and I had been to the toilet and was just coming back when the paratroopers broke in. I was thrown like a fish amongst the general fish whereas the ones the paratroopers were interested in were the men sitting at the top table and I suppose that helped save me. We were brought to Castlereagh but I had a full identity cover, having taken on this man's identity with his connivance. We were taken to Castlereagh where we faced a preliminary investigation by the Special Branch but there was none of the old hands there so none of them knew me. I had a slight disguise, a pair of horn-rimmed glasses and a slight tint in my hair, but nothing else.

The arrests took place on 11 October 1972. The troops had recovered arms and ammunition at Glentoran football grounds and at Coronation Park, Dundonald, where they also found two bombs.[18] On the evening of Gusty's arrest the UVF took a policeman and a soldier hostage. 'If any UVF men were harmed they would do them.' There was widespread rioting with crowds stoning troops and attacking Tennent Street RUC station. Shots were fired at the army in several parts of the Shankill. Riots followed in east Belfast. Catholic premises were attacked and St Anthony's Catholic church was ransacked and partly burned by youths.

While Gusty was in Castlereagh, he recalls:

> About twelve o'clock that night I spotted two men coming into the room in which most of the sixty people were ensconced. A detective sergeant from Special Branch, who had been involved in my case in 1966, came in. Ken Hagan was a pretty sizeable fellow and I got him to stand obliquely in front to give a half-side back-headed view of me. The detective might not have known me because something like six years had elapsed. He came in and had a good look round the room and seemed satisfied that I was not there. However my brother was there and Billy and I are not dissimilar, and they thought our Billy was me at first.

The men went through another series of interviews with the Royal Military Police.

I said to the young soldier who was taking details (all false of course), 'Now what's happening? I've my work to go to.' For all intents and purposes I was a BT engineer. He said, 'Between you and I, I think you are going to get released within half an hour or an hour.'

When we were released we went down into the reception area of Castlereagh barracks where men and women were making inquiries about their loved ones. A young cop, who was pretty nervous, said, 'Now don't forget and tell them up the road we've nothing to do with this. It was the paratroopers. It wasn't us.'

A young policeman offered us a lift home in a pig but we said, 'We'll make our own way home.' When we got into the public reception area, 'John' who was a senior UVF man said to this man, 'Right, have you got the car outside?' He said, 'Yes,' and 'John' says, 'Right, come on.' So the three of us, Ken Hagan, 'John', and myself, got in the car. We drove down the Castlereagh Road right into the middle of a riot. They were still throwing stones and they were besieging the RUC barracks. We got through side streets and were approaching the Laganbank Road. Coincidentally 'John' or Ken said, 'Well, Gusty, that's another one for the book. Michael Collins didn't do that!'

The driver suddenly realised who I was and mounted the footpath in a state of panic. He was a sergeant in the UVF and I told him, 'Wait till I tell you, son. I just didn't leave that place to be replaced back in it again.'

We were virtually facing Townhall Street which leads to Oxford Street. Says I, 'There's a policeman with a submachine gun standing down there and if he sees us acting in an erratic manner he's likely to open up on us.'

Gusty was brought back to Joseph Street:

My ma was there, God bless her, and her and me danced in the street. We had beaten them type of thing and they were halcyon days. I stayed in Forthriver [in the upper Shankill] that night and I was driven down to the lower Shankill to take a brigade meeting by Bob Hynds. A paratrooper stopped us at a roadblock but Bob was an ex-Green Jackets and talked his way out of it. The ironic thing was that most people knew me and I moved about loyalist districts freely. Things got a wee bit heavy at one time and I moved to east Belfast. The police were few on the ground and the troops even fewer. I was watching a parade one day when a wee woman came and pressed her key into my hand saying, 'Any time you want, Gusty.' I finished up with quite a number of front-door keys. Most people were extremely supportive.

'John' believes the authorities were content to have Gusty at large:

> While we were there we were searched and photographed – the usual pattern. Now Gusty has tattoos, and markings are well noted – they recognise you by your marks. We were sitting waiting to be interrogated and I was beside Gusty and a few others. Two detectives popped their heads in to look over at us and smiled.

John maintains they knew that it was Gusty Spence. 'We got out the next morning about five or six o'clock after interrogation, and it wasn't much of an interrogation.'

Gusty's tattoos confirmed his identity later when he was captured on 4 November 1972. The commanding officer of the Parachute Regiment, Colonel Derek Wilford, noticed that Gusty had dyed his hair but had been unable to hide the tattoo marks on his hands.[19]

At this time Lenny Murphy, a member of the UVF, was becoming notorious for brutal beatings and murders. He and his gang were active within hours of the Bloody Friday IRA bombing on 21 July 1972, killing a 34-year-old catholic, Arthur Matthews. In the context of mounting sectarian tensions the freedom of Gusty Spence made sense. 'John' said:

> I'm in no doubt that they let him out of prison to bring a bit of order to the UVF. If this had been successful they wouldn't have had wild dogs of renegades running about like the Shankill Butchers and others.

While Gusty was still at large, UVF men dressed in army uniforms successfully raided a military barracks in Lurgan on 23 October 1972. In all, a significant quantity of weapons and ammunition were successfully captured from the UDR and Territorial Army depot. The raid was meticulously planned. Four men in army uniforms overpowered the Territorial Army sentry, and a further eight soldiers were defeated when another ten UVF men arrived. Later that morning, however, the RUC recovered part of the haul from a Land Rover that had broken down. Later, in a statement, the organisation said, 'We would stress that these weapons are solely for the defence of loyal Ulster men and women and will not be turned on any of the security forces.'[20]

While on the run Gusty had a second heart attack. The UVF were so determined that he would not fall into the hands of the security forces that they contemplated flying Gusty out on a private plane. Gusty and Louie were staying in a flat at Glencairn and they knew there was a UVF unit stationed nearby. When Gusty took ill, Louie had to get help. Later she recalled:

> I was just learning to drive when he went on the run and although there was a car sitting at the door, when he took sick I had to run from the bottom of Glencairn to the very top to get a doctor. He swore the next day, 'That's it finished: you're going to learn how to drive.' So I learnt how to drive and it wasn't so bad then.[21]

Louie went to the officer commanding the UVF unit but they could not give much help. They got some tablets and the following day brought Gusty to see a doctor. Despite his heart attack, Gusty kept going:

> They were heady days and in many ways they were electrifying days. I was filled with all this patriotic verve and nothing was going to stop me. I was making statements like, 'Well if you don't have enough firearms, take them from the people that have the firearms.' I suppose that's what kept me going but I slowed down a few times.

Gusty was travelling throughout the whole of Northern Ireland swearing in new recruits and numbers were growing considerably. Billy Hutchinson was present at some of these meetings, but he was mainly concerned with new recruits to the YCV, the youth wing of the UVF. During this time an agreement was made between Gusty Spence for the UVF and John McKeague for the Red Hand Commando. This tied the two organisations together, an association which has lasted until today:

> I was behind the barricades that had been erected in the Witton Street area of the Shankill. I was staying in a safe house when there was a high-level meeting between the UVF and the Red Hand Commando. John McKeague and I made an agreement that the RHC would become an integral part of the UVF. Each retained their separate command structure, but in operational matters they took their lead from the UVF. Firearms and security matters would be shared and they would be looked upon as part of the one organisation.

I was unable to locate the original agreement made on 15 July 1972, but the agreement was revived in 1976. The first part read as follows:

The Ulster Volunteer Force / Red Hand Commando Agreement (1972)

Senior Officers of Red Hand Commando and Officers of the Ulster Volunteer Force Brigade Staff sat in discussion of various points relating to the UVF and RHC in July 1972, in which the following points were agreed.

1 Red Hand Commando shall be aligned to the Ulster Volunteer Force and shall work hand in hand in a joint effort to aggregate all resources of both groups and devote all their energies to the war against the IRA.

This alignment is taken because:

i Red Hand were in complete agreement with UVF policy on all matters.

ii The UVF recognises the right of Red Hand units to retain their own separate identity, as a regiment with its own pride and particular style of internal organisation.

iii It is deemed desirable that both groups become aligned in order to provide assistance and support to each other, politically, physically, financial or materially.

For a time the agreement had gone 'unhonoured', which was why it was updated in 1976.

Gusty's contribution to the development of the UVF is recalled in 'The Ballad of Gusty Spence', sung by loyalist prisoners in Long Kesh in 1975 and captured on tape by Winston Rea:

O gather round my comrades I'll tell you all a tale,
Of how we sprang a volunteer from out of Crumlin Jail.
I'll tell you of his story and how it came to pass,
That he was serving twenty years in the prison of Belfast.

'Twas in the reign of Terence O'Neill that he was put away,
For daring for to lift his hand against the IRA.
No evidence could they bring, informer for to say.
But the RUC imprisoned him in the town where they held sway.

A full six years he did endure in that great prison grim,
And though they tried they could not break the defiant heart in him.
I am a loyal Ulsterman my cause I'll not deny,
And yet I'll see my country free from the shoreline to the sky.

Then came the day he got a note to say his child be wed,
And could you come please father dear, 'tis by you that I'll be led.

And after all his duty done and parting filled with tears,
A voice did say you're not forgot by the Ulster Volunteers.
At the first great tide of evening as they drove back to his cell,
His car was stopped by three armed men who met him with a yell.
Brave lad you're free so come with us and ever from this day,
You'll lead us on to victory against the IRA.

So now he changed his prison grey for the bonnet of the blue.
Across the land he leads the fight with a heart that's ever true.
And well we know that victory's sure so long as we don't fail
The Volunteer we sprang that day from out of Crumlin Jail.

As new recruits swelled the ranks of the UVF, the previously strict vetting procedures became more relaxed. Both the UDA and the UVF attracted some recruits who turned out to have dubious backgrounds and whose motivation may have included exploiting their position for criminal gain. Most recruits, however, appear to have remained committed to the defence of their country, and Billy Hutchinson believes that there were relatively few with criminal intent as long as the UVF remained proscribed.

Billy Hutchinson had been outside the Brennan Street Club when Gusty was unwittingly apprehended. Henceforth, from approximately the end of July until Gusty was rearrested in November, Hutchinson usually accompanied Gusty. In fact, Billy was staying with Gusty on the morning he was rearrested. Billy recalls:

> On the morning that Gusty was arrested both of us were staying in the same place. He went out while I was still sleeping and someone knocked at the door and said, 'Gusty has been arrested.' I said 'He couldn't have been, he's still here.'

Gusty had been arrested by members of the Parachute Regiment: the security forces had been watching Gusty and at an appropriate moment they pounced. According to Gusty, his arrest highlighted the ambivalence of the Protestant community towards the loyalist paramilitaries:

> When the paratroopers captured me on 4 November 1972 on the Glencairn Road, people found it outrageous that I should be in a stolen car. Here's us, up to all types of hanky-panky defending Ulster to the best of our ability, and that meant in a physical way, yet people were outraged by this.

Shankill Road people were generally law-abiding. They felt under threat from the IRA in the context of an inadequate level of protection from the security forces. In this context paramilitary activity became increasingly accepted, but ambivalence remained. Ordinary crimes were frowned upon and the killing of ordinary Catholics was generally unacceptable, hence

> it was a terrible thing that I was in a stolen car. 'He was actually caught in a stolen motor,' they would have said. 'We'll shoot and kill and bomb and do all those dastardly things as long as it's within the law.'

12

Long Kesh

After his arrest, Gusty was taken to Black Mountain School on the Upper Springfield Road, where the Parachute Regiment was based.

> They suspected I was Gusty Spence but they weren't sure. Colonel Derek Wilford, Commanding Officer of the Paratroopers, interviewed me before I was brought to the guardroom of 39 Brigade in Thiepval Barracks, Lisburn. There they secured the help of Detective Sergeant Glass of the RUC fingerprint department. I gave them a thumbprint but much to their consternation he exclaimed that this was not Augustus Spence. There was another Augustus Spence living in Central Street off the Newtownards Road and his prints had been mixed up with mine.
>
> At that point I saw a little chink of light, but they put me against a wall opposite a door with a spyhole and someone positively identified me. I was kept for one day in the guardroom at Thiepval before being brought by helicopter to Compound 7 in Long Kesh where I was lodged with loyalist remand prisoners. All sentenced prisoners remained in Crumlin Road jail

and didn't move to Long Kesh until December 1972.

The prisoners then decreed that I would be Commanding Officer of both the UDA and UVF. I initiated a series of training schemes to get the men into shape, and the prison authorities didn't interfere.

There were still charges to be faced about the abduction but this unexpectedly brought some benefits:

I was charged with being unlawfully at large which entitled me to an extra visit each week to prepare my defence. This continued for two to three years until a new governor took over. He questioned why I was getting an extra visit and I told him why. He said, 'I haven't heard of that but I'll check up.' He came back saying, 'That case was withdrawn against you two years ago.' I protested. 'Nobody brought me to court in order to withdraw this charge against me.'

At the trial proper I dispensed with my solicitor and defended myself. I refused to recognise the court but I retained the right to cross-examine.

Major Mullin was rather uptight about being cross-examined by a prisoner but confirmed that I was a man of my word.

In my closing address to the jury I told them, 'I was heading back to prison when armed men detained me, just as I'm being detained by armed men now. Can anyone suggest what I could have done?' There was a ripple of laughter round the courtroom and I said, 'Ten thousand homes would have hidden me. I look upon myself as an Ulster Volunteer and I will continue as an Ulster Volunteer until some better way is found.'

The jury were hopelessly deadlocked. I was put back for another trial but this never happened because they didn't want to run the risk of another fiasco. They withdrew the charge against me behind my back.

Conditions at the disused airfield at Long Kesh were extremely primitive. Four Nissen huts and a toilet/shower unit were located within each compound; each compound housed approximately eighty to one hundred men behind a high-wire fence with a prison officer's hut outside each compound:

Republicans named the compounds 'cages' for propaganda reasons so that these poor Irishmen could be depicted as being stuck in cages. We usually called them compounds because that's how they were known in the army. Each Nissen hut was just a big open hut with beds and lockers arranged side by side along the walls. There were three or four convector heaters but I saw icicles on the inside of the Nissen huts – it was freezing cold.

It was not long before IRA prisoners beat one of Gusty's men.

> The authorities brought certain prisoners to and from the courts in a prison van and on one occasion a UVF man was handcuffed to one of five Provo prisoners. The five attacked and nearly murdered him so I went over to the wire because Provo remand prisoners were housed in Compound 8. I asked to see the senior republican and said, 'What's the score, Paddy? We had a no-conflict policy in Crumlin Road jail and I assumed the same thing would obtain here.'[1]

It was a gentleman's agreement in Crumlin Road jail that if anyone stepped out of line they would be punished by their own respective organisation, though not in a physical way. Patrick Serridge immediately agreed that the deal should apply in Long Kesh:

> From then on there were no problems between loyalists and republicans. There was a problem once between Martin Meehan and Joker Andrews, but that was soon sorted out. My men came down from Crumlin Road jail on 12 December and I moved in with the sentenced men.

The prisoners found the lack of order and basic facilities unsettling, and Gusty's men were in a state of depression in Compound 12:

> Everything was taken from them and a wilful attempt was made to humiliate them. Bob Truesdale was a hard governor. 'This is me, Bob Truesdale, and you'll do what you're told.' I found the men in a state of disarray and said, 'Right now, stand by your beds,' and one man said, 'It's like a breath of fresh air.' I told them, 'Look at the state of this place, we'll work until we get this cleaned up, shipshape and Bristol fashion.' We worked into the early hours until the lights went out. The following day the place was scrubbed out in British army fashion. There was a muster parade on the Monday morning and people had their own duties. That was the start of the regime in Long Kesh.
>
> We had about forty UVF and forty UDA men who got organised immediately that December. Any semblance of uniform had been removed so we started to get bits and pieces together so that a uniform and a signal mark of identification could be manifested. Then people could say, 'That's UVF, you know.' That was our main goal. We got uniforms. The human mind is extremely resilient. We were pitting our minds against sophistication. The army and the prison authorities were determined we would toe their line but we were equally determined we wouldn't be fucking toeing their line.

One former inmate told how Long Kesh was transformed:

> This hellhole is frustration, frustration and more frustration. The roof leaks, the rats are rampant and the food mostly cold and uneatable. There are no educational facilities, no relaxation or recreations provided. You have nothing except your own initiative. Thank God we had Gusty Spence. The man is a tower of strength to the Loyalist prisoners in Cage 19. As our Commanding Officer he ordered us, for our own good, to run our Compound on strictly British lines. We scrubbed, cleaned and polished that miserable hut until it shone like Aldershot Military Barracks. We painted the huts, hung curtains, polished boots, toilets, pots and pans, right down to the iron studs on our boots. We drilled, and we did PT and we even did 10-mile route marches inside a compound a few hundred yards square!! That, Loyalist friends, is how our Commanding Officer made us beat the boredom of Long Kesh Concentration Camp.[2]

Republicans in adjacent compounds initially were also impressed, as Martin Meehan told me:

> I was in the cage facing him. He ran a very tight regime in terms of discipline. I remember seeing them going out drilling, keeping fit and running round. Here's me, 'This man is running his regime on British army lines!'

For a time the IRA ran a similarly disciplined regime:

> It wouldn't have been as strict as Gusty's regime but when we first came in we were drilling too. We were actually mimicking loyalism and the British army, and this caused resentment among the men so I says 'Why should we be doing this?' Others said, 'We are republicans and should be educating ourselves. We shouldn't be marching up and down yards for two hours in the morning and two hours at night. Are we trying to impress by keeping up with loyalism?' About 1973 a decision was taken to do it no longer.
>
> Davy Morley was the commanding officer and I was his adjutant. He had a man standing at the bottom of his bed made up with everything laid out like the British army. Everything was checked. I didn't like that, we were playing the same game as loyalism. Davy Morley had been in the British army. He had been a drill major and he drilled our lads up and down the yard. He was good but it caused an undercurrent of resentment among our men who were saying, 'We should be educating ourselves and getting the books in.' That school of thought prevailed after 1973.

On one occasion the actions of Gusty and his men seemed to establish their credentials in the eyes of IRA prisoners. On 11 July 1972 a number of men associated with the UVF and UDA, committed a horrific crime upon a widowed Catholic mother, Mrs McClenaghan, and her son David, in Southport Street in the Oldpark area of Belfast.[4] They raped Mrs McClenaghan and murdered her educationally subnormal son while his violated mother struggled desperately to shield him.

A wave of horror swept through the community. While the men responsible were on remand in Crumlin Road, loyalists reportedly beat them. But this was not the end of the affair. When two of them were brought to Long Kesh to serve their sentences, republicans, including Martin Meehan, took care to observe the reaction of loyalists:

> They were expected to arrive at Long Kesh about half six that night, so after five o'clock about a hundred of us congregated at the wire. Gusty was in Cage 12 and I shouted across to him, 'See these boys coming in here? If you ones accept them into your cage there's going to be serious repercussions. They are not political, they're the scum of the earth. After what they've done nobody should accept them.'
>
> Negotiations went on with Gusty standing at the wire but he didn't commit himself to anything. Then, when the new prisoners pulled up in the bus, a few of our lads jumped over the wire to get them but they faced a big crowd of screws. They got the prisoners into Gusty's cage and the next thing was, for five or ten minutes we heard all sorts of banging and squealing. The hospital van then came and the men, who had had their arms and legs broken, were taken out of the cage in stretchers. That sent a message out that nobody was condoning that sort of behaviour. That went down well with everybody.

The rejection of the men who killed David McClenaghan and raped his mother had brought home to Martin Meehan that there was more to loyalists than he had thought:

> It showed a chink of light to me. The fact that they wouldn't accept them into the cage gave some sort of hope that, 'Hold on they've got a base line here.' Up to that stage we looked upon them as having no principles.

Great ignorance had always existed between the paramilitaries, as between the wider traditions in Northern Ireland. Gusty's influence was not confined to discipline and order within the camp and he was constantly stimulating new thinking and ideas. David Ervine, who first met Gusty in

1975, said that 'Gusty was always questioning and always forcing us to question', and was attempting to instigate the same kind of thinking outside:

> He was always drawing up papers and sending them out to the brigade staff of the UVF. In doing so he was not only engendering thought within the brigade staff but, perhaps even without realising it, he was beginning to take people down the path of political science.

The brigade staff occasionally dismissed Gusty's missives. They were facing a 'war' in which Gusty's ideas at times seemed inappropriate. Billy Mitchell agrees that Gusty had a very important influence but his ideas were sometimes rejected:

> Gusty was sending stuff out and when we considered it we didn't always agree. Many times we said to ourselves, 'Jail has made him soft.' Sometimes we even tore it up and one time somebody wrote 'bollix' across his document. But even though we sometimes tore them up and said, 'Ach, it's rubbish,' some of it was sticking in our minds.

However the thinking of the UVF on the outside at this stage was not all negative or sectarian. 'John,' who was a close friend, recognised the need for change and was ploughing his own furrow by challenging attitudes:

> I just cast the seed. I tried to cast the seed of doubt for a lot of people, and surprisingly a lot of them were picking it up although they couldn't grasp the full picture. A couple of them in latter years have said to me, 'You were right.'

Bo McClelland, a close friend of 'John' and Gusty, and the leader of the UVF at this time, sent a letter to Gusty in December 1972. It was a long letter written in cryptic terms. Bo apologised for his letter being 'overdue' and said he had been away from home himself (on the run?). He wished that things could be different:

> Recently I was speaking with 'the Red', and he told me he had spoken with you, though only for a few short minutes. It is good to see him in freedom, once again able to live as he chooses and not be governed by unfair authority, as he was for so very long. While it seems that quite a few of my old mates are home on parole, I have only actually met one and that one being young and the wearer of glasses. No doubt you will realise to whom I refer ... Since you left and I was left without the benefit of your

brainpower, I have been making all the decisions on my own. It has proved to be no mean task, but luckily and happily, up until now anyway, everything has gone all right.

Bo then wrote about the new black taxi service which had been brought into operation. Old London taxis were being driven, providing employment for the men and providing a public service during times of strife. Bo said, 'Up to the present time, your pet "people's service" is still going along as well as can be expected under the circumstances. Everyone still seems pleased.'

Pensioners could travel free but some chose to abuse the system:

As you know, the OAP free travel scheme has been a boon for our old folk, it really has. Could you please advise me re one old pensioner who is abusing the concession? He seems to spend his day travelling up and down the road for no other reason than to annoy drivers. One driver had him six times before lunch-hour. I know he is abusing the thing, but we do carry OAPs free, and at the outset we never stipulated anything about number of free rides per day. Up to now I have been very skilfully avoiding the issue, but sooner or later I won't be able to avoid it. So your advice would be welcome. Its comical too you know, for the old boy knows that drivers hate the sight of him, and he seems to enjoy that fact. Limit his travelling? Think of the bad publicity. We don't want that. How about buying him a car of his own?

Bo ended the letter with greetings, saying, 'there will be absolutely no surrender to the enemies of Ulster'.

The UDA and the UVF were together at this stage although in different huts but the 'half hut' was shared.[5] They issued a joint statement at the end of September 1973 which referred to the 'filthy and degrading Maze Prison'.[6] HM Prison Maze was the official name of the place, but, as Gusty recalls, the loyalist prisoners refused to call it that:

We called it the Kesh or Long Kesh. We got a Burco clothes boiler to make tea in and, as there were no eating utensils, they gave us little plastic knives and forks. It was scandalous. There was no milk, nothing. They were operating in an old army field kitchen and stringing wire all over the place for security lights. There were power cuts and the place was freezing. We literally had to carve out a living space. There was no hospital and a doctor only came intermittently. The prison camp was in its embryonic stages and beyond the authorities. No library, no education, nothing except oppression.

> The politicians from whom I got help were Alliance people like Bob Cooper and Oliver Napier who made representations to the NIO. The SDLP also helped. The unionists said they would do a number of things but did virtually nothing. After the fire they came down and squealed hard about how badly the loyalist prisoners were being treated and how they were being put under siege from republican prisoners. We didn't want that kind of crap. They were attempting to use us to score points and we didn't want it.

There were growing tensions in the autumn of 1974 as is evidenced in a letter addressed to 'The Leaders of the Loyalist and Republican Groups' on 2 October 1974 from Peter McLachlan, a Unionist member of the Northern Ireland Assembly. He was appealing to the leaders to help bring the tensions to an end. He said he was speaking on behalf of 'wives, mothers and relatives' who were 'extremely worried' about what was happening, including bans on visits and parcels.

Two days later, Gusty wrote to the Church of Ireland Bishop of Connor, Dr Arthur Butler, regarding two specific complaints. First, there were not enough suitable books. Second, they wanted a series of talks by suitably qualified people to provide mental stimulus for the men. Bishop Butler replied on 9 October saying he had approached the governor who was looking into the matter of the books, and that a series of lectures was being arranged. Bishop Butler asked to be kept informed and referred to 'other matters' which Gusty had said he was concerned about:

> It would seem from your letter that you are now worried about other matters, but you do not state what they are, and you refer to 'the unease which abounds universally in the camp'. I will be glad if you could give me detailed information as to what you consider are the causes of this unease and frustration. I will gladly do anything I can to help, and I hope to visit you before long.

I asked Gusty about the unease:

> We hadn't been long moved from Crumlin Road jail and the camp was absolutely bare and the prison authorities were extremely restrictive. For example, initially no handicrafts were allowed. If there hadn't been some easement there would have been violence and there was violence. People were getting turned out at two o'clock in the morning and told, 'We'll put you against the wire like kippers.' I said, 'Nobody will fucking put me and

my men against the wire like kippers. If you do we'll be dead kippers and you'll have to explain that to the world.'

Bishop Butler chose a rainy day to visit. Gusty later recalled:

> We couldn't have picked a better day for Bishop Butler to come up. He was kept waiting outside and had to tramp through puddles. He was absolutely saturated and we got him a hot cup of tea. In Compound 12 there was only a single brick wall. The bricks were porous so the water ran down the inside. One Saturday we were flooded out with two feet of water which had got in at one end and couldn't escape at the other.
>
> There was gradual change after Bishop Butler's visit. I give credit to Arthur Butler and to Bishop William John McCappin who succeeded him. They were old soldiers. Arthur Butler was in the Cornwall Light Infantry and Willy John McCappin was an artillery officer in the 4.2 Stokes Mortars in the Second World War. They knew how to handle men and how to appreciate men's complaints when there was manifest justification for them.

But Long Kesh had certain advantages compared to Gusty's small cell at Crumlin Road:

> Here you had a compound about forty yards by forty yards. We could exercise and get out into the fresh air where we could hear the twittering of birds and watch the seasons change. It was my first contact with life for a considerable period of time.

Loyalist prisoners engaged in military training. A document of 1972 which outlines the 'Working Day for Volunteers 8.30 a.m. – 4.30 p.m.' lists nineteen different forms of military training, including arms classes, explosives classes, map reading, fieldcraft, guerrilla tactics, riot drill, six-mile route marches, assault courses, first aid and personal hygiene. Some classes were held on a daily or weekly basis and some involved examinations. Reference was made in the same document to educational classes including English, Irish history, UVF history, political education, and police and army interrogation, as well as classes by outside teachers on psychology, sociology, anthropology and other topics. Language courses included German, French, Gaelic and Spanish.

There were two kinds of orders within the prison – the official rules and regulations of the prison, and UVF orders. UVF and RHC prisoners were to obey UVF orders first and foremost but 'if the UVF orders are complementary to, or run in tandem with, the prison orders, that was all right'.

> We had to become self-sufficient and develop expertise in various ways. This was in 1972–3 when a war was going on and some men serving shorter sentences were being made more militarily proficient. I never accepted that it was a 'university of terror', but it *was* a university of military training lasting eighteen months to two years from 1972 to 1974. Bomb making, firearms, phonetic codes, signalling, everything that makes a soldier proficient, was involved. We didn't have recourse to anything else and the only thing we had in common was that we were soldiers. We had a cause and we wanted to become more proficient in that cause.

Billy Hutchinson, who arrived in Long Kesh in 1975, remembers that decisions were the responsibility of the OC in charge of each hut:[7]

> There was an officer in charge of each hut and a hut sergeant responsible for everything within the hut. The officer was responsible for discipline and major decisions. In the headquarter compound, where Gusty was, there was a regimental sergeant major. In other compounds there was a company sergeant major. Then there was the OC of the compound in one of the huts and in another hut you would have had his 2 i/c [second in command]. Each would have had a sergeant responsible for discipline. If people wanted to watch a TV programme, he would have talked to them and organised a vote. This was the only time you would have a vote.

The prisoners felt it was important to display symbols of their identity. This need was felt particularly strongly in a prison setting where sources of identity were under threat. Erving Goffman, the sociologist, says that ordinary prisoners often resist cooperation with the authorities in order to preserve their perception of themselves. For loyalist and republican prisoners, the expression of identity was a pressing collective need. Northern Ireland itself was a contested space, and prisoners had acted in the name of one section or the other. They would not be treated as criminals, and so loyalists chose to exhibit symbols of Britishness:

> We made a union jack but it was taken from us. I spoke to an English governor. 'Do you not understand, can you not comprehend us? If we were in a South Sea island the first thing to make would be a union jack, should it be from palm leaves.' We then painted a big union jack on the inside of the hut and put UVF in three-foot high letters on it. Says I, 'Now remove

> them.' What were they going to do, bring the painters in and paint all over them?

Loyalist prisoners were at some disadvantage in terms of escaping. There were no safe havens available for them comparable to the Irish Republic for republicans (although a few UVF men did use the Republic surreptitiously). Gusty said that there had to be pertinent reasons for escape but, as he explained:

> There was a macho element in some of the escapes and attempted escapes. People often knew full well when they started digging that their tunnel would be discovered. Credibility could stem from an attempt and it could later be said that these fellows dug the tunnel and were only thwarted at the last minute.
>
> Loyalists were very dextrous and made all kinds of tools. We determined who the tradesmen were and, providing they weren't UVF officers, they were called pioneers. We had plumbers, joiners, electricians and others, and their expertise was called upon when needed. It could involve making wire-cutters or homemade shotguns.

I expressed surprise at the idea of making shotguns in prison but was assured that workable shotguns were manufactured in Long Kesh. They were 'very simplistic but very effective'. Other items included devices for making poteen:

> After the fire in 1974 when there was no electricity except the perimeter lights, young fellows, who seemed to be taking their lives in their hands, connected up from the perimeter lights and got power into the huts to watch the Muhammad Ali fight. They were also good at building tunnels, making air displacement systems, and installing electric lights in the tunnels. The authorities had heat-seeking equipment to detect people digging tunnels and a helicopter would fly over three or four mornings each week at five a.m., probably to keep prisoners on their toes.
>
> One morning a fellow wakened me up at 2 a.m. 'Sir, there's some very funny noises coming from the tunnel.' I said, 'It's probably water seeping in.' He says, 'No, it's not water.' 'Well, maybe it's a rat or something has got into the tunnel. Tunnels are dodgy places.' The last place I wanted to be at 2 o'clock in the morning was down a tunnel.

However, as commanding officer it was his responsibility to investigate:

> We went along a narrow tunnel lightly shored up underneath a nine-inch

skimming of tarmacadam from the old airfield runway. Water was seeping through from a natural water table in an old bog. Because of the flooding we had had to make pumps. It was in a terrible state but I had to crawl through it, and sure as shooting there were noises.

We listened very carefully and could hear muffled but distinct voices. It was the Provos who had lost their way and were digging into our compound. I shouted, 'Will you get to fuck away out of it, you're going in the wrong direction. This is Gusty here. You're coming into our tunnel.' They stopped immediately and later that day David Morley said, 'I know what you're going to say,' and we laughed it off.

Some of the inventions were marvellous pieces of work:

There were four huts in a compound and one was used as a dining hall in which there was a TV. But the men were not permitted to watch it after 9 p.m., which seemed unreasonable. They could have let the men have TV in their huts because when they're watching TV they're not digging tunnels. By 9 o'clock at night the interesting programmes only began. Most of the prisoners were twenty to twenty-two years old and were sports mad.

The prisoners devised a remedy:

We removed the TV before the compounds were locked up for the night. The TV then rotated every night. The UDA might have it on a Monday and the UVF on a Tuesday. We placed a dummy TV in place of the real one. When the screws came in I had always just switched off the TV. One prison officer was nicknamed Slipperfoot. He was a Highlander whose real name was Alex McGregor, and when I said, 'Turn it off,' Alex would say, 'Ah, ha, ha, you're not going to catch me that way. Turn it off at the mains.'

He pulled the plug out and that went on for months until one night there was a big fight on TV and the TV was too loud. Tommy Ervine, a prison officer who lived in our street, came to investigate and from the outside he saw that the UDA had a TV, which seemed strange. He went up to the dining hall and checked and the TV was there but on closer examination, he found it was a dummy. The TV was taken out, which was very petty.

Merlyn Rees met Gusty in Long Kesh before he took over as Secretary of State in February 1974:

I had an hour and a half with him and I found him very receptive. He guessed that the Labour Party would constitute the next government and wanted to find out as much as possible about Northern Ireland. I believe he had spoken to the PIRA in the camp and he definitely spoke to the Official

IRA. We discussed gangsterism in the paramilitaries and people in it for what they could get out of it.

On one occasion the prisoners stopped prison visits in protest at restrictions on facilities introduced after a PIRA man escaped from the visiting area. The visiting cubicles were now open and the area was arranged so that there could be no physical contact between prisoner and visitor:

> Conditions for the visits were atrocious so nobody took visits for twelve weeks. We refused to eat prison food but got some food from the parcels our families left in. All we were taking from the prison authorities at one stage was strictly rationed bread and milk. Cigarettes were also rationed. Whatever came into the UVF compounds was procured either by the commanding officer or the OCs in the compounds. It was pooled and distributed equally because some families couldn't afford a parcel and there were single men. No UVF man was going to get fat while another went hungry.

For up to fourteen weeks loyalist and republican political prisoners had no visits at all. The tensions grew and spread into the community outside, where bus burnings and hijacking took place. This first example of co-ordinated action by loyalist and republican prisoners at Long Kesh was successful. The OCs were assured of improvements and able to inspect the cubicles before visiting resumed.

According to Billy Hutchinson, the Camp Council would never have been formed had it not been for Gusty:

> The whole Camp Council idea came out of meetings between Gusty Spence, Francy Card and Billy McKee who continued to hold Camp Council meetings. The governors permitted this to go on. I'm not saying that the camp brought everyone along. It didn't because a number of things went wrong. However we had a Camp Council that could discuss serious issues about how to move things on.

'Robert' attended Camp Council meetings at this time and told me:

> We had weekly meetings attended by IRA prisoners to discuss how the camp should be run. Sentenced prisoners were there, as well as detainees. Gusty represented UVF sentenced prisoners, Jimmy Craig represented UDA sentenced prisoners, Ned McCreary was there for the UDA internees, I did the UVF internees, and Billy McMcKee represented the Provos.

The Camp Council, Gusty said, was composed of

the UVF, Official IRA, UDA, PIRA, and INLA [Irish National Liberation Army] OCs cooperating to bring about a more humane regime. We wanted a library and a comprehensive education system – all those positive things. We dealt with ministers and officials from the NIO and we had them squirming in their seats with embarrassment.

It was announced in the press in March 1974 that a united front had been formed between loyalists and republicans in Long Kesh and Crumlin Road jail. This story was a reference to the Camp Council and was the first public admission by loyalists of such cooperation, though the report said that the joint action only involved complaints and shared grievances. Even this was confined according to the report, to separate complaints being issued at the same time.[8]

Colin Crawford, a former prison welfare officer, described the accommodation in the huts as basic:

> Bunk bedding, sleeping areas partitioned by hardboard, a central corridor for meals and, given constraints upon space, limited area for recreational activity. The prisoners were in control of day-to-day activities within their own compounds; however prison staff had free access to patrol, search, lock and unlock individual huts morning and evening . . . While there was a very high level of prisoner autonomy, the prison was still effectively under the control of the Prison Service.
>
> Food was delivered to the compounds by lorry, having been prepared in the prison's central kitchen. The large metal containers were collected and distributed by the prisoners . . . In addition to institutional food (a source of complaint and even riot in some prisons), each prisoner received a weekly food parcel from family and friends and there were small cookers in the compounds upon which personal rations could be prepared.[9]

In August 1974 a loyalist prisoner complained about the quality and quantity of food being provided and this developed into a protest by all prisoners. They began throwing food over the wire. The authorities responded in September by banning food parcels, but food continued to be thrown over the wire. The 'Ho Chi Minh trail' was then devised. This was a pulley system for transporting food between the different compounds and was constructed from wire, ropes, cord and cloth:

> Loyalists sent stuff down to other loyalists and to the Provos in the lower part of the camp. Republicans sent stuff up to us. One super-Prod said, 'I don't want no fucking Fenian baps.' Says I, 'That's all right, you boy, a bap has no conscience.'

If there was a gap of sixty yards we got a piece of light string, made two holes in a tennis ball, pulled the light string through and threw the tennis ball across. This was followed with a longer plaited string or piece of rope. It was a pulley system back and forward with bags tied on it. It was wonderful. They were days of hope in many ways and we had complete cooperation.

Some prisoners found prison life very difficult to bear, as 'Robert' recounts:

There were fellows who physically couldn't handle it so we talked them through it. The first thing we did was to stop the prison officer coming round every night with a big tray of drugs. Prisoners could have whatever to hell they wanted because the prison warders preferred you sedated. We stopped this and we stopped people running to see the governor every morning on his visits. We gave him as much trouble as we could unless a prisoner really needed to see someone. There was trouble with kids and girlfriends so we talked that through, and some of the ones we talked to in those days are now active in the PUP and have done a good job.

Lecturers visited Long Kesh to provide some formal education. Gusty recalls:

The first person to introduce any kind of formal education on a voluntary basis was John Fairleigh from Queen's University, Belfast. He elected to ask some lecturers if they would come down and speak with us.

Fairleigh, who was deeply interested in the welfare of prisoners, initiated the idea because he wanted to see dialogue between the prisoners and top lecturers who could inspire the men with ideas. His work was to be greatly appreciated by both loyalist and republican inmates. The lecturers went on a voluntary basis. They found the prisoners to be an attentive audience. The venture was not confined to formal lecturing, and lecturers could stray into other areas, moving, for example, from psychology to creative writing. They thoroughly enjoyed the experience and often came away feeling sad to leave the men behind.

Fairleigh says there initially was some difficulty getting lecturers into the prison and he recalled a meeting with civil servants and Shirley Williams, the Secretary of State for Education and Sciences, at Stormont at which he pressed them to get lecturers admitted. The civil servants were not too happy about this but Shirley Williams could see no problem and so it began. Lecturers included Frank Wright, John Blacking from the anthropology department, Miriam and Jim Daly, and George Huxley. The authorities were on the whole quite helpful but there were difficulties at times, and lecturers could be kept waiting before getting to see the men. Gusty told me that at times the army kept lecturers late by going through their papers.

Miriam Daly was a lecturer in the Department of Economic and Social History at Queen's. She was a republican and this came through occasionally in her lectures at the university.[10] Despite her commitment to republicanism, Gusty remembers her being greatly appreciated by the loyalist prisoners. Her lectures to them sometimes lasted an hour and a half:

> Sometimes the army would have messed her about with searches and so on, so that she might only get in for half an hour. Before Miriam came to Compound 12, I was teaching Irish history in an amateurish way. After her lecture there was a short question-and-answering session, and she said, 'Gusty, thank God that question-and-answer only lasted ten minutes. I'll have to get back to the books because your men asked some very pertinent questions.'

One lecturer stood out as being of particular note. This was the late Frank Wright, who was from an upper-middle-class family in England and in his youth had experienced prejudice because of this background. He became a member of Corrymeela and was deeply interested in the Northern Ireland problem. (He was a young man when he died a few years ago after taking a post as professor at Limerick University.) Frank got to know Gusty very well and spoke highly of him. 'Robert' told me that it was while he was interned there in 1974 that Frank had come to Long Kesh:

> Frank gave us great assistance in our political thinking. His father was a British attaché who had been round the world fighting in every troubled spot where England was involved. Frank appeared at this opportune moment and gave us political guidance and that's when we got deproscribed.

Frank Wright's input was generally much appreciated, as Gusty indicates:

> Frank Wright has to be one of the most decent men I ever met. I first met him through John Fairleigh. I was eternally grateful for all those who came. They didn't have to and they came at their own expense. It was all right me

lecturing to the men and giving a perspective on Irish history but I wanted academics to do it because the boys would say, 'Ach well sure, that's only Gusty's point of view.' I wanted the academics to come to verify what I was saying and to provoke questions, and they did.

Frank Wright pulled no punches. When he first came he said, 'I want to make my position clear: at one time I was a member of the British Communist Party.' He laid his cards on the table, and my men took to Frank Wright. He was chronically honest and supportive and tried to understand who my men were, what they were doing there, and what their motives were. Frank Wright had a quicker grasp than anyone else as to what the UVF prisoners were about.

Wright's friendship with Gusty continued after the authorities stopped the lectures.[11]

Frank Wright then sometimes came up on visits and we shared many thoughts and explorations. I don't know how Louie took it because when Frank and I got into full flow she barely got a word in edgeways. Frank was conscious about that. We had a deep friendship and Louie was very fond of Frank because he had a humanity that was seldom seen.

He was suffering himself and had all types of problems. He sucked these sweets and the prison officers wanted to know what they were. On one of the last times he saw me, in Hopewell Crescent, he had a little box from which he had a constant flow of insulin. The man was in obvious pain but as sharp as a tack. Frank Wright and people like Paddy Devlin, Billy Blease and others, would have been my mentors.

In Crumlin Road, intercommunity dialogue was usually limited to individual contacts, and these were reduced by the camp structure. Nevertheless, there were opportunities for loyalists and republicans to meet each other, as 'Robert' explained:

If we were in the adjoining compound or they came to play football matches, we could talk to them. We also knew when they were playing matches and we threw messages over. The favourite method was inside a tennis ball. If we were next to the Provos and I wanted the message to go to another compound I threw the ball to the Provos who would throw it to the appropriate compound. Messages were never lost.

Indeed Gusty was seeking to establish contacts between republicans and loyalists but Bob Truesdale, the governor, told him:

'You're living in cloud-cuckoo-land.' I says, 'Bob, I want peace and I know

> the way to go about it.' 'There's naïvete there,' he said. 'There won't be peace until the politicians agree it.' Says I, 'That's OK, but let me work at it.' But he wouldn't. I wanted exposure of loyalists to republicans. I wanted them asking, 'Look, what's this all about here? Let's get down to real issues.'

Martin Meehan recalls that there were occasions when the warders appeared to be involved in attempts to stir up trouble among the prisoners:

> I was in the visiting box waiting for my wife coming in and the next thing is Gusty Spence came into the cubicle. I says, 'What did they send you here for?' 'Well,' he says, 'some of them screws are mixing [stirring up trouble]. They've allocated us the same box hoping that there would be a confrontation.' Then I said, 'I think we're a wee bit too wide for that.'

Gusty recalls shaking hands with Martin Meehan after this incident.

There had been some meeting of minds between the prisoners in Crumlin Road but Gusty was conscious that

> I hadn't got into the minds of the Provos at all. I knew Billy McKee and Proinsias McAirt but I hadn't got into their minds and they hadn't got into my mind. I also saw it as a positive thing for republicans and loyalists to meet and sit down with the Northern Ireland Office initially, and it was only initially, to talk about prisoners' rights and conditions. That eventually happened but perhaps I wanted it to happen too soon and was overambitious. I knew the dialogue would eventually turn to politics.

According to Gusty, intensive political discussion among loyalists only began when the detainees arrived in Long Kesh in 1973.

> Politics was spoken about in Crumlin Road but it was rudimentary because the UVF prisoners didn't really comprehend politics beyond the constitutional issue. The boys weren't *au fait* with socialism, especially as applied by the Official republican movement. It was bred into us that those things were anathema but with them being away from their old environment and by injecting a bit of politics here and there, people were becoming politically aware. The [informal] seminars began in 1973 and became intense between 1974 and 1977.
>
> The detainees grasped politics very quickly. They were the leadership of the UVF: they were no slouchers and they were invariably men of mature years.[12] It was with a sense of grievance that they were saying, 'Well, everything in Northern Ireland's not right so let's explore possibilities of

> making those things right.' They had a grievance against unionist politicians for not supporting the men on the outside and especially on the inside in pursuit of political status.

The compound seminars were about more than party politics, discussion on fundamental questions regarding the most basic issues of life took place:

> There were seminars about our origins; about the working class; about our lack of opportunity and disadvantage. There were seminars about the education we [never] received and where it lacked. It was obvious that coming from working-class areas, unless you had exceptional parents or were an exceptional person with exceptional ability, you weren't going anywhere.[13]

They were questioning the basis of their society:

> That's what Long Kesh was all about. It was about investigating our backgrounds; our attitudes to life and everything else including the way people have been manipulated through being told that they were 'the people'.

Prisoners were able to carry on a detailed debate because loyalists enjoyed some freedom in Long Kesh and were left more to their own devices inside the wire than they had been in Crumlin Road jail.

> We had a study hut where we stocked our own type of books – not military-type books – history books, sociological books, political books, all those geared towards making us a better society even in Long Kesh. It was a hard-earned education but when a thing's hard-earned it's terribly important. You have to seek yourself. You get the first key and open the first door, you present that key to someone else, you close the door behind you and you let them go through the door. It's no use you finding the way for them, but if they want counsel and advice you give it.

This kind of education arose directly out of the experience and needs of the men themselves and was not imposed:

> Someone forwarded a proposition, for example, that 'the Provos were right in the fight they were fighting'. We then had a mini Oxford debate. One of my favourite ploys was to ask, 'What are you fighting for? Give me it in five minutes.' The atmosphere had been prepared with all this demoralisation and searching. There had been an erosion of confidence, not only

in British justice and the British way of life, but with unionist politicians. The men were ready to be set on the path, not only of truth, but of some form of political ideology.

The huts were open from half past seven in the morning until ten o'clock at night and we were left to our own devices. The only thing that relieved the tedium of the day was a visit three times a week. Once we set up the seminars I responded to their questions but at the same time presented political arguments relevant to the situation in Northern Ireland. I drew analogies with communal disturbance in Cyprus where an indigenous population was split on ethnic, political, social, religious and race lines.

Some of the detainees wanted to learn, some were nosy, while others didn't care a damn but had nowhere else to go. Perhaps twenty to thirty-five people were involved and they were well-attended. I knew that once I presented a stimulus, I had to elicit a response. They would be presenting stimuli to themselves, which became more pronounced when they moved from Compound 11 to 14.[14]

David Ervine said the discussions were enjoyable as well as being deeply challenging. They opened up new worlds for those who became spokesmen for the PUP in the 1990s:

The debate was superb and I have to give you a confession. When I went to prison I couldn't conceive that people could have laughter and fun without alcohol. I don't mean I was an alcoholic, far from it, but it was that sense of letting your hair down when I had such a thing to let down. At the weekend I went mad ... And here I found myself in prison and at times I never laughed as much and certainly never debated as much in my life. We used to plot and scheme to wind somebody up in political debate, and we were provoking each other all the time. Out of that came the capacity to think on our feet, and the articulation, which comes from experience as well. Gusty unlocked the door for many.

Whether you walked through it or not and whether you took the political course was entirely up to you. Gusty was saying – for goodness' sake, understand this problem, then when you understand it do something about it, even if it's only within the ranks of a paramilitary organisation. He nurtured this, although I wasn't conscious of what he was up to until I came out of jail. I began to realise what was expected of me. It was almost like, 'Get out there and breed. Go and confront others as I confronted you.' That was never said and it was up to you whether you picked up the cudgel. In the case of Eddie Kinner, Billy Hutchinson, Plum Smith, Billy Mitchell and myself, we've all done that, not only in the political arena but in the streets and on the roads where we were resident. We have consistently questioned and argued and indeed, I think, helped to create a wind of change.

I asked Billy Mitchell why he thought Gusty's influence was so important:

He was there up to ten years before us so he had time to work things out in his mind. He was a cult figure or a folk hero, he was Gusty and he was the CO. In many cases he was the one that issued an order that debate would happen. The name 'Gusty', the word itself, speaks about movement and vibrancy, but there was also this image of the folk hero and a lot of people respected that. He was excellent at playing devil's advocate. He was brilliant at sitting down, putting himself in a republican position and grilling you. He could have put himself in a loyalist position to grill a republican ... he could have torn your views to pieces. He could let you ramble on and then subtly get you to change your mind.

Gusty and the progressive leadership of the UVF were probably rare in having reached such a stage of confidence that they could begin to criticise themselves and their assumptions. For many ordinary Volunteers, dialogue remained a problematic enterprise only to be indulged in surreptitiously, as Martin Meehan discovered:

One thing that struck me very plainly was that the prison hospital was neutral ground. Loyalists were in the same ward and you shared your parcel with him. You gave him the newspapers to read and he gave you the newspapers. He talked about his background and about his case. There was no point-scoring. To me it was neutral territory, like the Germans and the British soldiers playing football in between the ceasefire in the First World War.

Was this with ordinary UVF men?

It was every type. When you went to the prison hospital everybody treated it as neutral. You would share your parcel and use the same shower. Nothing was different. One thing struck me very plainly was that the loyalist and republican background was working class. Their upbringing was similar.

But it was different when a visitor came to the ward to see a loyalist. He would refuse to speak to me. This happened on several occasions and I was saying to him, 'What's the craic here? When you and me are on our own there's no problem. You treat me with respect and I treat you with respect.' But they were afraid.

They actually said to me, 'You don't understand it. If I was seen talking to the likes of you I would get a hard time.' I says, 'But talking to somebody doesn't dilute your principles or your objectives, it's educating yourself and showing a wee bit of respect.' He says, 'They would think I had betrayed them.' That was one thing I couldn't fathom. You get a loyalist on his own and there's no problem, but if there's anybody else in the equation, no way would he let the barriers down. They're always looking over their shoulders.

Inevitably word began filtering through to the outside world that Gusty Spence was meeting with IRA men. The average unionist, including some members of the UVF, found this almost impossible to understand, although some senior UVF men on the outside had met with IRA leaders to discuss ways of reducing the violence.

Gusty was circumspect in a response he made through the columns of the *Sunday News*. He said he had not talked with the IRA *on behalf of* the UVF and that there was no truth in this allegation. (Such reports were dangerous in an already volatile situation, and 'Robert' confirmed to me that the report was indeed untrue. There were weekly meetings with republicans through the Camp Council but these discussions were about how the camp was run, not political matters.) Gusty said he was not the leader of the UVF and did not speak on behalf of the UVF, which was also true. Another source quoted in the *Sunday News* report said the reports could be based on a misunderstanding of a letter sent to Francis Pym, Secretary of State, by Pat Duffy MP, seeking greater contact between the UVF, UDA and the IRA and their respective compounds. This approach had been made only in regard to prison conditions.

At Easter 1974 in the midst of these developments, Gusty's 78-year-old mother Bella became seriously ill. This was a very difficult period for Gusty. Since his imprisonment he had been deeply aware that, despite her outward defiance, she had suffered as much as he had upon his incarceration in Crumlin Road jail.

Two years earlier, on Mother's Day, 12 March 1972, he had sent his mother a card from Crumlin Road jail in which he wrote:

I know that the day I was imprisoned you also entered the cell with me and are 'doing time' the same as myself. Have no fear as we shall emerge victorious, triumphant and unconquered.

'NO SURRENDER'

Shortly after that Gusty and Bella had danced for joy in Joseph Street. Now she was about to die.

Geordie Dickson, the Chief Prison Officer, came to see Gusty on the night before Bella's death:

> 'Gusty, as you know, your mother's not well and we're taking you to the City Hospital.' When I arrived a big hospital officer who had orders not to take my handcuffs off said, 'Gusty, can I trust you?' I said, 'Of course you can.' He took the handcuffs off to allow me to embrace my mother. Despite the pain and dying she was really glad to see me. I always had an old saying when we met – 'Right now, Ma, no surrender.' But she said, 'I think I'll have to surrender this time, son.'
>
> The family weren't allowed into the ward but there were two swing doors and I could see them through the little panes of glass. When we got down the stairs the policeman half apologised. 'I have to search you, Gusty.' Says I, 'Yes, my dying mother always keeps a Thompson sub-machine gun under her bed!' It was hurtful.

Thus Gusty was able to see his mother for the last time before she died.

He applied for parole to attend the funeral but was turned down. Members of the Spence family wrote to the NIO protesting at this refusal. Mr A. Huckle, NIO Private Secretary, replied two weeks after Isabella Spence's death saying that, generally, parole or an escorted visit was granted. However:

> Regrettably, in the case of Mr Augustus Spence, the security implications involved in even an escorted visit to his mother's funeral were considered to outweigh the compassionate considerations. I am sorry that this decision caused distress to the family circle but it was taken in the knowledge that Mr Spence had not returned to prison when given parole on an earlier occasion and, by reason of the escorted visit to hospital on 10 April, had been enabled to see his mother before she died.[15]

Gusty's brother Billy complained about this 'discourtesy' and Huckle responded by saying that 'no discourtesy was intended'. Billy argued that more favourable parole terms were given to republican prisoners but Huckle said, 'each application is treated on its merits'.[16]

Gusty was not overly concerned. 'I saw her before she died, loved her all my life, loved every hour that God gave to her and me, and it didn't hurt me not being at the funeral. I was hardened to the callousness of others.'

13

Conflagration

In 1974, after years of reflection and inner debate, Gusty burned his bridges and rejected violence as a means of solving the problems of Northern Ireland:

> I realised that physical force was not the way forward. I hadn't become a pacifist, and I recognised that people need to have the wherewithal to defend themselves, but the continuing violence was not getting anyone an inch nearer peace. The UVF leadership wasn't good then, and once the UVF ceasefire went down the tubes I said to myself, 'What's the point?' I tried in my own way to sharpen people's awareness of politics in the hope, which proved not a vain hope, that they would lift the torch and run with it when they were released. It was a mental decision that I didn't reveal to anyone else.
>
> Whenever you'd spent as long as I had in the physical force game and seen what I'd seen, it was a bit of a wrench. I was a physical-force person. My whole life had been geared to physical force, in the army and in the

UVF. It was a conscious mental decision. I had always said, 'Who do you think we are? You won't take advantage of us.' However in 1974 I said, 'It's time this was stopped and we sat round the table.'

It was at this time that Gusty experienced what he referred to as a telling moment:

It was a Thursday night and pop music was blaring from the radio. I didn't go much for pop music, but rather than be a spoilsport I went out for a walk on my own. It was during winter months and the weather was rotten – as bad as it can be in the Lagan valley. As I walked round I felt lonely in the bleak night. Then I saw a lone figure from the republican hut less than a hundred yards away. The figure stopped at the wire and shouted, 'Is that you, Gusty?' I didn't recognise him, but replied, 'Is that you, Paddy?' He says, 'What the fuck are we doing here, Gusty?' I said, 'To be honest, I don't know. I'm questioning that at this moment and I've been questioning it for some time.' I never knew who that fellow was, nor did I enquire.

This experience seemed to crystallise things for him:

My disillusionment was with violence, never with loyalism and never with Britishness. It was never with what I saw as a legitimate political cause but with the means being used to pursue that cause. Many republicans were going through the same turmoil and asking, 'Where is violence getting us? There has to be another way.'

At this time Gusty was still carrying the burden of responsibility as commanding officer of the UVF in Long Kesh:

Command is a very lonely thing. It's a big responsibility. You're responsible for men's lives, for their welfare both physical and mental, and it's extremely difficult. I was grateful to those senior officers who relieved the burden to some extent, but I had to make the decisions and we faced a dangerous situation.

Although they would not admit it, republicans were also questioning violence:

I saw that in David Morley but he never said, 'I'm going through a bad period. I'm questioning violence.' However, by his whole attitude and body language he gave me the firmest of impressions that he was of the same opinion as myself. There had to be an alternative to violence.

We were still being looked upon as puppets of the British Government, and of an ascendancy. We were seen as misguided but there was a

> grudging respect because we acted with honour and professionalism as soldiers. If we said we would do a thing it was done. Mandelson referred to the IRA's 'rugged honesty'. There was a rugged honesty about us that republicans acknowledged.

Some UVF people had concerns about what Gusty was doing. They feared he was going too far. Gusty saw that David Morley had similar difficulties:

> There were whispering campaigns against Morley, who was light years ahead at the time. He did not fit in well with the republican leadership and he showed me a wee dirty letter saying, 'You're in receipt of British gold.' I thought Morley would have been first to come under pressure but it was me. They said, 'Ach, you're in dialogue with them dirty Fenian bastards.' People on the republican side said to Morley, 'Ach, you're negotiating with them dirty Orange bastards.'

In July of 1974, a UVF spokesman on parole denied reports of division amongst loyalist prisoners:

> When men in Compound 9 were attacked by troops on July 19 all the Loyalist prisoners joined forces to resist the troops. The army ... could have avoided the riot by negotiating with Loyalist leaders. They didn't attempt to speak to us and came in in force with the war dogs and Saracens ... They even followed up with cameramen taking a movie of the fighting ... we were all made to lean spreadeagled against the wire for several hours ...
>
> There were more than forty of us and we all took severe beatings, including a young diabetic whose case is now being investigated by the Assemblyman Mr Ernest Baird. As troops kicked the feet out from below the men, other soldiers standing immediately behind kicked and grabbed them by the hair and threw them up against the wire. Most of the men collapsed during the ordeal ... You won't believe this, but the war dogs were allowed to snap at us, urinate and defecate on us when we were down ... One dog went so mad it attacked a soldier and had to be bludgeoned by its handler.[1]

Brutality against loyalists occurred more frequently than was reported. Billy Hutchinson once told members of the Shankill Think Tank that he had once been severely beaten by military police. When he sought to make an issue of this he was opposed because 'it might lend support to republicans'.[2] Gusty recalled seeing a republican with bruises covering most of his body.

There was resentment when even the clergy refused to take issue with the authorities. Gusty recalls one clergyman walking into a cell at Crumlin Road:

> There were two prison officers knocking shit out of a prisoner. He apologised and walked out again. Later, when challenged, the clergyman said it was deplorable but he didn't know the full circumstances. The clergy were seen as an extension of the system.[3]

During October 1974, republican prisoners burned most of the camp to the ground. Prior to the fire, UVF prisoners had received a visit from the Roman Catholic cardinal William Conway, the same William Conway whom Gusty had once seen in Dover Street when he was a boy and Conway was a young priest. He came with a delegation of other churchmen, including the Reverend Jack Weir, a Presbyterian minister:

> Cardinal William Conway was a big, robust man. He was very astute in a political way and we did good business with him. He agreed to take up some of the things we raised about the prison with the Northern Ireland Office on behalf of republicans and loyalists. He said he would be presenting a universal, as opposed to a sectional, view because the bad conditions affected everyone.

Gusty tried to remind Cardinal Conway about the Protestant boys smoking in Dover Street, but Conway did not remember that moment from thirty years before. Nevertheless, there was considerable empathy between the two men, who had been born and bred within a few hundred yards of each other but separated by centuries of historical misunderstanding and mistrust.

After Gusty's rejection of violence in 1974, he considered resigning as commanding officer of the UVF:

> I realised that no one was going anywhere through violence. The more republicans pushed, the more the British government and loyalists responded. Loyalists were finessing their operations, and when the UVF ceasefire broke down a more militant group took over. I became absolutely disillusioned with violence and extremely disappointed because the 1973–4 ceasefire had failed.

A retrograde group now dominated the UVF on the outside so that relationships with Gusty broke down. The UVF Brigadier said, 'I won't go up and see that man because he embarrasses me.' Gusty did not see the UVF leadership outside prison for two or three years after the UVF ceasefire collapsed in 1974. When he did speak with them, he said, 'I didn't miss them and hit the wall, as far as my feelings were concerned.'

The writer Martin Dillon believes that the UVF leadership at that time were preparing to launch a new military offensive, claiming that only 'superior force' would ever induce physical-force republicanism 'to abandon their assaults upon ... Ulster Protestants'.[4] In what Dillon took to be an implicit reference to Gusty's contacts with republicans, the UVF leadership claimed they had been 'forced, as a result of political compromise and treason, to engage ourselves in a war effort against our enemies'. They then tried to justify their rejection of what they regarded as 'hypocritical' and 'humane methods of warfare'.[5] Gusty stayed his hand, realising that resignation could play into the hands of militants:

> Prison is like a society but like no other society. There are wars and rumours of wars, even within the different paramilitary groups. There are always people kicking against authority because they are in prison and suffering the depressions, disappointments and resentments of prison life. I was experienced enough to know that if I resigned there would be a power struggle and we didn't need that. I was still speaking to republicans and the Camp Council was working, but the UVF was not enamoured with either.

In September 1974, when Gusty spoke with the *Sunday News* about his discussions with republican leaders, he said they had discussed

> ... our common existence in this place but I have never talked to republicans about our politics or organisations. They are still the enemy but in here we have to live together and we have common grievances ... If society feels it is necessary to remove someone from that society it must also follow that society should provide a reasonably humane life for the person ... Among the prisoners' demands were ... the provision of vocational training and improved educational facilities, better laundry facilities, full food ration, a camp welfare committee and more favourable consideration for compassionate parole.[6]

These demands also appear on a list of thirty-four demands of the Camp Council. The demand heading the list was for a 'compassionate parole system (right across the board)'.

The Camp Council promoted the interests of all prisoners with the authorities. The three thousand prisoners formed a powerful lobby that could operate as one. This was illustrated in the 'stand to' practised by the Camp Council. On a given order:

> Everyone in the camp was standing facing the wire, which was frightening for the prison officers. There were alarm bells in the huts for prison officers if they were attacked. We rang them and at the sound of the bells everyone throughout the camp went to the wire. They didn't say a word and there were no commands. They stood facing outwards towards the prison officers as an act of discipline and cohesion.

As commanding officer of the UVF, Gusty could make decisions on the UVF prisoners' behalf, and when agreed with the republican COs they would be transmitted throughout the camp. The means of communication was informal. Meetings could be arranged by synchronising visits to the doctor or the welfare office where brief conversations took place. Alternatively written messages were passed between the leaders. Each OC would read the relevant document, note the comments, and pass them on. Documents were frequently typed, with carbon copies made. The OCs could not formally meet together except under the auspices of the governor or the NIO.

There were instances of the security forces, especially the army, coming into the camp and beating prisoners with little provocation. They would come in at 3 a.m., put the men against the wire, and call a head count. Even if the snow was lying two foot on the ground every man had to turn out and stand against the wire. The result was a decision by the prisoners to react with deadly intent:

> The commanding officers agreed that if the security forces came in to beat people without justification (that qualification was very important), the camp would rise and anything standing would be burned to ashes. The Camp Council comprising the UDA, UVF, INLA, Provos, Officials, including detainees, agreed on that. The camp would be burned, but there had to be real justification.

Early in October 1974, two republican prisoners attacked a prison officer after a relatively trivial argument. This was against the regulations of the Camp Council so David Morley ordered the offending prisoners to come out of the compound where they were (Compound 13). They refused unless Morley came to them in person. Morley told the governor, 'Let me go down and I'll order them out.' But Truesdale insisted, 'No, I'm the governor – I'll order them out.' The prison governor was looking for a chance to reassert his authority after the Camp Council had gained semi-recognition from the NIO and Gusty recalled that he demanded the men come out for punishment:

> I don't know what provoked the argument but men had masked themselves with pillowcases over their heads to beat up the two prison officers. The governor had a fair idea who was involved and ordered them to the punishment cells.

A statement from the Provisionals appeared in the press to the effect that the camp would be burned. The Camp Council had not sanctioned this so Gusty tackled Morley, saying the statement should not have been issued without agreement. But he suspected that the Provos saw the incident as an opportunity to grab world headlines and make political capital:

> I told them, 'We can't take any part in this because we did not make the decision as a Camp Council. This is a Provo thing.' I went on, 'David, you know what this means? This means that heads will be cracked.' The agreement was that if men were brutalised we would burn the camp but men had to be brutalised first. Even the Officials were stymied, and Peter Monaghan said, 'What are we going to do, Gusty?' Says I, 'Well, Peter, you're a republican and you can't stay out of it.' So the Officials burned their camp leaving one hut standing to give a bit of shelter to the men.
>
> The Provos wouldn't wait so I said, 'What's the score – does the no-conflict agreement still stand?' Morley said, 'Yes, my word was given that there would be no trouble between loyalists and republicans.' Morley issued the order in front of me – 'Loyalist compounds must not be touched.' I told David, 'I'll defend these compounds against you or the army.' There was a clear understanding, and David Morley didn't want to antagonise loyalists because his argument was with the camp authorities. I got my men into two compounds to give them a position of strength.

Most of the camp had been burned to the ground, and an ugly situation developed as soon as it became clear that the Provos would be beaten. Thousands of troops mustered and Gusty sent a squad of men to prepare the loyalist prisoners and tell them to 'leave everything and get up here on the double and form in three ranks':

> They were from compounds 9, 11 and 12, about 180 men in all, and I got them into a strong position in Compound 14. There were men in the hospital so I led a party of men through the Provos who were mustered on the football fields. We broke into the hospital and got our men to safety. I

was expecting the Red Cross but there was no one there. All the prison officers had gone, but a few who were unable to get out in time were brought into our compound and dressed in civvies until we could get them out.

That night I went up to one of the towers manned by the army. 'Radio the governor that I want to speak to him.' There was no response because they wanted to teach the Provos a lesson. I was reluctant to draw that conclusion and thought that an intermediary could have saved the situation. As it was, the screws had gone and we could be hung, drawn and quartered. There were all types of rumours, such as that Gusty Spence had been hung on a wire and big Jim Ervine was beheaded.

If the Provos had had firearms the perimeter guards would have had an excuse to open fire on them. They couldn't win because the place was being reinforced with paratroopers and marine commandoes. They were pouring in, and I could see the dark shapes of prison officers or army personnel.

That night I went down to no-man's-land. The Provos were on guard at the edge and one said, 'Where are you going, Gusty?' Says I, 'I want to stop this madness before it starts,' and he says, 'I can't allow you to go any further.' Says I, 'I respect that.'

The die had been cast, and there was an air of apprehension. As the loyalists waited, they posted guards:

Somebody described the compound as being like a galley ship with bodies lying everywhere. More than two hundred of my men were crammed into one compound designed to take eighty. I said, 'Waken me at dawn,' but at dawn there was still no sign of movement. I had been up nearly all night and told Jackie Whitten, 'I'll have another doze and if there's any movement waken me.'

At about half past eight Whitten said, 'You better get up, sir, there's helicopters and the fighting's about to start.' The Provos were on the football field wearing 'Long Kesh ponchos' made by cutting holes in blankets and putting them over their heads like Clint Eastwood. They tied them round their waists and carried some weapons.

The Provisionals had no chance against the army's superior strength:

There was vicious fighting with chair legs and planks of wood as batons but the army were able to stand back and pelt the Provos with rubber bullets. They threw punches from fifty feet and I thought there wasn't any strategy with the Provos. They fought in fits and rushes instead of sections and platoons and manoeuvring. Helicopters were dropping CS gas and everybody was being gassed. Rubber bullets were being fired and all kinds of things were happening in the confusion. It's called the fog of battle and it was absolute devastation.

The Provos had made weapons from the wooden stanchions in the compounds and nailed strips of bull wire with half-inch gaps to them. They sawed the stanchions through and set fire to some of them. The stanchions collapsed so the compounds were wide open. All lights in the camp were out so they were fighting in pitch dark except for the army searchlights. The army towers remained intact because there was a high wall and then another wall with the tower mounted on top of that. The republicans didn't have a chance. A blow was struck, but I thought it was a propaganda blow.

Loyalists kept clear of the violence, but some ventured down with Gusty:

The army pushed the Provos back up the camp where a lot of the fighting took place. I went up with John McKeague, Jimmy Craig, young Flint McCullough and about five others, carrying a union jack. We passed through the army ranks and some of them yelled at us 'Bastards' but I knew not to respond to the goading.

I went down and spoke to the senior army officer – 'I may or may not be able to get this thing stopped but I want to prevent further bloodshed.' He agreed and I found Morley in an exhausted state against the wire with a soldier's dog just about five inches from his genitals.

I says, 'David, this is absolute madness. You're beaten and the best thing is an honourable surrender. Think of Patrick Pearse in 1916. You've put up a fight but they're pushing more and more troops in and you'll be overwhelmed.' He said, 'Speak with the senior republican officer and tell him that I said that it's all over, go to their compounds and be ready for identification. I don't want any of my men brutalised.'

Gusty agreed to this and spoke with Morley's adjutant, Geordie O'Hara:

'Geordie, I give you my word that what I'm relating came from David Morley. Can you accept my word?' He says, 'Yes I can,' and I said, 'David says, "Surrender the men in orderly fashion, take them back to their compounds and allow them to be identified."' Geordie agreed that they were beaten, they laid down their arms and marched to their different compounds.

The senior army officer was then approached by Gusty and told that the Provos would surrender but there must be no vicious reprisals. The lieutenant-colonel gave his word but despite this the soldiers proceeded to brutally thrash the republican prisoners in full view of the loyalists:

> The marine commandoes behaved in a disgraceful manner so I ordered my men to turn away and told Billy Wright, the chief prison officer, 'Billy, this is fucking disgraceful. You must do something about it.'[7] He said, 'I'll do my best, Gusty, but when the army move in and take over, the civil authorities have no say.' I protested in the strongest possible terms. The officer I had first spoken with said that once the Provos surrendered he had taken up his own remit outside the camp and was no longer the senior army officer.

Most of the army brutality took place in Compound 20. The soldiers made men run while carrying bricks. The men ran gauntlets while soldiers beat them on the backs of their legs with batons. Some were forced to salute the Queen, and when one fellow refused they broke his arm:

> Although we had told Morley we would play no part in this, we attended to the wounded, no matter who they were. Joe Rafters from Ardoyne was smacked with a rubber bullet and was one of the first carried in. We brought them into our compound where they were identified. Whatever medication we could find we got it across to them and I put an old lighter, a pipe and a bit of tobacco in a cap and threw it across. Any food we had was also thrown across. After that we never got hot food for two or three days because the camp was in a state of complete disarray.

The IRA never forgot this humanity.

Once the camp began to stabilise, the prisoners distributed whatever food they had. There were bigots who would not eat 'Fenian baps' and super-Taigs who would not smoke 'Orange fags', but most cooperated.

The prisoners appeared to be running the camp themselves at this stage:

> The prison officers seldom came into the compounds where they had little authority, but we facilitated a head count in the morning and a head count at night, following army traditions. When the order 'Stand by your doors' was given, the prison officers came inside to count us.[8] The Provos, however, fell in outside and were counted as they walked into their huts at 9 o'clock at night.
>
> In the UVF compounds a UVF officer of the day and an orderly sergeant were responsible for food distribution and so on. UVF officers were served last, other ranks first. If a prisoner had a visit that morning, the orderly officer ensured that he was out of bed, washed, shaved and ready so that his visitors weren't kept waiting.

Conditions within the camp were slow to improve. Food was very poor and there were limited facilities for heating and light. Loyalists asked for firewood from Crumlin Road jail, where prisoners were employed in its production, but this was refused. Sleeping conditions were extremely primitive and it was believed that, 'someone was dragging their feet to teach the Provos a lesson'.[9] Loyalists felt they were being punished for something they had not done.

But there were changes. Formal education and qualifications were introduced, and people began studying Open University degree courses. UVF men went to classes along with UDA men and members of the Official IRA, but the Provos preferred to remain on their own. Gusty thought this reflected a determination not to let their human face be seen.

His new-found commitment to peaceful means went some way towards healing his relationship with his estranged brother Ned, wife Kathleen and their son Ronnie. At Christmas 1974, Gusty sent them a Christmas card in which he wrote:

> May God bless you at this Christmas time. Looking back on the years, one sees everything, the loves, the hopes and the stupid mistakes. With this knowledge, one looks forward . . . knowing the mistakes will never be repeated. Forgive me all my mistakes. Yours always and ever, Truly Gusty. 9th year in captivity. Spirit? Unbroken.

In January 1975 Gusty became seriously ill and was admitted to hospital. He had had a heart attack and had other medical problems:

> I had gall bladder trouble and ulcer trouble and was pretty poorly. Even Paisley came up to see me. I was semi-conscious and it was like a dream that I can barely remember. After they removed my gall bladder and treated my ulcers they moved me into secure Military Ward 18 at Musgrave Park Hospital. Professor Jimmy Grant performed the operation. He was a good man who had been in the Desert Army. At first he was bluff and gruff, but he and I had a respectful relationship and he recommended that the operation be carried out. After the operation I was moved to Nuffield Four, a civvy ward. It was heaven, being able to get good food and good conditions.

A plea for mercy was made to Merlyn Rees. In it Gusty's nephew Eddie Spence said that Gusty 'has done more than any man to improve relations inside and has repeatedly prevented outbreaks of violence'. Gusty was 'admired by other inmates and respected by prison authorities for his efforts to keep other militant prisoners in check'. Released prisoners claimed that but for the control Gusty exercised, there would have been more violence in prison.[10]

Gusty wrote to Ian Paisley towards the end of February 1975 regarding his medical condition. As a result, Paisley phoned the office of Lord Donaldson, Parliamentary Under-Secretary of State, on 3 March about the possibility of Gusty being examined by a consultant to be chosen by his brother Billy. Donaldson said that Gusty 'had been advised of the normal procedure for requesting a medical examination' and such a request would be carefully considered.

Before Gusty returned to Long Kesh he obtained a tape recorder and smuggled it into the prison. At Easter 1975, Winky Rea, Gusty's son-in-law, who was in Compound 18, made a recording addressed to Winston's mother and father, who had migrated to Australia. He told them how he intended to bring up his children in a land free from terror and hatred. '[We] must change the whole situation from what it is today into a land where all people, Protestant and Catholic, can live together proud of the name Ulstermen and willing to work towards a free and just land'.

A number of other loyalist prisoners spoke, and Gusty gave an epilogue in which he spoke about his surroundings:

> Long Kesh is a blight on the fair face of Ulster. And whatever the propaganda, whatever the attempted justification, it cannot be justified. It is a concentration camp in the worst possible sense. As I sit here in the study hut and look around me I see gun towers, hundreds upon hundreds of miles of barbed wire, special barbed wire, razor wire, guard dogs, prison officers, searchlights, rubber bullet guns, tear gas guns, soldiers with rifles and machine guns, helicopters. And despite the sophistication, loyalists have made escape attempts and escape attempts have been successful.

Gusty spoke about the young men in Long Kesh in 1975 being in the tradition of others who fought in foreign fields in Britain's cause. But he reflected on the futility of fighting and on his commitment to peace:

> I have been fighting all my life, mostly in the British army, and one questions fighting. A person doesn't fight for fighting's sake, and I want to put the fighting aside, I want to see peace in Northern Ireland. I want to see people sit down in peace and justice and hammer out their differences to make this country prosperous for everyone ... At present there is a ceasefire and I have hopes that the ceasefire will continue, because no one can

win this war. War is only necessary when one is attacked. Now that the attacks have finished let us have a true, just and lasting peace.

Gusty gave an oration in Long Kesh on the 12 July that same year, 1975. He called for the rejection of gangsterism:

> Gangsterism and corruption of whatever type must be resisted at all costs. Our aims must only be the wellbeing of the loyalist people and their defence. No organisation of the people can be allowed to become a tyranny or dictatorship exploiting the people just as the political hacks did before them.

He expressed hopes for a peaceful solution. This was significant because for some 'traditional unionists' there could be no political solution but only an illusory military defeat of the IRA. Gusty had begun to see things differently:

> Wise men will be helpful and hold a watching brief on the Convention discussions[11] and hope that a political solution will be found to our problems wherein all men of whatever calling can live in peace and justice with equal opportunity. But, equally, wise men will legislate for the day when an upsurge of violence could occur.[12]

In September, Gusty was medically examined. Part of the medical report says:

> He is a fit looking man of forty-two. He was discharged from the Army in 1960 with a partial disability pension because of bronchitis and asthma. He complains of shortness of breath from this. In 1970, he began to have episodes of pain in his chest and arm and on occasions, he was admitted to the Coronary Care Unit at the Royal Victoria Hospital ...
>
> Since 1970, the pain had recurred frequently, usually with effort but also occurring at night. He continues to be troubled with shortness of breath and wheezes. His shortness of breath is worst when he has chest pain. He has constant numbness in the outer aspect of his left calf and gets pain in his thigh on walking. His feet are uncomfortably cold. They may become swollen on occasions and feel abnormally hot ... He has a 'buzzing' constantly in his ears and had left-sided headaches for about one year ... In the cardiovascular system there was a fourth heart sound and a very weak ... pulse but no other abnormality.

Another medical report, from the Belfast City Hospital on 5 September, referred to heart problems and said that 'one could not with confidence state that a coronary attack could not occur at any time'. Reference was also made to a 'chronic duodenal ulcer'.

Despite his illness, Gusty gave a Remembrance Day oration on 11 November 1975. He referred to the purpose of Remembrance Day, which was, he said, 'to remind all men of the futility of war'. He pulled no punches as he told his men:

> War is too serious a game to be toyed with and death is very final so I will solicit you to put all romantic notions of war out of your heads. War is evil, inglorious and ugly and must only be engaged in as a last recourse instead of a first resort and constructive dialogue must always be pursued by righteous men. To ask a man to die for an ideal is outrageous but to ask him to die needlessly is criminal ... The Ulster Volunteer Force has had its share of donkeys and recently men have died needlessly when they were sent out ill-prepared and ill-advised to carry out misguided missions.

Gusty then asked how they could best remember the dead:

> I submit that we best pay respect to their memories by resolving that wars be eradicated – by removing injustice which invariably festers and bursts into violence – by ensuring that every man and woman and child in this province, disregarding race, creed or calling can feel safe from fear and walk all our streets unmolested and unhindered. The awful reality of the situation is that 1,300 people have been slaughtered in our streets, ranging from unborn babies to eighty-year-old women. What honourable war is this? What code of soldier-conduct prevails in such a war? Who can win when neighbour fights neighbour? – When children are booby-trapped and women tortured?[13]

He said the IRA would not get what they want and loyalists would remain British, 'despite all pressures from whatever quarter'. The Volunteers must remember all their dead, he said, and he read a list in couplets of forty-four names; twenty-two had died during the 1914–18 war while another twenty-two, with identical or almost identical names, were modern UVF men who had died between 1968 and 1975. He presented the names and read a poem, 'For the Fallen', ending with two minutes' silence.

The questioning of violence had become a central theme in Gusty's speeches. There had to be an alternative, and, drawing on the experience of the recent Ulster Workers' Strike, Gusty was convinced the first steps had to be taken by the warring men:

> Hardline unionist politicians, including Paisleyites, weren't going to do anything. They were on a high, thinking, 'Didn't we bring the government down?' Whereas I was saying to the paramilitaries, 'You have shown that you controlled most of Northern Ireland.' Even the IRA admired what loyalist paramilitaries had done. I was inciting the workers and paramilitaries together to go beyond that and seek ways to bring the war to an end.

The success of the Ulster Workers' Strike demonstrated that the principle of consent had to be accepted and that the British government would not pull the plug. According to Gusty:

> It was forcibly shown that you couldn't override the unionists in response to a silly remark by John Hume about lancing the unionist boil.
>
> After the UVF ceasefire of 1973–4 a hardline group took over and I wasn't getting much response. But the men inside wanted to see the violence stopped so they could get out of jail. There was also an enlightened element who reached the conclusion that violence only bred counter-violence. Even the IRA realised that. The British government wouldn't leave here in a million years and even if they did, I think the IRA knew, 'You can't beat these loyalists and even if you did they wouldn't know it.'

David Ervine, who became a respected exponent of loyalist thinking, recalls how he met Gusty after being arrested in 1975:

> I was transported from Crumlin Road prison while on remand and awaiting trial on an explosive charge. I was taken into Compound 21 which was a shell of a place. It had been virtually rebuilt after the fire and it was cold and not very pleasant. A group of us arrived and, as we found out later, the norm was that the commanding officer would address us. The CO in this case was Mr A.A. Spence, who I learned to call Sir, and I've never called him anything else.

Gusty's first question was – where did he come from? Ervine replied, 'From east Belfast,' and Gusty said, 'Isn't that where they eat the missionaries?' Shankill Road men were not too fond of east Belfast. The second question was, 'Why are you here?' Ervine thought this was a stupid question and said, 'I'm here because I was fighting for Ulster.' He still recalls Gusty's response:

> He says, 'No, no, no – why are you here?' Not the fact that I'd been caught with explosives, he wanted to understand why I was in the prison and

> what beliefs had taken me there. I found it an arrogant question and yet it was a question that began to unlock a door to a different idea. He was confronting my attitudes and was forcing me to question why. The question annoyed me and seemed arrogant because he seemed to know why he was there. Gusty had gone through that process and was rocking my justification. I then embarked slowly and methodically upon a process because, as I'm sure he has said to you, self-analysis is one of the most frightening and difficult things for a human being to do.
>
> I needed to understand what was happening to me in a society of which, frankly, there was little sense to be made. But once I'd stepped from it and was looking back at it – that was the breath of life. I was beginning to understand the human being that I was and why generations had been prepared to sacrifice their liberty or lives for the defence of republicanism or loyalism. Given that we're a zero-sum society, what fuels us most is not what we want, but our desire to make sure that others don't achieve what they want.

Gusty was also attempting to influence the IRA to say, 'Hold on a minute, there has to be a better way than this' and to think about sitting down and talking about it. Both sides had to recognise that violence could not end the conflict. Gusty's favourite saying to the UVF was: 'Off you go and kill a thousand Catholics, but what have you proved? Even if you kill a hundred IRA men what have you achieved – nothing but ranks of martyrs.'

14

Cooperation and Tackling Sectarianism

Loyalist and republican leaders began cooperating so effectively in the Camp Council that they began to see wider possibilities. As Gusty Spence later wrote:

> The paramilitary representatives attempted to 'export' this cooperation to the outside world through the medium of a 'downtown' office in Belfast wherein welfare groups interested in paramilitary prisoners could meet and maximise their welfare efforts on behalf of those people in whom they had an interest. Heaven only knows where such cooperation could have led Northern Ireland.[1]

The Camp Council achieved tranquility and understanding between bitter opponents. They found a *modus vivendi* enabling them to live and work in harmony despite their differences. If this atmosphere could be created under such uncongenial circumstances, it should be possible to find a way forward for the whole community. This was the vision that enthused loyalist and republican supporters of the downtown office:

> It was the ideal medium for stimulating our kind of dialogue on the outside. Paramilitaries could not be seen to be talking to each other, and such hypersensitivities were taken into account in the downtown office concept. A welfare representative from each group would have an office within a suite of offices. There would be a coordinator trusted by all the groups – Elizabeth Kennedy. She happened to be a Protestant who spoke Irish, which she deliberately learned so she could speak to the IRA in their own tongue.
>
> Some prisoners made smart-ass remarks to her in Irish, but Elizabeth was no pushover. She made a couple of remarks in Irish that left them smarting. Elizabeth was to be the first coordinator of the downtown office in Belfast but unfortunately she died very soon. She was very incisive and fought hard with the prison authorities for the prisoners.
>
> She was one of those 'don't-you-take-me-for-granted' people – blunt but good, honest and fair and she was to have an assistant coordinator. Returning prisoners and/or their families would go to their respective offices. The principals in those offices were to be from the different groups. They would come together to speak initially about prisoners and prisoners' families. That would naturally evolve and other people would be introduced.

Political discussions were also envisaged, according to Gusty:

> That's what it was all about. We were going to call in political scientists from Queen's University and other places. We hoped that ways and means would be found to develop a process. It was high-geared thinking.

David Morley had devised a scheme for republicans in June 1975 entitled 'Outline Scheme for Resettlement' which proposed an office in central Belfast under a coordinating committee with voluntary, probation and prison and paramilitary welfare group involvement. The loyalist document was entitled 'Proposals for a Resettlement Programme' and 'outlined in considerable detail many problems besetting prisoners and their families, both financially and emotionally during and after prolonged periods of imprisonment'.[2] Both documents were brought before the Camp Council which agreed on a submission to be drawn up by Gusty Spence for the NIO.

The office would provide:

> A place to which families of prisoners and others interested in their welfare, as well as discharged prisoners, could resort. There would be a suite of

> offices housing a probation office, a voluntary welfare office, a conference room and a waiting room. Within these offices could be fostered the relationships which we all desire, and which for too long have been absent.[3]

The downtown office plan had the private support of prison welfare officers who volunteered their services. Colin Crawford refers to it being a 'political forum' which would have facilitated increasing dialogue and cooperation between those who had engaged in violence. Most of the prisoners involved, including Gusty, saw it as part of the road to peace.

On 9 April 1976 a confidential memo referring to the downtown office was addressed to the UVF brigade staff from Gusty as commanding officer in Long Kesh. The project had faced a setback, but he remained confident:

> Unfortunately the negotiations concerning the Downtown Office and After Care, has been postponed and I am not surprised, in the light of the Provo attacks against the Prison Officers. But I am convinced that the Office will go ahead because the NI Office realise the potential, and will accommodate it.

Gusty went on to criticise David Morley:

> There is disgust amongst the different groups for the Provos and David Morley their Commanding Officer must resign. His credibility is gone. He should have stood up to his 'hard' men long since because I am convinced if the Camp Council's policies had been spelt out to all his men the more reasonable of them would have howled down the fascists.
>
> He has only himself to blame and you can see by the copy of his awful document that I sent you he is inconsistent and even irrational. I shall never forget his bland withdrawal in the face of the questioning by the NI Office and Prison Officials. I could never have faith in his word again and despite whatever else could be said about the republicans, in the past they were always reliable as far as their word was concerned. I am afraid gentlemen that this is symptomatic of our times because there are many so-called UVF men whose word I would not trust. I admit to being old-fashioned and believing in honour.

Gusty told me that David Morley had been constructive and enlightened but faced strong opposition from hardliners. Morley supported the downtown office concept but had to claw back when faced with virulent opposition. Hardliners did not want any form of cooperation with the NIO or other British authorities. However, the UDA, UVF, Official IRA and possibly even the INLA, remained committed.

But there were also unionist and other opponents. In May 1977 Conor

Cruise O'Brien reportedly attacked the scheme for 'giving status and dignity to murderers'.[4] Ian Paisley's Democratic Unionist Party (DUP) reacted with 'one message for the IRA – we seek their annihilation'. Harry West of the Unionist Party regarded such discussions as 'completely repugnant'. The Ulster Special Constabulary Association suggested that these 'secret meetings' could create 'total anarchy'.[5]

Nevertheless in August 1977 the UVF/RHC Special Category prisoners at Long Kesh prepared fifteen pages of detailed proposals for the NIO on a number of issues, including the downtown welfare centre proposal:

> We propose that a central office be set up in 'downtown' Belfast under the management of an accepted Welfare Officer. This Office could be used as a base where the representatives of the prisoners' voluntary welfare groups could meet, discuss and work for the common welfare of all prisoners and their relatives ...
>
> The downtown office would also provide a base or centre through which representatives of Prisoners' Voluntary Welfare Groups could carry on dialogue with representatives of the Northern Ireland Office, representatives of Official and Voluntary Welfare Groups and with each other ... The advantages of having these Groups based in a central office under the supervision of a recognised Welfare Officer would be tremendous ...

Despite Provisional rejection, Gusty felt they might still participate. He was a firm believer in what he referred to as the 'once-removed' form of dialogue. This meant that someone associated with something but not identified completely with it could be a representative.

But the promise of the downtown office was never realised. Gusty ascribes failure to

> Devious and unenlightened publicity, coupled with sensationalism. This went a long way towards thwarting our efforts and petty politicians scoring sectarian points made it easy for that little dictator Roy Mason to instruct his prison governors to ensure that there was no opportunity for prisoners' representatives to liaise and resolve the many problems they faced.[6]

In Gusty's view, a potentially important breakthrough was allowed to die. Reflecting on the demise of the hopes for the downtown office he wrote:

> There will be no way forward, no peace will reign and assimilation will not

take place, until the politicians, constitutionally and democratically elected, liaise, debate and resolve to end the torment which has beset us for so long.

The sharing of responsibility must become our aim, the removal of fear from our streets our task, the eradication of injustice, oppression and discrimination our sacred duty, and then, and not until then, will all our inhabitants walk forward in dignity, in pride and equality, knowing that all their aspirations are recognised, and that at long last they can attain and enjoy the happiness and contentment that has so long avoided them.

In the absence of political stability and justice there will be violence, and to achieve peace one has to be prepared to take that extra step – it's known as COMPROMISE.[7]

The advocacy of a form of responsibility/power sharing was not something that Gusty dreamed up after leaving Long Kesh. While in prison he had tried to explain why it was a good system. David Ervine recalled that as early as 1975:

I was talking to Gusty and he put forward a theory to a couple of us as we sat in the sun outside the study hut in Long Kesh. He came over and threw a 'hand grenade' into the middle of it to provoke debate. The one he chose that day was power sharing. I remember going off the wall saying, 'What? You must be joking.' He says, 'Hold on a minute, son, power sharing is the politics of the goldfish bowl.' A concept was being thrown to me and I'm trying to hone in on the 'politics of the goldfish bowl'. It means that politicians are there for everyone to see and if they are disingenuous it becomes obvious. Why not give it a try? Why not call the bluff of those who say they're alienated?

The bringing into use of the H Blocks in 1976 meant that informal contacts between loyalist and republican prisoners became more limited. Gusty said the cell system was different and people were no longer 'living cheek by jowl, they were semi-dependent. That's why prisons have cells, they divide people and this often means divide and conquer.'

While the downtown office was being discussed, the rate of sectarian killings in the streets of Northern Ireland reached alarming heights.[8] Killings perpetrated by the UVF were at an all-time high, and in 1975 UVF/RHC killings (100) for once outstripped PIRA killings (94).[9] Loyalist killings reflected deep concern about the intentions of the British government.[10] A cabinet subcommittee was then giving consideration to the possibility of withdrawal.[11] The sectarian killings were condemned in the *Orange Cross*:

> To those people perpetrating these heinous crimes we appeal to you to stop now. The Loyalist people do not want it and they do not condone or support the men carrying it out. It serves no purpose in ensuring our retention of the British link and most important of all, please remember – IT IS NOT A CRIME TO BE A ROMAN CATHOLIC.[12]

In a letter dated 17 January 1976 and signed by Gusty Spence as CO of the UVF in Long Kesh, reference is made to recent 'resignations within the Brigade Staff'. A demand was made that a new authority '*must* be constituted immediately before an irresponsible element is tempted to fill the vacuum'. While the men in Long Kesh had no particular bias in relation to the leadership, Gusty set out names of people who might constitute a 'Shadow Brigade Staff'. A new 'shadow' Brigadier was suggested together with four men as a 'Shadow Brigade Staff'. Two other senior officers could be co-opted if necessary.

A number of other roles had to be filled, the letter stated:

> Appointments to ATO [Armaments Technical Officer] and Armourer would be made from the most capable of our men whose task it would be to undertake an immediate inventory to determine just what arms, ammunition and explosives we have to hand and to ensure that these war materials do not fall into irresponsible hands.

The interim brigade staff would have the responsibility of appointing new battalion commanders including Paymaster and Quartermaster etcetera. Appointments would take place after discussion and would be a matter of discretion. The prisoners said their overriding concern was to act in the best interests of the UVF. The letter ended with a plea regarding the UVF: 'Please do not make it bleed any more.'

Billy Mitchell, former editor of the UVF magazine *Combat*, refers to a previous change in the outside leadership as a coup in which 'Tommy' had taken over. 'Tommy' was considered a weak leader and was ousted so that 'Mark' took over in a 'shadow' role. 'Mark', a veteran UVF man, was among those who had been interned in 1973.

'Mark' was to prove an able senior officer who saw the organisation through many difficulties and dangers. In his work he always had access to the wisest counsels available within the ranks of the Volunteers. Gusty remembers 'Mark' leaving Long Kesh:

> When he was leaving, he and I spoke at the wire. He said, 'What do you

> think I should do?' I asked, 'Do you want to become re-engaged with the UVF?' He said, 'Yes, I do.' 'Well,' I said, 'go to the UVF and say, "I want this job because I'm far more experienced and I have been there over a good number of years."' Give them all the valid reasons. The UVF had been elevating men who were completely inexperienced to senior positions. They hadn't got a clue. The UVF was drifting and all guerrilla organisations or military organisations need a political goal as well as knowledge of military and strategic ways, and that wasn't happening.
>
> When he went out, he told them that he wanted a senior role. He presented his case and was rewarded with a senior position. It wasn't as senior as his qualifications merited but at least he had a foot in the door. He was tolerant, he was patient, and ultimately he was rewarded, if 'reward' is the right term. I'm not sure getting a senior post, or the senior post within the UVF, was a 'reward'; believe you me, it's not. It is important but it's also a millstone round one's neck because you're on call twenty-four hours a day and you've to make all these awful decisions. Thankfully he was one of the men that eventually turned things round.

Gusty and other progressive elements within the UVF had been deeply concerned about the continuing sectarian killings and had tried to initiate an ongoing debate about how the killings could be eradicated or at least significantly reduced. Messages on the issue were now passed between the compounds and then surreptitiously forwarded to the British government. Permission was sought for prisoners, together with outside delegates, to hold a conference inside Long Kesh about the killings. Merlyn Rees consulted the governor and agreed, providing it was held in secret and the outsiders involved were not being sought for criminal offences. As a result the Anti-Sectarian Assassination Conference was held in Long Kesh in February 1976.

Two members of the clergy were present: Father Joachim, a Catholic priest and monk, and a Presbyterian minister, the Reverend A.N. Parker, who was a chaplain to Long Kesh and ministered locally near the Maze prison. Gusty chaired the meeting, and each paramilitary group sent two representatives or confidants from outside the camp. Gusty recalled that the commanding officers attending the conference were Jimmy Craig, UDA, P.J. Monaghan Official IRA, David Morley PIRA, Gusty Spence UVF and Frank Gallagher representing INLA. The accompanying two associates were considered necessary if they were to deal with the real issue.

According to writer Martin Dillon:

> When discussion began, Loyalists suggested that in return for an end to the killing of Catholic non-combatants, the IRA should cease killing off-duty policemen and soldiers particularly members of the Ulster Defence Regiment which had been set up as a replacement of the B Specials in 1970 as an integrated force of Catholics and Protestants to act in support of the British Army, but had soon become a force populated mainly by Protestants because Catholics were under threat of death from the IRA for being members of such a body. Catholic members were easily identified to the IRA, who lived within the Catholic community. The Provos insisted they should retain the right to kill police and members of the UDR when they were on the streets wearing uniform. There was no dissent from this proposition. Likewise each group retained the right to shoot members of each other's organisations while the war continued.[13]

The issue of legitimate targets was discussed in detail and some peripheral prisoner issues were briefly discussed. In Gusty's letter to Bob Hynds in 1981 he took a positive view of the outcome of the conference in the short term, but this advance was soon reversed:

> We were successful in eradicating the sectarian killing including the killing of off-duty UDR men until it did not suit other men's purposes that prisoners had so much power and things were manipulated so that everyone retreated back into their own wee trenches.

No minutes were kept of the conference but Gusty recalls:

> It was a frank meeting. It wasn't heated because everybody knew what they were there for. There was a level of cooperation but the minutiae of the issue were spoken about and I wasn't qualified to speak about that at all. That's why the two representatives from outside were present. There's no use a prisoner sitting down and saying 'I think certain things should be done' and this being rejected on the outside.

The majority of those present took a positive view of the conference but Sammy Smyth, a leading figure in the UDA, took a different line. He said that for him, a Catholic three-year-old child or a seventy-year-old Catholic woman were legitimate targets. Jimmy Craig, OC of the UDA, immediately told him to keep quiet. But he had signed his death warrant. Sammy Smyth had made injudicious remarks before and these caused him to be regarded with suspicion by members of his own organisation. Despite his sectarian views, he was paradoxically seen as being 'soft on republicans and dabbling in the politics of the left'.[14] Three weeks after the conference, on 10 March 1976, Samuel Smyth was shot dead by the PIRA.

The number of UVF/RHC killings fell from a total of 100 in 1975, to 71 in 1976. However IRA killings increased in the same period, from 94 to 139, as did UDA killings, which peaked at 50 in 1976 as opposed to 20 in 1975.[15] Clearly the Anti-Sectarian Assassination Conference had limited, if any, success in the short term. However, it was never Gusty's intention that a major change should be achieved after one short conference, and he continued periodically to raise the issue.

He addressed another letter to brigade staff on 9 April 1976 in which he referred to 'negative attitudes and confrontation within the prisons'. As far as Gusty's men were concerned, this had now come to an end. He also referred to attacks by the PIRA against the prison staff which, he said, 'alienated them even further from decent opinion'. He said the UVF must learn from the mistakes of the Provos and remove the remnants of the criminal element from their midst:

> I hope that you have gathered more opinion to your side so that you may put forward your more 'enlightened' policies. But you must not wait too long before moving. Sweep the last vestiges of that gangster regime away from about you and ensure that all our men see that democracy is once again amongst us. I for one do not desire a witch-hunt but those who have accumulated ill-gotten gains must not be allowed to enjoy them. Deprive them of everything and kick them out.

But how far had UVF men become more politically aware at this stage? In Gusty's view, only a small number had. Most were not interested in politics at all. However:

> The prison seminars involved men sitting down to explore and give a voice to UVF political thinking within the camp. We certainly had more time for political analysis, and opportunity to investigate radical ways forward. We also had some people on the outside, but unfortunately those of a political bent didn't have any command status at that time.

Yet the UVF outside generally reacted positively to Gusty's own questions and ideas:

> They were a bit nervous and always conscious of unionist politicians sniping at them and calling them communists and traitors. They expected Paisley to capitalise and say, 'Oh they're talking to the IRA and having secret meetings.' The UDA were nervous too because they had already felt

the sting of these people's tongues. They were trying to turn the people against the paramilitaries but the UVF and the UDA responded positively. Unfortunately it didn't last, but today loyalist paramilitary organisations have their own political outlets. Both the UDP and PUP are quite capable of taking on the so-called constitutional unionist politicians.

An article about Gusty appeared in the May 1976 edition of *Fortnight* magazine. The author, Anne Uprichard, in a reference to the Anti-Sectarian Assassination Conference, wrote about Gusty's efforts to negotiate an agreement between all paramilitary groups in order to halt sectarian killings:

Ironically, many people consider that Spence's release would be an unacceptable concession to extreme loyalism, when his influence seems most likely to be towards moderation and reassessment. As long as he remains in prison, his influence in any direction will stay limited.[16]

Gusty's approach, she said, had made him unpopular with some loyalist militants, and on a number of occasions his directions were virtually ignored by the UVF outside. During 1975, obscenities were scrawled over a document of his urging a ceasefire. Uprichard suggested that:

Time and voracious reading have changed his simplistic political views. To his colleagues, he hammers home the message that political development is vital for the Protestant working class; that the battle for Ulster is also about 'jobs and houses and schools and benefits'. Spence identifies strongly with the Protestant working class. Despite clear socialist sympathies, and friendly contacts with imprisoned Official Republicans, he has not been converted to Marxism, and continues to feel that Irish unity would undermine the interests of Ulster Protestants. He has to look for areas of common ground, which do not involve compromise of 'the ultimate principle'. These are easier to find within prison than outside it.[17]

This article also referred to Gusty's constantly 'trying to canvas some new scheme – most recently, the establishment of marriage counselling facilities in Long Kesh' to meet the needs of prisoners.

But central to all such developments was the need for discipline and order. Gusty had set out to establish a tightly disciplined regime inside Long Kesh and this in itself became, for some, a cause of resentment. One deputation came to him saying

'Sir, could we get reveille put back to half past eight?' I said, 'Yes, it would be the easiest thing in the world because it would be popular, but you're either soldiers or you're not.' 'Oh well, we're soldiers,' they said. Says I, 'There are children of five years old being wakened at half-past seven every morning, winter and summer, for school. Are you telling me that you're less hardy than five-year-old children?'

In prison anything that's new or that does not mirror yesterday, prisoners want to embrace it. Get the reveille put back to half past eight, and after that, 'If the lockers were on the wall it would give us a bit more room' – anything that diverts the mind from the sentence they are serving. I used to tell them, 'Look I could have you in palatial surroundings or in eighteen-carat-gold cells but you're still in jail and I can't give you what you want – freedom. I can't do that.'

Not only did I have to take a practical approach, I also had to take a psychological approach with the policies I was implementing. It was the practical coupled with the psychological. It had to be presented in a practical way but also finely tailored in a psychological way.

Billy Hutchinson confirmed Gusty's psychological approach:

While men were on the parade ground and Gusty had his back to them, he knew what they were doing because he knew his men so well. He knew their character and if someone was fidgeting, he knew who they were, and would have shouted, 'McCrea, stop that,' and McCrea would have wondered, 'How did he know? He must have eyes in the back of his head.' He had been inside so long he had worked out how people lived in prison.

He was a bit like Brian Clough and was someone who could manage men. He managed them because he knew the psychology of people. If you did something, you might have to clean out the ablutions or brush out the compounds. You might be given fifteen minutes or half an hour of fatigues. That's the way it was done. There was no brutality. Gusty's system wasn't about the strong surviving and the weak going down, it was about everybody working for each other so that everyone survived without bullying.

One ex-internee said, 'I was exhausted polishing boots and scrubbing floors and drilling but I realise now it brought us through and kept our self-respect.'[18] Everyone played his part in the scrubbing and cleaning. After David Ervine broke the rules, he recalls:

I had to sweep the yard, clean the toilets and things like that when I was caught, as I often was, infracting the rules. It was the cleanest place in the world. People said, 'You could have eaten your dinner off the floor.' They made sure it was absolutely spotless and it seemed they would plant dirt to make sure that someone was cleaning the place.

Ervine also told me:

Gusty was a man who tried to talk problems out. Numerous people were unhappy about the amount of military discipline in the compounds but Gusty did that for many reasons. Military discipline was there to keep people occupied and to achieve a sense of cohesive control and it was interesting for the authorities to see how this was achieved. It created a figurehead who could with great capacity negotiate for better conditions from a position of strength.

But of course not everybody was happy. When you have more than three people you never have a homogenous happy group. So in Long Kesh there were those who were detractors, and Gusty's approach was to listen. If you had a good argument he would hear it but in the end of the day he was the commanding officer. He would hear what you had to say but *he* made the decisions.

Billy Hutchinson was aware of the complaints about Gusty's strict discipline but he saw value in this:

If a lot of prisoners are hanging about without work they can get up to all kinds of mischief. Gusty tried to fill the day for them and to make sure they remained disciplined. He created a whole education system from which I benefited because I listened to him. One of the things Gusty always insisted on was the need, not just to exercise the body, but also to exercise the mind. If prisoners lie about all day and do nothing, the system wins. They had to beat the system by keeping physically and mentally alert. Not only did he give us this advice, he actually built the systems to work through. Long Kesh was like a microcosm of the outside world. Everything was there for us, and Gusty made sure we had access to books and the library. We had an education system, opportunities for physical activity with gyms in the compounds and football three times a week.

All of that was hard fought for and won and the system was brilliant. Some of the seminars were unbelievable. Gusty knew that certain issues would come up during Camp Council meetings so he would throw these issues into the seminar to hear people's views. Often people didn't know that they were giving him a view. People said 'Gusty doesn't listen to us anyway, he does his own thing.' But he didn't, he had ways of getting people's views and using them to get them what they needed. But not everybody saw the benefit of that.

Gusty's approach to discipline and organisation served to raise the status of loyalists even with the IRA:

> The Provos always saw themselves as the *crème de la crème* and they saw loyalists as a bit of a joke because they were politically immature. But there developed a grudging respect for the UVF because of their discipline, their turn out and the mere fact that they saw themselves as soldiers and behaved like soldiers.

A former UVF prisoner in Long Kesh wrote to a local paper saying that in his five years there 'I never once saw a man subjected to physical violence in a UVF compound.' He went on:

> ... what I did see was UVF men taught to keep themselves clean, disciplined and self-reliant. I saw them march and drill in a military fashion, which would have done credit to the brigade of Guards. I saw them detailed to pick up every scrap of cigarette ends and matchsticks. I saw them polish boots and wash clothes. I saw them clean pots and pans and other cooking and eating utensils till they shone and I saw them and took part with them when they proudly marched behind their union jacks and Ulster flags and regimental colours ...
>
> It would be difficult to say that one served a term of imprisonment 'proudly' – but to me it would not be difficult to say – indeed it would be true to say – that I was very proud to share a compound with some noble and true Ulstermen.[19]

Gusty took a pride in the fact that not one man was ever physically punished:

> The worst punishment was that a prisoner would have to leave the compound. I put some out of the compound for disobedience of orders. That was the biggest punishment I could apply. If you don't obey UVF orders you can't take advantage of whatever conditions men have fought long and hard for. We wouldn't permit it. Some people left voluntarily and they would come to me first. For some it was for domestic reasons, which was fair enough, but I required a statement to the effect, 'I am leaving the compound of my own free will.'

David Ervine confirmed that they avoided physical punishment:

> In the five and a half years I spent there I never saw the UVF carry out one physical punishment. Other groups did but there was no wee guy in the dinner queue being pushed out of the way by some bigger guy. That was

never going to be the case. All were to be treated as equal in Gusty's philosophy.

I found senior UVF people surprisingly tolerant of new ideas. This was in stark contrast to the suspicious intolerance found among some Ulster Protestant fundamentalists.

Billy Hutchinson agreed with this and with my suggestion that Gusty was compassionate:

> Gusty is one of the most compassionate people you could meet and even though he was the father figure he had time to talk with people. If someone's relative had died or they were ill he would have had a chat with them. That was a side that people didn't always see because he was always barking out orders. That was the way he had to do it because he couldn't 'run with the hare and hunt with the hounds'. That didn't mean that he didn't have friends. He would have come in and said, 'Are you going for a walk,' and I would have joined him. That was just the way he was. He always kept himself aloof, but that was because he knew that next day he might have to discipline someone.

A letter was sent from Compound 21, Long Kesh POW Camp, to UVF officers and men outside on 2 November 1976. It was signed 'A.A. Spence, Commanding Officer', together with the OCs of Compounds 18, 19 and 21, and the adjutant of the UVF/RHC personnel. They pledged to support their comrades throughout the UVF 'in freedom, in their struggle to resist the removal of "special category" status' from colleagues charged with offences committed after 1 March 1976, many of whom would be housed in the new H Blocks. They also pledged full support to the 'present leadership of the UVF' and declared their readiness to engage in 'extreme action' in support of political status.

Merlyn Rees, who had supported the introduction of special category status in 1972, announced its demise in February 1976, saying:

> This is the key to the restoration of control – the loss of control was the most objectionable feature of special category. The aimless existence followed by special category prisoners in compounds is no preparation for return to normal living. Henceforth all new prisoners will be required to work . . . While they are working, prisoners will be required to wear prison clothing and if they want to enjoy the privileges available under prison rules they will have to earn them.[20]

Clearly it was misleading to suggest that UVF special category prisoners followed an aimless existence at Long Kesh. Gusty rejected such views and had already demonstrated fierce resistance to 'control' in Crumlin Road jail. He immediately recognised the futility of reintroducing 'control'. He also rejected the assumption that political status and the compound system created indiscipline. He told journalist Alan Whitsitt in November 1976:

> Here in the UVF/RHC compounds fighting and bullying are non-existent. There are no 'tobacco barons' to live like parasites on the misfortunes of others. There are no cliques of 'hard men' to impose their will on their weaker colleagues. There are no schemers or skivers honing their wits in order to obtain more privileges than their fellow men. In our compounds the law of the jungle has been erased from the minds and thoughts of the prisoners ...
>
> We abhor meaningless work and would resist any attempt to have imposed labour forced on us. We are, however, willing to carry out meaningful duties, for such work breeds contentment. My men look upon their compounds as their homes, however reluctantly, and are as anxious and able to maintain and improve their homes as any householder on the outside.[21]

On 17 November 1976 the commanding officers of the PIRA, UDA, UVF, Irish Republican Social Party (IRSP) and Official IRA prisoners in the compounds proposed a series of seminars. Sixteen themes for debate were listed, including subjects such as reconciliation, political status and its phasing-out, Britain and the Irish Republic, culture and art in Ireland. Nothing came of the proposal. The governor, in Gusty's words, 'wouldn't entertain it'. This was because the government had recently withdrawn special category status from newly convicted prisoners: henceforth, prisoners convicted of political offences were to be treated as criminals, held in cells under the control of prison officers and made to work (see Chapter 16 for the battle over 'criminalisation').

On 19 November 1976 Gusty, as CO of the UVF prisoners, issued a letter from Compound 21 saying that he and his men supported political status and 'would not be found wanting when the struggle intensified'. During the previous week they had undertaken a publicity exercise through a local paper explaining the campaign and answering government propaganda. The compound prisoners retained political status throughout, a 'privilege' Gusty enjoyed until he left Long Kesh in 1985.

However, Gusty also explicitly told the UVF leadership outside that some prisoners were not, in his view, politically motivated and were abusing political status. Actions were being taken by the organisation outside that could not be defended and had 'brought the organisation into disrepute'. He called upon the UVF leadership to 'denounce these acts and their perpetrators lest our detractors be given genuine ammunition with which to beat us'. Gusty's reference was to the vicious sectarian murder campaign. He then asked for written answers to specific questions.

First, was the UVF leadership prepared to take 'stern disciplinary action against the "gangsters" within our own organisation?' They were engaged in robberies and 'atrocious murders' and there could no 'winking' or account taken of the personalities involved. Justice must 'be done and seen to be done'.

In a reply dated 26 November 1976 and signed 'Capt William Johnston', the UVF brigade staff said they were drawing up a code of conduct that would be enforced. They accepted there had been 'discrepancies' and said they would try to ensure that these would be eradicated. They requested access to any relevant information gathered during debriefing sessions. This should be forwarded to the 'committee'.

Second, Gusty asked the UVF whether, upon entering negotiations on political status, he would be given the rights of a plenipotentiary with 'full power to make a deal on behalf of the UVF', and if they were prepared to stick by this. Would they object to the UDA or republicans participating in such discussions, and would they supply 'two other men' to take part in the negotiations?

Gusty supported opting for political status but wanted to know if the UVF leadership was really behind this. Some prisoners who had lost political status now conformed to prison rules and regulations. Many had no prison experience to draw on, and Gusty believed a hunger strike was looming in the near future:

> I wanted to see what their determination was like. I had been through the mill myself for political status, and we wanted to be the architects because those moving into the H Blocks were relatively inexperienced. They knew very little about prison life or how to mount a strategic campaign and we had sincerely warned the NIO that ultimately there would be some catastrophic happening, culminating in a hunger strike.
>
> I was not sure of the calibre of men coming into the H Blocks because I didn't know them. I needed to know if they would see things through to

> their logical conclusion. We didn't want to be left with egg on our faces, and I was trying to get through to these people that they couldn't depend on any form of political support from unionist politicians. There was not a hope in hell of that, yet they needed some form of political clout or sympathy on the outside.

The UVF replied on the issue of political status saying that 'Jack', a senior UVF officer, had already suggested to Gusty that he try to open talks with the NIO on an acceptable compromise for all parties. A joint committee with the UDA had already been created to pursue all avenues to achieve political status. The UVF accepted the need for a united front and had no objections to the inclusion of republican groups in the negotiations. There was an emphasis, however, on the solidarity between the UVF, RHC and UDA on the outside, and they hoped this could be matched inside.

Gusty's third question was on the vexed question of sectarian assassinations. Sectarian killing was always in danger of spiralling out of control:

> Is the UVF willing to take part along with the UDA and republican groups in talks to investigate ways and means of curtailing or eradicating sectarian assassinations within our society, thereby enabling the recently advocated Ulster independence policy time to be properly investigated and digested by a war-weary general public as well as by those political groups really interested in finding a solution to our many and diverse problems? And if agreement is attained on the question of political assassinations, will you ensure and undertake repressive disciplinary measures against those wilfully disobeying direct UVF orders?

Gusty wanted the UVF to face the question 'Are they just a murder gang?'

> I had already had some dialogue with the republicans and with the UDA about setting up some form of seminar on these awful killings. We couldn't get them stopped but we could get them curtailed, and when the enlightened leadership took over they sent two men from the outside to take part in the seminar.

In reply to the question of a seminar about sectarian assassinations, the UVF leadership said that it would only take part in such a seminar in the context of 'A COMPLETE CESSATION OF ALL VIOLENCE'. This cessation would have to apply to the murders of UDR, RUC and army personnel, as well as to 'what the republicans term economic bombings'.

There were, however, to be no further anti-sectarian conferences. This was not because of any reluctance on the part of the UVF. Roy Mason had replaced Merlyn Rees as Secretary of State in September 1976, and he put a stop to all such initiatives. Gusty told me that Mason had 'knocked everything on its head' and would permit no dialogue between the different factions or even between prisoners and the NIO.

Gusty had raised the issue of independence for Northern Ireland in an effort to focus minds on politics. He never advocated independence and in fact saw it as a contradiction as far as unionists were concerned:

> When we read in the papers that the UVF were toying with independence it came as a big shock to us. Independence went against our principles; it even went against the very reason why the UVF had been formed in 1912 and perhaps why it was reconstituted in the twenties and the thirties and again in the sixties. It was worthy of investigation but not serious investigation.

The fourth question in Gusty's letter referred directly to Lenny Murphy, leader of the notorious Shankill Butchers, who was then imprisoned in the H Blocks. Murphy had also been in the compounds and while there he tried to team up with like-minded people. Gusty separated them and kept Murphy under discipline, but now that Murphy was in the H Blocks, he had become a law unto himself.

The brutal nature of the terrible killings in which the Butchers were involved represented a deep stain on the character of the Shankill Road.[22] Gusty asked the leadership:

> Will the UVF please clarify the situation concerning the structure of the UVF command in the H Blocks within Long Kesh because it has been brought to my attention that Volunteer L. Murphy presumes to be 'in command' and will take no orders from anyone except the 'outside' (whatever that may mean)? I have no wish to engage in personalities but I will not have this upstart telling prison authorities that 'he does not take orders from Gusty Spence'. I either command Long Kesh and those therein or I do not. I expect a direct answer from you and I want Volunteer Murphy informed of your answer, whatever it may be, so as again there will be no misunderstandings.

In reply, the UVF leadership did not mention Murphy by name but instead affirmed Gusty Spence's position as overall commanding officer.

> In order to clear any misunderstanding which may exist concerning H Block. H Block is part and parcel of Long Kesh, all UVF/RHC personnel in H

Block come under the command of the Long Kesh Commanding Officer ie A.A. Spence. We realise that there may be problems re communication with H Block but are confident that the CO will be able to overcome this.

In his letter, Gusty also referred to previous letters to the leadership, some of which had never been responded to, while others had been treated in an offhand manner or even 'lost' or mislaid. Gusty demanded feedback on the previous documents as well as an undertaking that in future the UVF leadership would keep prisoners fully informed on issues such as 'independence':

> Our men in Long Kesh did not know that the UVF were in favour of Independence until they read it in the pages of the Belfast *News Letter* and we also saw that we supported the RUC!! Common courtesy demanded that we should have been asked our opinions before such serious steps were taken ... Will the UVF in future consult 260 of their imprisoned Volunteers before such major policy decisions are finally implemented and published?

The UVF accepted that some documents had indeed been 'mislaid' or cast aside but said this would not happen again. 'In future any correspondence received from any camp will be discussed by Brigade Staff and Battalion Commanders and an explicit reply shall be sent back.' They added that they would try to ensure that everyone was kept informed on policy matters. The UVF would adopt whichever policies were in the best interests of Ulster loyalists.

Gusty also referred in his letter to a kidnapping case. It involved a publican's son who was held to ransom. Elements of the UVF leadership were thought to be involved but the man escaped, the leadership came crashing down and a more enlightened leadership took over, some of whom were veterans from the 1960s. Gusty said:

> I am very angry with all the retrograde publicity that will fall about the shoulders of the UVF. You must honestly ask yourselves – have we relegated ourselves to a purely gangster organisation? Where are we going and are we kidding ourselves on about being a military machine or are we becoming somewhat of a joke!

However he gave 'full credit to those men who had tried to pull the organisation from the gutter after a bunch of criminals put it there'.

Billy Hutchinson accepts that paramilitary organisations inevitably recruit some people who turn out to be criminally motivated. The UVF had however been relatively free from criminality until 1974 when it was deproscribed:

> When the organisation was made legal we got the problems because people could do it openly and freely. They could run about saying they were UVF men and not be charged whereas in 1972, before the recruitment drive, people wondered if the UVF was even in existence.

While Gusty clearly acknowledged that criminal elements were involved, in 1976 he said that the UVF were 'not mindless gunmen and criminals'.[23] They had carried out what they saw as their patriotic duty and would not 'accept the role of scapegoat'.[24] Politicians had incited them to violence and then failed to provide strong leadership, so guilt had to be shared.

On 14 December 1976 Gusty proposed that a 'full and impartial Court of Inquiry be constituted', composed of ten or twelve of 'our most senior officers', because of dissension within the UVF. The main cause of the unrest appears to have been the 'recent kidnapping case and the aftermath of that affair', in which the Brigadier had called for an inquiry, which was initially rejected.

An inquiry was eventually held but the centrally involved No. 1 Battalion would not accept its findings and the meeting ended in deadlock. The result was that 'In the interest of the organisation as a whole and the welfare of the prisoners, the Brigadier and the Headquarters Staff stood themselves down, and left the room.' A report stated that the issue remained unresolved and 'it would appear that the motto For God and Ulster no longer means anything'.

On 25 January 1977, five OCs – Desmond Grew of the IRSP, Gusty Spence of the UVF, James Scullion of the PIRA, William Sloan of the UDA and Adrian Clarke of the Official IRA – issued a joint statement which was smuggled out and became front-page news in the Belfast *News Letter.* The newspaper, somewhat confusingly in view of loyalist demands for segregation, said that the statement 'poignantly directs the way forward in Ulster in one word – integration'.

The OCs attacked 'separate schools, separate adolescence, separate places of entertainment, separate ghettoes and in many cases separate employment environs':

> In Long Kesh we, republicans and loyalists, have attempted to bridge the gap by engaging in constructive dialogue without conceding principles, but

now the Government no longer permits our representatives to meet and discuss our mutual problems ... The prison authorities played no part in making the peace except to accommodate a series of face-to-face meetings.

The OCs did *not*, however, accept integration within the prisons. This could only come about in the long term through the prisoners' choice: 'If integration was to come about it must be sought by the prisoners themselves, and it must be a gradual process, just like what Mr Mason is trying to do with the local politicians.' The prisoners had achieved mutual accommodation. This was not integration; rather, it involved circumstances in which dialogue became possible. As far as integration was concerned: 'It is the most natural thing in the world for people with different political, cultural and religious philosophies and affiliations to cling together in time of adversity.'[25]

Other new ideas and practices, related to education within the prison, continued to develop. This is evidenced by 'Prison Camp UVF Standing Orders' relating to education and library facilities dated 1 November 1978 and prepared by Billy Mitchell, the administration officer. A full analysis of these thirty standing orders is not possible within the confines of this book, but clearly they represent a radical approach to education within the prison. I quote directly from the document:

1 Education is an essential function of Society and the UVF has an obligation to create and maintain structures and services sufficient to attend to the educational needs of its personnel and to furnish them with the indispensable means for improving their academic and cultural level.
2 The UVF Education Programme shall be organised as an integral part of the 'compound culture' and shall be aimed at:
3
- Achieving the harmonious and full development of the human personality
- Creating opportunities for cultural and academic improvement
- Preparing personnel for social and community service upon release
- Stimulating political awareness
- Developing the spirit of human solidarity

Standing Order 19 states that 'The UVF shall not permit personnel to subject themselves to the interrogation or assessment processes demanded by the Prison Regime for those undergoing education courses.' Standing Order 23 lists a number of reasons why UVF personnel were not permitted to participate in the current Prison Vocational Training Scheme. Participation would mean, for example, that they would be forced to surrender political status and to 'criminalize themselves'. They would have to leave the compounds and enter the H Blocks, and the order states that 'the Prison methods of "control and punishment" militate against initiative and personal responsibility & create an atmosphere which is hostile to constructive training and work.'

In contrast, the prisoners' own educational scheme was to be largely self-motivated and self-organised by the UVF prisoners. Many had already experienced the negative and damaging effects of the state educational system before joining the UVF. Some had experienced at first hand the debilitating effects of 'failure' under the divisive selective system. It can be argued that the prisoners, by demonstrating their ability to organise this system inside prison, confirmed that talent outside was being wasted in a system geared to meet the needs of the middle class.

By April 1979, the prisoners' education system faced further difficulties in that, according to a detailed report by Billy Mitchell, a number of books were inexplicably censored:

> There seems to be no problem with third-rate trash such as novels dealing with sex and violence, but when it comes to educational books the censors seem to take a hard line.

Mitchell then listed nine books which the censors had rejected without explanation. Among these were a commentary on St Luke's Gospel by Lenski, *The Romantic Poets* by Graham Hough and various other serious works. A qualified teacher had donated all the listed books to the students at Long Kesh. Other books not listed were given by relatives but censored by the authorities.

The authorities had already demonstrated their pettiness over other reading materials. Gusty showed me a large pile of magazines in his home entitled *History of the 20th Century*. One copy dated 1968 had the words, 'Spence C. 21 Security' written on the cover. This edition dealt with the Home Rule crisis of 1912. It had been confiscated in 1977, presumably lest it encourage UVF ideas and activity. The magazines had been given to Gusty by his nephew, but this copy was withheld until his release.

15

Resignation

On the Twelfth of July 1977 Gusty delivered an oration to the UVF prisoners, again advocating dialogue and negotiation rather than war. He began by speaking about persecution in Ireland and asked, 'Should we not be defending the rights of all men, whatever their calling, in Ulster?'

> I submit that it is fear that makes one people oppress another, and until such times as we abolish fear in our society we are always going to have oppression and misguided persons to implement it. We are living in the most socially and legalistically oppressive society in the Western Hemisphere, the manifestations of which are strewn over that society like scabs. Polarisation complete, with one section or community cut off from the other except for some middle-class contacts which appear to be concerned more about their class than community. Jails filled to overflowing and legislation that the apartheid countries would envy ...
>
> The fears of the Roman Catholics will not go away because a bunch of

> bigoted unionist politicians say so, and make no mistake about this word 'Unionist' because we are unionists too, even though we could never agree with these fascists who hold the reins of power. Do they not realise that the IRA was a natural manifestation of Catholic fears just as the UVF/UDA were born from loyalist fear?

Gusty went on to speak about the intolerance, paranoia and scapegoating that had plagued Northern Ireland:

> We in Northern Ireland are plagued with super-loyalists who are not content to be ordinary. These people are the witch-hunters – Ulster's Senator McCarthys – who enter debate and the newspaper columns armed with the tar brush, the innuendo, the lie, and you will find that they can usually shout louder than most. If one does not agree with their bigoted and fascist views then one is a 'taig lover' at best or a 'communist' at worst. They are adept at labelling those who disagree with them.

Gusty called upon the paramilitaries to take the initiative in ending the futility of the 'war':

> The politicians seemingly cannot or will not give us the peace we so earnestly desire, so I therefore call upon the paramilitaries – all the warring factions – to call a universal ceasefire, to open dialogue with each other in order to pursue ways and means of making such a ceasefire permanent. Eventually loyalist and republican must sit down together for the good of our country if we claim to be patriots.

Those who consider themselves traditional unionists rejected this advice, but at the end of July 1977 two senior UVF men, Billy Hutchinson and Billy Mitchell, issued a letter from within the prison strongly supporting Gusty's position.

The letter illustrates the kind of tensions and struggles faced by the UVF as they tried to move beyond the violence. They said that despite rejection by the usual people, Gusty's sentiments 'must be commended to all true patriots who wish to see the present crisis in Ulster brought to a speedy end without loss of principle'.

They reflected upon the thinking of the UVF in 1974:

> Some of us held similar views as long ago as early 1974 but, to our eternal sorrow, did not have the moral courage to pursue these policies ... Instead we espoused the policies of 'populism' for fear that we would be branded as disloyal by the vast army of super-Prods who have so much to say and

> so little to offer concerning the violence and bloodshed that has ravaged our fair Province.

Advocating radical changes in 1974 had brought charges of betrayal upon the UVF leadership in the jail. Yet they successfully laid a foundation for the peace process of the 1990s. In their 1977 letter, Mitchell and Hutchinson went on to write, perhaps somewhat prematurely, about the changes sweeping the UK and Northern Ireland:

> The forces of modern-day enlightenment are shaking away old prejudices and uprooting ancient myths. An age of upheaval is undermining and toppling long-established systems of political and sectarian tribalism, status and belief. An older order is dying, with all the ugly brutality, turbulence and bloodshed that has attended other throes of change in the past.

Revenge and hitting back, they observed, represented the apogee of thinking for many unionists, who appeared to have lost the ability to think ahead:

> We are stumbling blindly, trapped by our own moral adolescence, and death. We are a land of 'patriotic' giants (super-Prods) and ethical infants. We know more about contention and strife than we do about contentment and love; more about tribalism and division than about unity and coexistence; more about killing than about living.

A two-day UVF seminar was held in Compound 21 on 5 and 6 September 1977 at the request of the CO, Gusty Spence. The intention was 'that a paper be prepared in questionnaire form for the consideration of Brigade Staff'.

On Monday 5 September, twenty-seven Volunteers were addressed by Gusty on the principles of democracy and policy-making within a paramilitary organisation. Other issues included the rate of UVF arrests, resources and weaponry, the objectives of constructive criticism, and the need for prisoner interest in the welfare of the UVF.

The first item raised by the Volunteers was whether the UVF would become more politically involved. Some felt they should become a ginger [pressure] group, while others felt the government would try to smash any attempt to 'go political'. The meeting agreed on the need for a political stance to attain 'respect and recognition within the community as a progressive and constructive patriot body'. This stance should be based on a 'social conscience' and identified with the social problems of the people.

Appropriate questions on these topics were to be forwarded to the brigade staff. If they agreed with the ideas, they were to be asked for plans 'to formulate a political philosophy'. If they disagreed, they were to explain why.

A discussion followed on disunity within loyalist paramilitary groupings. It was agreed that some form of unity was essential if they were to move towards a common goal. The brigade was to consider setting up a joint study group with other groups. Internal unity was discussed, and agreement was reached on 'strict military discipline' and the eradication of gangsterism.

Those present agreed that the membership needed to be pruned and the UVF required restructuring. Among the questions was one asking if the brigade was 'prepared to expel the gangsters from the UVF'. Issues related to the H Blocks were raised and it was agreed that a plan should be drawn up in support of those prepared to 'go on the blanket'. Among the questions for brigade staff was one on plans for booklets and pamphlets on prison conditions. The seminar was then adjourned pending a report to be drawn up for ratification.

Two months later, on Remembrance Day, 11 November 1977, Gusty gave an oration to the assembled UVF prisoners. He made a dramatic appeal to all paramilitaries to lay down their arms:

> We can never repay those who gave their lives for us and it is futile to try. We can, however, keep faith with those who have passed on, solemnly, and in a manner befitting their passing whilst at the same time promising that their sacrifice has not been in vain and further deaths are completely unnecessary in the name of patriotism.
>
> This is not a morning for overt militarism, but by our calling we are soldiers and therefore can only offer soldiers' often inadequate words. The only true testimony to the dead is the abolition of war, fear, oppression and injustice. The dead were no different from you or I, having the same hopes and fears, likes and dislikes, loves and hates, and simply aspired to a better life for their loved ones and themselves, and yet they were caught in the net and finished their lives bleeding to death in some place long forgotten. Sassoon comments thus:
>
> ... when soldier lads pass by,
> Sneak home and pray you'll never know,
> The hell where youth and laughter go.[1]

In the name of government we are expendable and simply cannon fodder, and no gentlemanly rules of war can gloss over the fact that war is evil ...

When we are labelled 'terrorists' we will smile the smile of the knowing and think that in a so-called 'legitimate' war we would be dressed in a uniform of their choice, having been stupid enough to have volunteered in the first place after having listened to their impassioned, patriotic and intimidating appeals, questioning our manhood if we had not willingly volunteered. The war situation in Northern Ireland has changed dramatically and requires serious and radical re-appreciation on the part of the paramilitaries.

Further violence is useless and counterproductive since the aim of the loyalists for self-determination has been achieved. There is a need for reconciliation with our neighbours, whose aspirations differ from ours. Negotiations and dialogue can fill the vacuum of violence. It will take courage, of course, and will mean give and take on both sides, but I am confident that with honesty and goodwill a breakthrough can be achieved in our present polarisation logjam.

He continued:

War is obscene and there is no glory in it, and in its wake there follows bitterness and recrimination, sorrow and heartbreak, hatred, contempt and vengeance.

It is so simple to be destructive and bitter and it takes very little courage, so let us therefore be courageous and constructive, even should we stand alone. We are all victims of the violence permeating our society. We are the living dead entombed in many cases for a lifetime, and a broken mind can be equated with the handicap of a broken body. Like that paraplegic we do not want pity, just understanding and patience.

The only true testimony to the dead is peace, otherwise their passing has been for no purpose and our tears will be false.

Let the rattle of oratory and the volleys of words be heard instead of bombs and bullets – we need the strategy of political policies in place of battle plans and let us face one another across the negotiating table as opposed to no man's land. Let us reconcile and permit the grass and flowers to grow over the battlefields just as they have at the Somme and Passchendaele. And lastly let us forget past dissensions and resolve to pass on to our children the fruitful lessons which cost us so high a price in life and human misery, so that they may never know the hell and barbarity through which we had to pass.[2]

Gusty's appeals for peace did not receive universal acclaim, although he retained the full support of his men in prison.

In a letter to the press he replied to comments that had been made about 'my men and myself' in Long Kesh. He said his men supported him one hundred per cent and went on, 'I have made two appeals for peace in Northern Ireland and for having done so I make no apology.'

Gusty had crossed a Rubicon and would not retreat on the commitment he had made in 1974. Rather, he became more determined than ever that there had to be a better way. It was at this time that Trevor West, a Dublin senator and academic at Trinity College met him at Long Kesh. West was already in contact with 'Alex', a former UVF man interned in 1973, who had studied at Trinity. 'Alex' was a rugby player who held pronounced Protestant views. He had appeared on TV during a St Patrick's Night debate in the 1970s and West found his views very progressive.

It was 'Alex' who West referred to in an article in *Fortnight* in 1978:

> A former inmate of Long Kesh, who already held a university degree, has gone so far as to remark that he learnt as much in his six months in Long Kesh as he had done in his four undergraduate years. There is little doubt that many of those who have been in Long Kesh have developed a much healthier respect for people 'on the other side'.[3]

West met 'Alex' on a number of occasions, and 'Alex' told him that if he wanted to understand hardline loyalist feeling he should talk with Gusty Spence. He explained that West could get into the prison on a family pass, so West contacted Gusty's son-in-law Winston Rea, now out of prison, and accompanied him on a visit to Long Kesh with Ulick O'Connor, a writer with a keen interest in northern affairs:

> Needless to say we didn't know the ropes. We were searched with everyone else and then passed to another hut then searched again and finally we arrived at a hut to be confronted by a man who was obviously the senior Prison Officer. I stood in front of him, stuck out my arms expecting another frisking, only to hear him say, 'At ease, men, I'm Gusty Spence!'[4]

Gusty had an agenda prepared and he and his visitors tried to get through it quickly. He wanted to hear southern opinion on the north. His visitors were flabbergasted to meet such an organised, humorous, optimistic, articulate and well-informed individual, whose enthusiasm for Irish history seemed to know no bounds.

West was so impressed that he wrote another article for *Fortnight* in December 1977, referring to 'prophetic voices' in the north. The liberals and politicos, he said, were now exhausted and without a forum, so it was necessary to look away from the churches and upper strata and 'right at the other end of the scale':

> A prophecy and a vision has emerged from (or been smuggled out of) the Maze Prison in Long Kesh ... In a Remembrance Day speech in November [Gusty Spence] made an appeal for Peace in Ulster declaring that further violence was useless and that the Loyalist aim of self-determination had been achieved ... He has helped to give dignity to the lives of those people who, however much we may abhor their actions, are human beings like the rest outside Long Kesh and who at some stage will have to be rehabilitated into society.

He went on to say that 'everything points to the need for a speedy and dramatic review of Gusty's case': 'The Peace People have said that "he is possibly a great man". From the South he looks like a saint. Dublin has its Matt Talbott, why not Belfast's Gusty Spence?'[5]

Gusty had this to say about Trevor West:

> I found him open-minded, warm, aye indeed affectionate, and extremely quick on the uptake. Whenever I was making points which would have been obscure to the normal person, Trevor was on them like a terrier. Meeting Trevor West certainly encouraged me to keep hammering away. I was still commanding officer when he came. He brought Ulick O'Connor, who was into Irish history, and I had a good warm relationship with him.

Ulick O'Connor had told West he wanted to meet Gusty after coming across Gusty's letter to Joe McCann's widow.

West remembers that one of the loyalist prisoners they met wore a Fáinne (a badge indicating progress in the Irish language). Gusty himself only gained a smattering of Irish, although some loyalists had become reasonably proficient in Irish.

Nevertheless, the extent of loyalist prisoners' knowledge of Irish was exaggerated in some press reports. One of these said that 'at least one hundred former and present inmates of the loyalist compounds at Long Kesh wear the badge denoting competence in the language'.[6] The author of this had probably misheard Gusty when he said that they had had a 100 per cent pass rate in Irish. In a letter dated 18 November 1977 dealing with a number of inaccurate reports, Gusty said:

> I have five men in my compounds, proud Loyalists, UVF men, who have attained their Fáinne in the Irish language. I also have sixteen other men studying the Irish language and who hope to attain their proficiency badges in the near future. Twenty others of my men are studying Spanish, French and German in accordance with an educational policy that encompasses remedial to Open University.

Gusty responded in his letter to another press inaccuracy suggesting he had donated £100 to a Sister Joannes (Molly Meenan):

> I believe in being unconventional since convention in Northern Ireland does not appeal to me at all, and it is time that we laid a few ghosts. I happen to know a lady who is a teaching nun and I am proud that she considered me a friend of hers. I have known her for over twenty years and have yet to meet a more sincere Christian. I would love to have given her £100 as reported, but I am afraid that I have not a hundred shillings in my account. Her name is Sister Joannes, she is teaching in Kitale in Kenya, and she abounds in courage and humanity.

The story of Sister Joannes is a fascinating one. She came from the Grosvenor Road close to where the Spence family lived in Hertford Street:

> There was a little shop half way up Elizabeth Street, at the corner of Selina Street, known as Wee Mary's, close to where we lived. It was our neighbourhood shop. John Meenan, a barrister who had a spinal problem, owned it. I believe his wife Molly was a civil servant at Stormont. [Mary J. Meenan was a shopkeeper and Justice of the Peace, according to the 1967 Belfast Directory.] They answered the needs of the neighbours at night with two ounces of cooked ham or whatever, or Molly might dress and comfort some wee girl after she had fallen. She was a very caring person and my children were in and out of the shop and she knew the whole family. Many a time I had a yarn with her. John the barrister died and I lost contact with Molly Meenan.

It seemed unlikely that Gusty would ever see Molly again. However, one day in Long Kesh in the mid-1970s Gusty was sent for. A nun had come up to see him.

> This appeared strange to some people but it didn't strike me as strange so I went down to see this nun. She was a teaching nun, and it was Molly Meenan after all those years. She wanted to remove the top of her habit so as not to cause me embarrassment. 'Me?' I says. 'Don't you dare; you keep that on.' She had taken the name of Sister Joannes and was a member of the

Sisters of Mercy of Clonmel, Tipperary. We talked over old times and she told many humorous stories.

But Molly also told Gusty she had cancer of the marrow:

'Gusty, I'm slowly dying but I want to do as much as I possibly can before I die.' She returned to her work in Kitale and later died in a nuns' home in Clonmel. The Mother Superior wrote to me to inform me that Molly had died.

Gusty's later years at Long Kesh were particularly difficult. He had rejected violence as the way forward for Northern Ireland and as far back as 1974 he had been tempted to resign as commanding officer but had he resigned then

I wouldn't have had the welfare of my men at heart. The fire had happened, there was a period of reconstruction and there was a Labour Government and a window of opportunity in 1974/75 for a more progressive way forward. It would have been criminal not to pursue it. There was a different atmosphere after the burning of the camp because the camp could have been burned again and again, and I think the British government realised that. I'm not saying it got them to the negotiation table because there had been talks and negotiations before that, but they were more amenable to some of the things the Camp Council were saying.

If I had resigned, all of that would have been lost. There would have been a power struggle and while the men couldn't have freedom, they wanted the next best thing, to do whatever they liked on the inside. They couldn't have that so I stayed my hand until 1978. Then I asked myself, 'Is my being commanding officer lending a stamp of approval to the violence outside?' That's when I decided to resign. A structure was left in place so I just didn't resign willy-nilly. The same policies would hopefully remain in place and there would be a certain amount of fine-tuning by the new leadership.

I reminded Gusty that I had a copy of a letter of his resignation dated September 1976. 'Yes, I kept the letter ready. It was always there and if things got too outlandish or too retrograde, I would have said, Right, there's my letter of resignation.'

The threat of resignation was used to good effect:

Whenever I waved it about it paid dividends. I would say, 'That's OK, I'm packing it in and you know what that means.' Not that I was holding a gun to people's head. If people didn't pay attention to some of the things that I and my men were saying there was no point in pursuing it.

Gusty's draft resignation letter of 1976 reads as follows:

Ulster Volunteer Force
Compound 21
Long Kesh Camp

Monday 20 September 1976

Ulster Volunteer Force
Belfast Brigade HQ
Belfast

Gentlemen,

It is with much reluctance and a large degree of sadness that I am exercising my prerogative as a senior officer of the Ulster Volunteer Force by tendering my resignation as the Commanding Officer UVF/RHC in this camp.

Quite easily and honestly, I could give my reason for resigning as ill-health but I am not that type of person. I am resigning because I am tired of the in-fighting that goes on within the loyalist ranks and because I am not prepared to attempt to be all things to all men. However that is not to state that I pay any attention to political or paramilitary pygmies yelping in the background levelling criticism without having the acumen or indeed the responsibility or integrity that constitutes genuine leadership. They fail to understand that true leadership entails legislating for every one of one's men without fear or favour and means making unpopular decisions when necessary.

I am grateful to my men for their unswerving loyalty and for their forbearance in the face of hardship and sacrifice down through the years behind bars without one word of reproach or complaint. It has been my privilege to have served with such men because it is only when men have had everything removed from them that they are seen in their true light. My proudest moments have been spent in such a deprived company and I am well pleased with their performance in the face of such strong adversity. I have learned much about human nature during my period of incarceration, and in the business of life I am still an infant.

> My so-called public image does not reflect my true self at all and so few people really know me outside of sensational newspaper headlines. Therefore, I am only concerned about those who are in command of all the facts to deliver judgement if it must be given.
>
> This resignation gives the lie to those who would accuse me or suggest that I am only concerned with personal power or publicity, and I hope they realise how foolish such accusations or suggestions really are. I have every wish to fade into the anonymity from which I sprang.
>
> I sincerely hope and pray that our society can very speedily attain that which the overwhelming majority of our people truly desire – a stable and just country wherein all our people can live without fear.
>
> I am confident that there are those in Ulster and further afield who will for their own reasons put their own interpretation on this resignation and quite probably will continue their practice of sneering comment and attribute me with squalid motives. If this be the case then so be it.
>
> My decision to resign is irrevocable but I am at hand always for counsel or advice on the understanding that I will advise as I, myself, would act.
>
> In conclusion I ask all UVF personnel to fully support whoever is delegated the responsibilities which I now relinquish and I beg them to try to understand the awesome and onerous task that they are required to shoulder.
>
> Yours truly
>
> Gusty Spence
> Loyalist Political Prisoner

An amended version was used by Gusty in 1978. He recalls:

> It was certainly along those lines and one of the deep motivating factors was that violence had to cease. I was disenchanted with a paramilitary organisation that in some instances was carrying out violence for the sake of violence. I had become quite disillusioned when the ceasefire by a reasonably enlightened leadership collapsed in the absence of a response from the IRA.

Gusty's resignation was from the leadership of the UVF in prison but, he says, 'It would be incomprehensible for a senior officer in the UVF to resign from a post and remain a volunteer.' In fact, among Gusty's notes, which appear to have been forwarded from Long Kesh to someone in contact with his nephew Eddie, he makes it clear that he had resigned from the

UVF itself. The notes are undated but are attached to other notes dated July 1981. They state:

> My resignation in April or May of 1978 was not only from the CO position but most importantly from the UVF itself. And it is completely true that I have broken off all contacts with that organisation and never again will they be resumed.

Billy Hutchinson was fully aware of the reasons for Gusty's resignation:

> I knew it was because he was at odds with the leadership on the outside and his health was only a small part of it. He wasn't going to listen to anybody and was going to do whatever he was going to do. At that time I didn't want him to resign because I felt that he still had a lot to offer, but at the same time he was entitled to have a rest if that's what he wanted.

Yet despite his resignation, Gusty retained a relationship with the UVF leadership outside Long Kesh. This was because he and a number of them had been comrades for a very long time and consequently, 'They trusted me and I trusted them.' Even when a bad leadership took over he could occasionally speak with them although there was a period of years when there was no contact whatever, by mutual agreement.

On 5 March 1978 the *Sunday News* reported that Gusty Spence had died – but only for two minutes. This happened not long after he resigned from the UVF. He was rushed to the Royal Victoria Hospital with a serious heart complaint.

> Details of his ten-mile dash for survival from the Maze Prison, near Lisburn, where he has served 12 years of a life sentence for murder, are being kept secret by hospital and prison authorities. Both departments are refusing to issue any statements about the case, but it is understood from a reliable hospital source that 45-year-old Spence technically died in a hospital examination room. His heart stopped beating, and it was only revived after a doctor injected a life-saving drug directly into the heart.[7]

I asked Gusty about his experience of dying:

> I have no recollection of it, none. There were no out-of-body experiences or white lights. I remember sinking and going unconscious.
>
> People's aspirations had been built up that I was going to be released after this but I never had any illusions about what the government would do. I took things whichever way fate dealt the cards because my health wasn't good. Not that I had given up hope – I always knew I would leave

> Long Kesh. This defiance within me said, Someday I'll be free and I will have thwarted those awesome powers that were machinated to put me in that place. I think at the end I became an embarrassment to the British government when Professor Grant said, 'I will not be responsible if anything happens to this man.'

Billy Spence wrote to Enoch Powell, MP for South Down, on 5 August 1978. In a previous letter (dated 29 July 1978) Billy had said that Gusty specifically mentioned Powell in relation to a possible release. Billy told Powell that his brother Gusty was probably 'the longest serving prisoner in Northern Ireland's history for a political offence'. Billy referred to the Great Train Robbers and the fact that some had been released despite having been sentenced for up to thirty years. He accepted that Gusty had political status and had been considered as 'the leader of a proscribed organisation', but said that IRA men had been released while engaged in open conflict:

> Prominent lawyers described his conviction as being carried out in the interests of political expediency – a view I would immediately concur with ... My principal reason for writing is the grave deterioration in his health and the length of time he has served ... To be truthful, Mr Powell, I have been rather worried about my brother for some time now and would be grateful if you would assent to raise the matter of his continued imprisonment with the British Government ...
>
> [Gusty] some time ago relinquished his leadership of UVF personnel in Long Kesh and now, I understand, takes little or nothing to do with the conduct of any business for that organisation in the prison. I could of course, give far more intimate details of his case history if given the opportunity of a personal meeting with you in Belfast.

In reply, Enoch Powell said he could 'see no reason to think that further representations in the near future would be likely to alter the decision' of the NIO. Contact should be made with Billy Spence's own MP. Billy replied saying he didn't know whether to interpret Powell's reply as 'a letter of advice or simply as a brush-off'.

He told Powell that loyalists in west Belfast had no representative in Parliament because Gerry Fitt did not reflect their views:

> If you, sir, had the slightest notion of how unfairly treated my brother was 12 years ago, then I do not think that you would have treated my original letter as abruptly as you did. Let me say also that I am not alone in thinking

> this way as thousands of Ulster Loyalist people think exactly as I do in relation to his case.
>
> Perhaps you could test this out in your own constituency of South Down. I am not writing this letter to you in any sense of recrimination for your abrupt reply, but in fact to let you see that people are not just beggars lying at the feet of Mr Powell pleading for some form of mercy. My brother nor I seek mercy from no one – but I feel we deserve justice or even a sympathetic word from a person with your knowledge and experience. It certainly seems on this occasion that I picked the wrong person. No doubt this letter will find its way into the nearest waste paper basket ...
>
> I am sorry I troubled you sir with the simple matter of an innocent man wrongly convicted of murder who is now serving a life sentence, which could shortly develop into a death sentence. Such trivialities to one such as you would, I am sure, be very boring indeed. If however you feel disposed to answering this letter, even in the most critical terms, please feel free to do so.

Enoch Powell's private secretary replied on 10 August 1978 saying that in view of what Billy had said, Enoch Powell 'thought it preferable to forward the correspondence to his colleague, Mr James H. Molyneaux MP, for information as Leader of the Unionist Parliamentary Party'.

Billy Spence had previously been in contact with Molyneaux so he wrote to him again and received a reply on 29 December 1978. Molyneaux told him he would write a personal letter to Don Concannon 'who is the Minister who deals with the Royal Prerogative of Mercy ... and see if he can find grounds for a reduction or remission of sentence'.

Molyneaux wrote to Concannon on 4 January 1979 enclosing a copy of Billy Spence's letter. In a reply dated 18 January, Concannon rejected any comparison with the train robbers, one of whom 'was recently released on parole from a determinate sentence of 30 years' imprisonment'. Gusty, he said, was imprisoned for life, and in passing sentence the judge had recommended he serve a minimum of twenty years before release on licence. Concannon assured Molyneaux that the case would be kept under review but said, 'the Secretary of State does not yet feel justified in fixing a date for Mr Spence's release on licence'.

Jim Molyneaux saw a glimmer of hope in that the Secretary of State had said that he 'does not *yet* feel justified'. But in the event Gusty was to spend five more years in Long Kesh.

After Gusty's resignation, a new, composite UVF leadership took over. This consisted of the OCs of the UVF compounds: 18, 19 and 21. Gusty remained available with advice, although 'the commanding officers had to make the final decisions'.

Bobby Spence, Gusty's brother, a former naval gunner and veteran of the Malayan and Korean wars, was one of the compound OCs who formed the composite leadership. Gusty says that the new leadership at first maintained discipline in the camp. Muster parades, ceremonial parades and hut inspections continued but less frequently. It soon became clear that

> The new leadership had nothing to offer except an opportunity to do as they pleased and impinge on the rights of others. The tradition of discipline and cleanliness went to the wall. Nothing good came from this leadership. It was a rudderless vessel that didn't know where it was going.

Later, Billy Hutchinson became commanding officer in Long Kesh. He says the men approached him saying:

> 'Look, you need to take over. The whole discipline is gone and the prison officers are laughing at us.' It was brought to a head by strip-searching when one of their friends stood up to the prison officers and nearly started a riot. I refused to be strip-searched so they took me to the cells. When I came back they asked me to take over and I did.
>
> On the first day a prison officer who was a Free Presbyterian came in and shouted, 'Everybody down to the canteen. We're going to search' and I shouted, 'Nobody move, stay where you are, the only orders you take are from the UVF and I'm the only person with the authority of the UVF in here.'

'Victor' was aware of the situation that led to Hutchinson being made commanding officer:

> Billy Hutchinson tried to bring it back to where Gusty had brought it. The big problem, and it's a big problem with the UVF everywhere and not just in prison, is that when the organisation gets too big it becomes harder to control. When it was controllable it was OK, and Gusty controlled it brilliantly even when the numbers were growing.

However, there was a coup against Billy Hutchinson, and discipline again began to decline, while political development was stifled. More alcohol was consumed and there were rowdy scenes and fights. UVF meetings stopped taking place and the progressive elements within the compounds began to concentrate on formal education.

Billy Hutchinson told me that sometimes when the men from

Compound 21 went out to play football, others, from Compound 19, came to the wire with stories:

> They were telling all sorts of yarns saying there was no discipline in Compound 19 so they could lie in bed all day. Our men got a bit annoyed because we were saying, Lights must go on at 9 o'clock in the morning and out at 12 o'clock at night. Bed packs were to be made at 9 a.m. and there was to be no lying in bed during the day. We carried on with those traditions.
>
> A couple of weeks later their OC sent for Trevor King and me saying, 'These people are going to kill me because I'm trying to impose the discipline you asked me to impose.' He came to us and we protected him. He was told they were going to kill him but I said, 'If you do that you're going to have to kill us as well.' They backed off and said, 'Our argument is not with you, it's with him,' but he hadn't the guts to stand up to them.
>
> They talked to the outside leadership who told them to appoint new people to take over. They voted in a new person. He was a nice enough fellow with a reputation of being a hard man but he wasn't going to stand up to these people or impress governors or prison officers. He was very easy-going. You could have put a bomb under him and you wouldn't have shifted him. He was just one of those people who wanted to sleep all day and do his own thing. Every time they wanted to do something they had a vote, which I thought was nonsense and refused to get involved.

Gusty himself was becoming increasingly disenchanted with the decline in discipline and in other aspects of the UVF. The leadership within the camp was 'virtually inarticulate' and the UVF leaders outside had allowed someone to usurp their authority inside. The consequence was that eventually, in 1981, Gusty felt compelled to write a bitter critical letter to the UVF leadership beyond the prison camp. This was intended to be his final word on the UVF and would mean that 'the last link has been broken'. The letter, dated 10 June 1981, was addressed to 'Jack' and sent from Compound 21:

> I have wasted my life and neglected my family for an ideal that at best was misguided and for a truth that no one is interested in or has been interested in since 1912. I still aspire to and emulate the dedication of those days and I still mould myself in those traditions.
>
> Complete and utter disillusionment has set in and I have become the original cynic. I belong to another generation in which duty, principle, truth, professionalism, sacrifice and loyalty (especially to one's friends)

were traits normally practised in those days, whereas today they are out of vogue and old-fashioned. I am too set in my ways to change even if I wanted to. Expediency is a stranger to me and a thing is either right or it is not – there can be no middle way or compromise on a principle.

Power is a whore who intoxicates, flirts, tempts and undermines but it is fatal to fall in love with power because she will cohabit with you for a while, let you taste her delights and then move off to newer pastures after betraying and leaving desolation in her wake. I never loved power and was thrust in against my wishes by fervent voices telling me to do my duty, and consequently I handled power easily and when it suited *me* I relinquished it voluntarily in 1978 and would have done so sooner only it would have caused chaos in here ...

I am now free completely without having freedom inasmuch as I have no other responsibility in here except to act and behave like a loyalist political prisoner who has not nor ever will sell special category status by allowing the prison authorities to assess, review or depoliticise me. I can now express a personal opinion and make an individual decision without reflecting the views of the UVF. I am now truly Gusty Spence – the man. Do you really know how much that means to me 'Jack'? One must never expect thanks or appreciation in return for patriotism – it is given freely or not at all.

I am not disappointed and I honestly pray that each of you when your time comes – as come it will – will take it as easily and laconically as I am treating my paramilitary demise. Please 'Jack' be sure to show this to 'Mark' and 'Big T' and I can assure you that this is my very last word on the UVF and the last link has been broken.

In April 2000 Gusty reflected:

I believed that the people on the outside should have said to the usurping leadership, 'You are in prison now but you will have to leave that prison and even though you're somewhat remote, we have long arms.' That's what soldiers would have done when the coup came into operation. I would have said 'Go ahead, that's OK, there's not a terrible lot we can do about it at the present moment, but when you come out!' But there was no comprehension. I shudder to think in what context their demands were put when they represented UVF prisoners with the prison governor. The UVF had permitted people to usurp and flaunt their authority.

I wasn't disillusioned with the loyalist cause, I was disillusioned with their perception of the loyalist cause. I was prepared to give my life for these people, I had left everything and my wife and family had taken second place. They betrayed this sacred thing – the UVF. It was a holy thing to me and to many like me and they had betrayed it. The same as some IRA men are saying to Sinn Féin, 'You are forsaking all those martyrs.' That's the way I felt.

This sacred thing had been something almost tangible to Gusty:

> When you're born and reared with that, it wasn't a myth – it was a reality. You were taught it was respectable and something that people had given their lives for and it was good and honour and truth and justice and all those things.
>
> People led us to believe it was a mystical thing, the same as republicans believe that 1916 and the bloodletting was a mystical thing, but it wasn't. The formation of the UVF was an incident in history when a whole people were prepared to say no and to die. These men inside and outside jail had declared to me that they were soldiers. I only know one way, that's a soldierly way. A soldierly way is sacrifice. A soldierly way is service, a soldierly way is duty and a soldierly way is honour.

The failure of the downtown office ideal, along with the unhelpful attitude by the authorities, compounded the effect of the decline in leadership inside the prison. All of this had a demoralising effect on Gusty's hopes. I asked Billy Hutchinson if he had been aware of Gusty's disillusionment:

> I was aware of it and I think that was when we had a number of disagreements and rows. That probably affected him and those who were close to him. It certainly affected me, and things got a wee bit sour, but we all worked through it and in the end it was OK. He was totally disillusioned about what was happening on the outside. He rejected the sectarian killings but he was also concerned about what was happening on the inside. He saw things being allowed to slip. I agreed but unfortunately the wrong people had been put in charge.
>
> His health was always bad but he started jogging and things like that and became healthier than he had been. That probably extended his life. If he hadn't started this and had continued in the leadership role, he would probably have died. Whether you recognise it or not, leadership brings a lot of stress.

Gusty had become determined to improve his health and achieved a surprising degree of success for a time:

> I said to myself, 'If I go out, I'll go out fighting' and once I had given up being CO I was free to do whatever I wished. I eventually took up a

> rigorous fitness programme. I started off in a commonsense way, small at first and then building up gradually. I was doing things that amazed myself, running marathons, running thirty miles. What I was doing, without even being conscious of it, was saying to those people who would have looked down on us, 'I'm doing it – you do it.'

As mentioned above, not a single man in the UVF compound had ever been physically punished during Gusty's time as OC. But a letter from Gusty on 10 June 1981 referred to fatigues being imposed on him by the 'retrograde' leadership in the camp:

> After this leadership took over, there was a meeting in the dinning hall where I spoke out forcefully. They were going to give me fatigues because I spoke against the leadership and I had been a senior UVF officer. They wanted me to go to an assessment board and I said, 'No, I'm not going to any assessment board, I've no need for it.' I never allowed the prison authorities to assess my men. I was the only person who assessed them but some were getting 'gate fever' and thought they saw a way out but it was only a black tunnel. They thought that by going to an assessment board they would get out quicker. It was a ploy by the prison authorities and the NIO to split the prisoners.
>
> I never pulled any punches with the UVF. Many times I said, 'Away and fuck yourself.' They took it from me because they respected me. I reflected a collective will but sometimes my men had to be guided in a way I thought was best for them. I was drawing on a wealth of experience. I was drawing on British army experience and on all those years in Crumlin Road jail, including the communication I had had with the IRA.
>
> There was more involved than just being a UVF man. I had to show the world and the republicans that we could be every bit as determined as they were and every bit as principled. We could make sacrifices if sacrifices were required.

Within the camp things continued to decline and eventually

> After I left prison in 1984 a large body of UVF men approached Billy Hutchinson to take over [again] as commanding officer. They had become disillusioned with this rag-tag putting themselves forward as leaders. It became abysmal inside at a time when numbers were diminishing. Most of the UVF were now confined to one compound and they were all lifers. Many didn't see any light at the end of the tunnel, and men in that situation do strange things. Those who remained in the compounds were Special Category status prisoners.

Billy Hutchinson remained UVF commanding officer in Long Kesh until he was released in 1990. He went on to play a significant role in the peace process.

16

H Blocks and Friendship with a Cardinal

Merlyn Rees had announced the building of the H Blocks at Long Kesh in February 1975. At that time the Camp Council was negotiating with the NIO on various matters, including the remission of prison sentences. Ideally the Camp Council would have liked two thirds remission, leaving prisoners to serve one third of their sentence. They knew that a quid pro quo would be expected and it was assumed the NIO wanted an IRA ceasefire, followed by a loyalist cessation. There had never been any talk of the dissolution of political status, Gusty insists.

> However, the NIO did mention that there would be a different format for the prison regime. We were against this for a variety of reasons. We knew that some idiot would attempt to impose prison regulations. I stayed after the meeting and begged the governor, 'Don't support this. It would be disastrous. There'll be protests and a focus of attention will be

kept, not only on the general war that the Provos are running, but on the brushfire wars. They need to fuel the big war with strip searches and so on.'

If protests get nowhere they will end in hunger strikes. You didn't have to be a prophet to see this in 1975. It was so predictable that I questioned myself, 'Do the British government believe that they have the IRA on the run? Do they feel that one more push will be enough?' Merlyn Rees didn't emphasise this, but his successor Roy Mason did. Every time he said the IRA were on the run they responded with another atrocity, so there was a feeling of despondency.

The Camp Council was invited to see the H Blocks and the five commanding officers of both wings of the IRA, the INLA, the UDA and Gusty inspected the new prison:

The only prisoners there were ordinary non-political prisoners – we would call them juveniles. The atmosphere, the building, the structures – everything was oppressive; and the funny thing is, it was the authorities themselves that named them H Blocks – a terrible blunder. It gave the impression throughout the world of an oppressive regime and that's what it was.

What the OCs rejected was symbolised by individual cells with thick walls keeping prisoners confined. It was about control through individual segregation. The government announced that special category status was being phased out, and that all paramilitary prisoners convicted for offences committed after 1 March 1976 would be held in the H Blocks rather than the compounds. This, according to former prison welfare officer Colin Crawford, ended

a form of imprisonment that had allowed for political and social accommodations between the paramilitary groups. That had led directly to dialogue and a desire for further dialogue. Instead of fostering this initiative the Government committed itself to criminalizing political prisoners, in a calculated act of provocation.[1]

There was no attempt, however, to criminalise the prisoners in the compounds or to move them into the H Blocks. According to Gusty:

It would have been a slaughtering match, a massacre, if they had attempted it, and they had nothing to offer as a sweetener. The H Blocks were set up purely as part of 'normalisation' policy. They had this anomaly of special category status, which sullied Britain's name throughout the world, so they wanted to portray the whole situation as a criminal undertaking in a normal prison regime. It was disastrous.

I begged the authorities not to do it and David Morley was as insistent as I was, from a different point of view. I'm still British. Even though I was a prisoner I was conscious of the Provo propaganda machine. The government handed it to them on a plate. If there were protests and a hunger strike in Crumlin Road to achieve political status in 1972, it was reasonable to expect the same in 1976 if they tried to abolish it.

The battle was fought out in the H Blocks. Loyalists were alarmed at a policy designed mainly to criminalise the Provisional IRA:

We saw it as a complete disaster and said, 'Listen, if you bring this into being, people will die.' A hunger strike was on the horizon as plain as Napoleon's Nose on a clear day. Serious upheaval was inevitable in the H Blocks.

Politically oriented prisoners will not stand for inequality. Whatever they achieve they want it for the rest of the prisoners in the same organisation. A wall divided the compounds from the H Blocks but a physical wall didn't divide them in ideology. You couldn't have one set of so-called ordinary prisoners while others were treated as special category prisoners.

According to Gusty, Bob Truesdale, the prison governor, saw criminalisation as the answer to all his problems:

'At last prison rules will be observed.' Says I, 'Bob I thought you were a shrewder man than that. That's a very silly statement. My men don't obey prison rules, they obey UVF rules, same as the IRA.'

The first IRA prisoner to face the rigours of the new policy was the late Kieran Nugent in September 1976. He resolutely refused to wear a prison uniform or be treated like an ordinary prisoner. According to Gusty, Nugent's response to the request to wear prison clothes was, 'No, I'm not wearing prison clothes. I'm not a felon so I'm not wearing the garb. They'll have to nail the clothes on my back.'

He wore a prison blanket instead and the authorities responded with loss of remission and the removal of furniture from his cell. He was forced to sleep on the floor but in spite of such hardships the number of protesters steadily increased. More and more convicted Provisionals, along with members of INLA, draped themselves in blankets and rejected the government's insistence that they should wear a prison uniform. They became known as the Blanket Men.[2]

The UVF in the compounds actively supported the struggle to resist removal of special category status. Little more than a month after Kieran Nugent's protest, on 2 November 1976 the UVF Camp Command issued a statement to their officers, staff, NCOs and Volunteers:

> The Camp [Command] consisting of the Commanding Officer, Compounds 18, 19 & 21 OCs, and Adjutant of the UVF/RHC personnel, do pledge that we shall support our comrades throughout the Ulster Volunteer Force in freedom, in their struggle to resist the removal of 'special category' status from our imprisoned colleagues who are charged with offences committed after March 1st this year.
>
> Further, we give the present leadership of the UVF our complete support in the task they have before them, and we are prepared to engage in extreme action within this Camp in order to give actual support to the fight for an acceptable settlement of the 'political status' issue.
>
> We are renowned for our responsible demeanour within Long Kesh, but we are equally renowned and respected for our determination and discipline if we believe that principles require specific action from us. In this instance we believe it may be necessary to embark upon drastic action in order to extract an acceptable formula; therefore we state that if it is warranted and necessary, the UVF/RHC contingent in Long Kesh shall not be found wanting in this respect.
>
> We wish you every success in the campaign for 'political status'.

This statement was signed by Gusty Spence as commanding officer and by 'James Strutt, OC Compound 18'; 'R. Warnock, OC Compound 19'; 'R. McCullough, OC Compound 21'; and 'I. King, Adjutant'.

By the following year, 1977, nearly four hundred republicans but only about twenty loyalists were engaged in the H Blocks protest. The loyalists were generally unsupported and felt badly let down by conforming loyalists in the H Blocks. They did, however, retain the support of their fellow loyalist prisoners in the compounds. That Gusty and the UVF/RHC leadership knew the dangers inherent in the abolition of political status is clear from a document prepared by Gusty, William Mitchell and Ronnie McCullough and signed by Gusty as CO on 31 August 1977:

> With loyalists soon to go 'on the blankets' and growing calls from the rank and file membership of both republican and loyalist organisations for

> 'more positive action' in support of the men in the H Blocks, it is evident that the conditions at the H Block control units will be the centre of a new wave of violent agitation within and without the prison system in NI.
>
> We believe that the problems of the H Blocks can be solved peacefully and reasonably without any great loss of principle on either side. We cannot put our full proposals on paper at this stage but we can assure the NIO that, once dialogue and negotiations are started, it can be arranged that the five Faction Leaders at Long Kesh will be empowered by their respective organisations to reach a settlement with the NIO on the H Block question.

Negotiations were not, however, the way of Margaret Thatcher and her Conservative government colleagues, so catastrophe seemed inevitable.

For a number of weeks at the beginning of 1978 most loyalists in the H Blocks were 'on the blanket'. However, once one OC took his men off the blanket, the others soon followed suit.

On the first day of 1979 Bishop Cathal Daly publicly said it was folly not to review the degrading situation in the H Blocks. Members of the Northern Ireland Prison Service expressed concern at a 'brutalising and intolerable way of life'.[3] Conditions quickly deteriorated, as former prison welfare officer Colin Crawford recorded:

> Republican protesting prisoners were at their most vulnerable when leaving their cells to slop out, as they would become open to abuse and assault (as witnessed by loyalist political prisoners). As a result they began throwing the contents of their toilet containers out of their cell windows. When the windows were blocked, they resorted to leaving the overflowing containers on the cell floor. The prisoners then decided to escalate their protest by smearing excreta on the cell walls.[4]

After visiting the protesting prisoners, Cardinal Tomás Ó Fiaich spoke movingly of his experiences. He said he would be horrified if animals were kept in such degrading conditions, and he repeated stories of the ill-treatment that prisoners said was being meted out to them. There was growing sympathy internationally for the prisoners. Yet in the midst of all this the PIRA began secret talks with the British government. Gusty reflected on the situation:

> We were in the compounds but we'd heard some horror stories coming from the H Blocks. Some of the men had been released including some loyalists who had been on the blanket protest. I probably would have been

dead if I had been on the Blocks. I give short shrift to those who don't see things through to their logical conclusion. It was always half-eaten sandwiches, nothing was completed, and it's still the case. Do you know why? They haven't suffered enough. It was different in the thirties with the hunger.

It's the same old routine. 'We've given them everything.' But what have we given them that they're not entitled to as people? They're entitled to oppose the unionist government or even Britishness as long as they don't oppose it with force of arms. That's when we [the UVF] come into play. If they oppose with force of arms, there will always be a counter guerrilla movement. It happens in every country.

I understood the position of Bobby Sands and those fellows. I was in the same position myself. It started off as a dirty protest, 'Fuck you, you're going to make my life miserable, I'm going to make your life miserable. If you deprive me of recognition as a political prisoner I will take steps to prove to the world that I am a political prisoner.'

It was a slow trundling steamroller heading towards the edge of the cliff. I could put my hand up to God as a loyalist and as a UVF commanding officer at that time that I did all in my power with the prison governors and the NIO to try to stop that steamroller before lives were lost. If it happened under milder conditions in Crumlin Road jail in 1972, it would happen under these harsher conditions nearly ten years later. When you close down everything else, a man is only left with his body. That's the only weapon he has to fight with.

Not long before Margaret Thatcher became prime minister in May 1979, her close friend and adviser Airey Neave was killed in an explosion on leaving the House of Commons car park. The INLA claimed responsibility, having used explosives made in the USSR and supplied by the Palestinian Liberation Organisation.[5] On 27 August, Earl Louis Mountbatten, the Queen's cousin, was killed with others at Mullaghmore, County Sligo. On the same day, eighteen soldiers were massacred by the IRA at Narrow Water near Warrenpoint, County Down. This was followed by an upsurge in killings of Catholics by loyalists. One month later, on 30 September 1979, the Pope visited Ireland and at Drogheda he appealed for an end to violence:

Do not believe in violence, do not support violence. It is not the Christian way. It is not the way of the Catholic Church. Believe in peace and forgiveness and love; for they are of Christ. On my knees I beg of you to turn

> away from the paths of violence and to return to the ways of peace. You may claim to seek justice. I too believe in justice and seek justice. But violence only delays the work of justice.[6]

Bishop Arthur Butler had remained in contact with Gusty. In October 1980 he visited him after his brother Bobby died in the compounds. Bobby Spence had been sentenced to fourteen years for his part in a UVF bombing. On the morning of his death Gusty had finished his run and was in the gym when Billy Hutchinson told him that Bobby had collapsed. There was no doctor on hand so they sent for a medical orderly, but it was too late.

Gusty's brother Billy had already died suddenly a few months earlier, in March. Bobby and Gusty had both applied for parole to attend Billy's funeral. Gusty's request was refused and Bobby's was granted, but Bobby had said, 'Ah no, if my brother can't go with me, I won't be going. If my mother's death didn't divide us you are not going to divide us now.'

After Bobby's death, Bishop Butler wrote to Billy Spence's son Eddie to say that he had visited his uncle:

> When I saw Gusty, he was in running clothes. As I expect you know, he has become a very keen jogger. I am glad to say that he looked very well and in much better form than when I have seen him on previous occasions. I have real sympathy for Gusty and feel that as he has served three-quarters of his sentence, a claim for some remission is not unreasonable. I will do what I can to help ... You will appreciate that the Northern Ireland Office just at present is much concerned about the H-Block issue and it might be wiser to delay a little before making a formal application.

During that same month, October 1980, six PIRA prisoners and one INLA prisoner in the H Blocks started a hunger strike. By December Sean McKenna, a PIRA man, was close to death, but negotiations brought his hunger strike to an end.

On 1 March 1981, however, a new hunger strike began in the course of which the first man to go on the hunger strike, Bobby Sands, stood for election as MP for Fermanagh/South Tyrone and won.

In the compounds, Gusty recalls:

> There was an air of anticipation and depression permeating the whole camp. One morning as I was going out for my run a screw came in and said, 'Bobby Sands has just died.' Again there was an air of dread about what might happen next. Was the IRA going to cut loose even more than

> they had done? It was a depressing time. I had been on hunger strike myself for something I strongly believed in. I had protested and sacrificed and I couldn't possibly have disagreed with what those men were doing or have no sympathy, I understood it wholly. There are people outside who don't want to understand that a boy from the back streets of the Shankill or the Falls could face an awful end for something he firmly believed in.

Ten hunger-strikers died, the last in August 1981. Those remaining ended their strike at the beginning of October.

Within three days James Prior, the Secretary of State, announced that prisoners would be permitted to wear their own clothes and have 50 per cent of their lost remission restored. The prisoners had won. They achieved everything they had sought but the political ramifications remained: the writer Jack Holland has remarked that, 'treating republicans like common criminals had turned them into politicians'.[7] As Gusty put it to me recently, the hunger strikes represented 'the blossoming of Sinn Féin under Margaret Thatcher'.

> Of course we hear people even now saying, 'We should have done the job right in 1969.' Who should have done the job right? It was working-class Catholics fighting working-class Protestants, with a smattering of arms. Those people who wanted 'to do the job right' were often ensconced in some leafy villa.

Gusty believes that Margaret Thatcher's actions had unexpected consequences:

> Despite her many blunders, she created a basis for the peace process. What happened was absolutely horrific and one expects governments to be astute and to have a finger on the pulse ready to move in an overt or covert way. The British government ham-handled the hunger strike, but without Margaret Thatcher's ham-handling we wouldn't have had the rise of Sinn Féin, wouldn't have had the political strength Sinn Féin gained. Consequently we wouldn't have had the peace process. So things can take an ironic turn.

It was early in 1981 that Gusty first acknowledged his commitment to socialism, which for him represented a caring society and was more of a commitment to the working class than a theoretical standpoint. He expressed this allegiance in a private letter to his brother Ned and his wife Kathleen after their son Ronnie, Gusty's nephew, was arrested in relation to the Official IRA. This letter was very different in tone from the postcard Gusty had sent to Ned and Kathleen at Christmas 1966. That had displayed an 'Orange arch, festooned with a variety of Loyalist motifs and inscribed, "This we will maintain."' Inside there had been an old message, 'I am what I am and I can never change.'[8] In 1981, however, Gusty pondered thus over Ronnie's arrest:

> Did he get four years because he was in the Official IRA or was it because he was my nephew? The papers made great play of it – 'Gusty Spence's nephew was in the Official IRA.' I remember even some UVF men passing remarks, 'Haven't you a nephew in the Official IRA?' 'Well,' says I, 'I'm not my brother's keeper.'
>
> Even within republicanism there are brothers in the Provos and other brothers in the Officials and even relatives who were Orange.

Within right-wing unionist paramilitary groupings like Tara, the fact that Gusty's nephew was a member of the Official IRA was used in attempts to damage the UVF. Some newspapers too seemed to delight in exposing the fact. Journalist Paddy Reynolds, writing in 1981, said that radio, TV and newspaper reports of the trial of Ronnie Spence stressed, 'without exception, that he was a nephew of Gusty Spence and revealed Ronnie's address'.[9]

Gusty says that at the time:

> I was commiserating with them because trouble had come to their door. Leaving that incident aside, those people who had complete faith in the police until it affected them always amazed me. All of a sudden they wanted changes and tried to stop the world with their heels. The only thing they got was sore heels.

Gusty respected Ronnie's decision to try 'to do something for our society'. He added in his letter that he would not pass judgement on the causes that people adopted.

The letter was sent from Compound 21 on 9 February 1981. He began by referring to the 'tragic events of young Ronnie' and suggested that 'our family perhaps personifies the whole situation and deep sadness of Ireland':

> As you know I have very much changed – not because of what prison has done to me but because of what I have done for myself. If I had to serve a lifetime in dungeons like these, I wanted to know for what reason, and I

> searched for the truth. In pursuit of that scarce commodity in Northern Ireland, my quest brought me into contact with all manner of people many of whom I now class – and they me – as dear friends.
>
> I feel deeply embarrassed when I think of my former 'truths' which when investigated did not stand up to scrutiny or fact. It would be easy to apportion blame in other quarters but that is beneath me. However, I could go on typing all night since I have so much to say on matters of ideology and politics.
>
> Needless to state that I have become a committed socialist for quite a period of years now, a declaration which, for me, would have been unthinkable ten years ago ...

Gusty had at last found freedom to own the word 'socialism', though his kind of socialism was far removed from the ideological socialism of his brother Ned:

> Socialism was a word that I had shied away from for a multiplicity of reasons. It wasn't an accepted word that I was born and reared with. Secondly, it wasn't accepted in the period with which I was acquainted and thirdly, it wasn't really accepted because of the awful abuses happening in socialist societies. I was a democratic socialist. There was nothing dogmatic about it and I had more in common with Groucho Marx than I would have with Karl Marx.
>
> I knew little about socialism and a member of the Official IRA said my approach to socialism was simplistic. Indeed he was right, but sometimes a simplistic approach is better than a dogmatic or complicated one. If someone was to ask for a word other than socialist, I would say a 'care-ist'. If you care about your society, for the old, the young and the sick, people may call you whatever they want. 'Socialist' is the common term.

Ronnie's father Ned (known as Eddie by his socialist friends) was for a time a member of the Communist Party. He was involved in the Civil Rights Association and took part in the first civil rights march from Queen's University in 1967, as well as the march in Derry on 5 October 1968. In the mid-1950s, Ned married a Catholic girl, Kathleen Price, much to the consternation of his parents and family. The couple decided to marry in England, while ostensibly holidaying in Wales. They went to Sheffield and later had a visit from Gusty. When Gusty came on the scene Ned thought they were going to be killed. Gusty spent an enjoyable week with them but his last words were, 'Take my advice and don't come back to Belfast.' This frightened Ned, but later he recognised that Gusty said this for his own good.

After receiving the letter, Ned Spence spoke highly of his brother Gusty:

> You have only to compare the things he said in the past to what he says today. For example in a letter he wrote in April 1967 when he was in Crumlin Road Jail, before he was transferred to Long Kesh, he stated, 'Tell the boys to make sure my [Orange] regalia is worn on all parades because my heart is always outside and only a shell remains here. No Surrender.' In another letter the same month he wrote, 'I am loyal because I AM loyal. I will put my loyalty to the test anytime – preferably in the Falls.'[10]

Gusty gained a greater understanding of his brother:

> As loyalists and unionists in the past, we never conceded recognition to anyone other than ourselves the right to be what they are. We never recognised republicanism as a legitimate political philosophy, just as unionism is. But if either is pursued through force of arms to change whatever status quo there is, that makes it wrong.
>
> Republicanism has always pursued its aims through force and that's why I suppose unionists, loyalists and Protestants never conceded recognition. They conceded recognition for nationalists but they never gave them much. At that time, because of my limited thinking, I refused to concede the right to my brother that he should be a Communist. He can be whatever he wants to be, providing he doesn't try to shove it down my throat.

Gusty had previously been deeply hurt by comments made in 1972 or 1973 by a senior Orangeman:

> I don't know who he was referring to in saying 'Isn't that fellow Spence a card-carrying commie?' He didn't say which Spence. What he was saying was true: that fellow Spence was a card-carrying Communist – only it wasn't that fellow Gusty Spence. It was that fellow Ned Spence, but most of his and my associates would not have known anything about our Ned, and so they would have attributed that to me.

In his 1981 letter to Bob Hynds, Gusty said:

> I have only one desire now, Bob, and that is to fade into the insignificance from whence I came and lead a very quiet and unobtrusive life in complete anonymity. No publicity – no reporters. Just Louie and I and a wee house in the country somewhere with access to the family and the lights of my life

the grandchildren. No amount of money could induce me to open up, and count yourself lucky that I have imparted so much to you ...

No memoirs – no nothing. I had fifteen years done on 27 June and don't let anyone kid you – it is two lifetimes and I want home. It's going to be interesting to see how long they intend to keep me. There is *no form* of resettlement for long-term prisoners in Northern Ireland and there never was, except for one governor with foresight, old Paddy Mullin.

It's about bloody time they were thinking about it and yours truly will act as guinea pig if the terms are acceptable. If there is a lesson to be learned in imprisonment – and I doubt it very much— fifteen years in the one classroom is enough. Even a soldier going back to civvy life has to be resettled.

During August 1981, Gusty formally set down his intentions, should he be released. These were forwarded to Eddie who in turn forwarded them to the NIO. In this document, Gusty referred to his having left the UVF, rejected violence and stated his desire for peace and seclusion in the bosom of his family:

It is my sincere wish and true desire to bury once and for all time the undeserved and unsolicited image and myth of the Gusty Spence often portrayed in the 'popular press'. I long for anonymity and peace and earnestly seek the opportunity to put into practice what I have written here.

In December 1981 Eddie Spence wrote to Jim Molyneaux thanking him for his help in seeking the release of Gusty. Eddie went on to say:

Gusty has severed all connections with the organisation which he has always been associated with, and has given his categorical assurance of future behaviour. I wonder how many released prisoners have ever voluntarily given this assurance? His behaviour in prison these 15 years has been exemplary and he has never in that time ever been disciplined, reprimanded or had one bad mark against him for breach of prison rules ...

In all his time in the Maze and Belfast prisons, not one sectarian 'punch' has been exchanged between the various prisoners, he has prevented the loyalist prisoners from assisting others to burn down the camp in 1974, he has been instrumental in forming many committees within the prison to implement prison reform, which has led to Gusty intimating to the welfare section of the Maze that he will be making application for employment to the Probation Service on his ultimate release be it sooner or later.

A number of other politicians responded over the years to the approaches of Billy Spence and his son Eddie. Among those who contacted the NIO or government ministers were the Reverend Robert Bradford, the Reverend Dr Ian Paisley and Peter Robinson of the Democratic Unionist Party, Oliver Napier of Alliance, and Harold McCusker, Ulster Unionist MP. Jim Kilfedder MP frequently corresponded with the Spence family and with government ministers. In 1980, Mairead Corrigan of the Peace People commended Gusty in the following words:

> Gusty Spence has proven that, with his unique experience, he can lead people towards rebuilding the broken fibres of their own lives – and that is a far cry from the taking of lives. I and many other people in Northern Ireland believe that Gusty Spence has well paid his debt to society and it is time he returned to his family and the wider family of Northern Ireland – we need all the help we can get to stitch together our torn fibres.[11]

In August 1981 she wrote to Humphrey Atkins, Secretary of State, saying:

> This prisoner has done untold good among young prisoners – as we have found directly – and which, no doubt, governmental welfare people can confirm. We are frankly at a loss to understand why the compassion exercised in other cases has not been extended to Mr Spence. We have even wondered if he is being penalised because of his stabilising and rehabilitating influence – making the prison authorities unwilling to lose him.

Prisoners regularly extended an invitation to VIPs to visit the compounds. Not all availed of the opportunity, and the authorities sometimes discouraged such visits. One of the few unionists to meet republican prisoners was Hugh Smyth, an independent unionist and now a leader of the PUP. Another was John Carson, an Ulster Unionist politician.

But Gusty wanted to extend the invitation list. There was one person in particular he wanted to meet – Cardinal Tomás Ó Fiaich:

> I applied to the prison authorities, saying we would like to put some grievances to him. We were told we were not of his flock and his visits were pastoral visits. They forgot that a previous Roman Catholic Primate had come to see us. Tommy Fee [Ó Fiaich] had a particularly green tinge to him – the man was a republican. He told me he was a republican and I told him I was a loyalist. But we were agreed that violence was not the way to further the interests of any section of the people.

Cardinal Ó Fiaich was visiting the Official IRA near Gusty's compound:

> He and I assumed that he would be allowed to visit the UVF compound. The prison authorities may have been apprehensive about the possibility of him being physically harmed but that would never have happened and I gave firm assurances. I said, 'Bring four or five prison officers along with him' but he would have said, 'Oh no, I don't want the prison officers with me. I'll feel free if I'm going into the lions' den alone.'

However the Cardinal was unable to meet loyalists face to face at this time:

> It was bloody awful. The authorities backed the van right up to the gate of Compound 20, which meant he could be whisked off immediately. But he came over to the wire where I could see him. I raised my right hand and he raised his right hand and there was an unspoken understanding that, 'We'll do something about this.' I got on to the Northern Ireland Office right away, 'You people are talking about peace. That man's trying to forge links and you people are thwarting him.'

Cardinal Ó Fiaich appealed to the NIO and in March 1980 he was able to see Gusty: 'I visited the UVF and met Spence and a number of other Protestant prisoners. They received me kindly and in a friendly fashion and in fact, we exchanged a few words in Irish.'[12]

The Cardinal was made very welcome by Gusty who recalls:

> He was amazed at our historical library, especially the Irish section, and at how *au fait* we now were with politics. We had a general conversation in the study hut where there was room for about twenty people. All the senior UVF officers were present. It was in my interest to have them there so they would be in a position to take the message to the outside. It was important that it was coming from sources other than myself, that this man was not only an enlightened man, he wanted peace and had a genuine interest in prisoners.

The Cardinal said that Gusty had told him that when he was growing up he had never had the opportunity to read Irish history. Gusty saw this first meeting as the start of a friendship based on mutual respect: 'He was a republican but he wanted peace in Ireland. He wanted to see an all-Ireland but there's only one way it could come about: through peaceful means. That's fair. He had his aspiration, I have mine.' During the conversation Ó Fiaich had said, 'You know, Gusty, including my own flock, you're the only one that has addressed me properly as "Your Eminence".' Gusty later recalled:

> I had moved on from 1966 ... I became friends with the Cardinal and I know he was friends with me. But when dignitaries visited Crumlin Road jail I always made representations to them because I saw it as my duty to represent my men to the best of my ability. I aimed to ensure that they achieved the best humane set of circumstances to lighten their load in prison. In any case meeting the Cardinal was a privilege and a pleasure.

On 4 August 1980 Ó Fiaich wrote to Gusty's nephew Eddie. He had met Gusty by this time and said the meeting had been 'friendly and relaxed but a little bit rushed as it was coming near closing time'. He had mentioned Gusty's name to the NIO as 'one that merited consideration for early release', and he said he intended to raise the matter formally with the Secretary of State. He thanked Eddie for his good wishes 'for a successful outcome of the discussions concerning H Block'. He said that if Gusty could be released, this would remove 'one of the great obstacles to the restoration of peace'.

The visits continued, and at Christmas they exchanged cards. Gusty recalls:

> Twice a year I allowed the boys to make poteen, on the Twelfth of July and Christmas Day, because generally alcohol and jail do not mix. I got my ration of poteen the same as everybody else; I used to steep my tobacco in it and then I would take it out in small quantities and let it dry out. It made a nice smoke.

He decided to share this delicacy with the Cardinal:

> He was a wee stout countryman, down to earth, and very amenable, very jovial, very affable. He and I got on like a house on fire. He was smoking cigarettes and coughing badly and I says, 'Your honour, it's them oul things, they're going to kill you.' 'Ach,' he says, 'but sure I love a smoke, Gusty. What am I going to do?' Says I, 'Did you ever try a pipe? Now don't get a straight pipe, get a bent pipe.' So the next time he came there was a whole trail of smoke behind him, like a smokescreen.
>
> I asked him, 'What's that you're smoking?' He said it was a mild tobacco and I said, 'Can I fill your pipe for you?' He says, 'Aye certainly.' So he gave me the pipe and I filled it and he took one or two puffs and said, 'God, that's a quare drop of stuff.' Says I, 'Well it's soaked in poteen.' Says he, 'Aye, I thought it tasted familiar.' So I said, 'I'll give you a couple of ounces away with you.' 'Ach no,' he said, 'I won't take anything from a prisoner,'

> but I said, 'Your Eminence I've got plenty to be quite honest,' and he took a couple of ounces. Fair play to him, he never came to the compounds without having cigarettes in his cassock to be dispersed to the prisoners. There wasn't many Prod ministers did that. Against the rules, you see. Later a fellow slipped up to me saying, 'His Eminence says if you had a wee drop of the other stuff he would be very grateful.'

Trevor West was among those who sought to secure Gusty's release. West saw Lord Gowrie, who had a house in the south of Ireland and was the Tory minister dealing with Northern Ireland prisons. West told Gowrie that the prison authorities were well aware of the constructive role Gusty played inside the prison and said what a force he would be for sanity if released.

Billy Blease met Michael Alison, Minister of State at the NIO, on 1 September 1981 to discuss Gusty and Robert Williamson, another life sentence prisoner. Alison replied on 11 September saying that the Secretary of State did not feel justified in fixing a release date for either prisoner:

> I did mention to you one particular difficulty which faces us in regard to Mr Spence. As you know he has remained in the UVF compound at Maze prison, whereas several years ago Mr Williamson asked to be transferred and has since served his sentence in a normal prison environment. It would be going too far for me to say, or imply, that if Mr Spence were to do the same now it would lead to an early decision to fix a provisional date for his release, but I hope you will understand that the present situation must give rise to a real problem in our reviews of this case.
>
> There is not much I can usefully add at this stage except to say, in regard to the question of home leave which you mentioned, that it has been the policy for a number of years now – under successive administrations – not to consider such leave for life sentence prisoners who have not been given a provisional release date. Nevertheless I took careful note of your remarks in relation to these two cases, and I will keep them in mind. Both cases will of course continue to be reviewed periodically – there is no question whatever of their being overlooked.
>
> Finally, I have reflected on your request that one of my officials would have a discussion about the cases with two people who are taking a close interest on Mr Spence's behalf. I am afraid that I do not feel able to offer such a meeting, but I hope that our exchange on 1 September, and the information in this letter, will be helpful.

The two people referred to as taking a close interest were Trevor West and Paddy Devlin.

In 1982 Gusty received his first parole since his daughter's wedding in 1972. He had now been in prison without a break for ten years – in total for approximately sixteen years. His parole lasted thirty-six hours.

> They let me out on Christmas Eve 1982, and I had to be back again on Boxing Day. I stepped into another world. When I was out on parole in 1972 the old Shankill was still there but in a terribly dilapidated state. Whenever I came out in 1982, the old Shankill was gone, and unfortunately a lot of the people too.

Louie was living at Hopewell Crescent in the Shankill.

> We had a big Christmas dinner together, the whole family circle, in-laws and all, were there. It was a mind-blowing time for me, after the years of solitude – all these kids, all running about shouting and pulling out toys and so on.

Six months later and Gusty again tasted freedom:

> The next parole they granted was in June of 1983, for our thirty-year wedding anniversary. Then they granted me parole at Christmas. I think it was a 72-hour parole that Christmas

Many close to Gusty felt that political considerations were involved in keeping him there. Nevertheless, they and others continued their efforts. Peter Robinson MP, deputy leader of the DUP, wrote to Nicholas Scott, Parliamentary Under-Secretary of State, on 26 September 1983, and in his reply Scott invited Robinson to meet him and to bring Louie Spence and their daughter Elizabeth Rea along.

Scott wrote to Robinson again on 27 April 1984 saying he did not feel able to recommend a date for Gusty's release. Robinson wrote to Scott on 22 August enclosing correspondence from Gusty's nephew. On 26 September, Scott made reference to medical reports saying that Gusty had been in the prison hospital and while there had had an asthma attack, 'during which an oxygen mask was applied'. Still Scott told Robinson he 'did not feel justified in fixing a date for Mr Spence's release on licence', but wrote 'all that you have said on his behalf will be kept in mind as we continue to keep the case under consideration'.

Gusty's nephew Eddie wrote on 16 August 1984 to W.J. McCappin,

Bishop of Connor, who replied saying that he had visited Gusty 'from time to time' and that he seemed 'to be a man who has prematurely aged, and whose wishes are for freedom, peace and quiet'. The bishop said he had taken the matter up with the NIO and had written to James Prior 'with a letter of strong support for the petition for the release of your uncle'.

Another politician who supported Gusty's release was Frank Millar senior, a North Belfast Assemblyman. He wrote to Douglas Hurd, who had become Secretary of State, on 11 September 1984, remarking of Gusty:

> He appears to have changed dramatically in his thinking and I cannot consider he would be a danger to anyone if released ... I cannot see him coming out of prison and taking control of any organisation.

Millar said he had met Gusty while he was out on parole and he had said he would like to help other ex-offenders on release:

> He wants to convince them – particularly first time offenders – that there is no future in such activities. If he could convince people that what they are doing is leading them on a road to nowhere, and that they will only end up in prison, then I suppose he would be better out of prison than in. The Government should also consider that he has done a fairly long stretch. If you take into account the 50 per cent remission granted to prisoners now he has served the equivalent of a 36-year jail sentence.

In September 1984, Gusty again put his intentions on paper and these were forwarded to his nephew Eddie. One of the topics he dealt with was his future accommodation:

> My wife lives alone since the marriage of my children and we intend to relocate ourselves in a more secluded, modest and anonymous residence but still within easy reach of our immediate family. We are very mindful of security requirements and we shall be circumspect in our selection of dwelling ...

On employment, Gusty referred to the restrictions imposed by his general state of health. However, he outlined a number of areas in which he felt he could make a contribution, including cross-community work, social work, citizens advice and community relations. He said he would also consider manual work if his health problems permitted this.

Louie's health had deteriorated and was giving cause for concern. Gusty wrote:

All of my decisions would have to take cognisance of what is ultimately best for her because her fidelity, love and steadfastedness over these long years demand primary consideration and my aspirations must become secondary.

He recognised that 'severe restriction shall be placed upon me on release and I find no difficulty in this respect'.[13] He reiterated his renunciation of paramilitarism and stated that he was prepared to state this publicly if necessary.

Gusty ended with the words, 'I have not written of atonement because one can only prove by personal example when given the opportunity. I need such an opportunity.'

Although the credit for Gusty's eventual release lies with many people including Cardinal Ó Fiaich, Trevor West and Paddy Devlin played a pivotal role. In 1996 I spoke with Paddy Devlin and he recalled:

Trevor West phoned and asked if I knew anything about Gusty. I said, 'No, I'm not in contact with him.' He says, 'He's been in there eighteen years and it's a life sentence which is normally only sixteen years. Everybody else that does a life sentence gets out after sixteen years but he's still there.' I said, 'I'll contact Jim Prior and the both of us will go and see him about it.'

So I contacted the Secretary of State and he arranged the meeting. Trevor came up and the both of us made the case to the Secretary of State that Gusty had been in for about eighteen years instead of sixteen. He says, 'I'll check it up and if that's the case I'll let him out.' So he was released and [afterwards] he came up to our house here and came in for a cup of tea. He thanked me and Teresa for the kindness shown towards him. Now that was the last I saw of him for quite some time and then occasionally I would come in contact with him. I remember during a debate we both had taken part in I realised how close I was politically to Gusty Spence.

It was after his release that Paddy Devlin really got to know Gusty. He developed a high regard for him:

I always felt he was an independent person, independent of the political parties, and even of the paramilitary organisations. He always had his own unique ideas on things, which had nothing to do with Green and Orange politics. It had to do with socialism, with the setting up of parties that would be dealing with political issues like they do in Liverpool or Glasgow.

> He was more a person from there rather than from here where he could quite easily become involved in the sectarian stuff. He was a non-sectarianist, which is a remarkable thing.
>
> I found him distinctive, wise in a way that I've never met a wise man in politics here. He had always an understanding, a great sensitivity in articulating political things ...
>
> I feel that while he's still on the Shankill, he is an obstacle to anybody that wants to create trouble. At the minute, he would be involved in closing down things in the middle of this bomb that went off.[14] I reckon that he would be a force for good in that sort of situation. He'd be closing down the militancy, and talking sense to them all the time and I reckon he would be doing an enormous amount of good.

I asked Paddy if he could understand how a leader in the UVF could move to a progressive position and if he could empathise with this.

> I can because that happened to me. I was in the IRA and I was jailed and when I got out, I headed to the middle of the road to deal with politics in the economic and social sense. I reckon that Gusty read and he felt the situations that I did and he would recognise the guys that were linked in with trouble and try to persuade them to knock it off. I would have great confidence in him.

Gusty had re-examined his whole outlook on life in prison. Could Paddy Devlin understand that also?

> I did that myself and I realised just what the factors were that he had to examine and then he had to bring his conclusions along. Gusty was an independent-minded guy from very early on and there was no question of bigots knocking him about or placing him into situations. He had an independent mind, he realised where the good of the community lay and he did something about it.

17

The Hammer Man Comes Home

When Gusty was finally released, on 13 December 1984, after eighteen and a half years' imprisonment, he was completely unprepared:

> I was out for a bit of exercise when one of the lads told me the governor wanted to see me. I went across and he told me, 'You have ten minutes to get out. I'm releasing you.'[1] I says, 'Ach no, I'll take half an hour. What's twenty minutes after eighteen and a half years?'
>
> So I went round and said cheerio to my friends. Coincidentally my wife and two daughters were up on a visit that morning and they were still in the visiting area. The governor broke the good news, and ... so the tap on the shoulder, which I had forecast, took place. The prison authorities were more concerned about Downtown Radio breaking the news with a whole barrage of photographers and flash bulbs outside the prison. Prisons are like that; they don't like too much publicity.

Gusty's daughter Elizabeth remembers the day of her father's release:

> My daddy hadn't been very well and my mother, myself and my other sister Catherine visited him that day. They let us leave a parcel and when we went to get searched we were told to go to the office. I thought sure there was something wrong.

Louie recalls that she was approached by a prison officer who asked, 'Could I speak to you, Mrs Spence?'

> I looked at the two children and thought sure something had happened. He was going to put them through to the visiting area but I insisted, 'No they're with me.' When he brought me into the office he says, 'We're going to release your husband.' I just looked at him and he said, 'Will you promise me you'll not tell the press until he's released?' I said, 'You can take my word on that. Nobody will know.'

The family had to wait in the office, telling people they were waiting for someone. When they got home Gusty phoned Sandra and Andrew at work and they cried on the phone. Louie said:

> Sandra was working in Gallaher's when she was told he was home for good. She went queasy and started squealing and people thought something had happened to her daddy. She says, 'My daddy's home for good, my daddy's home for good.' Andrew was the same so they let them out and the two of them came home. It didn't immediately hit the headlines until we had him home and that was when the press started coming. I lived in Hopewell Crescent and they were renovating the houses. I had all the carpets lifted and put in the back and the furniture was in the working kitchen so on the day he got released we hadn't a chair to sit on.
>
> Andrew lived two doors away and didn't the press come up to him and say, 'Is Spence in here?' Andrew says, 'No, Armstrong lives in here' – Armstrong was the name of his wife. They said, 'Somebody told us that you were Gusty Spence's son.' 'No' he says, 'I don't know who gave you that information,' and they said, 'Where does he live?' 'Two houses down there,' he says. 'There's a Spence lives in there but I think they've moved. But you can go and look through the window if you like.' They looked through the window and saw the house was empty. They never bothered again and that kept them out of the house in Hopewell Crescent.[2]

Some reporters went to Elizabeth's house and she told them: 'I've spoken to my father and he doesn't want to talk to reporters. He just wants to settle into a normal pattern of life. We are glad to have him home; it's been a long time and he wants to spend time with his family.'

I asked Gusty how he had felt being back with his family after nearly twenty years.

> My feelings were of overwhelming relief and love, of deep, deep emotion, especially when all my grandchildren were all around me, because the first place each of the grandkids had been taken was to Long Kesh, virtually as soon as they were born.

Gusty returned to a Shankill that had massively changed since 1966. Joseph Street and the Hammer had gone, though in his mind's eye Gusty could still picture every street. In reality, however, he said, 'I might as well have been in another town.' There was very little of the old Shankill left but he could see Clifton Street Orange hall – some things never changed.

He had told Bob Hynds in his letter smuggled out of Long Kesh in July 1981 that it would take him about ten seconds to be rehabilitated to outside life. He was right: he had no difficulty whatsoever. He remained as self-disciplined as ever, and after his release he maintained a rigorous fitness training programme. Every morning he was jogging on the streets of the Shankill from 6.00 a.m.

Soon after his release, 'John' organised a party to celebrate. Gusty told me:

> They held a 'welcome home' party in the *Orange Cross* club in the old Craven Street Unionist hall that was now a workingmen's club. I saw a lot of old faces that I hadn't seen for many years. 'John' and Ken Hagan did most of the organisation. They brought families home from far-flung places. Louie's brother came from Oldham and others came across from Luton and elsewhere. They paid their fares, found accommodation, and hid them until we walked in that night.
>
> Oh God bless us, it was mind-blowing seeing all these faces. My nephew-in-law from Dublin was there that night and Sheila said he was shaking because 'the boys' were there. The war was still on and they were all tooled up. Later in Luton he said to me, 'I want you to do me a turn. Are you still going to that wee club, the *Orange Cross*?' I said, 'Aye,' and he says, 'Will you look for one of the chairs to see if the big brown stain's still there?' Here was a fellow, Catholic born and reared in Dublin, who found himself in the midst of all this.

Gusty's brother Ned and his wife Kathleen were there with their son Ronnie. The reunion represented a coming-together of people from across the political spectrum.

Gusty soon decided to take up an invitation from Cardinal Ó Fiaich. He and Louie drove down to Armagh and met the Cardinal at his residence, Ara Coeli, beside the cathedral. Louie wanted to smoke but wouldn't in front of the Cardinal so Gusty said:

> 'Cardinal, would you give this lady permission to smoke. She's dying for a smoke?' He says, 'Smoke away there,' but she wouldn't. It was just part of the old tradition, out of respect. I had driven down but Louie was driving back because I knew the Cardinal was fond of a wee tipple and I'm fond of a wee tipple myself. The Cardinal said, 'What will you have?' as he opened a cupboard. 'Ah God bless us,' says I, 'what are you having?' He says, 'I'm having a wee drop of Crested Ten.' Says I, 'Well I'll join you in a wee drop of Crested Ten.'
>
> He turned to Louie. 'Mrs Spence?' Louie said, 'No, I don't drink, Your Eminence. I'll take a wee mineral,' and he said, 'What about a wee orange?' – his favourite tune was 'The Ould Orange Flute'. I slagged him about this and said, 'Was that because your man turned a Taig?'
>
> We got good work done and he had full knowledge of people within the Catholic Church who were talking to the Provos, talking to me, and talking to others. They were trying to give the Provos an alternative to physical force.
>
> These were some of the more enriching moments of my life. I was completely trusted by them as indeed I trusted them completely.

About this time I wrote to 'John', asking to meet Gusty. 'John' immediately arranged contact and I met Gusty in an attic room in the PUP offices on the Shankill Road on 14 June 1985. He was completely frank about his experiences and hopeful about the future.

A month later, on 10 July, Gusty agreed to meet Roel Kaptein at the PUP offices. I had come to know Roel through the Corrymeela Community. He had been a Dutch Reformed Pastor who became a psychoanalyst before developing a radical understanding of society and the Christian gospel, based on the writings of René Girard. In an article written in 1992, he made reference to his meeting with Gusty Spence:

> I two times met paramilitary leaders. The first time I went to the meeting I planned what to say &c. As soon as I saw the man I knew that my preparations were useless. We looked silently at each other for some time and then I said to him, 'I have decided to trust you.' He answered, 'I took the same decision. You can ask me everything. I will answer all your questions.' He did.[3]

I had intended to leave Gusty and Roel at this point, but Gusty insisted that I stay. He talked freely and admitted to having done 'desperate things'. Roel, like me, was deeply moved by the encounter.

After Gusty's release, he and his nephew were invited to lunch with Peter Robinson. Gusty didn't have a penny to his name. The only way he could thank Robinson was to present him with a Parker pen. Even that he could ill afford.

Another man who visited Gusty at an early stage was Dessie O'Hagan of the Workers' Party. Gusty recalled their first meeting early in 1985:

> I had known of Dessie O'Hagan and Dessie knew of me through my contacts with the Officials in prison. I think Dessie had a good understanding of where I was coming from and what we hoped to achieve. It was through Dessie O'Hagan that I met and developed a good friendly relationship with Cathal Goulding, Tomás Mac Giolla, John Lowry and Seamus Lynch.[4]

A relationship between some loyalists and members of the Workers' Party developed and remains to this day, despite serious political differences. A few people in the PUP, UDP and Workers' Party have been known to attend each other's conferences to their mutual benefit.

In September 1985, *Fortnight* magazine published an article by Andy Pollak based on interviews with Gusty. Pollak said Gusty was working on a political programme for the PUP, 'ad-libbing in the absence of a policy', but, Pollak added, when the policy was published there might be some surprises:

> The former UVF commander in the Maze, who now calls himself a socialist, is in favour of power sharing between unionist and nationalist parties, some form of Irish dimension, and a court to oversee human rights in Northern Ireland, which could include two judges from the republic.

Coincidentally, in the same magazine Danny Morrison of Sinn Féin said that no unionist leader would dare advocate power sharing and a friendly relationship with the south. But Gusty advocated both.

Pollak saw Gusty as being almost unique among unionists in regarding the intransigence of Unionist governments at Stormont as a central factor in instability. Gusty knew something needed fixed and, as with a blocked safety valve in a boiler, an explosion was almost inevitable in the absence of adjustment:

> We have to attain a society where nothing except the normal run-of-the-mill discrimination, which happens across the water and in other places, can be allowed to take place; where people can't say, 'I'm hard done by because of my politics or religion or whatever.'

Most of these ideas had been thoroughly discussed within Long Kesh and Gusty knew that a foundation was already being laid for change. The previous year, however, Andy Tyrie of the UDA had rejected compromise on the grounds that it would bring a united Ireland closer. Gusty respected Andy Tyrie as a progressive thinker in the UDA but disagreed, saying there was no possibility of Ulster integration in the UK or unity with the south. Each tradition had to be mollified to a degree, in the interests of a better society.

Gusty had also argued that integrated education at all levels was essential. Cross-border cooperation in areas like sport, energy and the economy was also needed and was already happening in areas like agriculture, fishing and tourism. It was the job of the PUP to point out that this cooperation had been going on for years and was nothing to worry about. Gusty was less happy with constitutional linkages with the south or a consultative role for the Dublin government.

He maintained that there could be security cooperation between the Garda Síochána and the RUC and, despite difficulties, between the courts. This could help in the fight against crime and terrorism. Referring to an issue that has blighted Northern Ireland, Gusty rejected the 'triumphalism' of Orangemen parading through Catholic areas. As far as the RUC was concerned, Gusty felt:

> It's a policeman's job to keep the peace without fear or favour. Loyalists look upon them as their police and are happy so long as they're doing what they tell them to do, and suddenly the police don't do exactly what they want and they [the Loyalists] become alienated.

Gusty saw no way forward without agreement and without some form of power sharing, and 'accommodation for an Irish culture'. This was what pluralism entailed, but such cultural expression should not be obnoxious to other people.

He favoured a Bill of Rights incorporating the European Convention on Human Rights. A European Court could oversee the implementation of human rights legislation. He accepted British government assurances that they would not pull out of Northern Ireland but added:

I'm not naïve enough to think that if the British government could possibly get rid of Northern Ireland with a wee bit of credibility and without leaving a civil war behind them, they wouldn't get out – of course they would.

But it would prove difficult for them to leave under any circumstances.

Let's assume the ultimate came and Britain said 'OK – withdrawal in fifteen years.' What does that leave? It leaves a recipe for civil war. But when the civil war is finished repartition was likely. You'd certainly have a big amount of death, but even after that subsided people still have to live here – so do you have another civil war, and another after that? You see, I don't think even when they talk about civil war, people are really contemplating civil war ...

Some people said years ago, we need a Beirut situation, we need big killing, and then people will come to their senses – such crap. If we'd had a preponderance of firearms in 1969 on both sides – on the nationalist side and on the loyalist side – there would have been such a slaughter that the whole situation – which is not completely irreconcilable at the moment – would have become completely irreconcilable.

Gusty was very critical of unionist politicians who called for Sinn Féin leaders to be shot and for the death penalty for those who committed violence. Other unionist leaders had been irresponsible in threatening loyalist violence should the British fail to listen to them. They were manipulating the fears of loyalists to force the British to withdraw from British–Irish talks. On southern Irish society, Gusty said:

The Irish Republic have a hell of a lot more to fear from us than we have to fear from them. I don't mean in the violence sense. Let's assume someone waved a magic wand and we'll have a peaceful 32-county Irish Republic ... whatever wee society they have down there, imagine what good radical Protestants could do to it. And they know it: you stop the average ordinary Southern person in the street and he'll say 'Jasus, we have enough problems of our own without incorporating those people up there – keep them away from us.'[5]

Gusty recognised that Sinn Féin was helping to meet the practical needs of the people on the Falls Road and they would have to be accommodated in any future political structures. People would resist sitting down with republicans, but they were elected representatives. Yet Sinn Féin had nothing serious to offer and he thought their *Éire Nua* document was only playing at politics. However there could be possibilities if unionists were magnanimous.

But there was little magnanimity. Unionists were captive to the fears they had fostered and they feared their inconsistency being highlighted. Northern Ireland was a sick society. Gusty had told the loyalist paramilitaries to 'grease up your guns and put them away'. This was one war that couldn't be won and Gusty said that only a Nazi would contemplate extermination or expulsion of the loyalist or nationalist populations. The only real alternative was accommodation. He then reflected on the role of Terence O'Neill and his 'timid moves' towards reform, which were seen by unionists as a sell-out:

> Maybe that was the inspiration for me joining the UVF in the first place – to fight against the sell-out. Sell-out? You must be joking. How much internal squirming I have done thinking how politically naïve I was ... Frightening people is nothing new in Unionist circles, because even then, immediately previous to elections, there was always a plot to assassinate a cabinet minister. In 1966 there was a plot to take over the City Hall and make another GPO, like 1916. What crap! But people actually believed it and here's one silly fool who really did believe that.[6]

On 15 November 1985, the Anglo-Irish Agreement was signed at Hillsborough. According to Bew and Gillespie, many unionists saw this as a cause for consternation:

> The Anglo-Irish Agreement ushered in an era of direct rule with a green tinge, symbolised by the permanent presence of Irish government officials at Maryfield, County Down. The Agreement was novel in its explicit acceptance of a role for the Irish Government in the affairs of the North as a defender of the interests of the nationalist community.[7]

The British had accepted that the Irish government had a legitimate interest in Northern Ireland. Peter Robinson of the DUP said they had signed away the Union and unionists were now on the window ledge of the Union. But he added, 'that does not mean we will jump off'.[9]

The focus of opposition was centred on Maryfield, where the Irish government officials in the Anglo-Irish Secretariat were permanently based. It symbolised Irish involvement, so a twenty-four-hour protest was maintained at the gates. Gusty saw this as futile:

> I said to the PUP and the UVF, 'What's so fucking holy or sacred about

Maryfield?' If they don't sit in Maryfield they're going to sit in Dublin or Timbuktu or North Korea. They're going to sit somewhere. It was the big thing to protest that nothing would happen unless Maryfield was abolished. But then there was a wee overrun of the trenches and they demanded its suspension for six months, then for three months ... and then everybody closed their eyes and pretended that Maryfield didn't exist.

Gusty told the UVF there should be no physical response to the Anglo-Irish Agreement.

There wasn't and I'm convinced it was because of this that the politicians realised that they could no longer manipulate the paramilitaries. My view, which I was giving to members of the PUP and loyalist paramilitaries, was, 'Let's sit back and see exactly what the agreement entails.' People were suggesting that it was joint sovereignty but it wasn't. It gave a neighbouring state an input into our state. On the other hand, if the British government wanted, it gave the British government an input into a neighbouring state also.

The politicians were making threats but I said, 'Sit back and relax and see what they're going to do' and of course they did nothing. They had a mass rally, quite a productive mass rally where up to a quarter of a million people turned up and it was 'never, never, never'.[10] But there was nothing after that. The UVF and UDA were quite placid. They too had come of age; they too were reading the political runes. Some had been through the supergrass trials with which unionist politicians had agreed, saying, 'Well, this is the way to put these fellows behind bars.' It was loyalists they were talking about but saying 'we only meant republicans' behind hands. Senior officers from both the UDA and UVF were being put away, a blasphemous passage in judicial terms.

Gusty saw the rejection of political change as a form of trench warfare. Trenches were dug with a determination never to yield an inch, but the 'enemy' always overran the trenches. The defenders retreated to dig more trenches with the same level of determination and the same result. Gusty was frustrated by this:

Let us put an end to it; let us do what we know to be right. Even Paisley knows that this is right, so let us do it. Let us purge the ghosts, and exorcise the spectres. Do away with the ritualistic incantations.

I asked Gusty if at that stage there was much radicalism left in the UVF:

When I came out of prison the supergrass thing was in full flow and the more enlightened UVF elements were languishing in jail. But there was continuity in their thinking. People were asking, 'Where are we going? How long is this going to last? What's going to be the end result?' They were questioning the futility of war and it was happening on both sides. People were saying, 'I don't want this for my grandson or my grandchildren. There has to be another way.'

I think it fitting and proper that all soldiers should think in that way, but leaders of paramilitary organisations could quite suddenly feel the need to purge the ranks. This happened in the past and people were conscious of purges in the UVF and the IRA. However enlightened Adams would want to be and however quickly he would move, he too has to be extremely careful. They have a southern contingent who really didn't understand the situation. That all changed when northerners got control. There are still notable IRA men in the south holding a certain amount of power who tried to embarrass Adams and the IRA after the first ceasefire in 1994.

I was watching the signs in the IRA. It's a very secretive organisation but at the same time it can be very public. Knowing who was moving and who wasn't and what they were trying to do and trying not to do. The body language and the language itself had changed subtly at that point. There was a change in language, just as there was a change in UVF language by the late 1980s.

One of Gusty's main roles was publicising the thinking of the PUP. They had talented people like David Overend, formerly of the Northern Ireland Labour Party, but they needed a higher public profile, so Gusty was 'broadening the empire a wee bit'. According to him, people from elsewhere began to come to the Shankill Road to seek interviews and to pursue some of the more positive things that were said. 'Sometimes I embellished it.'

Loyalists faced a difficult task, knowing that hostile reactionary forces would present any change as a sell-out. In July 1986 the PUP published a policy document entitled *War or Peace, Conflict or Conference*, in which some of Gusty Spence's thinking is evident. The Anglo-Irish Agreement sought a governmental framework for peace making but had not involved the unionist population. The PUP policy document, in contrast, stated:

> There can be no settlement to the political and social unrest in Ulster until there is a greater understanding by people – national and international – that the stony path to peace and reconciliation lies mainly in our small community just as it would at Toxteth or Finchley.

The document stated that the PUP was 'the only Socialist Unionist Party in this region'. Its members were fiercely British but felt that Northern Ireland politics should not be 'slavishly aligned' with either Conservative or Labour parties and should seek the best for this region. The Anglo-Irish Agreement had created an alienated majority of more than two thirds of the population, the document stated, adding:

> We do not want the joint authority rule that has been imposed WITHOUT CONSENT – and no democrat worth his salt can join with the collaborators in shaking hands with the devils that jointly imposed it.

The document called for a Bill of Rights for UK citizens, guaranteed by the European Court of Human Rights and the United Nations. Education should be integrated and north/south cooperation could be helpful. However, locally elected representatives should deal with issues requiring north–south cooperation. Nor should constitutional issues be permitted to rupture meaningful dialogue, hence a veto should be in operation.

The document listed areas in which cooperation was already taking place, arguing that the whole issue of north–south cooperation should be put on an open basis and not presented as a 'Council of Ireland' – a concept that it said had been fatally damaged in 1974. On violence, the document said that if the IRA stopped their attacks violence would be at an end. The document reproduced the PUP's ideas on devolution and said that the Assembly then in existence would require total restructuring:

> The main objective must be to obtain agreement, from all political parties if possible, on movement towards more general acceptability of sharing responsibility within a broadened structure of local government.

A year later, in early July 1987, a Unionist Task Force, to which the PUP contributed, reported on its findings to James Molyneaux and Ian Paisley, proposing an alternative to the Anglo-Irish Agreement. The report envisaged a power-sharing administration, but the two party leaders failed to respond. Gusty recalls speaking with Frank Millar, secretary of the UUP, who led the Unionist Task Force, together with Peter Robinson and Harold McCusker:

> I said, 'What happens, boys, whenever your leaders reject this?' Frankie Millar looked at the others. Harold McCusker was sitting to his right and Peter Robinson was sitting to his left. Frankie said, 'We're honourable men and we'll take an honourable course,' and he told me what happened to the

> Task Force report. He had tendered the report to Jim Molyneaux who put it in his inside pocket. He never read it but said, 'The two leaders are about to take an initiative here.' Frankie Millar resigned, not only from the Ulster Unionist Council, he resigned from the heap. Peter Robinson resigned from the deputy leadership and McCusker says, 'I'm ill, Gusty,' that was all.

Gusty began holding private meetings with interested people, including journalists. His first interview was with Jackie Redpath, then editor of the *Shankill Bulletin*, who published an article in November 1987 on Gusty's childhood background in the 1930s. Gusty also gave an interview to RTÉ:

> I wanted to speak first to the loyalist people of the Shankill Road. I wanted to tell them who I was, what I was, where I intended to go, and where I had been. I wanted to speak to the people of the Free State, to let them see a different face than they had seen on their screens, one prepared to admit some of the wrongs that had been done. If the people of the Free State would admit the wrongs they had done it would be a better world. I'm not just talking about Fethard-on-Sea; I'm talking about total amnesia about the First World War.

Gusty needed somewhere other than the PUP offices to meet with people from different backgrounds. The Shankill Activity Centre fulfilled this purpose, and it was here that I conducted my first interviews with Gusty in 1989–90:

> The Activity Centre aimed to give employment to returning prisoners. It was the forerunner of EPIC [Ex-Prisoners Interpretative Centre]. We were trying to say to the government, 'Listen, we have jobs for these men.' The centre also gave me a base, and Ken Hagan and myself planned it. This was unheard of on the Shankill Road and we had to take baby steps at first.
>
> I met Cooperation North, for example, and I went as a representative of the Shankill Activity Centre to meet Father Myles Cavanagh, working in the Brookfield Mill near Ardoyne. I passed a good hour and a half talking over matters of mutual concern, including political matters. I met Father Matt Wallace who was a leading light in community activity in the Falls Road. I was transmitting what was going on within my particular patch of loyalism and how thinking had changed.

Gusty viewed the technology suites at Cavanagh's and Wallace's centres and wanted to introduce something similar on the Shankill. Through computer technology they could teach skills to the young and unemployed and to those who had become redundant:

I found both men most enlightening and I felt sorry there weren't any Protestant clergy with the same interest. I suppose it goes back to, 'Well we're concerned about things spiritual as opposed to secular.' Catholic priests in contrast had a tradition of involvement in cooperatives in places like Donegal. There were exceptions like the Presbyterian Shankill Road Mission and some Methodists as well as the Salvation Army. But they would have been involved in charitable work. It seems nonsense to me that Irish church missions go to Africa to set up a village infrastructure so people can get clean water yet neglect these things at home.

Gusty sought to motivate UVF men and ex-prisoners:

I was speaking to the UVF saying, 'For flip sake, boys, wise up.' I was trying to persuade, and some of them were easily persuaded. The like of 'Victor' and 'Mark' and 'Jack' were sharp as a tack. Those fellows needed no convincing. What they needed was soul mates to carry it forward, and it paid dividends.

I asked Gusty how far he was able to work with the PUP and/or the UVF after his release?

It was the PUP who approached me. I said, 'I won't have any UVF involvement because that would cramp my whole style.' I didn't want any involvement in the UVF because I wanted to be in a position to criticise when criticism was required. A UVF man said, 'Oh you said you wouldn't do what the UVF tells you?' Says I, 'That's right, I won't do what the UVF tells me, I want to be a free agent.' I remember one UVF man saying to a councillor, 'You'll do what you're told.' That took away any freedom of movement. I wanted a free hand, but I did consult the UVF.

Gusty even met people from the then Soviet Union:

I spoke with left-wing papers – like *Pravda*, *L' Humanité*, the *Daily Worker*, the Hungarian papers and Czechoslovakian papers – which were mainly from behind the Iron Curtain. I said things that from a socialist perspective seemed strange. Socialism always fell back on Marxism, Leninism or Trotskyism or revisionism. They were all hung up with dogmas. I said – I'm a socialist and socialism should be caring and those people wanted to know more about this.

I was challenged about some of these things so I said, 'Well you're from Russia; you were the main directors of this philosophy. Here's a man from France and he would disagree with you and would say he's as good a socialist as you are. But he would disagree on many things. Here's a man

> here from England and he would probably disagree with the others.' I was chiding Russians and I was chiding anyone, including republicans and unionists, who were totalitarian and unshakeable or immovable in their views. It's shakeability that makes the world go round.

In February 1987 the Communist *Morning Star* paper interviewed Gusty, and in July that year the *Leninist* interviewed his brother Ned about him.[11] In the *Morning Star* interview Gusty is quoted as saying, 'If there was peace tomorrow our biggest enemies would be Paisley and Molyneaux.' He said they had to be challenged because theirs 'would be a sectarian state'. In response, the Reverend Martin Smyth MP, Grand Master of Belfast County Grand Orange Lodge, wrote, 'the use of the word "sectarian" as an indictment of our Province by supporters of a philosophy which manifests itself mainly in Russia and its satellites, enslaves millions'. Smyth went on to suggest that we should 'heed the call to turn away from the two "Rs" of perversion – Rome or Red – and towards the "R" of enlightenment: Reformed'.[12] This illustrates the kind of hurdle that was faced by the emerging PUP.

The Derry republican Shane Paul O'Doherty was released from prison on licence in August 1989. He had been sentenced in 1976 for posting letter bombs. Before being released he rejected violence saying, 'I came to the conclusion that injuring people and taking people's lives ... created a society of massive injustice. We became part of the problem.'[13] In 1992, Gusty met Shane Paul O'Doherty at the request of Ciaran McKeown of the Peace People. Gusty recalls:

> We shook hands and had quite a wide-ranging discussion. He seemed very knowledgeable, very capable. He had this exuberance, some would have thought arrogance, but he was speaking from a knowledgeable position. I was step by step with him and knew exactly where he was coming from. We spoke about the futility of violence, and he was responsible for some serious things like letter bombs.

He and Gusty received a request to address a meeting of the Irish Association in October 1992. The meeting took place at the Gresham Hotel, Dublin, and was chaired by Enda McDonagh, a theologian from Maynooth. Both speakers addressed their audience without notes. Gusty told them, 'I have the right to be a unionist, providing I pursue that in a democratic and peaceful way.' He received a standing ovation.

After Gusty had spoken, a man approached him and introduced

himself as Joe Colgan, saying that he had sent a card to Gusty in 1972. That was twenty years previously, but Gusty remembered the name and the fact that Joe had also sent him a book about old Ireland a matter of weeks after he arrived at Long Kesh. As a result of this meeting Joe Colgan later met other members of the PUP including William 'Plum' Smyth.

Gusty also spent some time with members of the Workers' Party:

> Cathal Goulding was there and I met Ruairí Brugha, whose father Cathal Brugha was an unrepentant IRA man who took the anti-Treaty side. He had come out of the Gresham Hotel, in which we were speaking, seventy years previously with both guns blazing and was cut down by Free State troopers. The hotel was convenient to the Four Courts and in my mind's eye I was trying to conjure up the situation in Easter 1916. Here was I speaking to the son of one of the main participants at that time. I finished up going to the Workers' Party club with my son Andrew. We had a few convivial pints with Tomás Mac Giolla and Cathal Goulding and a few others.

It was not surprising that questions arose in Andrew's mind:

> The ex-Chief of Staff of the IRA and the ex-Chief of Staff of the UVF were sitting together in harmony talking about issues like non-sectarianism. I remember him saying, 'Who are you, Da?' This had opened up a whole new vista to him. It wasn't really new to me because of my contacts in Crumlin Road jail, but it would seem quaint for someone confined to his or her own particular tribe.

I asked Gusty about his republican contacts after his release:

> One of the first men that came up was Brendan Mackin who had broken his ties with the Official IRA. We had this rampant unemployment and he and two or three others tried to do something about it. It was the first time a centre for the unemployed was set up anywhere in the United Kingdom. They could talk over their problems and receive assistance or give assistance in running the centre. This was unique, and I pay full praise to Brendan and people like him.

However, contacts with members of the Provisional IRA had not continued:

> To say there was hypersensitivity is an understatement. Here I was in the PUP virtually in daily acquaintance with UVF personnel. It would have not have been circumspect to do that although I was speaking to people who were speaking to the Provos. At that point they were on a bit of a high and

didn't seem interested in small fish. Loyalists didn't come into the equation because Provos were of the opinion that if the British government came to heel, loyalists would fall in behind. The Provos took a naïve view, considering 1974 and the Workers' Strike.

Maybe they thought loyalists were a spent force. There still is arrogance there but the arrogance is beginning to fade and in my opinion there is a growing respect amongst Sinn Féiners for the PUP and young Gary McMichael and David Adams and Frank McCoubrey and people like that because they know us to be genuine. I think one of their big questions was, 'Are these fellows real and are they genuine?' It's the same on the opposite side. Loyalists were saying, 'Is Sinn Féin real, are they genuine?' It's a question of being prepared to trust.

In June 1991, speaking as coordinator of the Shankill Activity Centre, Gusty addressed a conference on 'Community Development in Protestant Areas' at Duke's Hotel in Belfast. He told how a small Unionist Party elite had controlled and manipulated power in Northern Ireland from 1922 to 1972. There had been no delegation of power apart from a minimal amount to Belfast City Hall and the county councils where power was again abused. Those Unionists had betrayed the Union and manipulated the working-class:

The Catholic population was correct to criticise the absence of social progress or civil rights whereas the working class Protestant took all these abuses stoically lest their criticisms be seen as lessening confidence in 'their' Government and consequently endangering the 'Border'.[14]

Protestants who became critical were condemned as 'red flaggers' or 'closet republicans'. Yet Protestants on the Shankill lived in the same poverty. Even so they were told that discrimination did not exist.

Most pro-Union politicians had failed to address social issues and many relied on the same old rhetoric. The IRA still threatened and the rhetoric still worked. However, Gusty observed, a wind of change had begun to blow, and the abuses of the past would no longer be tolerated:

Ironically the proroguing of Stormont in 1972 was the catalyst that freed working class Protestants. The hypocrisy, abuses and pomp surrounding this unrepresentative monolith were wiped away by a stroke of a Conservative pen. At long last the working class could criticise. Many ordinary Protestants wised up and refused to respond to the clarion calls that 'Ulster will fight and Ulster will be right.' People who had responded blindly and landed in jail were later ditched by those who called them to arms in the first place. They played politics with their lives, a hard lesson that has not gone un-learned.[15]

At the conference, Gusty spoke of the need 'to show a more caring and magnanimous face of unionism' and to deal with the legacy of past abuses. All citizens had to be respected and treated equally so that trust and affection could take root and flourish.

Gusty argued that the RUC could not be classed as a normal police force: 'Little did the Catholic population know that we, too, the working class Protestant, looked upon the RUC with the same foreboding as did they because the RUC symbolised POWER.'[16] The Protestant Churches had 'consistently taken a pro-Government line' even when that government abused their powers. They failed to respond to social need because of an emphasis on individualism. They said little about unemployment, bad housing, inadequate education, hunger and state injustices, because they saw their role as spiritual. Only a few Protestant ministers demonstrated a social conscience by ploughing lonely furrows. The education system had failed working-class Protestants who were 'deemed fodder for the mills, shipyards and heavy industry'. The schools failed to teach Irish history, so generations of Protestants were ignorant of the history that had shaped them.

Other former UVF prisoners too were getting involved in building dialogue in unlikely places and discussing the PUP's ideas.

> When people like Billy Hutchinson, David Ervine, Billy Mitchell, Eddie Kinner, Martin Snodden and others came out of prison they started running with the ball themselves. Billy Hutchinson, for example, went right into the Bogside and got a standing ovation.

Gusty was in contact with Catholic priests from Clonard Monastery but could not be precise about how this came about. Certainly a prominent priest phoned him and began to visit his home.

> He used to come to our street. Now in this district we're still living in times when they'd say, 'The dirty bastards – they're bringing a priest into the street, they're selling us out.' Even now people are liable to come and set the house on fire.[17]

'Jack' was also in contact with the Clonard priests through the Cornerstone Community, a church-based reconciliation group. Gusty encouraged this contact, but 'Jack' told me he had always been a strong advocate of dialogue. He was a Methodist layman who established contact through the Reverend Sam Birch, a Methodist Minister in the Shankill.

'Jack' was once invited to attend a memorial service at Clonard Monastery for a woman who had worked in the area but died after returning to Scotland. He found it one of the most moving and enjoyable experiences of his life. These contacts grew and 'Jack' was able to pass messages between loyalists and the Catholic clergy, who in turn had contact with republicans:

> It wasn't widely known within the UVF that this relationship existed. I was relaying UVF thinking to the Clonard priest and he in turn was relaying it to the Provos and then coming back. It's been a long hard road, and some people are claiming most of the credit, but there are people who played a much greater part and put in a lot of hard graft – the unsung heroes.
>
> I was asked would we meet Sinn Féin. Now if that had been left to me I would have welcomed it, because dialogue always helps. It doesn't matter if you're talking for ten years. If nobody is being killed you just carry on talking. But the circumstances were never quite right.

A number of UVF men took risks that few outsiders could understand. Peacemaking in this context was a life-and-death matter and was not about cups of tea in genteel surroundings. It was at the hard end that change had to come. The Clonard priests also spoke with the UDA. Gusty says this was about 1985.

> Soon after I left prison I had a good yarn with the priest and we prayed together. I'm not a great pray-er, but hopefully I'm a Christian – my type of Christian. We were both of the opinion that it would be helpful if there were communication between ourselves initially and then with other people in a secondary manner to allow for hypersensitivity and misunderstanding. I would be speaking primarily about the UVF and he would be speaking primarily about the IRA, although he had contact with INLA.
>
> I believe the priest was dealing with Gerry Adams. Adams is a communicant and part of the Clonard priest's plan would have been to devise ways to get the IRA off the violent road and towards political movement.

On one occasion in the early 1990s 'Mark,' then a senior figure in the UVF, was shot and wounded by the IRA. Gusty immediately realised the danger in such an attack:

> I said to the Clonard priest, 'Tell the IRA and tell them this is from me: If they had killed this man, they would have killed a man in the leadership of the UVF who wants this conflict to end honourably and is working actively towards that end.'

The restraint of the UVF was not generally appreciated, and on one occasion when I commended 'Victor', a senior UVF officer, on their role in maintaining the peace, he said:

> Many people don't understand and don't want to understand that the UVF could have caused mayhem in this country. They could have precipitated a civil war in a flash. All they had to do was to go out and commit a major atrocity. People never give them credit for that.

Gusty met the priest regularly:

> We had a good understanding although people would have misunderstood where the priest was coming from. I never really questioned his politics but he would be the same as Tomás Ó Fiaich – a republican who wanted Ireland united without bloodshed.
>
> There was little point in me going to the priest with points of view if I was not confident they were accurate, though I could only go on what others told me. I was simply a willing conduit. I know the paramilitary mind and how diverse loyalist and republican paramilitarism can be. For example, if there was a 'successful' military operation and it went well it was claimed by the perpetrators, but not if it went badly.

Gusty eventually found he could continue in this role no longer:

> I said to the UVF, 'Look, you told me you don't shoot Catholics just because they are Catholics but yet you go across the road and shoot a building worker simply because he was a Catholic? I can't accept your word.' That was for me the straw that broke the camel's back and at that point in time I pulled out and the task was handed on to another person who I believe is still doing the job today.

John Hume and Gusty had met on a number of occasions while he was a prisoner. They also met after Gusty's release through the Cornerstone Community. Hume was also introduced to the UVF in relation to the peace process, as Gusty recalls:

> I'm speaking about a meeting that took place in the Cornerstone Community on the Springfield Road. At the meeting it was mooted that the UVF

were ready to call a ceasefire if the IRA did the same. Hume was then speaking with republicans and this was said so that it would be transmitted to the IRA. The UVF was present and I and others were there. We later met at the Everglades Hotel in Derry when a Clonard priest accompanied us.

When Gusty had first met this priest the IRA were not involved in the peace process:

I think Sinn Féin began to think along those lines when the Clonard priest and John Hume put propositions to them. I was only reflecting the views of one group and wasn't providing the full picture. I would have had more authority if I could reflect the wishes of all loyalists but I couldn't do that. I tried to get Protestant ministers involved in forming a consortium to speak with loyalist paramilitaries and facilitate a bouncing of ideas and a relaying of views.

My main task was to collate what was happening in loyalism and find the equivalent of the priest on the Protestant side. They listened intently to what I said but I never really got an answer. I think part of that stemmed from the bad experience Protestant ministers had after the Feakle talks.[18] I assumed they would need to go further up the ladder because the priest had the full authority of Cardinal Tomás Ó Fiaich. Bishop Cathal Daly was also cognisant of what the priest and I were doing.

The priest was the mainspring, although I was the theorist from my point of view. I wanted to see some theoretical ideas coming from loyalist paramilitarism, reflecting their innermost thoughts. This had to manifest itself in some political way as the priest was trying to do with Sinn Féin. I spent two days with John McMichael talking about the situation.[19] I'm not sure if John ever took up my suggestion that he speak to the priest in an exploratory way. I am convinced it did have some impact on him.

Gusty had met UDA leaders John McMichael and Andy Tyrie shortly after his release:[20]

I was closeted with John McMichael for two or three days, kicking the political situation about. When he and young Robinson produced the *Common Sense* document [which proposed a shared devolved government as an alternative to the Anglo-Irish Agreement], some of the things we had spoken about were in it. There were those in the UDA and the UVF who were looking beyond the violence. It had to stop – and there were people who recognised that when the violence stopped the situation couldn't be handed back to those people responsible for setting the scene that led to violence.

Gusty wanted to open discussions with Sinn Féin but this was more problematic:

> A message went from the higher echelons of Sinn Féin that they would like to speak to me. I had no problem in personal terms but my credibility had to be kept intact. I approached other [UVF] people and ... they weren't in favour at all at that stage. Now I believe that risks have to be run for peace but they have to be reasonable risks. The risks have to be evaluated and if, having done that, you see value in it, then go ahead.
>
> I could have spoken to Sinn Féin in personal terms. I could have told the UVF I was going to do it, but then again that would have been the whole lot up in the air. I would have liked to be able to go forward saying I had the word of the UVF and be able to stake my reputation on that, but I couldn't.

18

The Northern Ireland Peace Process

During the late 1980s and early 1990s Gusty and other members of the PUP were engaged in direct talks with the UVF, trying to elicit from them the minimum conditions acceptable to stop the violence. According to Gusty, 'We were trying to prepare the ground for a ceasefire to enable politicians to work for a settlement.'

> We put certain seemingly ridiculous propositions to them. Did they see the war lasting a hundred years? They thought this was ridiculous. Fifty years? Twenty-five years? Again they dismissed this. What was the least that they would accept for the war to finish? Firstly they said that the Union was safe and secondly that the IRA would fade into insignificance. There was to be no IRA violence and any ceasefire must be permanent and unequivocal. There was method in this because there were loyalist paramilitaries who said their violence was reactionary. That was wrong; the violence was a result of the Union being endangered.

On the question of human rights we found them extremely liberal. They didn't care who a person was or what he was. This was the UVF and Red Hand Commando and I think there was a mirror image in the UDA. Everyone was entitled to a fair slice of the cake. We found that very enlightening and it gave us something to work on.

Much of the discussions between the PUP and the UVF took place in sessions of what became known as the 'Kitchen Cabinet' which was set up in the early 1990s and met in Gusty's own home. Gusty regarded the venue as important:

It got us out of an office environment with constant interruptions through telephone calls and so on. Nobody knew where we were and it allowed us to concentrate. The discussions were hot and heavy, ties loosened and open windows to let air in. It was a hothouse, and it was radical and revolutionary in many ways. Sometimes we had to rein back radicalism coming from both the UVF and the PUP although there was some apprehension from the UVF at some of the things being said. We geared our analysis and attack along positive lines and we were taking the practicalities into consideration. Will the Irish government see the UVF and the PUP as pushovers? Well, we could disabuse them of that very quickly.

These meetings were seen by Gusty as being extremely important, involving as they did both the UVF and the PUP. 'getting their head round the political situation in Northern Ireland and how the war could best be brought to an honourable conclusion without concession of principle'. According to the journalist Peter Taylor, however, the Kitchen Cabinet was a paramilitary think-tank which came to the unanimous conclusion that in order to end the war it was necessary to escalate it.[1] While some members would have held such a view, military matters were not actually discussed. David Ervine is quoted by Taylor referring to 'the theories around our Kitchen Cabinet about escalating the war'. There is no denying that such theories existed among Kitchen Cabinet members, but members of both the PUP and the UVF were involved in the meetings and had a proposal been made to discuss UVF military strategies, Gusty assures me he would have rejected it. The reality was that the UVF generally remained relatively restrained when faced by extreme provocation in the form of IRA bombings and shootings.

David Ervine said in the same interview:

> In practical political terms we had the theories of the ceasefire in the bag. For the first time ever, this could be done. We had people thinking politically, people thinking strategically.[2]

It was not enough to have the UVF and PUP thinking strategically. The UDA and UFF also had to be on board. Gusty became engaged in talks with Ray Smallwoods of the UDA:[3]

> Ray Smallwoods started to come to my house and I think the goal of the UVF and the PUP was clear then. We had to await developments from the Provisionals and attempt to persuade the UDA, UFF and the UDP that there was a positive way forward here. So the Kitchen Cabinet was highly important.

Gusty felt that he and Smallwoods were 'travelling the same road'.

> Ray Smallwoods had this streak of independency within him, independent Ulster. Yet he saw how impractical that would be. He fell back on it from time to time but he was a good thinker. He and I had a good personal relationship and in political terms there was a *modus vivendi*. ... It was important to have two military men there, a senior UVF man and a senior UDA man. There was no use talking in political terms without attempting to bring the military men with us.

Gusty was meeting Smallwoods privately and it was only after the Combined Loyalist Political Alliance (CLMA) was formed that talks included leaders of the UDP like Gary McMichael and David Adams. Gusty found the UDP leadership very much on board and in his words, 'They were thinking along purely political lines, the end game, the outcome.'

The Ulster Unionist Party, however, was not yet on board, and by now many loyalists had come to reject the prevailing 'unionist family' idea. Billy Mitchell had done so long ago:

> There had been meetings with Paisley and other politicians and we believed we were part of the family. We didn't realise they didn't regard us as part of their family. All along we were the poor relations, yet deep down we could understand these people of a public profile and could stomach them saying 'We don't agree with your violence but you're part of the family, we'll look after you.' But instead they said 'You're scum, you're murdering dogs.' That's when we realised, 'Hold on, these people don't give two hoots about us. They use our violence, rattle the sabres, threaten the Protestant backlash, use us as cannon fodder, then dump us.' That's

when we realised we were not part of their family.

Gusty maintained that the Unionist Party would eventually come on board, but he recognised that loyalists had been, and would need to continue, setting the pace:

> We are driving the agenda. Those people either come along with it or they will be seen not to be pursuing positive lines. People will be in the position to say, 'Look at what the hard men are saying – why are you not saying this?' I believe we dragged unionism in by the ears but I keep on quoting the saying 'Only good people can say good things, bad people can't say good things.' I saw a big change in unionism when we came back from America and Molyneaux went out of office. Those positive elements shot to the fore right away, the Empeys, the McGimpseys, the Nesbitts, all those type of people. Trimble gave them the opportunity and took the opportunity himself with both hands.
>
> The greatest exposition of unionism that I had heard was from Michael McGimpsey speaking with the CLMC [the leaderships of the loyalist paramilitary organisations] in the Park Avenue Hotel. McGimpsey admitted things – 'Of course we have sectarianism. We are a broad party and we have the odd fascist or two.' That was a big admission on his part. It was an honest admission. When did you ever hear the SDLP or the Provisional IRA or anyone else saying it?

During the lead-up to the Brooke Talks on future political structures for Northern Ireland, the Kitchen Cabinet prepared the ground for the 1991 ceasefire. The UVF leadership was conscious of a mood for peace within the unionist community. According to 'Victor':

> A general feeling had been about for quite a while. The feeling was that we could claw each other all day and all night but we were really going nowhere and the people were bloody fed up by then. We had to ask – how could we do this in an honourable way so that it did not look like surrender or capitulation or appeasement? The feeling was so strong you could almost touch it. Just as when we knew our community had to be defended, we now felt the community was saying, 'Stop this.' I'm pretty good at picking up things like that and it was very, very clear. There were all sorts of rumours, with people coming and going all over the place. Every other week there was a different emissary or a rumour of something from some cardinal. There was always something on the go. Feelers were going out that the Provos were going to do something and this was going on for quite a while.

There was also a realisation among the UVF that 'Everything was pointing in one direction. The other road took you to nowhere or to a grave or Long Kesh.'

The public were unaware that this debate was taking place. According to Gusty:

> It wasn't quite a sea change but it was a tidal change if one was astute enough to gauge the demeanour of the UVF and listen to their statements. What amazed me, especially the senior officers, was their grasp on politics. For the first time I got an insight into how they were thinking, not only along strategic but along open lines. They were open, non-sectarian and using inclusive language. I found that extremely refreshing. The response, however, depended on the leadership of the time. There were some people in responsible positions who had completely closed minds and my motives would have been seen as squalid or questionable.

'Victor', then a respected senior figure in the UVF, said tactical considerations were invoked:

> We were caught between a genuine feeling that we wanted to do this and the use of strategic tactics. The strategic argument was, 'Well we can put the Provos behind the eight ball.' It was almost like what's happening now only on a smaller scale, 'Whose going to be left holding the baby?' The idea was, 'We'll float this and we'll see what way they [republicans] react.' They were probably floating something to see how we would react and after a series of kites being flown, the sky was full of kites. The next thing was it actually came to be real. So why not create a false momentum to get it started? That seemed fair enough.

According to Gusty, neither Ulster unionism as a whole nor the British government played any part in initiating the peace process or engaging with loyalist paramilitaries:

> Unionism *per se*, unionism *in toto*, did nothing to bring about the peace. They responded in part to the peace but they weren't speaking to the loyalist paramilitaries, although individual unionists were speaking to the loyalist paramilitaries. The British government, in relation to loyalism, did nothing to bring about peace. The Irish government did.
>
> The last people we spoke to was our own government, the British government. They underestimated us. Maybe they didn't think we were important enough to speak to or maybe they thought none of us were of

> the calibre to whom they could speak, *vis-à-vis* the Provisional IRA. There was arrogance in the British government. Prior didn't underestimate us but the then British government did.

In the view of Billy Hutchinson, the conflict should be resolved through peaceful means though

> If republicans continued their campaign we had to make sure we were able to match that. Republicans would have known this because I was quite clear about it. There was always this view and it wasn't a pacifist view. It was an approach to actually changing the war and moving it on from being a military campaign to one of politics.

Gusty and other leaders of the PUP visited the prison. The visit was not designed to gain the approval of the prisoners, though they gave their full support, but rather to acquaint them with what was happening. Gusty told me:

> The prison was a pleasant surprise to me but I was reluctant to go there. I'm a structured person and I saw that it was fitting that the UVF should inform the prisoners of what was happening but in no way seek their approval. The UVF didn't go to seek their approval, the UVF went to inform them and at the same time to receive feedback. UVF prisoners were just another company or battalion within the UVF. Whatever the UVF on the outside directed would have been adhered to.

Loyalists paramilitaries had come together as the Combined Loyalist Military Command. This was formed to enable them to act in concert, and it was based on the view that:

> Any ceasefire had to encapsulate all the loyalist paramilitaries. There was only one way to do this: they had to come together to achieve a universal ceasefire. They came together under the CLMC and if the militarists came together, the politicos would have to come together to map out a strategy. They did this through the Combined Loyalist Political Alliance. You couldn't have the PUP mapping out a strategy for the CLMC.

The CLMC declared a ceasefire on 17 April 1991 in order to facilitate political development. They sought 'a peaceful and acceptable solution to our political differences' and looked for 'accommodation' and a 'new beginning' but warned that if republicans acted to undermine the discussions, loyalists would retaliate.[4] The IRA rejected the approach, arguing that neither the Brooke Talks nor the ceasefire by 'pro-British death squads' were addressing 'the root causes of conflict'.[5]

The IRA at this time killed thirteen people, including a prominent member of the Orange Order. They launched devastating bombing attacks on Protestant housing estates in Cookstown and Donaghcloney. Loyalists saw this as a deliberately sectarian campaign designed to undermine their ceasefire, but the IRA feebly denied this, claiming that the Donaghcloney bombing was aimed at security force personnel.

The loyalist ceasefire, however, remained intact and ended only with the failure of the talks. The CLMC then said they had proved their desire for peace and had demonstrated their discipline by their responsible reaction to the sectarian attacks 'by republican murder gangs'.[6]

Loyalists were now playing a leading role. They tried to encourage fearful unionists to have confidence in themselves and get into the negotiations. They were not immediately successful and many unionists resented former terrorists claiming to set the agenda. Members of the DUP refused even to speak with loyalists in public.

Gusty recognised the potential consequences of a continued refusal to change:

> Ultimately if society was not going to change, we had the awful vista of a whole desolation and in my naïvety, I couldn't picture that. I pictured the alternative. I pictured a situation where people could say, 'I recognise you as a republican, and you recognise me as a unionist, so be it, let's reason together.' I didn't always believe that but definitely, from 1973 or 1974, that was what I had come to believe. Many times the UVF took fright and many times the IRA took fright with some of the things Morley and I and others were doing. They feared we had gone too far.

Early in 1993 loyalists opened indirect and ultimately direct contacts with the Irish government. Gusty suggested to me that the groundwork making this possible had been prepared by people like Chris McGimpsey and Ken Maginnis who took opportunities to speak at various gatherings in the Republic:

> They did a lot of pioneering work there because they realised a long time ago that unionism had this parsimonious, pinched, dour face and they were always looked upon as a mean and sour type of people and they are not that at all.

Loyalists still had had no contact whatever with the British government.

For Gusty, now co-chairman of the CLPA which represented the PUP and UDP, this was wrong:[7]

> It rankled me and other members of the Alliance. We were speaking to the Irish government, we'd been speaking unofficially to the American government, and we had even spoken with representatives of the South African government, but we hadn't spoken to our own government. Perhaps they thought we were not worthy of speaking to, or perhaps it was because we didn't put bombs in Balcombe Street and were small fish.
>
> When the first meetings took place with civil servants at Stormont [in early 1995], I didn't attend, though I had spoken to civil servants pre-ceasefire. I didn't attend any meetings until we met the Secretary of State and the ministers themselves. It was a case of, 'We'll speak to the organ grinder as opposed to the monkeys.'

The Reverend Roy Magee, who was to play a significant role in the loyalist ceasefire of 1994, introduced Gusty to a number of Dublin businessmen:

> Roy Magee said, 'There's some businessmen in Dublin would like to speak with you.' I agreed to meet them because things were moving in the right direction. The IRA appeared to be getting into the right frame of mind and loyalists had been in the right frame of mind for some time. There were people in the South that wanted to hear an authentic unionist voice. They wanted to get a 'warts and all' unionist perspective on life in Northern Ireland. The group came to the house here.
>
> One was a judge and a member of Fianna Fáil. One Belfast man showed more drive to get something done. He left his phone number and he had mine. Later he came to see me on his own, saying, 'I have certain contacts and I'll act the part of a conduit,' which he did. Later he opened doors to meetings with two taoiseachs and others.

Gusty's first meeting with southern Irish politicians took place in Belfast in 1993. David Ervine accompanied him. They met Fergus Finlay, Dick Spring's special adviser on Northern Ireland, along with Brian Fitzgerald TD. Both were emissaries of the Irish government:

> The southern government had approached us and asked, 'Are you prepared to meet Fergus Finlay and a delegation from the Irish government?' I said, 'I'll fall over backwards to meet them.' Aspects of what we said were included in the Downing Street Declaration. We told the Irish government through Fergus Finlay, 'We see this as a framework; there's nothing written

on tablets of stone here.' They agreed that it was a basis for dialogue. This was before the Framework Document came out.

Fergus Finlay and Brian Fitzgerald actually found their way into the heart of the Shankill. They spoke with Gusty and others in the Rex Bar. Gusty recalls asking Finlay and Fitzgerald if they were uneasy, but they assured him they felt safe.

After the ceasefire in 1994, Gusty was involved in a meeting with Albert Reynolds whom he described as 'a fixer':

> Albert Reynolds played it pretty straight, except for the decommissioning issue, which was discussed. We spoke about a Scandinavian country overseeing some aspects of decommissioning and a Canadian general was also mentioned. Someone said, 'What about money?' [That is, money to buy arms from the paramilitaries.] I said, 'That would be the biggest insult you could offer the IRA or the UVF,' and it was quickly shot down. The meetings were continuous and it was a mutual education. I found the Free State officials quite naïve whenever it came to Northern Ireland and what made loyalists or unionists tick.

Gusty also met John Bruton of Fine Gael, who replaced Albert Reynolds as taoiseach. Gusty found him to be a decent, open-minded man. But there were no meetings with the British government. However:

> Hugh Smyth, while Belfast Lord Mayor and leader of the PUP, met John Major on several occasions. Other people we had spoken to had a direct input into Major and Major knew the situation. I was pushing for the ceasefire to be declared when the Tory Party conference was in session, as indeed it was. The Tory Party was interrupted with the ceasefire announcement and there were bursts of applause all over the place. I wanted to maximise that opportunity.

Roy Magee liaised between the loyalists and the people in Dublin. According to Gusty:

> He spoke to the Combined Loyalist Political Alliance and the CLMC but I would not have been involved in that. When speaking to the Political Alliance he relayed whatever his contact in the South had to say and we would relay our response. There was quite a bit of that.

There were other Dublin contacts, and Gusty was indirectly involved in the links that led to several meetings between Chris Hudson, a Dublin trade unionist, and UVF men. An invitation was given to Gusty to speak at a meeting in Dublin in March 1993, but he was ill at the time and asked me to go in his stead. Those travelling to Dublin included Chris McGimpsey of the UUP, David Ervine, 'Plum' Smith of the PUP and a number of UVF people including 'Victor'. The meeting took place at Kinlay House in Lord Edward Street, Dublin. It was organised by Smith and Joe Colgan, Gusty's correspondent from 1972.

The meeting was preceded by a reception at Boss Croker's Inn on Arran Quay. John Robb, the Ballymoney surgeon and Dublin senator, chaired the meeting. Members of Republican Sinn Féin were present, as well as the son of the late Dáithí Ó Conaill who had been a leader of the PIRA. Their presence was inadvertent. They had offices beside the pub and Colgan had invited them along.

Joe entertained us generously, so much so that it took a full week to recover, but important contacts were established that helped facilitate the loyalist ceasefire of 1994. Gusty said to me that:

> 'Plum' Smyth later brought Joe to my home and Joe and I met on several occasions. The last time you were there and I returned his book *Tales of Old Ireland*. I endorsed it on the front in very affectionate terms.

At the Dublin meeting 'Victor', another UVF man and some PUP members met and engaged in conversation with Chris Hudson, who told me he had had contacts with loyalists many years previously. Ervine invited him to put his ideas directly to the UVF in Belfast. He agreed and met top people in the CLMC. He later liaised between the leadership of the UVF and Dublin ministers as well as meeting Gusty a number of times in Belfast. Chris tells me that: 'Even before I met the UVF I was beginning to question my typical southern Irish view of loyalist paramilitaries, in particular the UVF. The meeting confirmed that change of thinking.' Before meeting them he held stereotypical views of them as sectarian bigots with no political, moral or intellectual basis whatever. After his experiences he accepted that they had a legitimate political analysis and had adopted left-of-centre ideas. They wanted an inclusive Northern Ireland as long as the Union was safe, but if necessary they were prepared to fight the IRA to a standstill. They were not, however, losing sleep through fears of a united Ireland. Some had a deep interest in Irish history, and one UVF man expressed a deep love for Dublin, where he had spent his honeymoon.

Gusty says that in 1993 the UVF were trying to get a message across to nationalists:

They were saying to the Catholic people and to the IRA, 'Listen, this is a different ball game. We want to be reasonable and we want reasonability matched with reciprocity.' I'm not sure how much attention the IRA paid to the CLMC. I think they were more concerned about dealing with governments. A certain amount of arrogance had crept into Sinn Féin, you know – 'We are the true inheritors of the sacred flame.'

The need to involve community and political representatives on the ground in the Shankill was not neglected and in the early spring of 1994 the Shankill Think Tank was born. The Shankill Think Tank had developed from the Springfield Inter-community Development Project. Gusty was central to these meetings and although participants were exclusively Protestant, the chairman was able simultaneously to chair the nationalist Falls Think Tank.

Both groups were mixed in the sense that opposing views, political parties and ex-prisoners were included. In the Shankill Think Tank participants ranged from members of the DUP to the UUP, as well as the PUP, UDP and Independent Ulster people. At times the debate became heated. Some people were secular in their approach while others saw politics as being specifically about safeguarding Protestant religious traditions.

The Shankill Think Tank's first publication went to press within days of the announcement of a loyalist ceasefire and was entitled *Ulster's Protestant Working Class*, an exploration of Protestant identity from a grassroots perspective.

It was to be the political leadership of the CLPA, the confidants of the paramilitary groups, who launched the loyalist ceasefire statement of 1994, with Gusty reading the text. I asked Gusty if the paramilitaries themselves had been consulted in advance?

Yes. The procedure was this. The politicos would sit down, reason together and find a political way forward. A military representative from each of the organisations would come and the political representatives would spell out a viable strategy building up to a ceasefire. In the aftermath there would be some fine-tuning. Fair play to the paramilitaries, there were no major objections when we suggested there should be preparation for a ceasefire. We knew preparations were being made on the republican side. Intelligence told us that.

The UVF and the PUP were speaking through conduits to the Irish government. In September, one month before the loyalist ceasefire, the CLMC sought assurances on a number of issues – the permanence of the IRA ceasefire which had been declared on 31 August 1994, the intent of INLA, whether there were secret deals between the British government and the IRA, and the security of the Union. They also sought assurances that there would be no appearance of an IRA victory and that change would only come through dialogue and by agreement.

Loyalists had to break other moulds:

> Apart from Sinn Féin, one of the last political parties we spoke to was the Ulster Unionist Party. This happened after the ceasefire, in Belfast City Hall. David Trimble was present and we developed a good working relationship. Before we went to America, I met Jim Molyneaux, then leader of the Ulster Unionists, and Ken Maginnis. We could have had a good working relationship with the DUP if they had got off their hypocritical high horse but they refused to meet us. It's not as if members of the PUP were not speaking to the DUP behind closed doors. Indeed they were and reference has been made to the wallpaper and cups of coffee in their homes.

During the days leading up to the 1994 ceasefire leaders of the UVF and PUP spoke with a number of clergy and politicians. Some members of the DUP were unhappy with the prospect of a loyalist ceasefire and at least one spokesman suggested it should be delayed. A similar reaction came from a leading evangelical preacher who was not a Free Presbyterian. The UVF told him that they would not be giving up any arms, to which the pastor replied, 'Oh no boys, hold on to your arms.' This was not going to be an easy process.

In early September 1994, Gusty asked me to send copies of my thesis 'The Ulster Volunteer Force Negotiating History', in the production of which I had worked closely with him, to politicians in Dublin and London as well as to the NIO in Belfast. It had already been read by republicans and unionists. (James Molyneaux had told me in February 1994 that he and David Trimble were studying it with great interest.)

In my view the point of the exercise was to acquaint politicians with the new thinking in loyalism. The response of some Irish politicians was very enthusiastic. Tony Blair, who was then leader of the Opposition, replied somewhat condescendingly on 19 September through his assistant, Pat McFadden:

> Mr Blair was pleased to note that your group are seeking to work in harmony with your neighbours. Obviously at this time it is particularly

important that everyone concerned tries to ensure a peaceful future for Northern Ireland.

I asked Gusty what his motive had been in circulating the dissertation:

> It was laying on record who the UVF were and where they were coming from, and without overstating the case, 'The Ulster Volunteer Force Negotiating History', combined with some other things, proved pivotal because it allowed people like the Irish government to understand. They had their own intelligence sources but intelligence services tend to overestimate their own importance. Dick Spring read it from cover to cover without putting it down.

There was a lot of ignorance and misunderstanding and Gusty was at pains to explain that loyalism was not about any kind of dominance:

> Loyalists were not intent on discriminating against anyone – that was not their role at all. They weren't concerned about privilege for themselves or unionists. They were concerned about fair play. Society however is so blasé they believe what they want to believe, 'That's all right but they were killing people and yet they believed in equality!' It's easy for people who were not at the coalface.

Before the early 1990s there had been some reticence among unionists about the value of taking the unionist message to the United States. With the ceasefires on the horizon that began to change, and some Americans accepted that there were two sides to the Irish story.

On 6 September 1993, a group of Irish Americans, including Bruce Morrison, Niall O'Dowd, Bill Flynn and Chuck Feeney, began a visit to Ireland. They were collectively known as the Connolly House Group because they met Gerry Adams in the Sinn Féin headquarters on the Falls Road. They also met David Trimble, Chris McGimpsey, Jim Wilson and the Reverend Martin Smyth at UUP headquarters where they rejected views that they were following a nationalist agenda. They met John Hume of the SDLP as well as members of the Alliance Party but they were about to leave Northern Ireland without having spoken with loyalists.

Jim McDonald of the PUP arranged a meeting. According to Gusty:

> A PUP delegation met them about 7.00 a.m. in Duke's Hotel, Belfast, because they were flying back to America that morning. 'Victor', David Ervine, Billy Hutchinson, 'Mark' and myself were there. We said, 'Right, you say

you're impartial, we want to see your impartiality in action,' and we gave them whatever space and time we had. Bill Flynn referred to this as the longest breakfast he had ever had. For two to three hours we gave them a résumé of the situation and what could happen in the future. After they went back to America they had a reappraisal, saying these fellows have said something which is vital and has potential. Flynn kept in contact and was over on a couple of occasions.

The Americans found the Duke's Hotel meeting 'eye-opening, and saw that loyalists were serious about the peace process.'[8] According to Gusty:

O'Dowd and Flynn were searching in their questioning. They couldn't comprehend what we were saying until we went into the minutiae and told them how we had become involved in violence. They couldn't understand how as unionists we could be as radical and as different from the unionists they had listened to. They found that incomprehensible. Trimble was not in power then and we had had nothing but contempt for mainstream unionist politicians. 'These people will fight to the last drop of our blood and they'll lead from the usual position – from the back.'

They thought unionists were more homogeneous politically. We said it was the Union that drew disparate groups together, although our perception of the Union was different from [that of] the UUP, the DUP or Bob McCartney. The Americans found it puzzling but extremely interesting, and when they returned to America their goal was to achieve an IRA ceasefire. We threw a spanner into their stereotypical mindsets when we told them about the squalor and poverty we were born into. We challenged their perceptions but the biggest challenge was, 'Are you impartial?' 'If you are, you will extend to us the same courtesies and opportunities as you did to Sinn Féin and the IRA' and in fairness they did.

Bill Flynn was the leading figure in Mutual, the giant American insurance company. He was of Irish parentage and had been involved in a Derry conference on conflict resolution in 1992. Although an Irish nationalist, he was not prepared to see deaths for Irish unity. He had close friends in American law enforcement agencies and was an unexpected emissary to Irish republicans.

On the day at Glencairn in October 1994, when the ceasefire was announced, Gusty would discover Bill Flynn secreted in one of the Fernhill House rooms:

He was ensconced in a side room away from the media. All of a sudden, here's an American who must have had some prior knowledge, even though he was an Irish nationalist. They brought me into the room and I said, 'Bill, what to hell are you doing here?' He was talking to Andy Tyrie and I spent ten or fifteen minutes with him. That was after the ceasefire was read out.

Some loyalists must have telephoned Flynn and told him in a coded message that something momentous was going to happen and invited him over. Gusty thought Flynn was playing a positive role as far as republicans and loyalists were concerned, and he thought that they wanted him there at the end.

The journalist Conor O'Clery records that:

> The burly insurance executive was present in a back room, with the door locked, during the announcement, so that no one from the media could blunder in and discover he was there.
>
> 'I was the only Catholic invited,' he said proudly. 'The only nationalist or republican.'
>
> Flynn was serving a similar purpose for the loyalists as the full Irish-American peace group had for Sinn Féin. His presence was a guarantee of equal treatment for them in the United States.[9]

O'Clery claims that on the evening before the announcement, Gusty and six other loyalists were present at the Europa Hotel in Belfast drawing up the final version of the statement. Gusty was not present at that meeting, however. The only meeting he attended in the Europa was one with Father Sean McManus, another Irish American. During the former meeting, according to O'Clery, Flynn was in attendance and gave one piece of advice to the loyalists – that they should not change the sentence in which they apologised. He told them, 'I wish the IRA had said that.'[10]

The ceasefire was announced on 13 October 1994. The statement was drawn up and read out by Gusty, with some input by David Adams of the UDP in relation to the guaranteeing of Northern Ireland's position within the UK.

Seán Duignan, the Irish government press secretary, recorded in his diaries, 'I believe Spence – that's it; it's over – even though the Brits still won't accept it.'[11]

Two days after the ceasefire the taoiseach, Albert Reynolds, met Gusty and other loyalists face to face in Dublin. Seán Duignan recorded in his diary:

> I talk to Taoiseach in afternoon. He tells me loyalist heavies [he doesn't name them] met with him for two hours this morning. They discuss all aspects, including Articles 2 and 3 etc. They agree they don't matter very much, and that 2 is of no consequence. Any change should be to 3. Also that DUP doesn't speak for them. They say on radio that they may make submission to Forum [Forum for Peace and Reconciliation], but that at moment they won't send reps.[12] It may be that Gusty and [David] Ervine were among the guys that met Reynolds.[13]

The context of this first meeting with Reynolds was historic in that two Irish governments had been created in the same Dublin penthouse. Gusty recalled the meeting:

> Reynolds's daughter drove him to the Berkeley Court Hotel where he dispensed with his bodyguard. I then asked the intermediary to withdraw because we had other things to speak about, and only Albert Reynolds, David Ervine, and myself remained present. It was a businesslike meeting and we received assurances from Albert that they didn't wish to take over anybody. What they wanted primarily was peace and for the politicians to work it out, whatever way it had to be worked out.

Gusty had direct telephone contact with taoiseach Albert Reynolds immediately after the loyalist ceasefire. Some of Reynolds's comments were recorded in Seán Duignan's diaries on the day before the ceasefire came into effect:

> 'I've just had a chat with Gusty Spence,' says T. From Malvern Street to Merrion Street! He [Spence] was in at the start. Will he be in at the finish? Spence says David Ervine, himself, and one other, would like to come down to see Taoiseach. Will he see them on the same basis as Adams *et al.?* 'Absolutely,' says Albert, 'if you're going to make the right decision re present speculation that a loyalist ceasefire is on the cards.' OK. 'In Dublin?' asks T. 'Yes,' says Spence. 'Private?' 'OK.' 'Is this wise, Taoiseach?' I say. 'It's OK,' he says: 'I gather Fergus [Finlay] has already met them, so Labour will have to wear it.
>
> Also, the Brits have been bending the rules. John Major approved the recent meeting in the Maze of loyalist paramilitary leaders and loyalist prisoners there'.[14]

This might give the impression that Gusty contacted Albert Reynolds *before* the ceasefire. In fact the only contact made at that time was by the taoiseach's intermediary to Gusty on the day before the announcement.

Gusty recalls:

> I don't know how they got my phone number but there was a call from one of the intermediaries in Dublin and he says, 'A man wants to speak with you,' and the man was Albert Reynolds. Albert said, 'Can you come down?' I says, 'No I can't, Albert, because things have reached a very very delicate stage.' There were a couple of sticking points and we hadn't even met emissaries of the British government although we knew one or two unionists who had the ear of the British government. Anything we were inclined to relate would have reached our objective.

Gusty was conscious of the danger of politicians trying to leak the idea that Gusty Spence had been in Dublin with the taoiseach immediately before the ceasefire announcement. He declined a meeting, not wanting to upset any paramilitaries:

> Reynolds may have known that a ceasefire was in the offing, because there were also contacts with the UDA/UFF and with the UVF and Red Hand Commando. We knew my contact was relating whatever I had to say but I wasn't speaking for anyone. I was giving my opinion without betraying confidences.

According to Gusty, Reynolds 'was fully aware that the UVF would go back to war, with disastrous consequences, if there were attempts to alter the status of Northern Ireland without consent'.

Before the ceasefire announcement the leadership of the PUP had prepared a new party manifesto to be launched immediately after the ceasefire to capitalise on the interest generated by it. This was a progressive document reflecting the core values of unionism while avoiding many pitfalls. The PUP saw as folly the practice of placing tradition above first principles. While stating their commitment to the Union, the document said they also defended 'the right of anyone or group to seek constitutional change by democratic, legitimate and peaceful means'. They sought a Bill of Rights for Northern Ireland and wished to see 'an honourable and equitable society founded in democratic and accountable principles'. The PUP clarified their opposition to any resurrection of the Stormont system which nationalists so strongly opposed:

> We give our solemn pledge that never again in Northern Ireland will we willingly recognise or politically permit, as far as in us lies, a return to the

exclusive, divisive, abusive and corrosive political institutions of the past which were an affront to, and a blight on, the democratic embodiment and equitable concept of our country.

The Stormont system was gone for good and as far as Gusty was concerned

It was now a different ball game. Even Trimble recognised that Northern Ireland had been a cold house for Catholics. We said it first; we went even further in speaking about a corrosive and abusive machine. We knew full well that Sinn Féin would pull out the old red herring about 'a return to Stormont' but they quickly dropped that.

On cross-border cooperation the PUP manifesto supported the development of structures in which elected representatives 'could work together without interference in each other's affairs'. Other developments were taking place. A loyalist delegation was invited to the United States. Once again, Bill Flynn was involved. He asked Ed Kenny, an ex-FBI special agent working for Mutual, to look after the visitors. Kenny recalled:

He told me they were coming and were asking for the same courtesies as Sinn Féin and they would like to meet politicians and academics. The irony of the situation didn't escape me. Six weeks earlier I probably could have been surveilling these guys.[15]

The National Committee on American Foreign Policy, headed by Flynn, sponsored the visit. Taking into account the loyalist ceasefire and the kind of people inviting them, the White House waived any visa ban. Gusty recalls:

There were six of us there. On the UDP side there was Joe English, Gary McMichael and David Adams. On the PUP side there was David Ervine, Billy Hutchinson and myself. The American itinerary was pretty gruelling, with the last meeting being on Capitol Hill. They added a wee human touch. They knew I was an old soldier and brought us to the Vietnam War Memorial, which I found very moving.[16]

For Gusty, everything changed when they arrived in New York on 23 October 1994:

Going to America was a kind of pioneering. We didn't want to put on a dour parsimonious unionist face. We wanted to challenge America – 'If you are as fair as you say you are, why have the two sides of the coin not been viewed? You've certainly seen the green side, we're here to give you the orange side.' And we did, chapter and verse.

Conor O'Clery refers to the black humour from Belfast that was the order of the day when the loyalists 'came to dinner'. The new voices of Ulster loyalism, emanating from the back streets of Belfast and the Northern Ireland prisons, were being heard on a world stage. Gusty said:

> Whereas Gerry Adams met senators and others on Capitol Hill, we met staffers including Trina Vargo who was on Ted Kennedy's staff.[17] We had a good session with the staffers and were courteously shown round the Senate and House of Representatives. American hospitality was second to none, as far as food and accommodation were concerned. I will always be grateful to Bill Flynn, Bill Barry, and Ed Kenny and a multitude of others including Tom Moran, who invariably worked for Mutual of America. They accepted us for what we were and made a diagnosis that these fellows were straight shooters.

The hospitality was freely given, otherwise the loyalist team would have found it well nigh impossible to be there: 'The Americans paid the expenses. We didn't have two pence and we didn't fear anyone saying, "Ach, they became bought men because the Americans brought them across and wined and dined them."' The loyalists were introduced to Tom Donahue, a Democrat and deputy head of the USA's biggest trade union:

> We had a working breakfast at 7.00 a.m., at which we put our perspective on social and working conditions in Northern Ireland and how they could possibly help. We made some positive suggestions. We said that America needed to come over to Northern Ireland, especially in an era of peace, to survey the place with an economically unjaundiced eye and see how they could help to cement the peace. We mentioned the depletion of the shipyard and other things, and we got a good reception and suggested that the sooner a trade union delegation came to Northern Ireland and met fellow trade unionists and political parties the better.

The powerful nature of American business organisations left an indelible impression on Gusty:

> My first impression of America, especially of Manhattan and Wall Street, was of overwhelming power exuding from every sidewalk. It was a service society; it was all tipping and a 15 per cent service charge. It amazed me the amount of food that was eaten. I spoke with some of the drivers employed

by Mutual. They all seemed to be ex-New York cops or FBI and some were special police whose job was to guard visiting VIPs. We struck up a rapport with these fellows with Belfast banter and these fellows responded to it.

We were brought to the Irish embassy where we met President Mary Robinson and Dermot Gallagher, the Irish ambassador. I was looking through the window when I said something about Paisley: 'Aye there's a bast-ion of virtue.' They thought I was going to say something else and got into a real panic.

We were putting forward a reasonable case that many Americans didn't know. They thought it was just a matter of England occupying Northern Ireland and the need to 'get the Brits out'. But when we said, 'But we're the Brits,' they found this extremely difficult.

Conor O'Clery said the visit opened a new door into the heart of Irish America:

They made an unexpectedly good impression on the Irish-American activists who encountered them in the Irish-owned Fitzpatrick's Hotel in Manhattan with the Irish tricolour flying over the entrance or at Gallagher's Restaurant on 54th Street and Seventh Avenue, where they relaxed with Flynn, O'Dowd, Kenny and others, exchanging banter and making short speeches.

'It was the greatest tribute to Bill Flynn that this happened,' said O'Dowd. 'We had contacts with loyalists going back some time. The first loyalist community leader we met was Jackie Redpath from the Belfast shipyard. We talked to him in a room in Duke's Hotel in Belfast on our first visit. What he said blew us away. It was the first time I heard an articulate account of who they were, where they were coming from, and of their anger at the arrogance of the IRA killing people. My thoughts were that we must engage these people ...'

Ed Kenny thought the loyalists very astute, and despite their polar opposite backgrounds, the ex-FBI agent and the former loyalist guerrillas got on well together. 'Fortunately there was pretty good chemistry there, or it could have been a very long week for me,' he said, ruefully. 'They were genuine and very decent guys, and they enjoyed themselves. There were some sessions at the hotel bar, after which I had to do with one to two hours' sleep a night.'[18]

Gusty was very happy with the reception they received:

We were treated as unionists, not as deluded Irishmen. They found a different aspect of Irish culture from these unionists who for the first time in a combined effort came to get a particular story across. We saw this again when the American Committee on Foreign Policy set up a series of meetings for us.

I remember one of the first ones was in their own establishment in 57th Street. Father Sean McManus and the leading Irish Americans were there. An address was given and then we responded to questions. One wee gnarled man on a stick said to me, 'Gusty Spence, how can you say that you're Irish and British?' Says I, 'I take it, sir, that you're an American?' He sarcastically retorted, 'Yeah, how did you guess?' Says I, 'I take it you're also Irish?' 'Too true.' Says I, 'If you can be Irish American why can't I be British Irish?' That shut the wee man up. He came to me later and said, 'You made a point, you stimulated me. I never thought of it in those terms.'

The Belfast loyalists were determined to give a good account of themselves on their American trip. Gusty recalls:

We told our hosts, 'Right, we'll pull no punches. Bring us wherever you want and we'll give them chapter and verse.' They brought us to Boston, to the leading Catholic College in America, where we were well received. There was heckling from one fellow who went on about the Famine being genocide. He was quoting from some document as if it was an official document and David Ervine kept saying, 'Who wrote it? Tell us who wrote it?'

Gusty challenged Bruce Morrison:

Loyalists didn't call a ceasefire until six weeks after the IRA. Morrison said the police should move in to close down the loyalist paramilitaries. I challenged him on that, saying, 'Why didn't you say that the police should move in and close down republican paramilitaries? What fairness is this?' Two young fellows accompanied him and David Ervine said, 'I see you've got your Connolly Association badges in.' They took their badges out but David said, 'Don't take your badges out, we don't care what you are or who you are, it makes no difference to us,' but they were quite nervous.

These back-street loyalists would not be easily taken in:

We're not impressionable people and the Americans weren't out to impress us, that's just the way they are. Their diplomatic police were stopping traffic and going through lights. It felt unreal – 'Stop the car, stop the damned car', that type of thing. Getting us to the airport was a nightmare. Horns were blaring and they were travelling up verges and stopping traffic, but they got us there with a few minutes to spare.

Gusty found the tour extremely tough physically:

> America exhausted me. I couldn't go to the last meeting on Capitol Hill. My ankles swelled up and I had these wee pains. I had to stretch out on the bed. Everything had been helter-skelter starting from 7.00 a.m. and on one occasion it was five in the morning to catch a particular flight. We spent four or five days at Washington, Boston and New York.

Before the loyalists left, Gusty spoke with a former Northern Ireland girl, Rita Mullen, who was on Senator Gillman's staff:[19]

> 'Right, Rita, how do you reckon we did?' She says, 'You have done extremely well, Gusty. You came in cold, no previous hype, no fanfares, no nothing, and you talked the talk and you walked the walk.' The Americans were pleased because we were open and had nothing to be guarded about. We were telling it as it was, warts and all, and we took a pint of porter. I'm not saying we took the Americans by storm but it certainly was an eye-opener for them.

On their return to Ireland they were immediately confronted by antagonism:

> The garda told us, 'There's a reception committee waiting on you.' It was FAIT [Families Against Intimidation and Terror], I believe. I would have spoken to them but they weren't in a speaking mood. They said, 'Have you got your pickaxe handles and your duty free?'

Bill Flynn, however, had deeply appreciated the work of loyalists. On 20 April 1998, shortly after the signing of the Good Friday Agreement, he wrote to David Ervine congratulating him and Gusty on their support for the peace process. He said that the initiatives they had been involved in 'were critical to advancing a peaceful resolution':

> I join my fellow Americans, particularly those of us of Irish heritage, in expressing gratitude to you and Gusty for your willingness to give so much of your time and effort to achieving the peace that has so long eluded the people of Northern Ireland.

In early 1995, Gusty Spence and I discussed the Dublin Forum for Peace and Reconciliation which was intended to provide a vehicle for all Ireland's democratic political parties to consult together on the political way forward. It had opened the previous October, but was being boycotted by unionists. Gusty recognised there was a need for unionist voices to be heard but loyalists were not yet ready for this step. I told him I would be prepared to go, and so with Gusty's encouragement I travelled to Dublin, as an Ulster unionist speaking in a personal capacity, to present a submission. Colin Crawford, prison welfare officer at Long Kesh from 1974 until 1979, had been nominated by loyalist prisoners and former prisoners to articulate their views at the Forum so that the views of loyalists/unionists were heard.

There had been little direct contact between loyalists and Sinn Féin outside the prison context. The tendency was to communicate through intermediaries. However in August 1995 I was invited to share a platform in Conway Mill in the lower Falls with Martin McGuinness of Sinn Féin, former taoiseach Albert Reynolds and others. I again discussed this with Gusty and decided to accept the invitation. Immediately prior to the meeting I received a message of encouragement, indirectly, from senior figures in both the PUP and UVF.

In August 1995, less than a year after the loyalist ceasefire, the CLMC said that as long as the rights of the people of Northern Ireland were respected, loyalists would not return to war, 'There will be no first strike.' They went on, 'It is inconceivable for the Combined Loyalist Military Command to decommission weapons with a fully operational, heavily armed republican war machine intact and refusing to relinquish their arsenals.'[20]

According to Gusty:

> Although loyalist paramilitaries had called a ceasefire there was prevarication on the part of the IRA on the question of permanency. It was in order to put a certain amount of pressure on the IRA, to say or do something and to establish their own bona fides that the loyalist paramilitaries said there would be no first strike. It did put the republican movement under pressure.

On 9 February 1996 the IRA ended its ceasefire with the bombing of Canary Wharf in London. Republicans placed the blame for this on the shoulders of prime minister John Major and his government. For months, confidence in the peace process had been fading at a time when unionists were not prepared to engage in dialogue.

There were, however, some private contacts of which Gusty was fully aware and to which he gave his support. For example, a group of five unionists met leading Sinn Féin people in Belfast on 15 November 1995. The Sinn Féin group included Jim Gibney, Siobhan O'Hanlon, Barry

McElduff, Bobby Lavery and Joe Austin. There were two unionists, Norman Porter and myself, a member of the PUP, a former UDA member and a non-aligned unionist.

At the meeting, fears were expressed by Sinn Féin that we appeared to be nearing the end of the peace process. They were convinced that the British government was seeking an IRA surrender. The republicans made clear that nationalists would not accept a return to Stormont. They were then told, with the loyalist rejection of Stormont in mind, that there were unionists who also rejected Stormont. The republicans were then asked if, in view of this, they could envisage a solution short of a united Ireland. The response was that such issues would take us into the realm of negotiations and they were not then prepared for that.

19

The Good Friday Agreement
The End of the Beginning

On 1 November 1996 Gusty and I set out for Monaghan and Cavan with Dr Tony Buckley, an anthropologist with the Ulster Folk and Transport Museum in County Down. We had two missions, one happy and the other a sad duty. First we had to collect a number of historical artefacts, including an Orange banner, from a leading Orangeman near Monaghan. This done, Tony Buckley then headed home while Gusty and I continued on our journey to Cootehill, County Cavan. Jim Lynch, who in the 1950s had been an IRA commander in Cavan and Monaghan, had died. Gusty wished to honour his old enemy by attending the funeral.

Incidentally, the preservation of the Orange artefacts would have been approved by Jim Lynch who for years had been involved in the campaign to have the Boyne site properly resourced as an historical site commemorating the battle of 1690. He had told me, 'From the point of view of Ireland, the Battle of the Boyne could be thought of as a civil war in as much as Irishman fought Irishman; father fought son and brother fought brother.' Jim remained a republican but he had rejected violence and had vigorously campaigned for an end to the IRA campaign and the support it received from the United States.

We met Jim's widow Norma and members of the family who had gathered in the small terrace house near the centre of Cootehill. We then travelled to the Roman Catholic church in which a moving service was held, after which we followed the coffin to the burial ground.

Jim's son-in-law unexpectedly asked Gusty to say a few words at the graveside. Gusty immediately agreed, and his words were a moving tribute to a former enemy. He spoke about Jim having many unionist friends and he used some of the words of the traditional British military lament: 'Age shall not weary them nor the years condemn. At the going down of the sun and in the morning, we will remember them.'

Jim Lynch had also been a friend of Cardinal Tomás Ó Fiaich, and in a letter dated 31 March 1995, he had told me:

> My late great friend Tomás Ó Fiaich thought very highly of Gusty and always told me that the great hope for peace on the loyalist side was Gusty. What a pity that the Cardinal didn't live to see how right he was in his belief and respect for Gusty.

Gusty had been introduced to Jim Lynch by Chris McGimpsey of the UUP.

> There was a cross-community/cross-border group, in which good people would have taken kids from the Shankill Road down to County Cork. It was started through a big fellow called Alfie Midgley and his wife Minnie who was a welfare officer in the jail. There was a connection with Billy Hutchinson, and my daughter had also gone down.

The group in Belfast was based on the Agnes Street Community Centre in the Shankill area. It was called 'Between' and was formed in the early 1970s by Criostoir De Baroidh and others at Cork University. Billy Hutchinson confirmed his own involvement and told me that he had taken UDA and UVF families to holidays in Cork. Jim and Norma Lynch had become involved. Gusty said:

> They brought separate parties of Catholics and Protestants on alternate weeks to Cork. They wanted to let people from the Shankill and the Falls know that there was life beyond their own boundaries. Cork was a very different place. Jim Lynch, like myself, had little of material value but after

he had left violence behind, he wanted to do something positive. He became friendly with Ken Maginnis and Chris McGimpsey and it was Chris who said, 'Jim Lynch would like to have a word with you and meet you some time.' I was willing – it was old combatants together. Chris asked permission to give him my number and he phoned me and we had copious telephone conversations, Jim telling me what he was trying to do and I telling Jim what I was trying to do.

He had informed me he was coming to Belfast early in 1995. He and his wife and a party of them stayed at the Forte Crest Hotel, Dunmurry, and he asked if we could meet. I agreed and we had a good conversation. He came down to the caravan with his sister and an American. His sister was a teaching nun, Sister Eileen from Liverpool. We had a pleasant day and they saw the countryside and Belfast Lough from County Down. I became very fond of Jim and in our conversations he used to relay to me the doubts he had, and of course I had the same doubts.

I had been at Catholic funerals before but never at a graveside oration. Jim's son-in-law approached me during the funeral and asked if I would say a few words and of course I did. I stated the facts, that Jim was a non-materialistic type of person but he was rich in friendship. He had been through the mill and we of the unionist tradition respected him for what he was. He respected us for what we were. I suppose we're living in an abnormal society when people thought it strange that old combatants would pay respect to one another even in death.

One day he said to me, 'We have a mutual friend.' I said, 'Who would that be?' and he said 'Cardinal Ó Fiaich.' He had met the Cardinal on several occasions and we spoke at length about him.

The IRA ceasefire that had broken down in February 1996 was re-established in July 1997. By that September unionists had entered talks, facing republicans across the table. The leaders of the UDP and the PUP, in a dramatic show of solidarity, accompanied the Ulster Unionists walking into the talks.

Gusty told me that 'Sinn Féin found that incomprehensible' and had said to them, 'Sure, you've nothing in common with those people?' But loyalists like Gusty Spence, despite their criticisms of the unionist establishment, remain resolutely unionist.

The DUP and UK Unionist Party (UKUP), in contrast, found the prospect of facing Sinn Féin unacceptable and left the talks for good. In Gusty's view, this significantly helped the process because the negotiators would no longer have to face constant puerile attacks and bad manners:

When the DUP and the UKUP walked out, we moved on apace. Obviously the UKUP and the DUP would say, 'Ach well, the real unionist opposition wasn't there." But listen, we are hard men who have been through the mill. We were at the coalface; we chopped that coal out and we sucked in that stinking dank air. We came out black at the coalface and I'm talking about a paramilitary sense. Nobody was going to pull the wool over our eyes.

We came up in the back streets where you don't let your bone go with the dog and we monitored everything that happened. We wanted it cut to the core to get at the ultimate outcome, with hard bargaining all round on issues like the release of prisoners, the formulation of executives and the distribution of seats. It was hard going. The first document that came out – the one that John Taylor said he wouldn't touch with a forty-foot pole – we wouldn't have touched either.[1]

After discussions, summaries were circulated and read. We sought to clarify points, as in normal negotiations. That document wasn't disastrous, but as Abraham Lincoln said about his Gettysburg address, 'That speech didn't scow.' When the plough doesn't turn the soil it doesn't scow – it didn't go down well. George Mitchell's first document didn't scow, at least with the loyalists. It had to go back and we were in right away, hammering our points. We thought that George missed some of the nuances peculiar to Northern Ireland. And of course the Ulster Unionists unleashed shots too, fair play to them.

During the negotiations Gusty and other loyalists tried to ensure that the British government did not make too many mistakes in their contacts with unionists. In Gusty's view, loyalists were uniquely capable of relating to politicians:

We are working-class back-street people who educated ourselves. We are articulate, we have a strategy and we're not unreasonable. Our speech is honest and straightforward and we call a spade a spade. Consequently any meetings we had were good, let it be with the Irish government or George Mitchell and Harry Holkeri [the former prime minister of Finland] and General John de Chastelain, and their staff.

One of the aides to George Mitchell was Martha Pope, a very bright girl who could see all sides. She provided a wealth of information for George Mitchell because she contacted the different parties. Some anti-Agreement unionists were abusive towards her.

Loyalists on occasions used street language, but Gusty said the Americans found no difficulty with this:

I was no more circumspect than Davy, but David Ervine gave it straight from the shoulder if a thing was not right. He would say, 'It's a load of balls,' but after he came off with 'balls' a few times I said, 'We'll have to find a better word than balls. Right, in future use the word *cojones* – it's Spanish for balls.' The *j* is silent and pronounced *h*. So I says, 'In future when you want to say "It's a load of balls," say it's a load of cojones. It won't be offensive and they'll certainly get the message.'

George Mitchell and Martha Pope never blinked an eyelid. They knew our origins and knew we weren't being offensive. It's not that our language was crude, and Americans would accept the term as expressively demonstrative. They would use the term 'bullshit', or more politely 'bull'. We saw Mitchell lifting the eyebrows. It was one of those amusing moments that helped to lighten up the very serious things we dealt with.

We were concerned with only one thing: pushing the agenda forward. The agenda revolved around two questions – was there to be governance of Northern Ireland and was there to be a relationship with the South? Cut through the crap, ask the two questions and get them answered. Is there going to be governance in Northern Ireland? Yes, there is. Right, that's a starting point. What will be the shape of governance in Northern Ireland?

It had been a particularly stressful time before the DUP left because they had challenged every full stop and comma. Gusty recalls, 'I remember a half day being given over to one word. Should it be *and* or *with*. It was inconsequential as far as I was concerned. It was filibuster, it was feet-dragging and it was the worst possible form of negotiation.' As a consequence loyalists opted for smaller meetings:

The big group was no use, with people having to push buttons to get talking. We wanted a more condensed group, we wanted blood on the floor, looking each other in the eyes, seeing the whites of each other's eyes, having a frigging good row. Getting to know one another. This was very important and Mitchell ran with that. It's no use a smaller group sitting in the same room, so we moved into a smaller room.

The plenary, as it was called, was always there. We could go into plenary any time but we had a sub-plenary in a smaller room across the passageway. People sat cheek by jowl, shoulder to shoulder. This was extremely important because people then began to engage. Some even began using first names. Sinn Féin always did that and we always called Sinn Féin members by their first names. There was never any problem with Sinn Féin, none whatsoever, because they were mirror opposites.

Contrary to what opponents said, Gusty has insisted that the negotiations were genuine and based on the assumption that the result would be an inclusive system of devolved government. At the final hurdle on 10 April 1998, a significant number of UVF people were present and fully briefed by the PUP delegation:

> When the last draft came down there were many UVF men present. Something like fifty-seven people were sitting in the PUP room and we went through that agreement letter by letter, dotting the i's and stroking the t's. The PUP and the UVF accepted it. There were things we were unhappy about but being practical people we knew there had to be give and take. It was foisted upon no one. It was the people's agreement. There were things we were unhappy about but we saw no real threat from cross-border bodies. The only threat there might have been was that cross-border bodies take a life of their own and by-pass whatever legitimate executive came forward. We couldn't have a state within a state.

Jeffrey Donaldson of the UUP walked out of the talks at the very last moment. It appears that his main concern was decommissioning. Certainly, to Gusty, he did not seem overly concerned about the release of prisoners:

> He spoke to a PUP delegation in their offices at Castle Buildings, Stormont, at three o'clock in the morning and said that if we could make a deal with the government on prisoners, the UUP could live with it. I think Donaldson didn't really believe we could make such a good deal. He underestimated us and underestimated the republicans too. Little did he know that the SDLP and the Irish government were pushing for the same thing. The Unionist Party's big concern was decommissioning but I think it was with a certain amount of arrogance that Donaldson said [that to us]. When Donaldson walked out, he walked out of those talks on the decommissioning issue.

Gusty Spence had been reared in the poverty-stricken back streets of the lower Shankill. He spent almost nineteen years confined within Northern Ireland's prisons, yet he lived to play a central role in the unfolding momentous political developments.

He once told me that he had walked with kings and princes but he was not talking about political leaders. He was speaking of those who came from the same back streets, many of whom had also been through the prisons. By their courage and example they demonstrated that a better way was possible. The role he was able to play in the peace process had a particularly deep effect on Gusty: 'Sometimes whenever I'm sitting talking to you I can't really comprehend it all. There's an air of unreality around what happened. It's hard to believe that I took part in those things.'

Gusty can become impatient with those who pour cold water on all that has been achieved. He can be exasperated with the small-mindedness that cannot accept that change is with us, who cannot accept that it was really the small people who brought it about:

> How do the people think this peace came about? Do they think that somebody waved a magic wand and all of a sudden it happened? If the initiatives for peace had been left to the DUP and people like that, we would have had continuous war. People wanted peace and these people were at the cutting edge. They were determined that other ways be found to bring this to a peaceful conclusion.
>
> I weary sometimes. Do people want war, or do they want peace? If they want war, are they going to fight it? No, they won't. They'll leave it to the security forces while they sit on the sidelines and tut tut. If they want peace, are they prepared to go for it? Fifteen years ago I said that people in Northern Ireland were not ready for peace and peace would come when the people wanted it. We still have 49 per cent of Ulster Unionists and 100 per cent of the DUP who do not want peace. Now they'll tell you they do but they want it on their own terms. No unrepentant terrorists, no unconverted terrorists – that type of thing.

Long years of marking time in Northern Ireland's prisons have left their mark on Gusty and on all the prisoners of the Troubles. He has nightmares:

> Even today there are certain things I don't do – stupid things. I would never ever read the *Sunday Post*. It was a jail paper and too reminiscent of the past. I would never watch Esther Rantzen on TV for the same reason. The nightmares take a similar shape. I'd be in jail and I wasn't getting out. It could be Crumlin Road jail but sometimes it was Long Kesh. Sometimes it was a jail that I didn't recognise. Sometimes it wasn't a prison but it was somewhere detached from my family and I wasn't leaving. This was the main theme in my dreams – I wasn't getting out.

The nightmares reflected decades of waiting:

> Every morning as I wakened the first thing I saw was the bars, or their shadow. If there was any light at all, the shadow of the bars reflected on the wall. That greeted me every morning with a bell ringing at 7.00 a.m. The

second reflective thing was lying without sleep and smoking in the middle of the night, my mind racing in every direction.

It was an eerie feeling, and it's not peculiar to me. Ex-prisoners waken up soaking with sweat. During the first few months or perhaps even the first year after my release I wakened at night with Louie saying, 'My God,' as she went to get towels to dry me. They were soon soaking with sweat, the bed was soaking and had to be changed. It was pure perspiration. There wouldn't be a week go by that I didn't have a nightmare.

Crumlin Road jail was a particularly bad experience because a big part of my day was spent in complete isolation. We got up to all types of things. We had pieces of string or thread and swung a sock outside from one cell to the other with maybe a cigarette in it or a paper or whatever.

Gusty returned to Crumlin Road prison on 20 June 2000 – after it had been closed down. I had arranged to meet him later that evening but the experience had proved too much. He had found it emotionally and physically draining.

Of Long Kesh, he says:

We were living in a community establishment with thirty-two people in each hut so while there were bars on the windows, those bars were a joke. It was a tin hut, but we could have a yarn, whereas in jail we were locked up at 7.00 p.m. until seven or seven thirty the following morning. In Crumlin Road it was only when we went to work, and during the first seven months I didn't work, or when we had association for about two hours at night, that we could meet together. We just sat about in a yard, that's all – it was just a yard. A group of IRA men were in one corner and about eleven of us in another, we were able to speak and we spoke each other's language but we had no private space to speak about private matters. If we went into a dining hall there were forty or fifty other people.

Gusty had been determined to have something better in Long Kesh:

I wanted to build up an infrastructure of interdependability, each man depending on his comrade. We asked for paint but they didn't give us paint, so we bought it with our own money. Our families brought it up and we brightened up the place. It was no longer a Nissen hut or a prison – it became a loyalist barracks, a barrack room that had to be respected. It had to be clean and tidy. I had set out to reverse the roles, which Bob Truesdale called broadening the empire and wasn't far away. Whereas in Crumlin Road jail we were largely dependent on the prison officers, in Long Kesh they became dependent on us.

Had it not been for the humanity, imagination and vision of prisoners and paramilitaries like Gusty Spence who could rise above their circumstances and see beyond immediate problems, the hope for a better way would have long since diminished. David Ervine remarks:

> One of the things that strikes me most is that he's got to be getting tired. He's not in great health and I feel terribly, terribly guilty because when I telephone the house and Louie comes on I can almost tell how Gusty is by Louie's voice. I'm asking him to do something for me and I feel it's unfair at times to ask. He is so valuable because he is still the devil of devil's advocates. He has a way of looking at things in an abstract manner that pulls us on to a broader vision. Even now, at times events and pressures have the capacity to constrict your view. I have never seen Gusty under pressure and yet there have been hard times. His capacity to keep a cool head is excellent.

Martin Meehan told me that as a republican, he had also gone through a personal transformation over a twenty-year period. His experience in many ways parallels Gusty Spence's own journey and he recognises the significance of Gusty's leadership:

> I think he has made a significant contribution to the political philosophy of the UVF and guided them on the road we're on now. There's no doubt about that whatsoever. Sometimes it's hard to shake off the past. People look at me as a sort of hard Provo militant. I was a militant republican and I don't deny that one iota. I did believe in armed struggle and that armed rebellion would achieve the objective.
>
> We are all human beings. When I see my wee grandson now, he's my pride and joy. I've eight grandchildren, but this wee one lives with us and the impact that he has had on me is just unbelievable. He's everything that's good in life and you want the best for him and if we can find a way through this process even though there's hurdles and difficulties to get over, then we should try.

The similarity between Gusty Spence and Martin Meehan is remarkable. Both men encapsulate the tragedy and the hopes for this society.

David Ervine says:

> We unionists have lived for years with our feet implanted in concrete, deluded that we didn't have to do anything and that our numbers secured our position. Our relationship with the British government was, we thought, the be-all and end-all. Absolute nonsense, the world is an evolving

> place and unionism, if it doesn't evolve, will be left behind. The need is to create a unionism that is vibrant and sensible. This begins with the recognition that if unionism doesn't embrace a new generation and doesn't embrace that sense of evolution, then it's in demise and is going nowhere. It will slowly but surely die.

Nevertheless many people do not see things this way. For them, any form of change, let alone compromise, represents sell-out and surrender. Some would prefer to go down fighting and dying for a chimera, rather than live and work for a new Northern Ireland at peace. Those who seek to embrace a new way forward may be confronted with virulent opposition.

I conducted virtually all the interviews for this book with Gusty at his home on the Shankill Road. But during the summer of 2000, I felt growing tensions within the area. Houses right beside his were damaged. Nationalists were blamed for these attacks, but later it became clear that supposed 'loyalists' had carried them out.

On my last visit to the house, on 15 August 2000, garish sectarian slogans had been painted at nearby Carlisle Circus. That evening Louie suggested I leave by a different route because a large number of youths had suddenly gathered at the corner of Denmark Street and Carlisle Circus. It was then only a matter of days before serious violence erupted on the Shankill Road.

Gusty's home and the homes of members of his family and others were systematically attacked. One frightened old woman exclaimed that it was the Nazis once again. Luckily Gusty was not at home – otherwise, Louie is convinced, he would have defended his home and consequently would have lost his life.

Despite the risks Gusty did return to his home the following day and spoke publicly:

> It is no part of my purpose to exacerbate an already volatile situation. I am appealing to those cool heads, to those honest, decent people, especially in the UDA, to knock this on the head.[2]

But his words were not heeded. As the violence continued, a number of people were killed and more than 250 families were forced to flee from their homes in a matter of weeks. The suffering of many of these people has been horrendous. Gusty says:

> I know, as sure as the sun rises and sets, that those people who were the

> perpetrators of these things, perhaps not today but tomorrow certainly, will come to think as we are thinking. That which they have done will cause them the gravest embarrassment.

Permeating this book is the wish that one day this society, riven and divided though it be, will at last be at peace. We long for the day when we can become a normal society, but we must ask ourselves, How many people are prepared to place themselves in the firing line, to emerge from our own perceived herd and to have the spotlight of attention focused on them?

In writing this book it was not my intention to glamourise or lionise Gusty Spence, nor would he want this. This book does not spring from a desire to capitalise on an extraordinary life. I have tried to approach the story with sensitivity and compassion. It may help us to challenge our prejudices, to question our sacred myths, and to shed old comfort blankets. The time has come for us all to break the old moulds.

NOTES

ACKNOWLEDGEMENTS

1. This was on 19 August 2000 when violence broke out on the Shankill Road after a loyalist parade. Gusty is unlikely ever to return there to live.

1 INTRODUCTION

1. The CLMC represented the following loyalist paramilitary groups: the UVF, Red Hand Commando (RHC), Ulster Defence Association (UDA) and Ulster Freedom Fighters (UFF).
2. These ideas are decidedly not Marxist but can best be seen as a movement favouring the interests of the working class and the poor and the promotion of a new relationship with Irish Catholics.
3. Progressive thinking within loyalism has a long history and much of it has been associated with the PUP and UVF, as is reflected in this book. The UDA has also engaged in new thinking; this is reflected in publications of the New Ulster Political Research Group and the UDA: *Beyond the Religious Divide: Papers for Discussion* (March 1979) and *Common Sense* (January 1987). See also James McAuley, 'Cuchullain and an RPG-7: the Ideology and Politics of the Ulster Defence Association', in Eamonn Hughes (ed.), *Culture and Politics in Northern Ireland*, Open University Press, Milton Keynes, 1999, pp. 45–68.
4. Contrary to rumours it is possible to resign and leave the UVF. The manner of leaving would of course be important, in that members would have information that could potentially damage other members and so trust is essential.

5. The Maze prison is better known among the prisoners as Long Kesh or 'the Kesh'.
6. The loyalist ceasefire was preceded on 31 August 1994 by a republican cessation of military operations. The latter ended with the Canary Wharf bombing in London on 9 February 1996, but was reinstated on 20 July 1997.
7. Sinn Féin chairman Mitchel McLaughlin, writing in the *Examiner* of 27 March 2000, said, 'It is only through working with each other that we will ... reach a level of understanding and trust where statements of regret can be offered in the confidence that they will be accepted in the spirit in which they will be offered.'

2 THE CRADLE OF THE ULSTER VOLUNTEERS

1. On 12 July each year, Ulster Protestants celebrate the anniversary of the Battle of the Boyne in 1690.
2. Interview with Gusty Spence by Bob Hanvey, the Ramblin' Man, Downtown Radio, 18 April 1995.
3. Jonathan Bardon, *A History of Ulster*, Blackstaff, Belfast, 1992, p. 527.
4. Paddy Devlin, *Straight Left: an Autobiography*, Blackstaff, Belfast, 1993, p.5.
5. *The Times*, 12 October 1932, quoted in Bardon, p. 528.
6. Ibid., p.529.
7. Seán Cronin, *Frank Ryan: The Search for the Republic*, Dublin, Repsol Publishing/Skellig Press, 1980, pp.55–6.
8. See Chapter 6.
9. *Irish News*, 13 July 1935, quoted in Bardon, p.540.
10. A.T.Q. Stewart, *The Narrow Ground: The Roots of Conflict in Ulster*, Faber and Faber, London and Boston, 1989, pp.140–1.
11. Gusty Spence, *Shankill Bulletin*, November 1987.
12. Ibid.
13. Ibid.
14. Ibid.
15. Ibid.
16. Ibid.
17. Bardon, p.591.
18. Ibid., p.533.
19. Gusty Spence, *Shankill Bulletin*, November 1978.

3 DARK RECESSES OF SECTARIANISM

1. Roy Garland, 'Courageous Campaigner carries History of Hope', *Irish News*, 23 August 1999.
2. The Irish tricolour is intended to symbolise the two major traditions in Ireland, the orange representing the Protestants and the green the nationalists. The white in the middle denotes an aspiration for peace. However, Irish tricolours have seldom been used to promote peace. Rather they are interpreted by many unionists as symbolising aggression by Irish nationalism, as was reflected in the claims in articles 2 and 3 of the Irish Constitution. Archbishop McQuade, the Roman Catholic Archbishop of Dublin, largely framed these articles. (See John Cooney, *John Charles McQuade – Ruler of Catholic Ireland*, O'Brien, Dublin, 1999.) Some Protestants reject the claim that the tricolour stands for peace, arguing it was coloured green, white and *gold* (or yellow). The yellow and white were the colours of the Vatican with green for Ireland, reflecting, in their view, a form of Roman Catholic imperialism.
3. Some Catholics were unhappy that a religious festival like Our Lady's Day should be celebrated with bonfires in a similar way to the Protestants' Twelfth of July.
4. Roy Garland, 'The Ulster Volunteer Force Negotiating History', MA thesis, Department of Social Anthroplogy, Queen's University Belfast.
5. These nightmares appear to have been a common experience over generations. Sometimes the nightmares became reality, as when the author's father was taken and deliberately left on the Falls as a youth by a van driver.

4 MARRIAGE AND MILITARY SERVICE

1. Bo or Sam McClelland became leader of the UVF after Gusty was imprisoned in 1966.
2. *Belfast Telegraph*, 24 September 1959.
3. This meant having their time card marked by a machine to prove that they were at work.

5 POLITICS AND PERSONATION

1. Lundy is seen by many Protestants as the archetypal traitor because he was prepared to accept terms for surrender during the siege of Derry in 1688–9.
2. According to Liam Clarke, *Sunday Times*, 12 November 2000, a republican woman was awarded a plaque for achieving sixty-seven votes in Derry during the Stormont election of 1982.

6 THE FORMATION OF THE MODERN UVF

1. Brian Barton, *Brookeborough, The Making of a Prime Minister*, Institute of Irish Studies, Queen's University Belfast, 1988, p. 31.
2. Ibid., p. 31.
3. Ibid., pp. 33–4.
4. Paul Bew, Peter Gibbon and Henry Patterson, *Northern Ireland 1921–24: Political Forces and Social Classes*, Serif, London, 1995, p. 245.
5. Barton, p. 31.
6. Patrick Buckland, *Irish Unionism 1885–1923, A Documentary History*, HMSO, Belfast, 1973, pp. 446–7.
7. Arthur Hezlett, *The 'B' Specials: A History of the Ulster Special Constabulary*, Tom Stacey, London, 1972, p. 91.
8. Buckland, pp. 442–3.
9. Michael Farrell, *Northern Ireland: The Orange State*, Pluto Press, London, 1976, p. 224.
10. Jonathan Bardon, *A History of Ulster*, Blackstaff, Belfast, 1992, p. 631.
11. William McGrath, *What Then*, Christian Fellowship Centre and Irish Emancipation Crusade, Belfast, 1962. William McGrath was to become leader of Tara, a loyalist paramilitary group, in 1969. Many years later, in 1981, McGrath was jailed for sexually abusing young men at Kincora Boys' Hostel in Belfast.
12. Published in the *Protestant Telegraph*, 11 November 1968, and quoted in Dennis Cooke, *Persecuting Zeal: A Portrait of Ian Paisley*, Brandon, Dingle, 1996, p. 148.
13. From notes given to me by Art McMillen in 1999. Art also told me that their grandfather had been a Protestant and a Master of an Orange Lodge.
14. O'Neill had of course to consult the late Brian McConnell, Minister of Home Affairs, before embarking on such a venture.
15. Bardon, p. 630.
16. The Democratic Unionist Party (DUP) in the early 1970s managed to attract people from the left of the political spectrum into their party.
17. Sarah Nelson, *Ulster's Uncertain Defenders: Loyalists and the Northern Ireland Conflict*, Appletree, Belfast, 1984, p. 61.
18. Interview with Downtown Radio, 18 April 1995.
19. Roy Garland, 'The Ulster Volunteer Force Negotiating History', MA thesis, Department of Social Anthropology, Queen's University Belfast, 1991.
20. Taken from a document in my possession and verified by Gusty Spence.
21. Ibid. Such incidents were unsuccessful in 1966 but they did succeed in toppling O'Neill in 1969.
22. Ed Moloney and Andy Pollak, *Paisley*, Poolbeg, Dublin, 1986, p. 136.
23. *Belfast Telegraph*, 21 May 1966.
24. *Belfast Telegraph*, 9 June 1966
25. Garland, 'Negotiating History'.
26. David Boulton, *The UVF 1966–73: An Anatomy of Loyalist Rebellion*, Torc Books, Dublin, 1973, p. 52.
27. The basic tenet of evangelicalism is an emphasis upon an individual response to the Christian gospel. The Roman Catholic view is believed to neglect this, in favour of a person being admitted to the Church through infant baptism. Evangelicals emphasise the need to be 'born again' in order to become a true Christian. The growth of a Catholic evangelical movement, which shares many of the views of Protestant evangelicals, has made the distinction less clear. Both Protestant and Catholic evangelicals tend to be fundamentalist, meaning that they adhere to certain beliefs and doctrines believed to be central to the Christian faith. See Glenn Jordan, *Not of this World: Evangelical Protestants in Northern Ireland*, Blackstaff, Belfast, 2001.
28. Garland, 'Negotiating History'.
29. *Belfast Telegraph*, 21 May 1966.
30. *Belfast Telegraph*, 11 June 1966.
31. William McGrath, *The National Crisis of*

Faith, Christian Fellowship and Irish Emancipation Crusade Faith House, Wellington Park, Belfast, 1969.

32. The word 'ecumenical' has received a very bad press in Northern Ireland. It has become a byword for those who are deemed to have betrayed the faith. It is seen as having political as well as religious connotations in that the *raison d'être* of unionism, as understood through the eyes of political Protestantism, would inevitably be undermined through an ecumenism that is perceived to recognise a commonality with Roman Catholicism. The head of the Catholic Church was widely believed to be usurping the place of Christ. The whole Roman Catholic system in this view was sometimes identified with the biblical 'Mystery Babylon the great, the mother of harlots and abominations of the earth' (Revelations 17:5). This identification was almost placed on a par with orthodox elements of the Christian faith such as the Trinity. Thus this almost constituted a core belief, rather than a matter of interpretation, and Free Presbyterian congregations could sing what became dubbed a 'hymn of hate': 'Our Fathers knew thee Rome of old, and evil is they fame. Thy kind embrace the galling chain, thy kiss the blazing flame.'
33. Claims were later made that William McGrath himself was working for the communists.
34. *Belfast Telegraph*, 3 October 1966.
35. Boulton, p. 42.

7 TRIAL AND IMPRISONMENT

1. 'They Were Biggots', BBC Radio Ulster *Talkback* special, chaired by Brian Garrett, 1988.
2. There is another copy of these on ordinary notepaper with what seem to be minor differences.
3. The 'sentry' referred to was normal during all Orange lodge meetings. There were actually two of them and they were referred to as 'Inside Tyler' and 'Outside Tyler'. Some lodges dispensed with their services, which in any case were mainly of a ceremonial character.
4. Quoted in David Boulton, *The UVF 1966–73: An Anatomy of Loyalist Rebellion*, Torc Books, Dublin, 1973, pp. 50–1.
5. Good-living was a Belfast street term for a 'born again' Christian. It was sometimes greeted with scepticism with the phrase, 'Good-living for a living'.
6. Boulton, p. 56.
7. Gusty had written on the sheet of paper, 'This was written by a man who is now dead. A deathbed declaration?' His comment was signed 'Gusty Spence 1975'.
8. Boulton, p. 50.
9. A grand jury was later used in relation to a republican in the 1980s in Derry, and Gusty says that when complaints were made about this they pointed out that a grand jury was used to convict Gusty Spence.
10. Gusty Spence, *Orange Cross*, Vol. 1, special edition, May 1972. The *Orange Cross* was a loyalist prisoners' support newspaper associated with the UVF.
11. Terence O'Neill, *The Autobiography of Terence O'Neill*, Hart-Davis, London, 1972, p. 85
12. Peter Taylor, *Loyalists*, Bloomsbury, London, 1999, p. 44
13. Louie Spence, personal notes.

8 PRISON LIFE: RESISTANCE AND NEW BEGINNINGS

1. After Billy died in 1980, his son Eddie continued the campaign for Gusty's release.
2. Roy Garland, 'The Ulster Volunteer Force Negotiating History', MA thesis, Department of Social Anthropology, Queen's University Belfast, 1991.
3. Ibid.
4. Ibid.
5. Erving Goffman, *Asylums*, Penguin, Harmondsworth, 1961, p. 24.
6. Garland, 'Negotiating History'.

9 HUNGER STRIKE

1. Louie Spence, personal notes.
2. Patrick Mackin appears to have been the target, and his wife died trying to protect him. The IRA later issued a statement saying that other prison officers would be removed from their

2. Ibid.
3. Smallwoods was gunned down in 1994.
4. Quoted in Brian Rowan, *Behind the Lines: The Story of the IRA and Loyalist Ceasefires*, Blackstaff, Belfast, 1995, p. 21.
5. Ibid., p. 22.
6. Ibid., p. 23.
7. The Combined Loyalist Political Alliance gave political advice to the CLMC.
8. Conor O'Clery, *The Greening of the White House*, Gill and Macmillan, Dublin, 1996, p. 57.
9. Ibid., p. 149.
10. Ibid.
11. Seán Duignan, *One Spin on the Merry-go-round*, Blackwater Press, Dublin, 1996, p. 151.
12. But they were fully aware, through Gusty, that I was going to present a submission, which I discussed with Gusty, to the Forum for Peace and Reconciliation.
13. Duignan, p. 151.
14. Ibid., pp. 150–1.
15. O'Clery, *Greening of the White House*, p. 181.
16. Gusty had already been to Capitol Hill, but at the time of the final visit he was so exhausted he decided he couldn't make it. America he said, 'had nearly killed him'.
17. Vargo is described by Conor O'Clery as, 'a petite staffer with an infectious laugh who was acknowledged as the leading expert on Ireland on Capitol Hill'. O'Clery, *Greening of the White House*, p. 59.
18. Ibid., pp. 181–2.
19. Rita Mullen was a civil rights activist from north Belfast, working at Little Rock in the USA as a public health lecturer. See Ibid., p. 17.
20. Quoted in Paul Bew and Gordon Gillespie, *Northern Ireland: A Chronology of the Troubles 1968–1993*, Gill and Macmillan, Dublin 1993, p. 114.

19 THE GOOD FRIDAY AGREEMENT

1. This was a draft document meant for discussion in April 1998.
2. *Belfast Telegraph*, 21 August 2000.

Index

target lists, if they made known to the IRA their resignations from the prison service. A 22-year-old man was jailed for the killing in 1980. See David McKittrick, Seamus Kelters, Brian Feeney and Chris Thornton, *Lost Lives: The Stories of the Men, Women and Children Who Died as a Result of the Northern Ireland Troubles*, Mainstream, Edinburgh, 1999, pp. 775–6.

3. Peter Taylor, *Loyalists*, Bloomsbury, London, 1999, p. 109.

10 POLITICAL STATUS

1. Roy Garland, 'The Ulster Volunteer Force Negotiating History', MA thesis, Department of Social Anthropology, Queen's University Belfast, 1991.
2. Ibid.
3. Ibid.
4. Ibid.
5. Richard Deutsch and Vivien Magowan, *Northern Ireland, 1968–73: A Chronology of Events, Vol. 1: 1968–71*, Blackstaff, Belfast, 1973, p. 74.
6. Ibid.
7. They were said to have marched out again with a cargo of Official IRA guns, which fell into the hands of the PIRA. The Official IRA lost a significant amount of armaments in the curfew. See David Sharrock and Mark Devenport, *Man of War, Man of Peace*, Macmillan, London, 1997, p. 81.
8. Billy McKee was named by Major General Farrar-Hockley, the most senior British army officer in Northern Ireland, as one of five Provisional IRA men. Others he mentioned included an uncle and a cousin of Gerry Adams. *Éire Nua* was a plan for a federal Ireland devised by Ruairí Ó Brádaigh and Dáithí Ó Conaill in 1971.
9. When the author was employed during the mid-1970s in the Royal Victoria Hospital with working-class fellows from the Falls, my predominant impression was of a very similar lifestyle and culture, with which I was at ease. Only once was this questioned, and that was during the playing of Irish music when they did a wee dance and I suddenly felt somewhat intimidated.
10. Garland, 'Negotiating History'.
11. From the text of a speech given by Tomás Mac Giolla, Republican Clubs Conference, at Carrickmore, Co. Tyrone, in July 1972.
12. *Orange Cross*, January 1972.
13. Garland, 'Negotiating History'.
14. *Orange Cross*, May 1972.
15. Ibid.
16. Ibid., June 1972.
17. This was not the Billy Wright killed by the Irish National Liberation Army (INLA) in the Maze prison in 1997.
18. *Orange Cross*, 12 July 1972.

11 ABDUCTION

1. Smuggled interview made in Long Kesh, Easter 1974.
2. Loyalists had no confidence in the will of the security forces to defeat the IRA.
3. David McKittrick, Seamus Kelters, Brian Feeney and Chris Thornton, *Lost Lives: The Stories of the Men, Women and Children Who Died as a Result of the Northern Ireland Troubles*, Mainstream, Edinburgh, 1999, p. 1475.
4. The author does not find it easy to refer to killings in statistical terms. Each and every killing, whether by paramilitaries or the security forces, represents a terrible human tragedy.
5. IRA killings were generally aimed at members of security forces whom they regarded as legitimate targets. However many part-time members of the security forces were local farmers and others who sought to protect life and property, often in remote border areas. Many people regarded such killings as being motivated entirely by sectarianism, although a significant number of IRA killings were of Catholics.
6. Richard Deutsch and Vivien Magowan, *Northern Ireland 1968–73: A Chronology of Events*, Vol. 2: 1972–73, Blackstaff, Belfast, 1974, pp. 191–2.
7. Ibid, p. 192.
8. Ibid p. 193.
9. McKittrick *et al.*, pp. 210–11.
10. David Boulton, *The UVF 1966–73: An Anatomy of Loyalist Rebellion*, Torc Books, Dublin, 1973, p. 170.
11. Ibid, pp. 170–1.
12. *Orange Cross*, 12 August 1972.
13. Boulton, p. 3.
14. Ibid., p. 172.

15. Ibid., pp. 172–3.
16. Sarah Nelson, *Ulster's Uncertain Defenders: Loyalists and the Northern Ireland Conflict*, Appletree, Belfast, 1984, p. 146.
17. Ibid., p. 174.
18. Deutsch and Magowan, p. 227.
19. Ibid., p. 236.
20. Jim Cusack and Henry McDonald, *UVF*, Poolbeg, Dublin, 1997, p. 105.
21. Louie Spence, interview with Maura Lee.

12 LONG KESH

1. A 'no conflict' policy or 'non-aggression pact' was reaffirmed in September 1976 as existing between the UVF and the UDA after disturbances in Long Kesh.
2. *Orange Cross*, February 1974.
3. David Morley was very sensitive to his past in the British army and Gusty would occasionally chide him with, 'Sure you're British army anyway.' Morley would ask him to keep quiet.
4. See David McKittrick, Seamus Kelters, Brian Feeney and Chris Thornton, *Lost Lives: The Stories of the Men, Women and Children Who Died as a Result of the Northern Ireland Troubles*, Mainstream, Edinburgh, 1999, pp. 217–18.
5. 'Half hut' refers to one of the huts in each compound which was partitioned. One half was accommodation and the other was used for recreation.
6. *Sunday News*, 29 July 1973.
7. Billy Hutchinson went on to develop good working relationships with some leading republicans and played a central role in bringing about the loyalist ceasefire of 1994.
8. *Sunday News*, 24 March 1974.
9. Colin Crawford, *Defenders or Criminals? Loyalist Prisoners and Criminalisation*, Blackstaff, Belfast, 1999, pp. 29–30.
10. The author attended some of her lectures and heard her refer to the British army as an 'occupation army'.
11. John Fairleigh said the lectures stopped after the fire in 1974.
12. They included 'Robert' who, according to all reports, had been solely involved in the political development of the UVF before being interned in 1973.
13. Roy Garland, 'The Ulster Volunteer Force Negotiating History', MA thesis, Department of Social Anthropology, Queen's University Belfast, 1991.
14. Ibid.
15. Letter addressed to 'The Spence Family' from the NIO, dated 26 April 1974.
16. Letter addressed to 'Wm Spence Esq' from the NIO, dated 8 May 1974.

13 CONFLAGRATION

1. *Sunday News*, 28 July 1974.
2. On 9 October 1976 Gusty Spence addressed a letter to the UVF brigade staff in Belfast in which he referred to brutality by prison officers who were dressed in full riot gear during an altercation with the UDA. An earlier letter, dated 16 September 1976, refers to prison officers who 'beat (UDA men) in their compounds'.
3. Roy Garland, 'The Ulster Volunteer Force Negotiating History', MA thesis, Department of Social Anthropology, Queen's University Belfast, 1991.
4. Martin Dillon, *The Shankill Butchers*, Arrow, London, 1990, p. 46.
5. Ibid.
6. *Sunday News*, 29 September 1974.
7. Billy Wright, not to be confused with the militant loyalist of the same name from Portadown, was later shot dead by the Provos as he arrived at his Lyndhurst Drive home from the prison on 3 December 1979. Gusty told me that Billy had been a welter weight champion boxer of Ireland. He had also been next in line to the governor, of Long Kesh and had received the British Empire Medal before his death. Billy Wright had served with the Royal Marines and reached the rank of colour sergeant. He had escaped death once before, in October 1978, when he was shot at as he drove home from prison.
8. From 1972 until 1974 there were no cubicles and the order had been 'Stand by your beds', but then the huts were sectionalised with partitions. There were no doors on the cubicles, but each man stood by the entrance of his cubicle, which was curtained, to be counted.
9. *Orange Cross*, No. 63, n.d.
10. *Sunday News*, 12 January 1975.
11. The Constitutional Convention was

elected in 1975 'as a means of keeping local political forces harmlessly occupied'. It was during the convention that William Craig proposed an 'emergency coalition' to include the SDLP. See Paul Bew, Peter Gibbon and Henry Patterson, *Northern Ireland 1921–24: Political Forces and Social Classes*, Serif, London, 1995, p. 200.

12. *Orange Cross*, No. 80, n.d.
13. *Orange Cross*, No. 88, November 1975.

14 COOPERATION AND TACKLING SECTARIANISM

1. Gusty Spence in a pamphlet, *The Third Force*, Hand to Mouth Press, Co. Antrim, 1986, p.4.
2. Colin Crawford, *Defenders or Criminals: Loyalist Prisoners and Criminalisation*, Blackstaff, Belfast, 1999, p.45.
3. Ibid., p.46.
4. *Irish News*, 18 May 1977.
5. *News Letter*, 11 May 1977.
6. Spence, p.4.
7. Ibid, p.5.
8. There had been contacts between leading members of the UVF and the IRA in early 1974. These were aimed at reducing killings of UDR men and Catholics. The UVF called upon loyalists to cease sectarian killings in February of that year after the IRA said they had stopped killing off-duty UDR men. The UVF said they would have been happier had the IRA decided to stop regarding all UDR men as legitimate targets. See *Orange Cross*, No. 45, n.d.
9. David McKittrick, Seamus Kelters, Brian Feeney and Chris Thornton, *Lost Lives: The Stories of the Men, Women and Children Who Died as a Result of the Northern Ireland Troubles*, Mainstream, Edinburgh, 1999, p.1475.
10. The IRA was believed to have the ear of the British government because of their violence, so loyalists were determined to show that they also were capable of extreme violence. Loyalist violence was also designed to put pressure on the IRA to stop, by hurting the nationalist community.
11. Paul Bew and Gordon Gillespie, *Northern Ireland: A Chronology of the Troubles, 1968–1993*, Gill and Macmillan, Dublin, 1993, p.99.
12. *Orange Cross*, 12 July 1975.
13. Martin Dillon, *The Shankill Butchers*, Arrow, London, 1990, p.42.
14. McKittrick, *et al.*, p.632.
15. Ibid., p.1475.
16. Anne Uprichard, 'Gusty Spence, the Man and the Myth', *Fortnight*, No. 127, 21 May 1976.
17. Ibid.
18. Ibid.
19. Unfortunately my copy of the printed letter has no indication of the date of publication or of the newspaper involved.
20. *News Letter*, 16 February 1976.
21. *News Letter*, 17 November 1976.
22. Despite this, Lenny Murphy once made a beautiful leather wallet for Martin Meehan, who was a militant republican. The wallet displayed a Red Hand of Ulster on one side and a shamrock on another.
23. From an article by Alan Witsitt in the *News Letter*, 17 November 1976.
24. Ibid.
25. *News Letter*, 25 January 1977.

15 RESIGNATION

1. Siegfried Sassoon, 'Suicide in the Trenches', 1917, *The War Poems*, Faber, London, 1983.
2. Full details are also in *Peace by Peace*, 18 November 1977.
3. Trevor West, in *Fortnight*, 20 January–2 February 1978.
4. Taken from notes given to me by Trevor West.
5. Article by Trevor West in *Fortnight*, December 1977.
6. *Peace by Peace*, 18 November 1977.
7. *Sunday News*, 5 March 1978.

16 H BLOCKS AND FRIENDSHIP WITH A CARDINAL

1. Colin Crawford, *Defenders or Criminals: Loyalist Prisoners and Criminalistaion*, Blackstaff, Belfast, 1999, p.51.
2. Jack Holland, *Hope against History: The Ulster Conflict*, Hodder and Stoughton, London, 1999, p.147.
3. Crawford, p.57.
4. Ibid, p.58.
5. Holland, p.150.
6. Paul Bew and Gordon Gillespie, *Northern Ireland: A Chronology of the Troubles 1968–1993*, Gill and Macmillan, Dublin 1993, p.134.

7. Holland, p. 159.
8. *Sunday Press*, 1 March 1981.
9. Ibid.
10. Ibid.
11. *Peace by Peace*, 28 November 1980.
12. *Irish Press*, 22 December 1980.
13. Release in these circumstances does not mean a clean slate. The sentence remains on the books, and should a serious crime be committed, the prisoner would serve out the original sentence. Pension entitlement may be nil because contributions were not made during the years of confinement. The return of the prisoner adds to the financial and other difficulties faced by the prisoner and his family.
14. The bomb referred to was probably the previous month's Canary Wharf Bombing on 9 February 1996, which brought the IRA ceasefire of 1994 to an end.

17 THE HAMMER MAN COMES HOME

1. Secretary of State Douglas Hurd had signed the release papers about five days before this.
2. Original tapes of an interview with Maura Lee used in the RTÉ documentary *A Tap on the Shoulder*, 25 April 1996.
3. Roel Kaptein, 'Ethnocentricism in Northern Ireland, Its Escalation into Violence and Terrorism' (unpublished paper), 1992, p. 22.
4. Goulding was Chief of Staff of the Official IRA from 1962 until his death in 1998.
5. *Fortnight*, No. 225, 23 September – 6 October 1985.
6. Ibid.
7. Paul Bew and Gordon Gillespie, *Northern Ireland: A Chronology of the Troubles 1968–1993*, Gill and Macmillan, Dublin, 1993, p. 189.
8. Ibid.
9. Ibid., p. 190.
10. The words 'Never, never, never' were spoken by Ian Paisley at the City Hall rally in Belfast City Centre on 23 November 1985.
11. *Morning Star*, 7 February 1987; *Leninist*, 17 July 1987.
12. From *The Twelfth 1987*. *The Twelfth* is a booklet produced and sold each Twelfth of July by the Belfast County Grand Lodge Publications Committee.
13. Shane Paul O'Doherty, quoted by Conor O'Clery in *Ireland in Quotes: A History of the 20th Century*, O'Brien, Dublin, 1999, p. 196.
14. *Community Development in Protestant Areas: a Report on Two Seminars Held During 1991*, Community Relations Council, Belfast, 1991, pp. 63–9.
15. Ibid.
16. Ibid.
17. In fact Gusty's home was attacked and the bulletproof windows, provided for his protection at the time of the Good Friday Agreement, were smashed and some damage was done inside during what has been described as a loyalist feud in August 2000. At the time of writing more than 250 families have been driven out of their homes.
18. At Feakle, County Clare, on 10 December 1974, Bishop Arthur Butler of the Church of Ireland, Jack Weir, Clerk of the Presbyterian General Assembly, Eric Gallagher, former President of the Methodist Church, Stanley Worrall, retired headmaster of Methodist College Belfast, Ralph Baxter, Secretary of the Irish Council of Churches, his assistant Bill Arlow, and two officers of the British Council of Churches met with the leadership of republicanism in an effort to stop the violence.
19. John McMichael, a senior loyalist in the UDA/UFF, was killed by an IRA booby-trap bomb on 22 December 1987. The author had been in contact with him shortly before his death and heard him speak of tackling racketeering within the UDA. One of the people involved in the rackets, and also apparently working for RUC Special Branch, was Jim Craig who apparently passed details about McMichael to the IRA. It was claimed in the *Sunday People* (15 October 2000) that John McMichael was sacrificed to save RUC mole Jim Craig.
20. Andy Tyrie was a prominent loyalist until March 1988 when he resigned from the chairmanship of the UDA.

18 THE NORTHERN IRELAND PEACE PROCESS

1. Peter Taylor, *Loyalists*, Bloomsbury, London, 1999, p. 217.